Oxford and Cambridge

Oxford and Cambridge

Christopher Brooke
and Roger Highfield

Photographs by
Wim Swaan

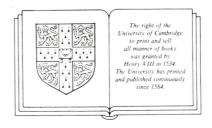

The right of the
University of Cambridge
to print and sell
all manner of books
was granted by
Henry VIII in 1534.
The University has printed
and published continuously
since 1584.

Cambridge University Press

Cambridge
New York   New Rochelle
Melbourne   Sydney

Published by the Press Syndicate of the University of Cambridge
The Pitt Building, Trumpington Street, Cambridge CB2 1RP
32 East 57th Street, New York, NY 10022, USA
10 Stamford Road, Oakleigh, Melbourne 3166, Australia

First published 1988

Printed in Great Britain by BAS Printers Limited, Over Wallop, Hampshire

British Library cataloguing in publication data

Brooke, Christopher
Oxford and Cambridge.
1. University of Oxford – History
2. University of Cambridge – History
I. Title II. Highfield, Roger
378.425′74′09   LF509

Library of Congress cataloguing in publication data

Brooke, Christopher Nugent Lawrence.
Oxford and Cambridge.
Bibliography.
Includes index.
1. University of Oxford – History. 2. University of Cambridge – History. 3. University of Oxford – Description
– Views. 4. University of Cambridge – Description – Views. I. Highfield, J. R. L. (John Roger Loxdale)
II. Swaan, Wim. III. Title.
LF509.B75   1988   378.425′74   87-10280

ISBN 0 521 30139 4

BM

Ever since I heard that they had a Printer in Cambridge, I did greatly fear this and such like inconveniences would follow . . . I think it very convenient that the books should be burned, being very factious and full of untruths . . .

Archbishop Whitgift, 1584, quoted in *CC*, p. 49

I was a modest, good-humoured boy. It is Oxford that has made me insufferable.

Max Beerbohm, 'Going back to School', in *More*, 1899, p. 155

1   *Cambridge, Emmanuel College: the chapel front and long gallery, by Christopher Wren, 1667–77*

Contents

Contents

Illustrations

All photographs are by Wim Swaan, except for the endpapers and plates 86, 98, 122, 126–7 and 204. Marginal numbers in the text refer to the numbers of the plates.

Front endpaper The Sheldonian Theatre, Oxford, by Christopher Wren (see pp. 198–9); engraving by David Loggan, *c.* 1675 (photograph by courtesy of the Syndics of Cambridge University Library)

Illustrations

Final endpaper Clare College, Cambridge, from the east: engraving by David Loggan, *c.* 1690 (photograph by courtesy of the Syndics of Cambridge University Library)

Maps

Sources and acknowledgements The maps have been specially drawn for this book by Reginald and Marjorie Piggot. The Cambridge maps are partly based on maps in Willis and Clark 1886, esp. IV, map 1; Lobel and Johns 1975; Darby 1938, 1974; and Heffers' Map of Cambridge. The Oxford maps are partly based on Catto 1984, maps 1 and 2, and on the maps after p. 159 in A. R. Woolley, *The Clarendon Guide to Oxford* (5th edn, Oxford University Press, 1983).

Preface

In a delicious passage of *Sense and Sensibility*, Jane Austen makes her hero proclaim: 'I was therefore entered at Oxford and have been properly idle ever since.'[1] This is one of the characteristic *mots* on which the general image of the ancient English universities has been modelled. The author would have been much amused to learn it has been taken seriously, for she herself came out of the Oxford establishment – her father and brother were both fellows of St John's and her great-uncle Theophilus Leigh had been master of Balliol – and was doubtless enjoying a quip at her family's expense. Her only known comment on Cambridge was to send two of her most disreputable young men there: Mr Wickham in *Pride and Prejudice* and Mr Crawford in *Mansfield Park*. But even that may not express her full meaning, for it is possible that she flirted with a fellow of Emmanuel and just possible that she named the hero of *Northanger Abbey* after a fellow of Caius.[2]

The great *History of the University of Oxford* is now at large – three volumes of the eight have been published; and even in Cambridge the history of the university is astir. It seems a good time to dispel some of the mists and legends, and tell the story again; and in one respect the general image is not at all astray. Our cities are places of great beauty, and we hope that all our readers will enjoy the revelation of their beauty in the art of Wim Swaan. Those who are historically inclined will reflect on the way this beauty is a mirror and a revelation of their history. For Cambridge in particular nature did little or nothing; man has done all. In Oxford the challenge may have been less but the response was equal; and in spite of their proverbial rivalry they have often co-operated. Thus Christopher Wren was Professor of Astronomy in Oxford and author of the Sheldonian and Tom Tower; but he left some of his finest monuments in Cambridge too, the fruits in particular of his friendship with his uncle Matthew Wren, for whom he designed Pembroke Chapel, and Isaac Barrow of Trinity, for whom he designed the Trinity Library. In a more modest way, this book has grown out of old friendship, and out of a wish to display the beauty and expound the history of our dwelling places.

The immediate aspiration from which this book grew was the wish of Christopher Brooke and Wim Swaan to collaborate once again as they had in *The Monastic World* (1974) – in a book on Cambridge and Oxford. When the opportunity arose in the mid 1980s they sought out Roger Highfield to unlock the doors and expound the secrets of Oxford, and thus the present collaboration was formed. We have tried to unfold our tale of

[1] *Sense and Sensibility*, chap. xix.
[2] See Brooke 1985, p. 185, and refs., esp. to F. Stubbings in *Emmanuel College Magazine, Quatercentenary Issue* (1984), pp. 77–81, on Samuel Blackall.

two cities as a plain unvarnished history, first of the towns, then of the universities, and above all of the colleges which have grown up in their midst and given them their fame; to deploy them so that their story is intelligible as a piece of living history to which the buildings are constant silent witnesses, while the dons and undergraduates among whom we work are less silent heirs and exponents of a tradition equally alive.

In the recent volume of *The History of the University of Oxford* on *The Eighteenth Century* (1986), Howard Colvin's brilliant chapter on 'Architecture' is tucked away between Anglo-Saxon Studies and Paintings, and the patient reader has to pass over 800 pages before he reaches it. Doubtless he will encounter many fine passages in the process; the whole book is full of riches. Our book is conceived in a different philosophy, which sets the buildings of Oxford and Cambridge in the forefront of their history, as prime expressions of the changing tastes and aspirations of the dons and their patrons, as eloquent witnesses to their past.

We owe many debts. In all our work Dr Rosalind Brooke has been both helper and critic, generously advising and correcting our plans and drafts. The Syndics of the Cambridge University Press undertook publication of the book, and we owe much kindness to their staff, especially Michael Black and William Davies, and in its production, Lyn Chatterton, Paul Chipchase, Reginald and Marjorie Piggot and Jane Williams. Wim Swaan's visits to Oxford and Cambridge were made possible by the hospitality of Merton College and of Gonville and Caius – and in Caius, where he was also at work on a parallel venture (Brooke 1985), by a generous understanding with the Master and Fellows we were allowed to share some of the photographs taken for the other book. With Wim Swaan we owe special thanks, not only to our two colleges, but also to Sir John and Lady Pilcher, and to Mr and Mrs Gordon Bishop and their colleagues. In preparing the book we have had generous help from friends beyond counting: we particularly thank Dr Paul Binski, Mr Thomas Braun, Dr Jonathan Clark, Dr Alexander Cooke, Dr David Cressy, Professor Ralph Davis, Dr Eamon Duffy, Dr Felipe Fernández-Armesto, Mrs Catherine Hall, Dr Vijay Joshi, Mrs Ann Kemp, Miss Betty Kemp, Mrs Anne Lonsdale, Dr Roger Lovatt, Mrs C. MacNicol, Mr Francis Maddison, Dr Dorothy Owen, Mrs Edna Pilmer; the present Warden of Merton and his predecessor, Sir Rex Richards; Dr Miri Rubin, Miss Alison Smith, Mr John Sturdy, Mr Richard Symonds, Miss Belinda Timlin, Dr John Twigg, Mr Malcolm Underwood, Sir Edgar Williams, Dr D. Worswick. In pursuit of the quotations which head our chapters the authors of *Cambridge Commemorated* had been before us: we acknowledge this and many other debts to the fascinating anthology by Laurence and Helen Fowler.

For permission to take the photographs which adorn the book we are indebted to the ready concurrence of the Governing Bodies and many officers, especially the Bursars, Senior Bursars and Domestic Bursars, of the colleges here represented: in Cambridge, Christ's, Churchill, Clare, Corpus Christi, Downing, Emmanuel, Fitzwilliam, Girton, Gonville and Caius, Jesus, King's, Magdalene, New Hall, Newnham, Pembroke, Peterhouse, Queens', Robinson, St Catharine's, St John's, Selwyn, Sidney Sussex, Trinity, Trinity Hall and Wolfson; in Oxford, All Souls, Balliol, Brasenose, Christ Church, Corpus Christi, Exeter, Green, Hertford, Jesus, Keble, Lady Margaret Hall, Lincoln, Magdalen, Merton, New College, Nuffield, Oriel, Pembroke, Queen's, St Catherine's, St Edmund Hall, St Hilda's, St John's, Somerville, Trinity, University, Wadham and Worcester. We are also grateful to many university officials, especially Bodley's Librarian, the Librarian of the

Cambridge University Library, the Directors of the Ashmolean and Fitzwilliam Museums, Mr Richard Barlow-Poole, Senior Esquire Bedell and Assistant Registrary of Cambridge, and Mr Graeme Rennie, Senior Assistant Registrary, the Registrar and Deputy Registrar of Oxford University, the Curators of the Sheldonian Theatre and of the Museum of the History of Science, the Committee for the Scientific Collections, University Museum, Oxford; and to many individual officers in the colleges, among whom we must make special mention of the Master and Lady Kornberg in Christ's; Mrs Margaret Gaskell in Girton; Mr John Drury and Mr A. Mundell in King's; Mr Brian Watchorn in Pembroke; Mr Richard Langhorne and Mr Malcolm Pratt in St John's; the President and Mrs Oxburgh, Mr Iain Wright and Dr John Twigg in Queens'; the Master and Lady Huxley, Mr T.C. Nicholas and Dr Timothy Hobbs in Trinity; Dr J.A. Cremona in Trinity Hall; and Dr Michael Franklin in Wolfson. We are also grateful for the kind help of the Surveyor of The Queen's Pictures, Sir Oliver Millar, and the Keeper of Drawings at Windsor Castle, the Hon. Mrs Jane Roberts, and deeply appreciate the kind permission of Her Majesty The Queen for the reproduction of plate 98. For plate 97 we are much indebted to the kind permission of the Dean and Chapter, and the Receiver-General, of Westminster Abbey.

Wim Swaan took a period of leave from an exceedingly busy architect's practice in New York, to stay with us and take the photographs. No one who has not witnessed Wim practising his art can calculate the energy, enthusiasm and toil which lie behind these photographs – a sacrifice of time and effort which we warmly and deeply appreciate. But the results are for all to see, and we hope others will share our pride and pleasure in deploying the work of an artist himself intent to display some of the noblest works of man.

CHRISTOPHER BROOKE
ROGER HIGHFIELD

1 *The Cambridge region,*
including major roads, Roman,
medieval and eighteenth-century

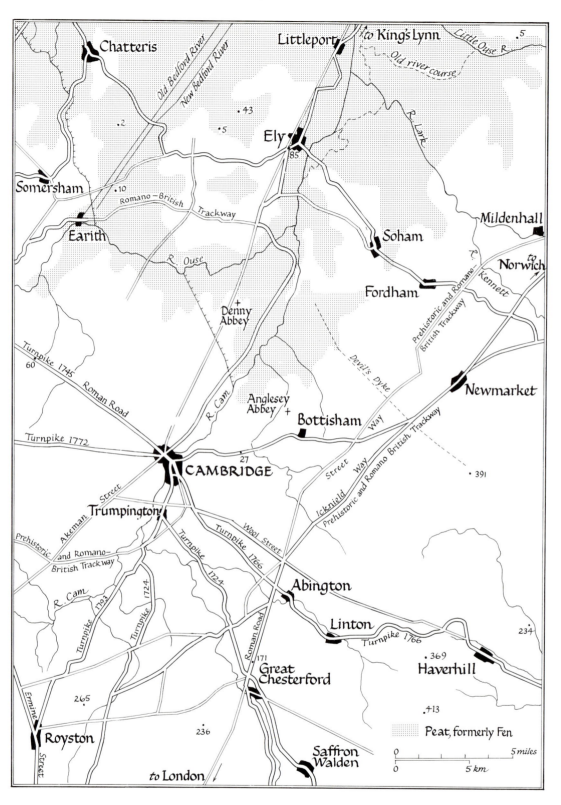

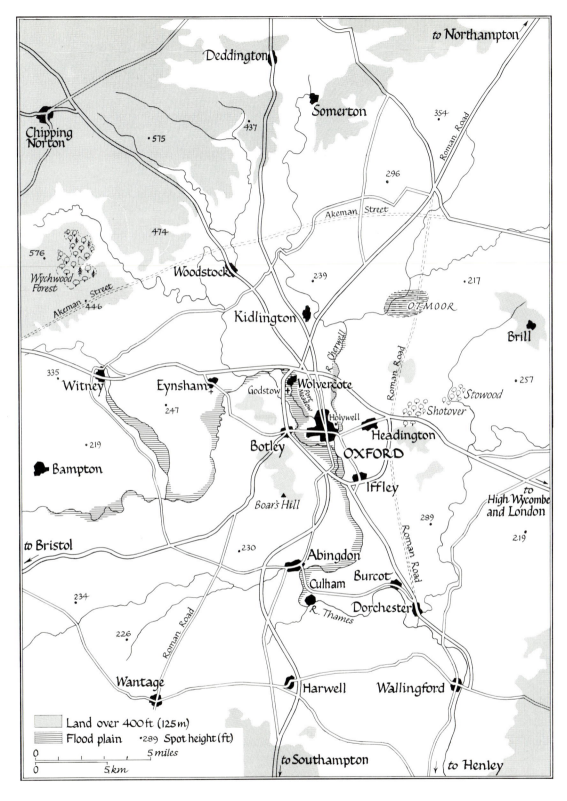

to Northampton

Deddington

Somerton

Chipping Norton

•575

•354

•437

Roman Road

•296

474

576•

Akeman Street

Wychwood Forest

Woodstock

•239

•217

OT·MOOR

Akeman Street •446

Kidlington

Brill

•257

Stowood

335•

Witney

Eynsham

Godstow

Wolvercote

R. Cherwell

port Meadow

Roman Road

Shotover

•247

Holywell

•219

Botley

OXFORD

Headington

to High Wycombe and London

Bampton

Iffley

Boar's Hill

•289

to Bristol

•230

•219

•234

Abingdon

Roman Road

Burcot

Culham

Dorchester

R. Thames

•226

Roman Road

Wantage

Harwell

Wallingford

Land over 400ft (125m)

Flood plain   •289 Spot height (ft)

0   5 miles

0   5 km

to Southampton

to Henley

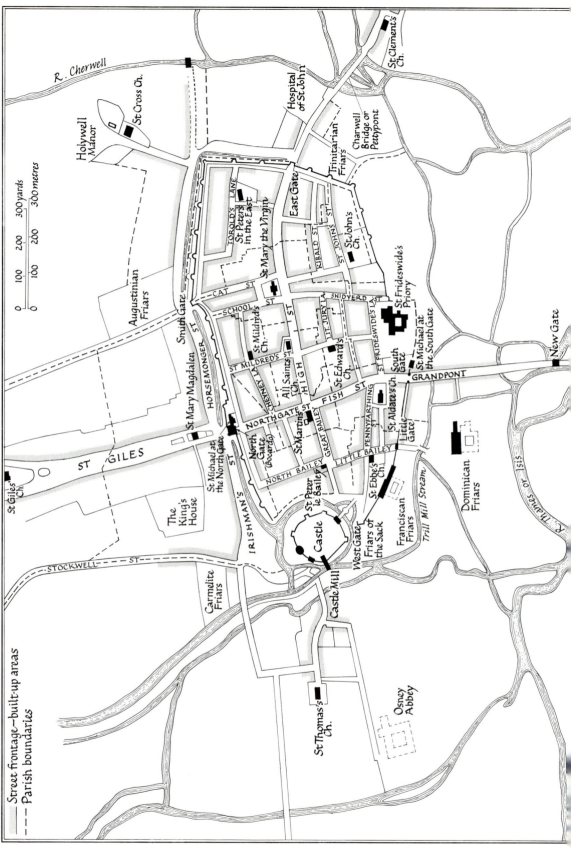

3 *Oxford before the colleges.*
c.1250

Street frontage—built-up areas
— — Parish boundaries

0   100   200   300 yards
0   100   200   300 metres

R. Cherwell

St Cross Ch.

Holywell Manor

Hospital of St John

St Clement's Ch.

Augustinian Friars

Charwell Bridge or Pettypont

Trinitarian Friars

TOROLD'S LANE

St Peter's in the East

St Mary the Virgin

East Gate

KIBALD ST

St John's Ch.

St John's ST

CAT ST

SCHOOL ST

St Mildred's Ch.

SHIDYERD

St Frideswide's Priory

St Mildred's ST

CHENEY LANE

ST JURY LA

St Edward's Ch.

ST FRIDESWIDE'S LA

St Michael at the South Gate

St Mary Magdalen

HORSEMONGER ST

South Gate

Smith Gate

HIGH

All Saints Ch.

FISH ST

ST ALDATE'S LA

GRANDPONT

New Gate

NORTHGATE ST

St Martins ST

St Aldate's Ch.

Little Gate

St Michael at the North Gate

North Gate (Bocardo)

NORTH BAILEY

GREAT BAILEY

LITTLE BAILEY

St Ebbe's Ch.

PENNYFARTHING

Dominican Friars

ST GILES

St Giles Ch.

The King's House

IRISHMAN'S

St Peter le Bailey

Castle

West Gate

Friars of the Sack

Franciscan Friars

Trill Mill Stream

R. Thames or Isis

STOCKWELL ST

Carmelite Friars

Castle Mill

St Thomas's Ch.

Osney Abbey

XX

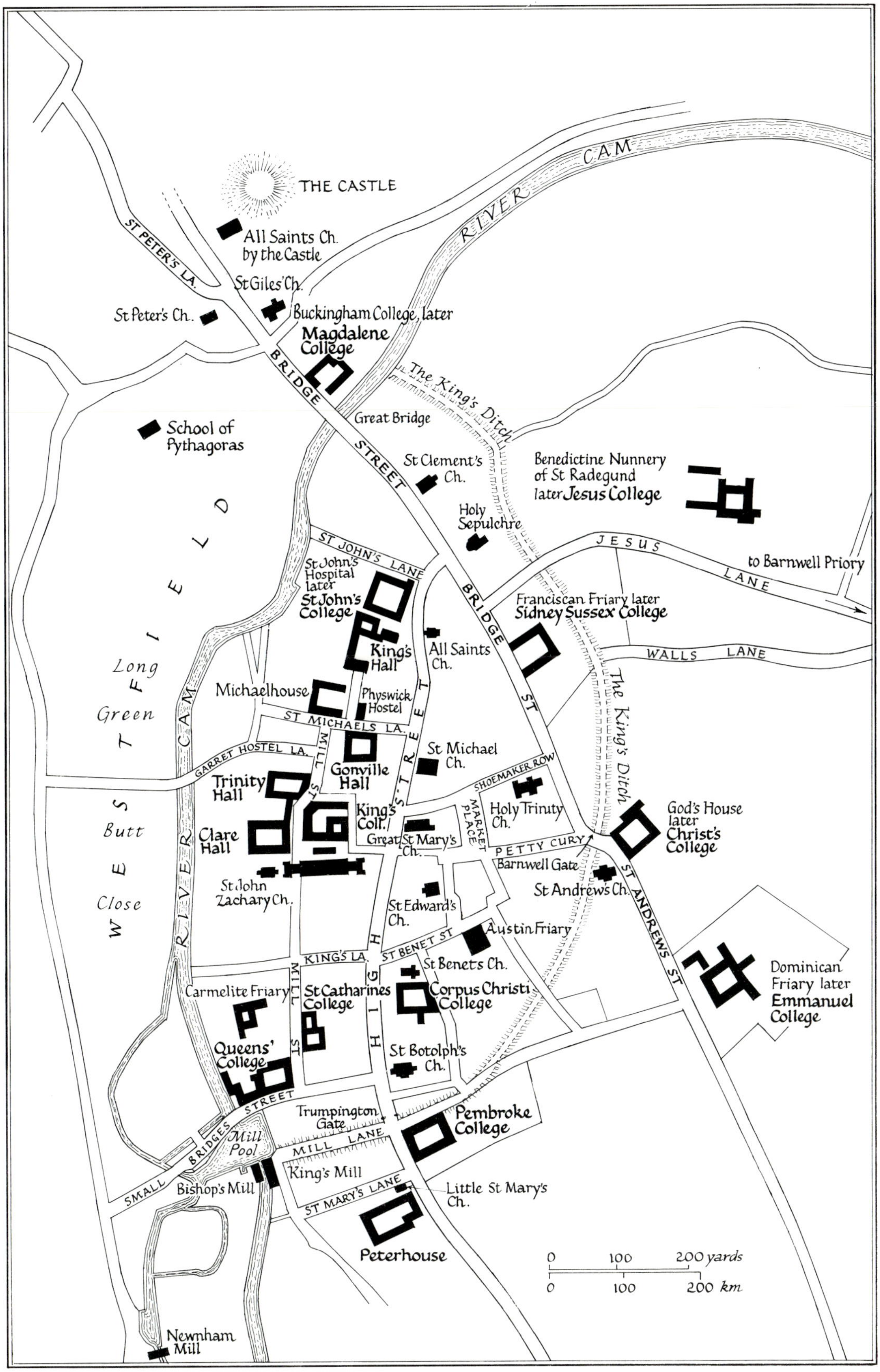

4 *Cambridge to 1500. Churches and colleges are shown: the university schools formed the quadrangle almost encircled by King's*

THE CASTLE

RIVER CAM

ST PETER'S LA.

All Saints Ch. by the Castle

St Giles' Ch.

St Peter's Ch.

Buckingham College, later **Magdalene College**

School of Pythagoras

Great Bridge

St Clement's Ch.

The King's Ditch

Holy Sepulchre

Benedictine Nunnery of St Radegund later *Jesus College*

JESUS LANE

to Barnwell Priory

BRIDGE STREET

ST JOHN'S LANE

St John's Hospital later **St John's College**

Franciscan Friary later **Sidney Sussex College**

WALLS LANE

King's Hall

All Saints Ch.

Michaelhouse

Physwick Hostel

ST MICHAELS LA.

St Michael Ch.

GARRET HOSTEL LA.

Trinity Hall

Gonville Hall

SHOEMAKER ROW

Holy Trinity Ch.

God's House later **Christ's College**

Long Green

Butt Close

WEST FIELD

RIVER CAM

Clare Hall

King's Coll.

Great St Mary's Ch.

MARKET PLACE

PETTY CURY

Barnwell Gate

St Andrew's Ch.

St John Zachary Ch.

St Edward's Ch.

Austin Friary

ST ANDREWS ST

Dominican Friary later **Emmanuel College**

KING'S LA.

ST BENET ST

St Benet's Ch.

Carmelite Friary

St Catharines College

Corpus Christi College

HIGH ST

MILL ST

St Botolph's Ch.

Queens' College

BRIDGES STREET

Trumpington Gate

MILL LANE

Pembroke College

Mill Pool

King's Mill

ST MARY'S LANE

Little St Mary's Ch.

Bishop's Mill

SMALL BRIDGES

Peterhouse

| 0 | 100 | 200 yards |
| 0 | 100 | 200 km |

Newnham Mill

xxi

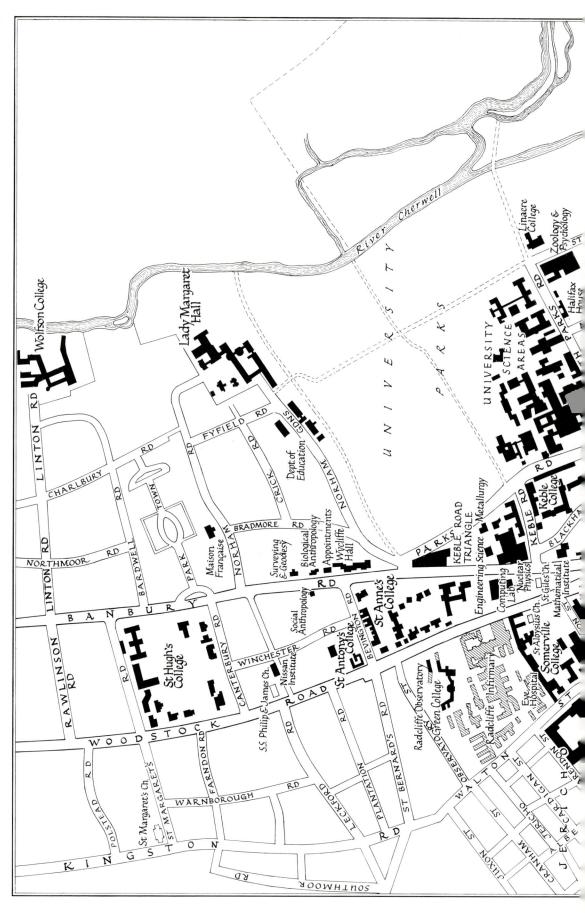

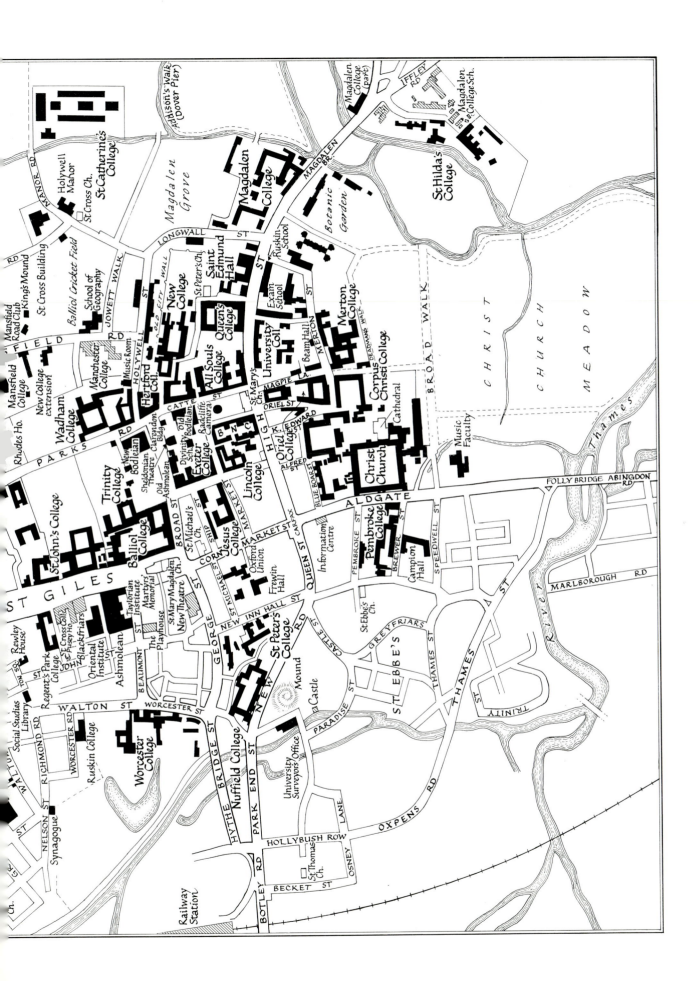

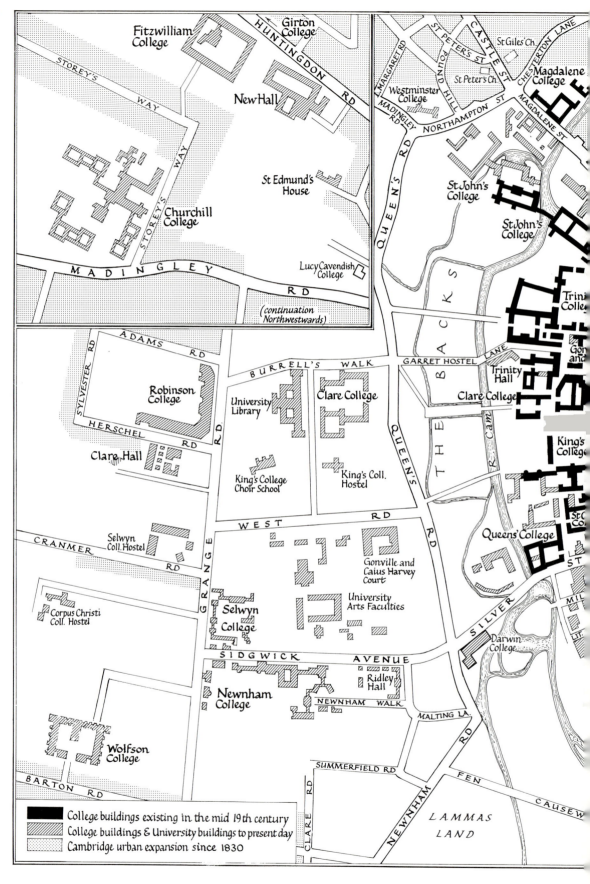

College buildings existing in the mid 19th century
College buildings & University buildings to present day
Cambridge urban expansion since 1830

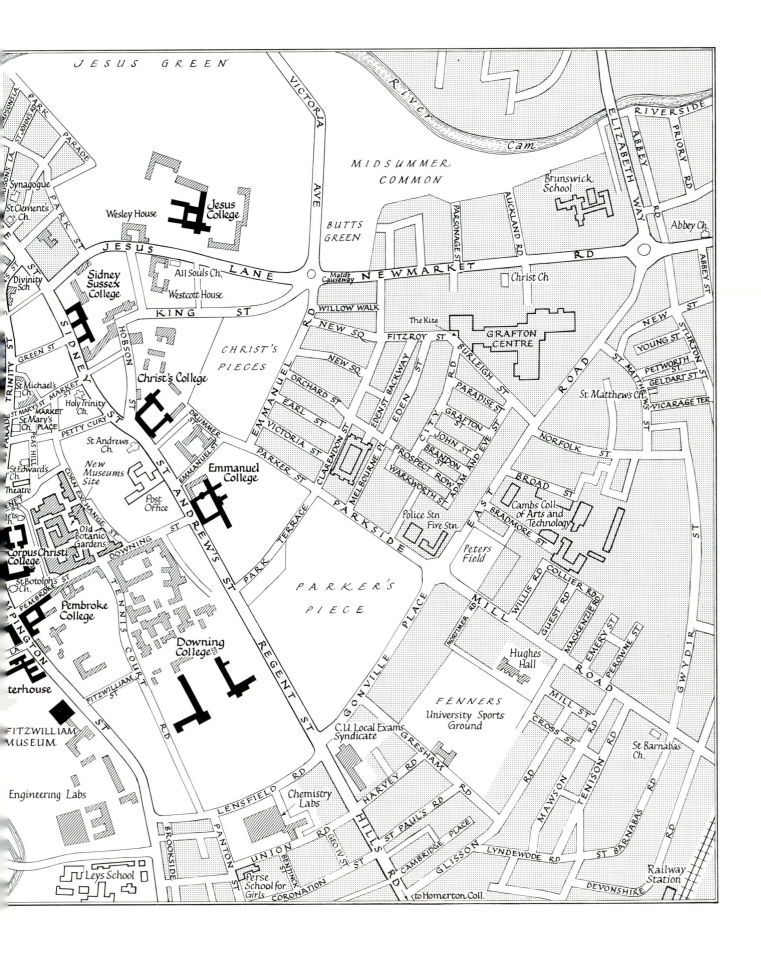

1 Cambridge

'Tis true Cambridge is very ugly, she is very dirty, and very dull; but I'm like a cabbage, where I'm stuck, I love to grow.

Thomas Gray, 20 March 1738, quoted *CC*, p. 133

For Cambridge people rarely smile,
Being urban, squat, and packed with guile.

Rupert Brooke, *Grantchester*

Vulgus Cantabrigiense inhospitales Britannos antecedit, qui cum summa rusticitate summam malitiam coniunxere – The common folk of Cambridge surpassed the Britons for being inhospitable, the Britons who combined the height of malice with the height of boorishness.

Erasmus, urbanely quoted by Maitland 1898, p. 7, in his Ford Lectures at Oxford

The old centre of Cambridge, the academic quarter between the medieval High Street and the river – with the lawns and meadows and trees of the Backs beyond – is one of the most beautiful in Europe. But it is man's doing. All that nature provided was a slow-moving, muddy river, a great expanse of marshy ground about it, in some of the flattest and dullest country in the land.[1] As we know it, this academic quarter was chiefly made between the fifteenth and eighteenth centuries, and the best and the worst that man could do in the nineteenth and twentieth centuries has not spoilt its beauty. But even if its creation was primarily an event of the late Middle Ages and later, it owed much to its prehistory back to Roman times, and its existence, and survival, are closely linked to the fortunes of the modest market town which grew up long before the scholars created a university in it.[2]

Already in Roman times it was a centre of communications. The Roman settlement and fort at the top of Castle Hill, from the first century to the fifth, lay beside a crossing of major roads, and not far from a notable prehistoric route, the Icknield Way. The Romans chose the most practical river crossing for their bridge and bridgehead, with gravel on both sides and Castle Hill to the north – a brief space before the banks of the Cam became engulfed in the fens. To the east lay much dry land; and just before the Roman settlers and the Roman soldiers had abandoned the fort, approximately in the fifth century, heroic attempts seem to have been made to stem the advance of the Anglo-Saxon invaders coming in from the

[1] See the classic studies of Fox 1923, Darby 1938 and 1974, and Taylor 1973.
[2] For the general history of Cambridge, there is a useful account with splendid maps in Lobel and Johns 1975; and an admirable survey by Helen Cam in *VCH Cambs*, III, 1–149 (with contributions by Susan Reynolds). Also most valuable are Maitland 1898, *RCHM Cambridge* and Hall and Ravensdale 1976; for the archaeological evidence, still woefully sparse, see Addyman and Biddle 1965; for other references Brooke 1985a.

2 *Cambridge: the river and
Clare Bridge, 1639–40, by
Thomas Grumbold*

3 *Magdalene Bridge from the river: the present bridge of 1823 replaces many earlier structures*

east; hence the great earthworks we know as the Devil's Dyke and the Fleam Dyke. But the effort failed: Roman Cambridge was abandoned and the earliest Saxon settlement there – 'the settlement by the Granta' – sat beside the little deserted fort, the Grantacaestir where, as Bede tells us, the monks of Ely found an ancient sarcophagus of white marble in which to lay the uncorrupted corpse of the abbess, Saint Etheldreda. It has recently been suggested that a new fortress town was established on Castle Hill by Offa, the great Mercian king of the eighth century.[3] The case has been most interestingly argued, but remains speculative; the story of Cambridge in this era is totally obscure. But by 875 the bridge had been restored, and the place had become 'Grantabridge', which did not take very long to corrupt itself to Cambridge – so that the river itself is now both Granta and Cam. This bridge formed the centre of the new Cambridge, and over it passed the old Roman Road from Colchester to Huntingdon and beyond, whose line can still be clearly traced, with a slight detour round the castle. At a very early date the meandering High Street (now Trumpington Street, King's Parade, Trinity and St John's Streets) came to meet it; and it is the junction of these

[3] Haslam 1982–3, esp. pp. 13–17. For the sarcophagus, Bede, *Hist. Eccl.* iv.19.

4

roads, and their progress over the bridge and up the hill, which formed the centre of Saxon Cambridge.

That is the surest and clearest fact of its topography, and so of its early history. Another is more difficult to interpret. On the north bank, not far to the east of the fort, lay the royal manor of Chesterton – the ton or settlement near the *castrum* or fort. The fields of Chesterton lapped right up to the boundary of the fort, and Cambridge never tried, or was never allowed, to encroach upon them. As soon as they enter the light of day – from the eleventh and twelfth centuries on – the open fields of Cambridge lie in two great expanses west and east of the city; but hardly to the north and not at all to the north-east. It has been very plausibly suggested that Chesterton was lopped off the original fields of Cambridge at an early date, perhaps even so early as the eighth century.[4] In any case the shape of the east field has been a major element in the strange story of the growth of the city; and immediately, it invites us to speculate that early Cambridge, between the ninth and the twelfth centuries, was growing up mainly to the south of Magdalene Bridge.

[4] Haslam 1982–3, p. 17. For earlier arguments about the relative chronology of Cambridge north and south of Magdalene Bridge ('cispontine and transpontine'), Cam 1944, pp. 1–18.

5   *St Benet's tower, c. 1000*

If we wish to plot the growth of English towns between the dark age of Alfred in the late ninth century and the relative daylight of the twelfth, we do well to look at the pattern of their parishes and churches.[5] It is a well-known feature of many English towns that they proliferated parish churches in the early Middle Ages to a degree hard to parallel on the Continent. By about 1200 London had 99 churches within the walls, well over 100 in the

[5] Brooke 1985a, and for all that follows on the churches.

6

whole precinct of the city; even Winchester, never a large town, had 50.[6] In the main street
of Cambridge – from just outside the Trumpington Gate which stood between St Botolph
and Little St Mary's, up the High Street and along the Roman Road until it was past the
castle and pointing towards Huntingdon – there were twelve parish churches in the Middle
Ages. Beyond the Market Place, which still sits where it did perhaps a thousand years ago,

[6]   Brooke and Keir 1975, chap. 6; Keene 1985, pp. 106–36.

lay three more churches, aligned along the southern limb of the Roman Road. Probably a number were of pre-Conquest origin. Great St Mary's stands on a central site between the Market and the High Street; and if one had to guess which is the mother church of early Cambridge, it has the most obvious claim. But there is no specific evidence to prove it earlier than about 1200. St Clement, whose church is near the bridge, has the dedication most favoured by Christian Vikings of the eleventh century. St Edward, king and martyr, died in 978, and his cult had its apogee in the early eleventh century; St Botolph was one of the Old English patrons of East Anglia, especially popular among the English about and soon after the Norman Conquest – there are hints here of the eleventh century, as with the two churches of All Saints, a favourite dedication of that era. But these are no more than hints. We can be much more certain that St Benet's tower is not much later than 1000 and represents a proud urban community in touch perhaps with the Benedictine monks of Ramsey; and that St Giles was founded and built in the 1090s.[7]

Thus the churches strongly suggest that the urban community of late Saxon and early Norman times was growing up on both sides of the bridge, though more extensively in the more convenient lands to the south. There was at one time a controversy as to whether Cambridge at the time of Domesday Book (1086) lay wholly to the north or mainly to the south of the river. The late Carl Stephenson propounded ingenious arguments in favour of a small settlement huddled round the castle. No one doubts that there was a substantial town in this region. There were ten wards at that time, and out of two wards 27 houses had been destroyed to make space for the Norman castle, whose mound or motte still sits on a corner of the Roman fort and commands a fine view over the town. But these 27 houses formed so substantial a part of the settlement in this region that the two wards had been reduced to one by 1086 – and such indications as we have place most of the others to the south, in cispontine Cambridge. In a famous paper the late Helen Cam demolished stone by stone Stephenson's argument, and concluded in triumph by drawing his attention to the tower of St Benet's, which indicates a prosperous Anglo-Saxon community in the deep south of medieval Cambridge.[8] What is certain is that the churches and early parishes show a modest urban community clinging tightly to the two great roads and the space between, and that the early Norman period saw the formation of a group of small and middling religious houses which came to dominate the religious life of Cambridge, and a part at least of its social life too, in the later Middle Ages.

In or about 1092 the Lady Hugolina, the pious wife of the Norman sheriff Picot, induced her husband to build a modest church dedicated to their favourite French saint, Giles, on the lower slopes of Castle Hill, and gather a small community of canons to serve it.[9] After twenty years or so the modest scale of the church – whose chancel arch still survives leading to a side chapel in the Victorian successor of medieval St Giles – and the presence of the soldiery on the hill above, made the place unsuited to a house of regular canons, as it had become; and they sought refreshment and peace around the ancient well of St Andrew a mile down the river. Here Barnwell Priory was built, the most considerable of the religious houses of medieval Cambridge. At about the same time or soon after, a small community of canons also gathered in the churchyard of the ancient, lost church of

[7] On St Benet's and St Giles, Brooke 1985a, pp. 55–6, 70–1; Taylor 1965, pp. 129–34.
[8] Stephenson 1933 and Cam 1944, pp. 1–18, esp. p. 18.
[9] Brooke 1985a, pp. 55–6, 71–2 and references.

St George and built the round church of the Holy Sepulchre, a symbol of their tiny order.[10] In the course of the next two generations or so the canons faded away, and so did St George's, leaving the round church a parish church, and a living symbol both of the cult of the Holy Sepulchre in the age of the Crusades and of the medieval fervour of the Cambridge Camden Society which restored it in the 1840s.

But the greatest mark on the topography of Cambridge was made by the foundation

[10] Brooke 1985a, p. 70; Gervers 1972, p. 363; *RCHM Cambridge*, II, 255–7.

8   *The chapel, formerly the nuns' church, interior: thirteenth-century arcading, restored by Pugin; the organ case, stalls and woodcarving are all by Pugin, 1846–9*

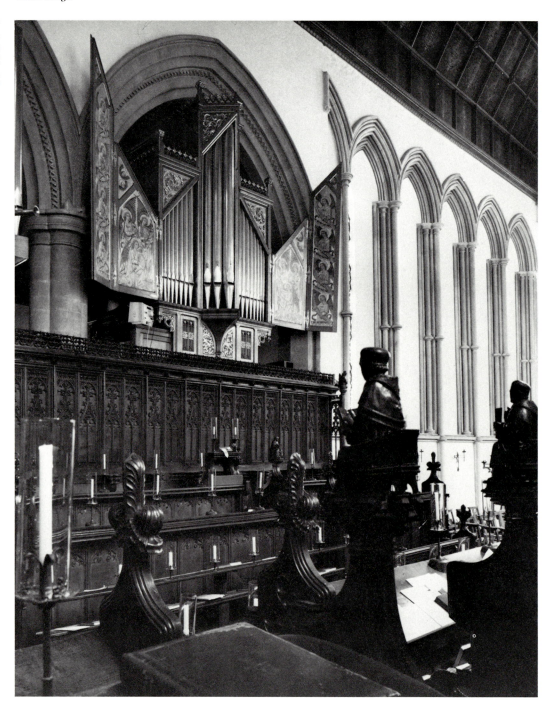

about 1150 of the convent of nuns of St Radegund.[11] The first endowment came from a rich goldsmith of the city called William the monk, and he may have taken the initiative in interesting two great notables, Constance, Countess of Boulogne, daughter-in-law of King Stephen, and Malcolm IV, Earl of Huntingdon and King of the Scots, to provide it with water and fish and the plot of land just outside the city rampart where it came to be built.

[11] For what follows, Brooke 1985a, p. 72 and references, esp. to Gray 1898; *VCH Cambs*, II, 218–19.

9 *The entrance gate, c. 1500 or rather later. The cocks on the coat of arms to the right form the 'rebus' of the founder's name, John Alcock*

The nuns' church and cloister, now the heart of Jesus College, forms the most splendid remnant of the medieval houses of Cambridge today; and about it lies the ten-acre precinct granted by King Malcolm and the surviving meadowlands of the east fields of Cambridge, Jesus Green and Midsummer Common; and thus it was that a great area of grass has been preserved so near the city centre. But the nuns were less fortunate in their destiny than their grass. In the late fifteenth century it was alleged that 'the house was reduced to ruin financially and, apparently, morally, owing to the proximity of the university' – and this was followed by the briefest of attempts at reform by John Alcock, Bishop of Ely, who in 1496 turned out the nuns and founded Jesus College in their stead.[12] The academic college represented the fashion of its day; women religious had no powerful friends at court; and the women had to wait another 350 years before anyone seriously thought of providing a college for them.

Soon after 1500 John Fisher followed the example of John Alcock and converted the old Hospital of St John into a college.[13] This ended the career of one of the central and most characteristic religious institutions of medieval Cambridge. The rapid urban growth all over western Europe in the eleventh and twelfth centuries had brought much new prosperity and grave social problems in its wake; the urban poor and their physical sufferings – poverty, ignorance and disease – came as a new shock to the religious conscience and consciousness of western Christendom. Charitable citizens and church-men combined to provide a stable base for poor relief in the institution of hospitals, which were intended to serve those who could not serve themselves – the very young, the sick and the old. Social service in the church's eyes comprised equally pastoral, spiritual care and physical aid; and pastoral care was one of the major impulses behind the growth of orders of canons in the twelfth century. There came to be a close link, not easy for us to trace, between the canons of Barnwell and several parishes; and even the nuns of St Radegund provided in the nave of their church for the parishioners of their precinct, at least from the late thirteenth century.[14] The first hospital was set up for lepers in the mid twelfth century outside the further boundary of Barnwell – a safe distance from the frontiers of the city, as was the practice; and although the leper hospital faded away in the thirteenth century, its charming chapel, a gem of Norman architecture, still survives, a lone example of the tiny Romanesque churches which filled the streets of Cambridge itself in the same epoch.[15]

About 1200 a group of citizens united with the Bishop of Ely to establish a Hospital of St John. It provided a focus for the charity of many citizens of large or modest means, and for many in the villages about Cambridge; it offered a home for a small group of urban poor and for the sick. It performed other functions too – pastoral care of unspecified extent by a small community of canons; and a modest banking service, providing loans for those who needed capital to buy houses or to go on pilgrimage, or to escape from their debts to Jews, the chief bankers of medieval Cambridge. But the Hospital of St John was scarcely off the ground before some of its functions were overtaken by the arrival of the friars.[16]

At one time or another six orders of friars had houses in Cambridge, and their presence came to be the most characteristic witness of the work of the religious orders in the eyes of the citizens. They made up for the deficiencies of the parish clergy – if such there were – by preaching and pastoral work; they provided for civic amenities by improving the water supply and in other ways; and they quickly forged a link of their own both with the civic community and with the university. In the long history of love and hate which forms the main theme of the tale of town and gown the friars formed a third party, themselves in intimate rivalry with both. But in Cambridge as in Oxford the friars above all fostered the

---

[12] Knowles and Hadcock 1971, p. 257; cf. Gray 1898, pp. 42–5.
[13] For what follows, Rubin 1987, esp. pp. 294–5; for the college, Miller 1961, chap. 1; Underwood 1979, 1982, 1983.
[14] Brooke 1985a, pp. 56–8, 69–72.
[15] Plate 10; Rubin 1987, pp. 111–18; Brooke 1985a, p. 74; *RCHM Cambridge*, II, 298–9.
[16] For the Hospital, see Rubin 1987; for the Friars, Brooke 1985a, pp. 60–1, 73–4; Moorman 1952; Hinnebusch 1951, p.89; F. Roth 1966, I, 250–3; *VCH Cambs*, II, 269–91.

10 *The leper hospital of St Mary Magdalene, mid twelfth century*

academic community and provided a mendicant model for the early colleges; and their story lies in another chapter.

A traveller coming south along the Roman Road from Huntingdon in the thirteenth century passed first the ancient Roman fort turned castle, then as now the centre of the shire, symbol of a wider jurisdiction. From castle bailey, now Shire Hall, and from the keep or mound or motte, now a grass hillock, Picot and his successors surveyed the most troublesome part of their little empire.[17] As the traveller pressed on down Castle Hill he came to the great bridge, now Magdalene Bridge, and the true centre of medieval *3* Cambridge. Where Bridge Street and the High Street met, around the church of the Holy Sepulchre and the Hospital of St John, he entered the Jewry.[18] Between the late eleventh century and the 1270s the economic life of the city depended heavily on the Jews, who offered a money-lending service which fostered its trade and helped many a householder and business man to his feet. Like all such communities who thrive in the act of bringing prosperity to a larger native population about them – our own third world is full of tragic examples of the same phenomenon – they were suspected as aliens and profiteers; and an intolerant Christian Church did little to protect them. The Holy Sepulchre in their midst was an ironical reminder of their homeland – for to many of them it must rather have been a reminder of how the Crusades had issued in many parts of Christendom in a heightened

[17] *VCH Cambs*, III, 3–5, 116–18.
[18] *VCH Cambs*, III, 95–6; Lobel and Johns 1975, p. 10.

anti-Semitism and in massacres of the Jews. Nor did the Jewish community long survive in Cambridge, for in the mid 1270s, well before the general expulsion of the Jews by Edward I in 1290, the king and the citizens of Cambridge agreed with the queen-mother, Eleanor of Provence, that as an act of piety they would expel the Jews from Cambridge – a sad example of the cruel forms which piety can take.[19] Yet in the two centuries at most in which they had lived in the city, the Jews had left their mark: Holy Sepulchre and All Saints church opposite the Hospital of St John were known for centuries to come as 'in Jewry' – and one of the community, Benjamin the Jew, who had a substantial house near the Guildhall, was long remembered, for his house became first a prison, then a Franciscan convent, and finally the Tollbooth – and always the documents specify that it was 'formerly of Benjamin the Jew'.[20]

Benjamin had lived near the Market Place, and this, for all the vicissitudes through which it has passed, remained the commercial and economic centre of Cambridge for many centuries, for Cambridge was essentially a small market town – small, and so close to its fields; it wore, as Maitland strongly emphasised, a very rustic look; many of its citizens had plots in the field and some of them worked there. But it was also a town, and essentially this was based on the market place, which then as now formed a centre for the produce of a wide agricultural region. The main artery of the city was the river, which served both the market and the fields. For the Cam – such is the persistence of man – was navigable up to Cambridge. The main wharves lay below Magdalene Bridge, but some craft went further, and along its banks where the lawns of King's now lie were wharves in the central Middle Ages.[21] Above the wharves lay the mills: a whole group of them is recorded in Domesday, lying between the end of Mill Lane, where the mill pond still races, and Newnham Mill.[22] This was the main factory for the corn of the fields of Cambridge, and must have served a wider area too; the mills were the industrial heart of the town.

The parish churches show that early settlement sprawled especially along and about the High Street, and around the Market Place; but there was also a little grid of streets between the High Street and the river, with its centre in the parish church of St John Zachary – John the Baptist – which lay near the west door of King's Chapel and was the one church between the High Street and the river. It sat beside the main street of this region, Mill Street, which was parallel to the High Street, and ran from the site of Michaelhouse to Queens' – that is, from the corner of Trinity Lane, along what is now Trinity Hall and Clare Lane, across the heart of King's, to end in Queens' Lane. All this was Mill Street long before any of the colleges was thought of, and about it was ample space not only for the substantial church of St John, but for a scatter of citizens' houses, including some of stone, set there in the twelfth and thirteenth centuries. The remains of one such, near the northern end of Mill Street, survived as the main building of Gonville Hall, to be engraved by Loggan at the end of the seventeenth century and abolished by eighteenth-century improvers.[23] Only one of the great medieval houses still stands, away to the west, across the river, now engulfed in the Cripps buildings of St John's: the splendid 'School of Pythagoras', a monument to the ostentation and social ambition of the two families of the Dunnings and

---

[19] *VCH Cambs*, III, 96.   [20] Brooke 1985a, p. 73: this was near the Guildhall, not in the Jewry.
[21] *RCHM Cambridge*, I, p. l; for the formation of the area west of the river, see esp. Hall and Ravensdale 1976, pp. 80–7; Lobel and Johns 1975, pp. 4, 9.   [22] *VCH Cambs*, III, 5, 64; Stokes 1910; Hall and Ravensdale 1976, pp. 46, 65–6, 80–2, etc.
[23] For the early history of Mill Street, Addyman and Biddle 1965, p. 101–3; for the houses incorporated in Gonville Hall, Brooke 1985, front endpaper (Loggan), p. 14 and n. 30, and p. 173; Willis and Clark, I, 159–60; IV, plan 8.

11   *Old houses in Magdalene Street*

the Blancgernons, who alternately occupied it in the late twelfth and thirteenth centuries.[24] As they fell into debt, they were bought out by that great speculator in mortgaged property, Walter de Merton.

In the present state of knowledge we cannot be sure how extensively peopled the region of Cambridge west of the High Street became in the twelfth and thirteenth centuries. We can only presume that it prospered modestly for a time and then decayed; that rents were always highest next to the High Street and fell off somewhat further to the west; but that the land by the river, originally marshy, had been extensively drained and built over by the thirteenth century. In the late Middle Ages Cambridge, like many English provincial towns, declined in population.[25] It is hard to assess this decline, for it went hand in hand with the rise of the university and the foundation of a group of new colleges which did

[24] *VCH Cambs*, III, 122–3; Maitland 1898, pp. 163–7; Gray 1932.
[25] H.M. Cam in *VCH Cambs*, III, 12–13; Rubin 1987, chap. 2.

12 *Town turned college: King's bridge (by William Wilkins, 1819–20) and the river*

13 *King's chapel and the Gibbs building, 1724–31*

much to replace what was lost to the town, but also shifted the balance of town and gown in the university's favour.

In 1352 the citizens had shown their interest and pride in the university by founding Corpus Christi College; and though the college was also to be first object of their hate in the rising of 1381, the university at large has remained one of the principal economic supports of the city – even if less so in the last two centuries than in earlier times – and the chief ground of its fame in the world.[26] The constant presence of a rowdy element of highly privileged youths, in the naturally riotous context of a medieval town, led to frequent bloodshed. But that was the stock-in-trade of medieval towns where any life is to be discerned, the English and academic counterpart of the feuds of Verona portrayed in *Romeo and Juliet*. The relationship of town and gown has always been one in which love and hate,

[26] H.M. Cam in *VCH Cambs*, III, 6–12.

18

intimacy and estrangement, have been mixed. What is most remarkable is the way in which the town allowed a whole segment, essentially the area between the High Street and the river, to be torn away from it and given over wholly to academic pursuits. This was partly due to poverty: rents declined in this region and it may have become depopulated. Partly it was the effect of a great act of power by Henry VI, who stripped a large area to make way for King's, demolishing numerous houses, moving a college – God's House – outside the Barnwell Gate where it was later enlarged to become Christ's College – and resiting the parish church of St John Zachary to the north of his precinct.[27] Partly it was due to the movements of the land market in the hands of rich speculators and rich founders. However it may have happened, it determined the history of the city in a marked way, for it compelled it to extend, not to the west, which has been in substantial measure college land since the Middle Ages, but to the south and east. *12* *19* *63*

Many generations were to pass before the town needed to expand. That is not to say that the sixteenth and seventeenth centuries saw no change in Cambridge. In the 1530s the religious houses were suppressed. This did not mean, in the long run, any great diminution in the stock of celibate clergy in the town, for the fellows of colleges were forbidden to marry till the 1860s or later. But it very much sharpened the difference between town and gown by removing communities who had their roots in both, especially the friars, who had performed a pastoral role as well as an academic – and the fashion for uniting college chapels with parish churches, so marked a feature of fourteenth- and fifteenth-century Cambridge, also declined.[28] Celibacy did not extend to the heads of colleges, and they came to form an aristocracy in the town, commonly, if not invariably, a little apart from the city patriciate itself. In the late sixteenth century and later the master's lodges of the richer societies became substantial gentlemen's houses, with long galleries such as those of John's and Queens' and Emmanuel, or stately homes like the Master's Lodge in Trinity.[29] *93* *71–2*

In the late Middle Ages the population declined and the citizens complained (as did those of almost all English towns, even the most prosperous) that they could not make ends meet, let alone pay the taxes the government required.[30] But whatever may be the truth of this, the essential basis of the town's prosperity survived: it was a market town at the head of a rich agricultural region, which grew steadily richer as the fens were drained in the seventeenth century and later; and its prosperity had its centre in the weekly market and the celebrated fairs. The fair at Reach, ten miles from Cambridge but presided over by the Mayor and Corporation, Garlic Fair near the opening of Jesus Lane, and Midsummer Fair, which still in a nominal form exists, all went back far into the Middle Ages and survived into the modern world; they were characteristic annual fairs of modest importance. But Stourbridge Fair was one of the greatest in Europe. Like the others it probably goes back to the twelfth century; and it was only abolished in 1934. But its heyday lay in the sixteenth and seventeenth centuries, when it occupied part of August and most of September, drew merchants of cloth of every kind known in Britain, and dealers in food and wine, 'pitch, tar,

---

[27] J. Saltmarsh in *VCH Cambs*, III, 386.

[28] See below, pp. 92–4, 152, 168; Brooke 1985a, pp. 64–8.

[29] Willis and Clark 1886, I, 21–36 (corrected by *RCHM*); II, 248–63, esp. 260–1, 606–27, 704; *RCHM Cambridge*, I, 62, 64, 66; II, 168, 174–6 (redating the Queens' gallery), 187–8, 194–5, 229–31; Twigg 1987, pp. 131–2 (on Queens').

[30] *VCH Cambs*, III, 12–13: complaints of this kind were a stock-in-trade of late-medieval towns; but they are not the only indications of declining population. It is greatly to be hoped that Cambridge will receive the detailed topographical study Dr Derek Keene has given to Winchester (Keene 1985), and he and his colleagues are now extending to the city of London (cf. Keene 1984; Keene and Harding 1985).

14   *The garden and lily pond,
Emmanuel College, probably
deriving from the fishpond of the
Dominican friars: its present lines
are of 1964*

15 *Merton Hall: the new wing of the School of Pythagoras, of the sixteenth and seventeenth centuries*

coal, charcoal, faggots, salt, hay and grain' to quote the proclamation of 1549; and the lay-out of its booths still marks the street-names of the region where it lay.[31] This great fair reflected the convenience and importance of Cambridge in national and international commerce; but the town remained relatively small, the home of farmers, brewers, masons, tailors, shoemakers, small tradesmen and dons. The area occupied by houses expanded very slowly between the sixteenth and the early nineteenth centuries. The space between Sidney Street and Trinity Street, the angle between the two ancient roads, became a densely populated slum. Slight expansion occurred elsewhere. But it is characteristic of the history of Cambridge in the seventeenth and eighteenth centuries that the notable changes in its face lay in parks and gardens and college buildings, not in the building of citizens' homes or great shops or warehouses. A notable exception is Merton Hall, or the School of Pythagoras, to which fine extensions were made in the sixteenth and seventeenth

13

[31] As summarised in *VCH Cambs*, III, 93.

22

centuries. Otherwise Cambridge is notably deficient in large houses of this period, though modest houses of great beauty of the seventeenth and eighteenth centuries – and a few which are earlier – abound on some stretches of the old High Street and its purlieus – and once made Petty Cury one of the enchantments of the city. But Cambridge was still the centre of an agrarian region, and its wealthy citizens are to be found in many houses out in the country, in Madingley Hall and the two halls of Trumpington, and at Fen Ditton and elsewhere.

Town and gown co-operated to preserve its open spaces to a remarkable degree. Between the sixteenth century and the eighteenth the colleges by the river developed the meadows and the gardens beyond them into the Backs, one of the celebrated landscape beauties of Europe. It was a piecemeal creation to which many hands contributed; and after a while colleges vied with one another in beautifying the landscape – whether to create the stately lawns of St John's and Trinity, or to preserve the rugged meadow of King's, now often

17   *The river and the Bridge of Sighs, St John's College, 1827–31, by Henry Hutchinson. On the left the Old Library (plate 95) with the letters ILCS for Iohannes Lincolniensis, Custos Sigilli – John Williams, Bishop of Lincoln, keeper of the great seal*

18 *Trinity College Library, by
Wren, built 1676–90, from the
Backs*

70

cropped by regal-looking sheep; just as the head gardeners of the colleges today compete in the culture of daffodils and crocuses and trees. In essence, the Backs was the creation of the seventeenth and eighteenth centuries, though it owes much to earlier days; and when Capability Brown came to Cambridge in the 1770s he devised an alluring scheme for turning the whole of the Backs into one park, widening the river to improve the show of water, and imparking the fields which lay beyond. But Cambridge is a federation, and the university had neither power nor will to enforce so grandiose an amalgamation upon the jealous cantons, the colleges. He had already been allowed by the fellows of St John's to replan the Wilderness, their garden; but that was all. The college and the university sent him on his way, sorrowing, burdened only with two handsome pieces of plate.[32]

[32] Stroud 1984, pp. 171–2, 181–2, and pls. 56–7; for the formation of the Backs cf. *RCHM Cambridge*, I, p. liii; Willis and Clark 1886, I, 89–92, 117 (Clare bridge, 1638–40, walks and avenues laid out 1691), 349–50 (King's); II, 5–6 (Queens'), 235–9 (St John's), 406–9 (Trinity); for their prehistory, Hall and Ravensdale 1976, pp. 80–7.

Meanwhile, as the colleges took in hand the Backs and beyond, they encountered islands of alien territory; and in 1613 the town conceded Garret Hostel Green, the ample space now presided over by Wren's great library, to Trinity.[33] In exchange the college gave the town 25 acres of land south-east of the city centre, which had been leased in 1587 to the college cook, one Edward Parker, whose name was thus immortalised in Parker's Piece. This rapidly became one of the two great areas of common carefully preserved by the civic authorities close to the heart of Cambridge – the other comprises the combined extent of Midsummer Common and Jesus Green, ancient common meadow lapping round the extensive lawns of St Radegund's or Jesus College along the river to the edge of the old ditch and rampart. About these two large stretches of grass the Cambridge of 1800 began to grow. It was, as it has always been since the early thirteenth century, a divided community, its division reflected by this time in the two poles of political authority. The town was politically dominated by John Mortlock and his patron the Duke of Rutland. Mortlock and his sons enjoyed the office of mayor with very few interruptions from 1784 to 1820. The university was subservient to its leading member, the younger Pitt, until his death; and thereafter the star in its firmament, or at least in Westminster, was Lord Euston, George Henry Fitzroy, M.P. from 1784 till 1811, when he succeeded his father as Duke of Grafton.[34] In his honour the central artery of the new Cambridge of his day was and is called Fitzroy Street.

Cambridge is an ancient market town and a city of shopkeepers; and it has two shopping centres. The more ancient is obviously the Market Place, which is set about by churches and colleges and public buildings; there in the 1780s the chief architect of the day for town and gown alike, James Essex, set up the new Guildhall, which was destroyed in the 1930s to give way to its dull but dignified successor.[35] The old market could only expand in recent centuries along and beyond its satellite the little market, the 'Petty Cury', destroyed in the 1960s to make way for the first of the new shopping centres of the late twentieth century, which stretches south over Lion Yard. The region to the south-east, round the Kite, is a monument to the expansion of the city in the early nineteenth century. In 1801 there were 252 souls recorded in the parish of St Andrew the Less; by 1851 there were 11,776, rather more than in the whole of Cambridge fifty years before.[36] From this centre Cambridge has continued to grow, and the natives of the city came to regard this as its true heart and core. When the dust of conflict had settled after the Lion Yard development had been completed, another argument of equal violence blew around the Kite; this too has now subsided, and out of the ruins another characteristic monument of late-twentieth-century development has appeared, the Grafton Centre. In the process the dual core of Cambridge as a shopping town has been preserved; and the Kite and the Grafton Centre stand at the heart of what was the new Cambridge of the early and mid nineteenth century.

The most spectacular development of Cambridge in the nineteenth century lay thus to the south and east; and the occasion for this was the enclosure of the east fields in successive acts between 1801 and 1807.[37] To the north-east lies Chesterton, and its development for the most part came later; to the west lay the academic quarter, and over

[33] Willis and Clark 1886, II, 407–14; *VCH Cambs*, II, 111.
[34] H.M. Cam in *VCH Cambs*, III, 72–6; *DNB* (Fitzroy, George Henry).
[35] *VCH Cambs*, III, 120; on Essex, see Cocke 1984.
[36] *VCH Cambs*, III, 98.
[37] J.B. Mitchell in Darby 1938, pp. 170–1; *VCH Cambs*, III, 98; *RCHM Cambridge*, I, pp. lvii–lviii.

the west field the colleges kept their grip until much more recent times.[38] Extensive development in Madingley Road and Grange Road and elsewhere came when fellows were allowed to marry in the late nineteenth century and saw the need for new housing beyond their own particular Backs. But the great step forward of the nineteenth century had been over the fields of Barnwell. The earliest monument to this expansion lies in a pleasant housing development of the 1810s and 1820s along Maid's Causeway, which made the name and fortune of Charles Humfrey, architect and mayor – and father-in-law of Professor Robert Willis, the engineer and architectural historian; in Humfrey, town and gown made a happy meeting.[39] In 1845 the Eastern Counties Railway, after long negotiation, established the fine arcaded station which still survives, much modified, with the immense single platform nearly a quarter of a mile long adjacent to it. Why Cambridge has but a single major platform is a historical mystery on which rivers of ink have flowed.[40] But the site of the station clearly marks the limit to which Cambridge had reached in 1845. Much of the residential quarter on either hand of Hills Road – that part of the old Roman Road which leads towards the station and beyond, up to the foothills of the Gog Magog Hills – was not filled with houses until the 1880s. In that era the colleges were struck by the agricultural depression and found relief in selling off tracts of land for housing.[41] Meanwhile the town was expanding fast. The many streets from Bateman Street to Harvey Road, which commemorate the worthies of Trinity Hall and Caius, reflect development in the 1880s and 1890s. Further out came the railway itself, which inspired the development of Romsey Town from Great Eastern Street to the end of Mill Road. In the mid twentieth century the colleges have yielded more land to the builder's trowel, most evidently marked in the last fifty years in St John's' Wilberforce and Clarkson Roads to the west, and Trinity's Newton, Bentley, Barrow and Porson Roads to the south. In a famous passage in his *Autobiography* Eric Gill compared the two towns of his youth, Chichester, square and rational, the product of town planning by Romans and Normans, and Brighton, a nightmare (as he saw it) of suburban sprawl. Few cities have a shape so absurd as Cambridge, stretched out like a great piece of elastic from Girton to Cherry Hinton, from Chesterton to Trumpington; yet revealing in its oddities of plan the whole story of its growth, from the little fort on Castle Hill of Roman origin, revived by the Saxons, spreading rapidly in Saxon times amid the marshes south and east of the river, and between the two great roads, the Roman Road and the Saxon High Street; through the formation of the noble academic quarter in the fifteenth and sixteenth centuries to the nineteenth century, when its circumstances prevented growth round most of the northern and western rims and encouraged it to the south-east – and when town and gown united to preserve the ample open spaces which come so near its heart.

19   (opposite) The High Street and Pembroke College chapel (by Wren: see p. 222)

---

[38] For the background to this, see Hall and Ravensdale 1976, pp. 57–76, 80–7.
[39] Colvin 1978, pp. 438–9; Pevsner 1970, pp. 224, 250, 539 (index); *RCHM Cambridge*, I, p. xcv; II, 361–5, etc.
[40] Between *c.* 1850 and 1863 there was a 'timber island platform to the east; the single platform has been lengthened at least three times' (*RCHM Cambridge*, II, 311–12; Pevsner 1970, p. 238).
[41] Brooke 1985, p. 252; Howard 1935, pp. 233–4; cf. J.B. Mitchell in Darby 1935, pp. 162–80, esp. p. 167.

2 *Oxford*

All the citizens of Oxford have in common outside their wall a meadow for which they pay six shillings and eight pence . . .

Domesday Book, I, 154

The far-famed city of Oxford, being sweetly hugged in the pleasant arms of those two pure rivers, the Thames and Cherwell whose timely floods enrich the meadows with excellent herbage.

Thomas Baskerville's Account of Oxford [1683–6], ed. H. Baskerville in *Collectanea*, IV, OHS, XLVII, p. 179

John Leland, the antiquary, wishing to praise the Thames-side palaces of his patron, Henry VIII, wrote a Latin poem attributed to a swan setting out from Oxford towards the mouth of the river. The many branches of the river embracing the watery side of the city are well described.[1] Restricted on all sides except the north by flood meadows, which are in their turn surrounded by low hills not more than 600 feet high, it stands more or less in the centre of England. A long series of gravel terraces running north and south between the Thames and its tributary the Cherwell had, since before the tenth century and perhaps as early as the eighth, provided a dry site for a Saxon borough at what was to become the frontier of Mercia and Wessex. The rivers had made the site defensible; thus it had been fortified by Alfred and refortified by Edward the Elder. Its eleventh-century street plan is striking.[2] With its rectilinear form and central crossing at Carfax it is a gridiron and not a spider's web. Someone made it more or less rectangular, a distinction which it shares with Wallingford and which distinguishes it from most Anglo-Saxon towns. Its compact block of royal lands was regarded as the equivalent of eight yardlands, which were still known as the king's eight yardlands in the twelfth century.[3] The phrase emphasises the interest which the king had in it from its earliest days; indeed he may well have been responsible for its first settlement. This royal interest continued when its importance was recognised in the Old English period by its becoming a shire town with a hundred of its own. Already by the eleventh century it had become a place of royal residence. Ethelred held meetings of the royal council there and Harold his gemot.[4] Under Edward the Confessor it paid the king and Earl Ælfgar yearly about £33 and in 1086 £60.[5] Its interest for kings was further enhanced when in the reign of Henry I the Norman king made a manor at nearby Woodstock one of his favourite residences, and subsequently when he built a 'new hall' at Oxford itself just

---

[1] *Cygnea Cantio* in Leland 1745, pp. 9–10.   [2] Biddle and Hill 1971, p. 8ĭ; and cf. Salter 1936, p. 8.
[3] Stenton 1947, p. 522.   [4] Whitelock 1979, p. 247: Salter 1936, p. 16.
[5] Salter 1936, p. 20.

20 *Oxford: the city wall (mainly thirteenth century) and the tower of New College (1396–1405) (p. 33)*

outside its walls, the so-called 'Beaumont Palace'.[6] From his time and perhaps much earlier Oxford had the rare right, with London and Winchester, to help the King's Butler at the coronation feast.[7]

The town was important not only as an occasionally garrisoned fort, for instance against the Danes, but also because it lay on the ancient road which since the tenth century had connected Southampton via the crossing of the Thames at Oxford with Northampton and beyond. This road coming through Hampshire and Berkshire crossed the river by a series of fords and streams lying immediately south of Oxford where now are the Abingdon Road and Folly Bridge.[8] Here it entered the town. Here too the existing route was developed by Robert D'Oilly, one of Oxford's earliest Norman inhabitants, into a causeway and bridge, known as Grandpont.

Trade flowed along the road and also along those stretches of the river immediately above and below the town which were navigable in the twelfth century, and until the

[6] Colvin 1963–82, II, 986–7.   [7] Salter 1936, p. 18.   [8] Davis 1973, pp. 258–67.

21 *The castle and D'Oilly's tower, late eleventh century*

building of many weirs had a damaging effect on navigation. At that time the town to which the scholars were to come still seems to have been prosperous and important. Under Athelstan its mint had four moneyers and in the reign of Edward the Confessor it had been about the fifth most important in England.[9] By 1050 the town had two portreeves or bailiffs.[10] Moreover between the tenth century and the time of Domesday Book (1086) it had become necessary to extend its limits; it has been estimated that by 1086 there were

[9] Davis 1973, p. 266.   [10] Kemble 1839–48, IV, 285.

some 600 houses within the walls and over 340 outside, even if some of them were waste and unoccupied.[11] Already in the twelfth century it had at least two guilds which paid a yearly fee to the king; one was of weavers and the other of leather-workers ('corvesers').[12] Their shops were on the east side of Northgate Street, now Cornmarket Street. The 'Drapery' where cloth was sold is mentioned in the reign of Henry III.[13] The initiative of which the town was capable is suggested by its attempt to form a commune in 1147. It failed then, but eventually succeeded by 1191.[14] Henry II had granted it a generous charter in 1155. Its municipal seal is the earliest in England.[15]

Although some of its trade was in transit, much more was the result of the fact that Oxford was a market town, at first the only market for this part of the Upper Thames Valley. It was to remain an agricultural market town with a higher proportion than Cambridge of traders to farmers until industry swept over both in the twentieth century. Straw, pigs, wood, earthenware, gloves, white bread, dairy produce, fish, tanned hides and corn, among much else, were daily brought into town. Just outside its northern walls horses were sold in Horsemonger Street, now Broad Street.[16] The widths of the cross of streets made up by Queen Street, Cornmarket Street, High Street and St Aldate's are there to remind us that they were all market streets – elongated market places. The houses fronting them often had narrow fronts with ranges behind them, approached through 'entries'. This arrangement reflected the value of the sites. The market was to become of almost as much interest to the university as it was to the town. For the former gained privileges over it which were valuable and much resented by the townsmen. The resentment was understandable, especially as the rights of the university over the market may well have had a restrictive influence.[17] This aspect of town and gown hostility – although easily exaggerated – was to have a long history.

The present town walls are of the early thirteenth century and were only moated in part. *20* They are a sign that Oxford's prosperity survived at least until then. To judge from archaeological evidence they probably followed the line of their Anglo-Saxon and Norman predecessors, even though in the tenth and eleventh centuries, to judge from the Burghal Hidage, the Anglo-Saxon town was smaller. At the North Gate the walls incorporated the town prison – 'Bocardo' – and further west linked up with the walls surrounding the Castle.[18] From 1199 when the burgesses leased Oxford from the king for £63 0s 5d annually[19] they undertook to repair the walls. These were proudly displayed on the seal of the municipality. There were six gates – North, South, East, West, Littlegate (at the end of St Ebbe's) and Smith Gate (at the north end of Cat Street). Their keys were kept by the town's bailiffs who locked them up at night except during St Frideswide's Fair, when the duty devolved upon the prior.[20] Beyond South Gate on D'Oilly's bridge was a seventh gate, the fortified 'New Gate', and a drawbridge, which were built perhaps before 1200 and were to become in due course Folly Bridge.[21]

The cramped nature of the town's site was no doubt an early stimulus to the

[11] Salter 1936, p. 23.
[12] Salter 1936, pp. 31–2. Only London and Winchester similarly had two guilds. For the corvesers cf. *VCH Oxon*, II, 253–4.
[13] *VCH Oxon*, II, 187.   [14] Davis 1973, pp. 266–7.   [15] Cf. Salter 1936, p. 38.
[16] Salter 1936, p. 78.   [17] Lawrence 1984, pp. 136–7; but cf. Salter 1936, p. 57.
[18] Davis 1973, pp. 265–6. For a possible eastern suburb between the line of the gutter of Magpie Lane and the East Gate, enclosed after *c.* 911–19, Hassall 1971, p. 45, and cf. Catto 1984, p. 157.
[19] Salter 1936, p. 41.   [20] Boase 1887, pp. 70–1.   [21] Salter 1936, p. 15.

development of suburbs, the more particularly because the 'civitas' covered an area of about eight virgates,[22] of which perhaps half lay outside the walls. Already by the time of Domesday there were over 340 houses outside.

It is notoriously difficult to describe Oxford's boundaries outside the walls. Let us start on the south where it is easiest and work round the environs in a clockwise direction. To the south there were houses outside the walls between South Gate and the river, and Grandpont had extended beyond D'Oilly's bridge (hence its name, the 'great bridge') and along his causeway. On the west expansion took place on the island opposite the castle and the Castle Mill. This was to become the parish of St Thomas in the twelfth century. The most important possession of the town outside its walls was the great pasture of Port Meadow which it had owned since Anglo-Saxon times: in 1086 the town paid the king 6s 8d yearly for it.[23] It lay to the north-west of the castle on the east bank of the Thames opposite Binsey. Its owners in the reign of Henry I were an oligarchy of burgesses – more specifically the merchant guild of the freemen who had the right to graze their beasts there.[24] From the time of the first mayor, Laurence Kepeharm, soon after 1199, the size of the stint of cattle and other beasts which might graze there was settled annually in April. Kepeharm, as mayor, could graze four or six beasts, the aldermen less than six, and freemen one or two each.[25] Round Port Meadow lay six manors in private hands. South of it the manors of North and South Osney belonged to the abbots of Rewley and Osney respectively. West of it on the other side of the river lay the manor of Binsey, the property of the prior of St Frideswide's. East of it were the two manors of Walton, one of which belonged to the abbot of Osney and the other to the abbess of Godstow. In all these manors the lords exercised their rights, such as the View of Frankpledge, and townsmen settling within the bounds of these manors had to reckon with seignorial jurisdiction. From the hythe on the river just north of the castle a street ran up to the North Gate and St Mary Magdalen church outside the walls. This was Irishman's Street, later George Street. But directly north of the North Gate was the Northgate Hundred.[26] This had once been part of the manor of Headington and contained the three open fields of Oxford. They were farmed by those who lived in the parish of St Giles. The hundred had split off from the manor and at the end of the sixteenth century was bought out by the city. Here was the site of the twelfth-century church of St Giles and between the North Gate and the church a suburb grew up on both sides of the road leading northwards. This was Beaumont, 'the fair mount', which paradoxically covered a flat area on either side. Just beyond its westernmost extremity lay 'Beaumont Palace' which was strictly speaking not in Beaumont at all.[27]

Continuing the clockwise survey, to the east of Northgate Hundred and outside the walls lay the manor of Holywell. Here a village grew up round the church of St Cross and the manor house and farm which from 1266 belonged to Merton College.[28] Beyond the East Gate of Oxford stood the Hospital of St John the Baptist; and further east still Charwell Bridge or Pettypont[29] led over the Cherwell to the suburb of St Clement's. Here was a chapel and here too roads branched off for High Wycombe and Henley. St Clement's was in the manor of Headington, a village a mile or so to the east of Oxford where there was an important stone quarry. This was only one of several quarries in the neighbourhood. They

---

[22] Salter 1936, p. 27.   [23] Salter 1936, p. 26.

[24] Salter 1936, p. 26. For the freemen, cf. Salter 1928, pp. vi–xiv.

[25] Salter 1936, pp. 49, 73.   [26] Salter 1936, p. 76.

[27] Salter 1936, pp. 75–6.   [28] Highfield 1964, p. 41.   [29] Salter 1936, p. 29.

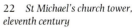

were especially to be found in the foothills of the Corallian limestone escarpment of the Cotswolds, as at Taynton near Burford. But they also occurred to the east of Headington at Great Milton, for example. Headington, however, was easily the nearest. These quarries were to ensure that Oxford was not simply to be a town of thatched houses of wattle and daub; its more important buildings were to be of stone. In 1907 there were still 39 quarries in use in Oxfordshire.[30] Stone was used for the tower of the oldest surviving Saxon parish church – St Michael at the North Gate – for the crypts of the early Norman chapel of St George's in the Castle and of St Peter in the East and for St Peter's south doorway. Two of *23* the early seals of Oxford show the stone towers of the two most important religious houses, Osney and St Frideswide's.[31] The latter seems to have been a Saxon church or monastery which remained a centre of pilgrimage because it contained the shrine of the patroness of *24*

[30] *VCH Oxon*, II, 268.
[31] *VCH Oxon*, III, 88 (plate II); 100 (plate III). For St Frideswide's cf. Stenton 1936, pp. 103–12; Hassall 1973, pp. 270–4; Mayr-Harting 1985, pp. 193–206.

23   *St Peter in the East (now the
library of St Edmund Hall),
Norman door, twelfth century*

the town. In 1122 it was transformed into a priory of Austin Canons, and in the sixteenth century it became one of the new cathedrals of Henry VIII. Osney, founded just outside the walls in 1129, was a great Augustinian priory, later an abbey, whose site now lies largely under the railway line just short of Oxford Station on the London side. The abbey is recalled today chiefly by its recast bell – Great Tom – which rings out each day at curfew time from Tom Tower in Christ Church. Osney and St Frideswide's were, as will be seen, centres of monastic learning. On a much smaller scale was the joint Cistercian abbey and house of studies of Rewley, established with the backing of Edmund, Earl of Cornwall, probably in 1282, on a western site well beyond the city walls.

85

Of the friars the Dominicans were the first to arrive, in 1221.[32] Their order had only been founded four years before, when Dominic had made his great decision to turn his back on the heretics of Toulouse and scatter the twenty or so members of his order over Western

[32] Catto 1984, p. 194; Hinnebusch 1938, pp. 57–82; Hassall 1973, pp. 286–94.

36

24 *Christ Church cathedral, formerly St Frideswide's Priory, shrine of St Frideswide, fourteenth century*

Europe. He had chosen Paris and Bologna as the centres of its activity on the basis that universities made ideal recruiting grounds. Now the Dominicans looked beyond Paris to Oxford. They made straight for the main pool of students in England and chose a house situated in the Jewry south of Carfax. By 1229–30 they had opened a school. Soon afterwards, in 1235, they began to build a new house outside the walls on a site of fifteen acres between the Trill Mill stream and the main river. Nor at this date was there a parish church in the area.

The Franciscans or Friars Minor came on their heels; they too quickly made for the universities. They founded in Oxford what was only their third house in England. Led by Brother Agnellus of Pisa they were at first put up by the Dominicans as they had been in London. Like them they found that their first site – in St Ebbe's parish on the south-west inside the walls – soon proved inadequate. In 1229 they were provided with better quarters which included a house and beyond the walls grounds which extended down to

25   *The cathedral nave: Norman
capital, twelfth century*

26   *(opposite) The nave vault:
the fifteenth-century lierne vault
over the twelfth-century arcade*

the Trill Mill stream.[33] The main church was built astride the wall. Here was the great
house in which Adam Marsh was to preach. Here too was the library to which Robert
Grosseteste, who lectured to the Minors, was to give his books.

   The Carmelites followed the Franciscans in 1256 and took up a station on the north-
west outside the walls at Stockwell Street. They were lucky to be able to transfer from it in
1317 to Beaumont Palace as a result of the vow which Edward II made to build a Carmelite

---

[33] Hassall 1970, pp. 10–18. The friars were allowed to build up the north wall of their church as part of the city wall; cf. also
       Brooke 1985a, p. 61.

house if he escaped from the battle of Bannockburn.[34] The Austin Friars also found a good extra-mural position when they arrived in 1266–7. This was to the north of Smith Gate on the present site of Wadham.[35] Short-lived communities of Friars of the Sack and Crutched Friars came in 1261–2 and 1342.[36]

The secular clergy ministered to eighteen parish churches and chapels inside and outside the walls in 1200 and to two which were non-parochial, Holy Trinity over the East Gate and St George's in the Castle.[37] Eight of the parish churches can be shown to have been already in existence at the time of Domesday. Seven can be shown from a list of churches given to St Frideswide's by Henry I to have been established by the early twelfth century. Two more took their origins in the twelfth century and can be fairly closely dated. St Giles was set up beyond the North Gate between 1123 and 1133.[38] St Thomas's was established by Osney Abbey between 1187 and 1191,[39] west of the town on an island between the Castle Mill and the Osney Mill streams.

Oxford's twenty churches and chapels can be compared with Chester's nine, the fifteen or so at Cambridge and more than fifty at Winchester or Norwich. Considering the lateness of Oxford's settlement the multiplication of churches matches that of other Mercian towns, while Winchester had been a most important town in Wessex, and Norwich was for many years the second city in the land.[40] Although none of Oxford's churches had very extensive revenues, presentations to them were to be often enough important sources of income for principals of halls and fellows of colleges. The Jews lived from the twelfth century on either side of Jury Lane, a turning off Fish Street (now St Aldate's), south of Carfax. Here was their synagogue. They eventually spread on to the west side of Fish Street as well. They were a small but quite prosperous community, probably never more than 200; some of their number were closely related to the Jews of London. Their burial ground was outside the walls and eventually became part of the site of the present Botanical Garden opposite Magdalen.[41]

Once the university had been established in the twelfth century it had to adjust itself to the social and economic conditions of Oxford and its inhabitants. Since there were no purpose-built residences, teachers and taught alike lived anywhere they could among the existing townsmen and women. They might even live in an inn. There were several in Cornmarket Street like the Bull and the Cross (later the Golden Cross), or in the High Street like the Ram.[42] Or they might be 'chamber deacons' who hired separate rooms, like Chaucer's 'Hende Nicholas'. But this situation began to change and to be restricted early in

---

[34] Sheehan 1984, p. 195.   [35] Sheehan 1984, p. 195.

[36] Sheehan 1984, p. 194. *VCH Oxon*, II, 148–50. Both orders were reckoned by the ecclesiastical authorities to have been extinguished by the Council of Lyons of 1274, and the Friars of the Sack died out soon after 1300; the Crutched Friars maintained a shadowy existence elsewhere till 1538.

[37] Salter 1936, pp. 113–14. The eighteen churches or chapels were St Michael at the North Gate, St Martin, All Saints, St Mildred (daughter of Merwald, an Anglian ruler on the Welsh border and granddaughter of Penda (cf. Attwater 1979, p. 246)), St Edward the King, St Peter in the East, St Peter le Bailey, St Aldates (unidentified), St Ebbe (dedicated to St Ebba, a Northumbrian abbess of Coldingham Abbey, Berwickshire (Panton 1980, p. 1)), St Michael at the South Gate, St Frideswide, St Budoc (perhaps a Welsh missionary bishop of the sixth century; he was popular in Brittany and Cornwall: Attwater 1979, p. 76), St John the Baptist, St Mary the Virgin, St Mary Magdalen, St Clement (a dedication popular in Scandinavia), St Giles and St Thomas.

[38] Salter 1936, pp. 114–15.   [39] Salter 1936, p. 114.

[40] For Chester see Harris 1979, p. 18. There were between 49 and 54 churches and chapels in Norwich in 1086, 61 churches in the late thirteenth century (Campbell 1975, p. 3), and for Cambridge see Brooke 1985a. For the multiplication of parishes, Campbell 1979, pp. 126–7, and Brooke 1970, pp. 59–83.

[41] For this paragraph see Roth 1951.   [42] Salter 1960, 1, 6, 10–13, 181.

the fifteenth century when the university first sought to insist that all its undergraduates should live in academic halls under the eye of a supervisory 'magister'.[43] This regulation temporarily enhanced the position of the halls and was to lead towards the abolition of the chamber deacons in the sixteenth century.[44]

This happened against a background of declining prosperity. Already by the first half of the fourteenth century houses were reported to be falling into decay.[45] The Black Death of 1348–9 undoubtedly hastened an existing trend. In 1370 there was a mandate to put a stop to the pulling down of houses.[46] But this was evidently ineffective. William of Wykeham, for example, was able to buy up thirty halls or houses on the site of New College,[47] and Merton acquired many houses on the south side of Merton Street which were in a decaying condition. The cartularies and rentals of Osney and the Hospital of St John the Baptist tell a tale of decreasing rents.[48] In the early fifteenth century when the university's population has been estimated at well over 1,600 persons[49] this must have represented a notable proportion of the total urban population, perhaps as high as a quarter.

Not until the sixteenth century does there seem to have been a reversal of this tendency to urban decay. In the middle of that century a concerted effort was made to pump new life into the cloth industry with a scheme to turn the deserted buildings of Osney Abbey, after the Dissolution, into a cloth-making industry employing 2,000 people.[50] But this came to nothing and the cloth trade continued to decline into the seventeenth century. More successfully, a university press was founded in 1584–5 with the aid of a loan from the university.[51] Another industry associated with the university which can be seen to emerge at this time was paper-making. This was eventually to result in the foundation of the Wolvercote paper mill by 1666.[52] Book binders who had flourished especially in Cat Street, once the home of manuscript illuminators, and in Shidyerd Street in the later Middle Ages, received a great boost to their trade with the foundation of the Bodleian Library in 1598.[53]

From the mid sixteenth century attempts were made to improve communications both by road and river. Apart from the road from Southampton to Northampton, already noticed, there were roads to Witney and Chipping Norton on the west and north-west and to High Wycombe and Henley on the east and south-east which were to become the great turnpikes of the eighteenth century.[54] The main London Road went up Cheney Lane, Old Road and over Shotover. Members of the university coming from London to Oxford would catch sight of it for the first time as they rode on horseback or from the top of a coach from half-way down Cheney Lane. Two of the bridges, those over the Thames to the south and the Cherwell to the east, had been maintained throughout the Middle Ages, the first with the help of the bridge hermit of St Nicholas' chapel who lived just south of the bridge.[55] Now in 1540 the seven bridges to the west linked Oxford by a new road with the village of Botley, even if the bridges were only wide enough for one vehicle at a time.[56] In 1555 the first public and general statute had been passed to provide for the maintenance of the highways.[57] The preface alludes to the 'noisome and tedious' conditions resulting from the

---

[43] Gibson 1931, pp. 208, 226–7.   [44] Gibson 1931, pp. 392, 419.   [45] Salter 1936, p. 87.   [46] Salter 1917, p. 146.
[47] Salter 1960, I, pp. 147–50.   [48] Salter 1936, p. 87.   [49] Aston 1977, pp. 6–7.
[50] This was an enterprise of William Stumpe, clothier of Malmesbury (*VCH Oxon*, II, 244).
[51] Carter 1975, I, 19–21.   [52] *VCH Oxon*, II, 240.   [53] *VCH Oxon*, II, 237.
[54] For the Faringdon Road see Lambrick 1969, pp. 79–81. For the roads to Chipping Norton, Henley and Wycombe cf. Falkner 1899, p. 300.   [55] *VCH Oxon*, IV, 286; Graham 1972.   [56] Bourdillon 1938, I, 15.   [57] Coleman 1977, p. 40.

growth of traffic. To judge from a reference by John Stow, the Tudor antiquary, this traffic was now often carried by long-wheelbase wagons with four wheels.[58] These helped out the traditional carts, packhorses and wains provided by the carriers. Acts of 1555 and 1563 established the repair of roads by parish labour.[59] When this was inadequate a bill of 1622 was introduced which sought turnpike toll finance for repairs.[60] Stage coaches followed in the same century. They can be seen in several of the illustrations of Loggan, and Anthony Wood tells us that he went in one to London in 1667, though it took two days, and he had to pass the night at Beaconsfield.[61] Regular flying coaches which performed the journey in a single day followed soon afterwards in 1669.[62]

Carriage of goods on rivers had a very considerable advantage over land carriage, measured by price per ton mile, and it is not surprising to find that in the reigns of Elizabeth and James I a concerted effort seems to have been made to seek to improve the river navigation between Oxford and London. Up to this time many goods, such as coal, seem to have been brought as far as Henley or Burcot up the Thames to be offloaded and carried the rest of the way expensively by road.[63] It seems that the river was open as far as Culham by 1562 since in that year Abingdon Corporation paid 4s 8d for the carriage of a hogshead of wine 'from London to Culheham in ye barge'.[64] By the early 1580s the river upstream from Oxford was open for at least eleven miles.

In 1580 indeed an approach was made to William Cecil to encourage a survey of locks and weirs from Maidenhead to Abingdon and to establish Oxford's right to sell goods free of toll in London.[65] In 1606 an Act of Parliament was passed for 'clearing the passage by water from London to and beyond the city of Oxford' and in the following year it was decided to inspect the river from Clifton Hampden to Cricklade.[66] The commission of eighteen members which was appointed succeeded more than has been recognised in improving matters upstream from Oxford. But for success with the major task of opening up the stream between Iffley and Burcot several more years had to elapse. Meanwhile timber from Stowood and Shotover intended for the project to make the Thames navigable from London to Oxford was redirected for use in the construction of the Bodleian Library.[67] However at last, after an Act of 1624 had set up an Oxford–Burcot Commission, three locks were built at Iffley, Sandford and Culham and the first barge to use this route successfully reached Oxford in 1635.[68] Trade began in the carriage of corn, stone and timber downstream and of coal coming upstream from London. Yet there were still hazards to be undergone, as Bishop Fell explained in a letter to Vice-Chancellor Bathurst when the latter was fitting up St Mary's church in 1676 with one of the latest Father Smith organs. 'The lowness of the river is a disadvantage', Fell wrote, 'that may hinder the organ and other materials from being brought at the usual rates and with the accustomed speed.'[69]

The fact that Holywell began to be built up in the early seventeenth century may be explained perhaps by the need for those displaced by the building of the Bodleian and the New Schools to find alternative homes. However, the assessment of Oxford for £100 for Ship Money[70] and the existence of seventy different kinds of token which have been identified as circulating there between 1647 and 1672 – a number only exceeded by

[58] Coleman 1977, p. 40.   [59] Coleman 1977, p. 41.   [60] Coleman 1977, p. 41.
[61] e.g. Loggan 1675, pls. III, IX, XV, XVI, etc.: for Anthony Wood, see Wood 1891–1900, II, 109.
[62] Falkner 1899, p. 301.   [63] Prior 1982, pp. 109–10, 113.   [64] Preston 1935, p. 307.
[65] Prior 1982, pp. 116–17.   [66] Prior 1982, p. 118.   [67] Philip 1983, p. 21.
[68] Scargill and Crosby 1982, p. 32; Salter 1936, p. 17.   [69] Falkner 1899, p. 219.   [70] Falkner 1899, p. 219.

Norwich and Exeter[71] – both suggest that the population was growing, as we know it to have been in the country as a whole. The university itself was more or less stationary at about 2,500 at the time of the parliamentary commission of 1648.[72] Meanwhile the town became the temporary seat of Parliament after its adjournment in 1625 and again during the Civil War for the royalists and in 1681. It was also the royalist capital during the Civil War and a refuge for the court of Charles II at the time of the Plague of 1665; and thus it was demonstrated that it was capable of accommodating substantial additional bodies, even if there were often loud complaints of cramped quarters from its temporary inhabitants. The siege of Oxford in the 1640s clearly interrupted any increasing prosperity while it lasted. Since the fortifications were slighted when it was over they have left comparatively little mark. Part of the King's Mound can still be seen and Dover Pier, named for the royalist garrison commander, the Earl of Dover, in the water walks at Magdalen has retained its fame under another name as Addison's Walk. After the war, trade seems to have picked up fairly soon. At all events the Oxford–Burcot commissioners were able to repay in 1667–8 and again in 1681–2 part of the money which they had borrowed from the City of London and the University.[73]

In post-Restoration Oxford, brewing, which had been a thriving industry at Henley and Oxford in the Middle Ages, expanded once more. Thomas Tesdale, joint founder of Pembroke in 1624, had made a fortune as a maltster at Abingdon.[74] Under Charles II great quantities of ale were consumed. Dr Lamphire is recorded as having told Anthony Wood that there were over 370 ale-houses in Oxford – the 'Meanes to create idleness and debauch scholars' as the antiquary sharply observed.[75] The second half of the seventeenth century also saw Oxford in closer relations with the capital. The stage coaches brought newspapers. Then coffee shops appeared where the papers could be read and read out. The first (1651) seems to have been run by Jacob, a Jew, at the Angel opposite the end of Queen's Lane.[76] Another – Arthur Tilliard's (1655) near All Souls – was much frequented.[77]

During the eighteenth century the roads which the coaches had to use were greatly improved. Between 1760 and 1770 existing roads to Faringdon and Witney were further developed. In Oxford itself the New Road to the west running past the castle was constructed in about 1770.[78] Then as a result of the Mileway Act of 1771 the East and North Gates were pulled down, the bridges on the Botley Road were widened and Magdalen Bridge was rebuilt (1772–8).[79] A wide variety of other improvements were begun including the construction of the Covered Market.[80] The main London Road to the east now ran directly up Headington Hill and took the place of the old route up Shotover. Along this new turnpike ran a variety of fast coaches: Bew's Flying Machine, the Worcester Fly, run by Samuel Manning, and the Burford, Witney, Oxford and Thame Fly. This last regularly carried passengers from Oxford to London for 10s. That meant that it was still an expensive journey. But the cost was halved for outside passengers.[81]

Since the 1760s there had been efforts to encourage the building of a canal between Oxford and the Midland coalfield near Coventry. This was finally opened in 1790.[82] It brought the price of coal down from 3s 3d to between 1s 2d and 1s 6d per hundredweight.[83]

[71] Salter 1920, p. 359.   [72] Burrows 1881, p. cxxxi: admittedly an untypical occasion (see p. 173 below).

[73] Prior 1982, p. 128.   [74] Macleane 1900, p. 51.   [75] Wood 1891–1900, II, 404.   [76] *VCH Oxon*, IV, 439.

[77] *VCH Oxon*, IV, 97.   [78] *VCH Oxon*, IV, 477.   [79] *VCH Oxon*, IV, 287.   [80] *VCH Oxon*, IV, 307.

[81] *VCH Oxon*, II, 206 and n. 5.   [82] Bourdillon 1938, I, 16; Prior 1982, pp. 186–7.   [83] Prior 1982, p. 190.

If ever the canal froze, as it did in 1795, the price shot up again.[84] The trade led to the development of wharves at Hayfield and Worcester Streets and at New Road. A fresh supply of bargees was added to the existing colony of fishermen at Fisher Row to form an expanded watermen's community.[85] Another was formed at Grandpont by Folly Bridge. Until the railways came, the Thames and the canal remained of the greatest importance for the carriage of goods which were not in too much of a hurry.

In the meantime Oxford had acquired its own newspaper, *Jackson's Oxford Journal*, which had opened its columns in 1753 and provides a vivid commentary on the life of the town. That it had enough potential readers to make a profit is suggested by the first census figures of 1801 which show the population of Oxford alone, without its hinterland in which the paper also circulated, to have been a little under 12,000 inhabitants.[86]

The nineteenth century brought a positive explosion of population. Numbers had doubled by 1851 to reach over 25,000; but by 1901 they had almost doubled again and stood at over 49,000.[87] The city by this date still remained as it had been in the Middle Ages, fundamentally an agricultural market town whose additional population was encouraging the development of market gardening in the immediate neighbourhood. In the first decades of the century the increase was relatively moderate. But it was enough to give rise to speculative building. This might be grand like the houses in St John and Beaumont Streets (1828–37) between St Giles and Walton Street, or it could take the form of jerry building. Often enough, tiny houses were built in terraces of two- or three-storey brick cottages as in St Ebbe's.[88] Then between 1853 and 1855 S.L. Seckham became the architect of a private trust which built the Park Town Estate off the Banbury Road on an isolated site originally designed for a workhouse. This proved to be the first notable extension northwards since the twelfth century and heralded the development of the well-to-do suburb of North Oxford.[89] Much of the land belonged to St John's College and the expansion was carefully controlled. Seckham was also the architect of one of the college's two planned developments – the Walton Manor Estate of 1856–60; William Wilkinson took over the completion of Walton Manor from Seckham and became the architect of the other, the Norham Manor Estate.[90] Together these formed a kind of garden suburb. If to begin with their occupants were chiefly leading tradesmen, subsequently the popularity of the estates and of their successors owed much to the changes brought about by the arrival of the married don. Between Walton Street and the canal meanwhile, and in west Oxford, some attempts were being made to provide working-men's accommodation. In the area known as Jericho – the 'Beersheba' of *Jude the Obscure* – they formed terraces of small houses, many of them occupied by employees of the University Press which had acquired new buildings in 1826–30.[91] In west Oxford they included a great block of buildings erected by Christ Church.

A gas works had been established about 1818 and it was almost certainly gas street lighting which was to provide the 'outmost lamps of the town' which winked their yellow eyes dubiously at Jude as he walked into Oxford from Cumnor Hill and along the Botley

[84] It was 4s 8d per hundredweight, only to fall to 1s 6d per hundredweight after the thaw: *VCH Oxon*, II, 205.
[85] Prior 1982, pp. 202–58.   [86] *VCH Oxon*, IV, 181.
[87] Scargill and Crosby 1982, p. 41; *VCH Oxon*, IV, 182.   [88] Panton 1980, p. 11; *VCH Oxon*, IV, 195.
[89] Saint 1970, p. 84; *VCH Oxon*, IV, 197.   [90] Saint 1970, pp. 57, 71, 84–5; *VCH Oxon*, IV, 197.
[91] *VCH Oxon*, II, 235; Sherwood and Pevsner 1974, p. 274. The architects were Daniel Robinson and Edward Blore.

27 *Folly Bridge, 1825–7,*
replacing D'Oilly's bridge and the
South Gate

Road.[92] Though the gas works lit many lamps in the new streets which were springing up, it discharged its effluent into a river which was being polluted also by the larger quantities of sewage drained into it from the expanding town.

Oxford had had a reasonable supply of water since the early seventeenth century when, in 1615–17, Otho Nicholson, a London lawyer, had ensured that water from a reservoir of 2,000 gallons at North Hinksey was carried to two conduits in the centre of the town, one of which stood at Carfax.[93] In 1694 the City Council itself had added a scheme of its own whereby water was supplied from a works at Folly Bridge.[94] This water was drawn from the increasingly polluted Thames. Moreover the houses in St Ebbe's and St Clement's which continued to rely for the most part on wells had often dug them too close to cesspits. Outbreaks of cholera and of typhus drew victims especially from these parishes. At last in

[92] Hardy 1895, part 2, ch. 1.   [93] Bourdillon 1938, II, 304, and Appendix, p. 475.   [94] Bourdillon 1938, II, 304–5.

1867 the Thames Conservancy was set up and it at once sought powers to prevent the pumping of raw sewage into the Thames; in 1873 the city introduced a comprehensive sewage system.[95] A hospital to deal with infectious diseases was built thirteen years later.

A big change in communications came with the railway in 1844. First mooted in 1837, its arrival was slow. This was not the fault of the railway company. The university authorities were reluctant to admit it at all: it stood for closer links with the corruption of the capital. Thus there was a period of four years, 1840–4, when undergraduates, as in *Tom Brown at Oxford*, coming to the university from or via London could only get as far as Steventon on the main line to Bristol some seventeen miles away. There they had to hire horses or flies to bring them over the last stage of the journey through Abingdon to Oxford. One result of the deferred decision has been that generations of Oxford passengers have had to endure comparatively poor cross-country rail communications.

The Oxford Railway Company did eventually establish a station in 1844.[96] It lay just south-west of Folly Bridge and west of the Abingdon Road. But although its position enabled a junction to be made with river traffic on the wharves by the Thames, the line was a cul-de-sac. Then the London and North-Western Railway Company built a station on the western edge of the city in 1851.[97] This station, disused since Beeching pruned the railway network in the 1960s, still stands as an interesting piece of industrial archaeology and is now a tyre depot. Part of it was made with prefabricated material in the manner of the Great Exhibition. The line ran from Oxford to Bletchley where it linked with trains from Euston to Manchester and Glasgow, while beyond Bletchley it carried passengers and freight to Bedford and Cambridge. Generations of undergraduates and examiners passed up and down between the two universities but never enough to make it pay. Mr Verdant Green (the hero of Cuthbert Bede's account of Oxford life) still made his entrée into Oxford behind the four horses which drew the Birmingham and Oxford coach.[98] This made its final run in the last week of August 1852, coinciding with the opening of the Great Western Railway Company's station in its present position in that year. Thus Oxford was put on to a main line to Birmingham and a year later found itself on another running through to Worcester and the Severn Valley. The railways in fact brought to Oxford the real threat of industrialisation. This was at its most dangerous in the 1860s when the Great Western Railway Company wished to set up its carriage works at Oxford. The university authorities resisted the proposal, which also raised a furore in the press. As a result the works went to Swindon, and, contemplating them, one may be grateful that this first attempt at industrialisation was a failure. Oxford stagnated a little during the agricultural depression of the 1880s although this did not stop – but rather stimulated – St John's College development of the northern suburbs.[99] The motor-car, not the railway, pitchforked Oxford into an industrial existence.

In the twentieth century Oxford's expansion has proved steady and for the period between the wars exceptional in comparison with that of the nation as a whole. The population ran up from 49,336 in 1901 to 98,747 in 1951 and has since passed the 115,000 mark. This has been largely the result of the development of the motor-car industry and in particular of the Morris Motor Works and its associated factory run by

[95] Bourdillon 1938, II, 321.   [96] Bourdillon 1938, I, 22.   [97] Bourdillon 1938, II, 408.   [98] Bede 1853, p. 36.
[99] See p. 301 below; and cf. especially the work of W. Wilkinson and H.W. Moore in Banbury, Bardwell, Chalfont, Farndon, Frenchay, Kingston, Linton, Norham, Northmoor, Plantation, Polstead, Rawlinson, St Margaret's, Southmoor and Woodstock Roads and Norham Gardens.

Pressed Steel Fisher Limited (from 1926). Starting from a cycle shop in the town, William R. Morris, the future Lord Nuffield, acquired in 1912 the buildings of the bankrupt Military College in Cowley as a base for his operations. The new company burgeoned after the First World War and still more after the Second, when it became part of the British Motor Corporation. By the 1950s the two companies were employing over 22,000 men.[100] The Service Division of B.M.C. covered about 1,000,000 square feet. For east Oxford this spelt a revolution. Oxford attracted workers especially during the years of the slump in the 1930s when to a large extent it escaped the worst effects. Cowley, Headington and Iffley took the brunt of the expansion and were themselves taken into the city of Oxford along with Wolvercote and Cutteslowe in 1929.[101] The new residents came especially from the south-west, but also from South Wales, London and the Midlands. The new communities of east Oxford as a result lacked the coherence which had typified the older suburbs of St Clement's and St Ebbe's. A whole new world with a shopping centre of its own grew up in Cowley, a world largely indifferent to the university and in some ways resenting the hold which it maintained on the centre of the town. There were new opportunities for bad relations between town and gown. Moreover slum clearance between 1953 and 1963 added to the pressure for new housing estates. The population of the university grew from 1,300 c.1850 to 4,600 in 1931 and over 12,000 in 1984.[102] But even so it never reached as high a proportion of the urban population as between 1300 and 1640.

An unexpected result of the arrival of Morris Motors has been the series of benefactions which the owner rained down upon the hospitals of Oxford, and finally the foundation of Nuffield College.[103] Having wished to do medicine himself, Lord Nuffield became deeply interested in encouraging the study of medicine at Oxford. Thus the profits of industry have directly furthered research and teaching both in medicine and in the social sciences. No less than four Nuffield chairs were based on the Radcliffe Infirmary (and one at the orthopaedic centre). Thus a great stimulus was directed to orthopaedic surgery, obstetrics and gynaecology, anaesthetics, surgery and clinical medicine. The statutes setting up the chairs (in 1936) left open the possibility for teaching undergraduates. This chance was grasped by the regius professor of medicine, Sir Farquhar Buzzard, and in the years following the Second World War it became possible to establish a complete School of Clinical Medicine which has since won international recognition for the quality of its instruction.

The urban revolution did not occur without some steps being taken to try to prevent the ancient city from being overwhelmed by industrialisation. One was the private initiative which led to the setting up of the Oxford Preservation Trust in 1927.[104] This had already by 1932 achieved the notable acquisition of part of the Morrell Estate so that St Clement's is separated from Headington by the green expanses of South Park, an achievement which was enhanced by the addition of Headington Hill Park, the Morrells' demesne on the north side of the London Road. The Trust was also able to buy up part of Boar's Hill to the south of the city and the old golf course on its north-eastern slopes. Here the landscape itself changed a little when Sir Arthur Evans had the Jarn Mound constructed in order to provide

[100] Sherwood and Pevsner 1974, pp. 323–4.
[101] Scargill and Crosby 1982, p. 41.
[102] For c.1850 cf. Pantin 1972, p. 12. In 1985–6 the total number of undergraduates and graduates was 12,863 (*Oxford University Gazette* (14 July 1986), p. 95).
[103] See pp. 324, 326 below.   [104] *Town and Gown* 1982, p. 34.

work during the depression and a suitable viewpoint from which to admire the landscape described by Matthew Arnold in *Thyrsis* and the *Scholar Gypsy*.[105]

Another attempt to save the ancient city is represented by the conservation areas. Part of the Norham Manor Estate was so designated in 1968 and proved to be only the first of twelve such areas which had been established by 1977. Within their boundaries there are the severest limitations on development.

More spectacular still was the concept of the 'green belt', which was written into the Town and Country Planning Act of 1947. Eleven years later a green belt round Oxford was taking effect. A buffer of undeveloped land was to be preserved between the city and the villages of Kidlington, Yarnton, Garsington and Horspath. The outer part of this belt had been approved by 1975 and it is hoped that approval for the rest will follow.[106] Thus to the constrictions placed upon the expansion of the city by the flood meadows and by the ownership of much of its centre by the university and colleges, has been added another restraint. This operates on the surrounding country for a depth of about a dozen miles from Carfax. Beyond it, where building is less restricted, suburbs have replaced former villages, as at Kidlington to the north, while outlying ancient towns like Witney and Woodstock have become dormitories for Oxford commuters. Indeed since the rail and road links with London have greatly improved in recent years, Oxford has itself become a centre for commuters to London and this has added yet another element to the city's burgeoning population. The constrictions on building have led to soaring house prices so that in chosen suburbs, like North Oxford, they may be compared with those in favoured parts of London. The wide range of modern building controls, coupled with such defences as green belts and conservation areas, may yet prove inadequate to protect the heritage of city and university.

[105] Scargill and Crosby 1982, pp. 58–9.   [106] Scargill and Crosby 1982, p. 73.

3 *The formation of the universities*

This Edmund [Rich] was born at Abingdon beside Oxford. He fared as the olive tree that holdeth itself the bitterness in the rind and holdeth out to others the sweetness of the oil.

Ranulf Higden, *Polichronicon*, quoted G. Bone, *Came to Oxford*, Oxford, 1952, p. 38.

> . . . Imagination slept,
> And yet not utterly. I could not print
> Ground where the grass had yielded to the steps
> Of generations of illustrious men
> Unmoved.

Wordsworth, *Prelude*, III, 260–4 – on Cambridge

Oxford

Unlike many continental universities which owed their origin to the definite act of a pope or king, Oxford became a university gradually by the wills of its teachers and students in what appears to have been a natural process. There was no specific moment of genesis. We are told that Theobald of Étampes, a schoolmaster 'who had been a "magister" at Caen . . . was teaching at Oxford before 1100 and in the early twelfth century'.[1] He acquired a following of some sixty to a hundred pupils, and was still teaching in 1119. Another teacher, Master Robert Pullen, who occurs in the annals of Osney, a theologian in the tradition of Anselm and a future cardinal, began to lecture in 1133 on the Bible.[2] By 1139 he had transferred from Oxford to Paris where he taught John of Salisbury. If Gervase of Canterbury is correct, Vacarius, a 'magister' of Bologna and the first civilian to lecture on Roman law in England, delivered law lectures at Oxford.[3] But when did this happen? It could hardly have been in Stephen's reign. Perhaps they were given in that of Henry II. Whether there was a migration of teachers directly from Paris to Oxford at this date is doubtful. But the wars of Henry II must have made it much more difficult for the English to study in France. On occasion the king specifically forbade clerks to cross the Channel. There may also have been a pull towards Oxford by learned local residents. Such were Walter, archdeacon of Oxford and provost of St George's in the Castle, evidently a senior friend of Geoffrey of Monmouth, and two canons of St George's, Robert Chesney later Bishop of Lincoln and patron of his fellow canon, Geoffrey of Monmouth himself, as well as Wigod, prior and subsequently abbot of Osney, and the first two priors of St Frideswide's,

---

[1] Salter 1936, p. 91; Southern 1984, pp. 5–7.   [2] Southern 1984, pp. 6–7.   [3] See Southern 1976, esp. pp. 266–73.

49

Wymundus and Master Robert Cricklade.[4] Osney, it is true, appropriated St George's in 1149 and put an end to the appointment of any more learned canons, but it is difficult to see in this step, as Salter does, the crushing of an embryonic school.[5] Osney was itself, it seems, a centre for the study of theology and the scriptures in the second half of the twelfth century. Master Walter of Ghent (Gant), a canon, became abbot of Waltham in 1184.[6] He was one of several known 'masters' about this time at Oxford. It is not easy to prove that any one of them was specifically a teacher of an arts course. There was even a period about 1180 when it seemed more likely that Northampton would develop a university rather than Oxford.[7] However by 1187 it seems that there were several faculties (or branches of learning) at Oxford. In a well-known passage of his *Autobiography* Giraldus Cambrensis describes how, when he had written his *Topographia Hibernica* (1186), he went to Oxford and for three days read it to assembled audiences.[8] These included the doctors of diverse faculties and those among the scholars who were well known, as well as those who were not, and the knights and citizens of the town. Giraldus often exaggerates. Nevertheless it is hard to avoid the conclusion that by the time of Giraldus's visit (*c.* 1187) the faculties of arts, canon and civil law and theology were all operating.[9] Two major canon law texts from Oxford of the 1190s actually survive. That theology was positively flourishing is strongly suggested by the fact that Alexander Nequam, a grammar master of Dunstable, transferred thence to Oxford in 1182 and eleven years later was giving regular courses on the Psalms, Ecclesiastes, Proverbs and the Song of Songs.[10] It is even possible that there was a faculty of medicine. The earliest arts lectures of which we have knowledge were those of Edmund of Abingdon, the future saint. He was lecturing on Boethius's *Arithmetic* and Aristotle's *Sophistici Elenchi* about 1200, and continued to lecture on arts for six years as a regent.[11] The system of regency reflects incipient organisation by which graduates, as a condition of their graduation as masters, promised to lecture for the university for a set number of years, thus guaranteeing that tuition would be available and continuous. Organisation is also reflected in the appearance in 1201 of John Grim, regent master in theology, as Master of the Schools – the same title, significantly, as many cathedral dignitaries carried. In the late twelfth or early thirteenth century it was replaced by the title of chancellor. Later (in 1210) we hear of a 'rector scolarum'. What did these officials do? One thing they may well have done is to have organised the teaching of grammar.

Of all the seven subjects that made up the liberal arts – grammar, rhetoric and logic (that is, the trivium), and arithmetic, geometry, astronomy and music (the quadrivium) – grammar was the most important, and indeed a *sine qua non*. For a knowledge of Latin was necessary to enter on any clerical career or to follow any of the university courses. It was taught to boys as well as to students, as it was to the young Edmund of Abingdon, who went to a grammar school at Oxford at the age of twelve, probably in the last decade of the twelfth century.[12] There were lectures on grammar in the embryonic university also. They were controlled by the archdeacon of Oxford and might be given by 'magistri' or 'non-

---

[4] Southern 1984, p. 8; Brooke and Dumville 1986, pp. 43, 97; Emden, *Oxford*, III, 1971–2 (Walter of Oxford); I, 406 (Chesney); III, 2108 (Wigod); for Wymundus see Wigram 1895–6, I, p. xiii; Emden, *Oxford*, I, 513–14 (Cricklade).

[5] Salter 1919, pp. 382–5.   [6] Emden, *Oxford*, II, 749; Knowles, Brooke and London 1972, p. 188.

[7] Southern, 1984, p. 11.   [8] Southern 1984, p. 13.

[9] As is confirmed by the researches of Dr Emden (esp. *Oxford*, I, 37–9) and Father Hackett (1984, pp. 37 and 39). For what follows, Boyle 1984, pp. 531–2.   [10] Southern 1984, pp. 22–5; on Nequam, see Hunt and Gibson 1984.

[11] Southern 1984, pp. 22–5. For what follows see *ibid.*, pp. 28–9; Hackett 1984, p. 41 n. 3.

[12] Southern 1984, pp. 27–8.

magistri'. Grammar masters often presided over grammar halls although grammar was not to become a faculty of the university.[13]

Oxford was the centre of an archdeaconry, and one of the leading Oxford glossators, John of Tynemouth, was archdeacon of Oxford.[14] From the archdeacon's court went an increasing flow of appeals to bishop, archbishop or pope. In the mid and late twelfth century the pope came frequently to send these cases back to be settled before local 'judges delegate'.[15] These judges required lodgings and brought with them their retinues. St Frideswide's and Osney alone generated a considerable amount of business: there were no less than thirty cases affecting them between 1155 and 1195.[16] All these needed the appointment of papal judges delegate who met in Oxford. The cases also required the presence of trained lawyers, several of whom can be identified by name.[17] The courts had to have graduate lawyers and the lawyers may have practised in the courts, where local custom was as important as canon or civil law. Practising lawyers had the opportunity to take pupils. By about 1190 a combination of practice in the courts and instruction in the schools was beginning to draw students of canon and civil law to Oxford. The *Liber Pauperum* of Vacarius 'quickly became a bible for the students of civil law'.[18] However it was the study of canon law which was to be the more important branch of legal study at Oxford, no doubt because it was the needs of the ecclesiastical courts which the successful students were to supply. The great Abbot Samson of Bury St Edmunds in 1197 gave a dinner at Oxford for a party of 'magistri'.[19] By 1200 the masters had begun to organise themselves.[20] These are two of the signs that at the turn of the twelfth and thirteenth centuries a *studium* was forming. But the incipient courses in arts, canon and civil law and theology were to receive a sharp setback with the great dispersion of 1209.

This took place as the result of the murder of his mistress by a clerk, who then absconded and could not be found; the mayor and townsmen arrested in his place two clerks who shared his lodgings, and in their anger, and with King John's permission, hanged them outside the city walls.[21] In January 1209 the 'magistri' instructed the members of the university to disperse. The number of 'magistri' involved may well have exceeded seventy. This action itself reflected a considerable degree of sophistication in the existing organisation. Those who failed to obey were noted down for disciplinary action. Some 'magistri' who came from Cambridge went home and set about founding the university of Cambridge.[22]

King John had been in collision with Pope Innocent III since 1206, as a result of the election of Stephen Langton to the archbishopric of Canterbury and the king's refusal to confirm the appointment. Since 1208 England had lain under an interdict. When after a long struggle John eventually capitulated to the pope in 1213, the mayor and townsmen, as royal protégés, found themselves without a patron. They also decided to come to terms with the church and sought out accordingly the papal legate, Nicholas de Romanis, Cardinal Bishop of Tusculum.[23] The heavy penance which he required was accepted and the legate drew up the terms of peace in an ordinance on behalf of the university. This document of 1214 is at once the earliest charter of the immunities and privileges of the university and a statement of its powers *vis-à-vis* the town. Half the rents of all hostels and

[13] Hackett 1984, p. 68.   [14] Southern 1984, p. 20 n. 1; Emden, *Oxford*, III, 1923.
[15] Southern 1984, pp. 16–19.   [16] Southern 1984, p. 16.   [17] Southern 1984, p. 19.
[18] Southern 1984, p. 9; Boyle, p. 533.   [19] Southern 1984, p. 20.   [20] Southern 1984, p. 28.
[21] Southern 1984, p. 26.   [22] Hackett 1970, p. 44.   [23] Southern 1984, pp. 26–7.

houses let by townsmen to clerks were to be surrendered. The rents were to remain at their present levels for ten years. The town was to pay 52 shillings annually to the university for ever and to entertain a hundred poor scholars on St Nicholas' Day. Then a most important point: the scholars of the university were to be placed under the authority of a chancellor, called 'cancellarius scolarum Oxonie' at one point and 'cancellarius Oxonie' at another. In addition the exemption of all university clerks from lay jurisdiction was confirmed.[24] That meant that there had to be a special ecclesiastical jurisdiction exercised on their behalf. By 1221 we know that it was the chancellor who exercised it.

Armed with the strong defences of the ordinance of 1214, backed up by the authority of the pope, the university began to reassemble with remarkable speed thereafter. The friends of Edmund of Abingdon successfully persuaded him to return to Oxford from Paris in order to lecture on theology. Soon after his return he probably incepted as doctor of divinity, the earliest known example at Oxford.[25] The law school meanwhile was re-established. The study of Roman law was not dropped, as it easily might have been. The study of the old *Liber Pauperum* continued alongside that of canon law. The tradition of 'utrumque ius' was maintained. The two schools did not become rivals. Students of civil law were, in principle, being prepared for a career as practising canonists. Students of canon law were to be trained in civil law as well.[26]

It was probably in the 1210s that the Master of the Schools at last became chancellor. Long after, in 1295, Bishop Oliver Sutton recalled that one of his predecessors had refused the title of chancellor to the greatest figure of the early history of Oxford, Robert Grosseteste. The truth is obscure, and it may be that the first man called chancellor was Geoffrey de Lucy, a relative, perhaps an illegitimate son, of Godfrey de Lucy, Bishop of Winchester. He was chancellor by 1216. It is very likely that Grosseteste was chancellor in the 1220s; and he was himself Bishop of Lincoln from 1235 to 1253.[27]

That the master and scholars were rapidly becoming a corporate society is suggested by a letter of the Legate Guala of *c.* 1218 addressed to 'all the masters and scholars living at Oxford'. In 1226 papal judges delegate used the term 'chancellor of the university of Oxford' and the royal clerks of Henry III in 1231 drew up the king's remarkable grant of privilege for the university in the person of its chancellor.[28] By 1244 the chancellor was in addition to have such a grant of civil and (by 1255) of criminal jurisdiction as was eventually to give the university, through him, almost complete control of the town. The jurisdiction was to be exercised through a court which was at once of first instance and of appeal, an ecclesiastical court which by the end of the thirteenth century was to meet at St Mary's church if not daily at least weekly. He was also to fulfil the functions of arch-deacon, chancellor of a cathedral chapter school and rector of the university. He was to be much more than the bishop's vicar general. He had no meaning apart from the university whose 'magistri' elected him, as they still do. He was to be a regent master himself or a member of one of the superior faculties. As Father Hackett has put it 'he was its head, chief justice, and chief executive officer'.[29] Since he was a regent master, that meant that he resided in the university – at least until 1230, when we hear of his appointment of a commissary to act on his behalf. This was Elias de Deneis. Quite soon afterwards (1258) the commissary is referred to as vice-chancellor. This officer had at first slight authority. His

[24] Southern 1984, pp. 29–32.   [25] Emden, *Oxford*, 1, 6.   [26] Boyle 1984, pp. 534–5.
[27] Southern 1984, pp. 29–33.   [28] Hackett 1984, p. 49.   [29] Hackett 1984, p. 70.

great days were to come when the chancellor ceased to reside in the university in the fifteenth century.

Another sign of corporate existence was the appearance of students' lodgings and the emergence of the proctors. By the legatine ordinance of 1214 rents of lodgings were to be assessed by taxors. By 1231 we learn that this has come to mean that rents were settled by two masters and two burgesses elected by the proctors.[30] This makes it look as though the

[30] Hackett 1984, pp. 82–4; *VCH Oxon,* III, 2–3.

proctors' origin dates back to the first ordinance and that they were the first taxors. At all events they had come to stay and were referred to again, it seems, in a royal charter of 1248. They turn up also in a university statute of 1252.[31] We learn that there are to be two proctors, elected annually at the first congregation of regent masters after Easter, representing the northern and southern nations. The division between the two turned on whether a man came from north or south of the river Nene. Strange though this division appears, it divided responsibility more evenly than would have been the case if the boundary had been drawn further north. Irish and Welsh students were counted as southerners.[32]

Another result of the 1214 ordinance was the emergence of congregation as the supreme governing body of the university. The decision to disperse in 1209 had been the result of concerted action by the 'magistri', and the ordinance itself seems to presuppose that the regent masters were meeting regularly. The taxors referred to in the ordinance had to be elected by the regent masters in what was in fact a meeting of congregation. Moreover this practice was recognised as valid by the representatives of the town. The regents coming together in such meetings were to make up the governing body of the university until gradually between 1250 and 1280 the non-regents were included for specific occasions. By 1279 the non-regents had acquired a more definite status: meetings of regents and non-regents were known as 'great congregations'. In due course they were to be 'convocations'. When they occurred it was customary for the regents in arts to meet together on the day beforehand to consider the agenda. These meetings were known as black congregations, taking their name from the colour of the artists' garments. The ordinary administrative business of the university continued to be managed by the congregation of regents or lesser congregation. It is to this body that the name 'congregation' has adhered.

The earliest surviving register of the university, Registrum A, dating from the fifteenth century, refers to *statuta antiqua*.[33] How old were these ancient statutes? The earliest surviving statute dates from 12 March 1253 but in an accord of 1252 aimed at preventing riots between the Irish and the northerners there is reference to *antiqua statuta*. Thus it seems likely that there was already university legislation in the first half of the thirteenth century. By the middle of the thirteenth century a few more officers had appeared and the university was beginning to secure some property. For buildings of its own it had to wait until the early fourteenth century, when Thomas Cobham, Bishop of Worcester, fitted out a Congregation House at the north end of St Mary's church with a chamber over it which was to house the university's library.[34] But this is to anticipate. In the thirteenth century, congregation met in St Mary's church itself. Among the additional officers were the proctors' assistants, in the shape of two bedels (later their number was raised to six). They were elected in the same way as the chancellor. There was also a chaplain to celebrate masses when these were required by custom or statute. In 1240 Robert Grosseteste as Bishop of Lincoln instituted an arrangement whereby the common chest of the university, known as St Frideswide's chest, should be looked after by three custodians, a canon from the priory and two regent masters in arts.[35] The regents were to be elected in the same manner as the proctors. This was only the first of 21 chests which were to provide loans for

28

[31] Hackett 1984, p. 82.   [32] Emden 1964, pp. 2–6.   [33] Hackett 1984, pp. 52–3.
[34] Hackett 1984, p. 57. On St Mary's church, see *VCH Oxon*, IV, 390–4.   [35] Hackett 1984, p. 89.

members of the university during the late Middle Ages and thus to act as a kind of primitive bank.

By the middle of the thirteenth century the university was undoubtedly flourishing. Its magnetism was such that it drew to itself the Dominicans and the Franciscans in the 1220s, even if soon it was the friars who were stirring Oxford. The civil war of Henry III's reign only temporarily held back this efflorescence. It in no way prevented the founders of early colleges from concluding that Oxford was a place to which they should turn their eyes.

Cambridge

Why Cambridge? In Oxford there was a tradition of learning; her schools had flourished now and then in the twelfth century; the favourite royal hunting-lodge at Woodstock was near enough for the scholars to look for royal protection and patronage, and in the thirteenth century they were not to look in vain. Cambridge had no such tradition, and as a centre of learning could not seriously compete with Oxford before the fifteenth century. And yet already in the early thirteenth there was a university there, and in the course of the century its position was secured by a like protection from the king. To Dr Caius, writing in the sixteenth century, the answer was plain. Long before Oxford had been thought of, the ancient British prince Cantaber had established a favourite academy at Cambridge as an offshoot from Athens; and long before the days of Geoffrey de Lucy or Robert Grosseteste, St Amphibalus himself was installed as chancellor.[36] Dr Rashdall, the Oxford historian of the late nineteenth century, scarcely pausing to observe that neither Cantaber nor Amphibalus had ever existed, attributed Cambridge to a crisis in Oxford leading to a migration of scholars to places more obscure; and even though the eminent Cambridge mathematician and antiquary Dr Rouse Ball made a spirited case for an origin of Cambridge independent of Oxford, Rashdall's view has prevailed.[37] But the story of the migration depends on the word of one of the least reliable of chroniclers, Roger of Wendover; and much scholarly inference and some conjecture have had to be added to his text to account for a foundation so unlikely. Many a flourishing market town, especially Northampton and Stamford, both less than fifty miles from Cambridge, and many a cathedral city, might have aspired to be the homes of universities.[38] It is astonishing that the university of Cambridge was founded – and, once founded, survived.

But the circumstances in 1209 were unprecedented. King John had quarrelled with the pope over the election to the see of Canterbury, and Pope Innocent III had laid an interdict on the English church: the churches were empty, the sacraments in abeyance and many clerks without occupation. The see of Lincoln had been vacant and the new bishop did not take up office till the interdict was over; there was no one to control or protect the Oxford clerks; and Eustace, Bishop of Ely, an old royal servant, who had consented to become the pope's agent in the recent negotiations, had prudently escaped from England when they failed.[39] The clerks of Oxford and the Bishop of Ely's staff seem to have engaged in a measure

[36] *Historiae Cantabrigiensis Academiae lib. i* in Caius, *Works*, p. 12. Much of this goes back to Nicholas Cantelupe in the early fifteenth century and was repeated in John Fisher's address of welcome to Henry VII in *c.* 1506 (Parker n.d., pp. 1–3; Fisher in Lewis 1855, II, 267; cf. Hackett 1970, pp. 41–3).   [37] Rashdall 1936, III, 276–7; Ball 1918, pp. 181–6.
[38] Lawrence 1984, pp. 127–32. For the migration of 1209 see Hackett 1970, pp. 44–5; Roger of Wendover 1886–9, II, 51.
[39] Hackett 1970, pp. 43–8; Emden, *Cambridge*, p. xii.

of self-help. There were riots in Oxford and clerks were hanged by the secular authorities; the schools were closed in 1209 and only resumed their business after the end of the interdict in 1214. The scholars went elsewhere, some abroad, some to other parts of England. A group of learned clerks in the service of the bishop of Ely, so it seems, had the idea of occupying their idle days and replenishing their impoverished purses, by opening schools in the county town of Cambridge – for Ely itself was little more than a village, no place for a community of scholars to lodge. When the bishop returned and Oxford reopened, the scholarly community in Cambridge had been established, though it must have been very small and relatively obscure for many years to come.

The next stage is equally obscure. In the course of the reign of Henry III (1216–72) the king issued various privileges to various schools, including Oxford, Cambridge and Northampton; but at some point, for some reason or reasons unknown, he decided to close the schools of Northampton and allow royal protection only to Oxford and Cambridge.[40] Without rights and privileges, without royal protection against greedy and riotous townsfolk, permanent communities of scholars could not hope to flourish; and if self-help by students and masters was of the essence of the founding process, royal protection was equally decisive in enabling the universities to survive. The details are totally obscure; but to the question – why did a university arise at Cambridge in the thirteenth century? – the general answer is plain enough: because a community of masters and students won royal approval, and because King Henry III determined to give Oxford and Cambridge a monopoly, for the time being, of university status in England. It was not until the fifteenth century that Scotland acquired universities, nor till the nineteenth that the English universities multiplied. This gave Cambridge a breathing space of 600 years to establish itself; nothing lasts longer than a temporary fiat.

The annals of the university for its first 200 years tend to read like a catalogue of riots and crises.[41] But this is largely due to a defect in the evidence; a peaceful academy made a modest showing in the chronicles and records of the age; tumult and litigation brought it to the fore. None the less, some of the tumults are instructive. In 1261 a riot between northerners and southerners, students from the north and the south of the kingdom, reveals to us that they were coming to Cambridge from far and wide.[42] An enquiry in 1270, presided over by the Lord Edward – the future king – himself, upheld the university's privileges in the matter of rent fixing for student lodgings and in other ways, and shows that the university was cutting a figure in the land. In 1276 the Bishop of Ely was determining the boundaries between the jurisdiction of the chancellor and of the archdeacon – to the chancellor the clergy of the university, to the archdeacon the clergy of the town; but plenty of ground remained for co-operation and friction. In the early 1280s the same bishop, the ex-monk Hugh of Balsham, was seeking a religious context for a small group of students he wished to provide for. First he tried to lodge them in the Hospital of St John which was in spiritual matters under his jurisdiction; but the canons or the old people and the students proved ill-matched. So in 1284 he took them right out of the town into the southern suburb beyond the Trumpington Gate – and founded St Peter's College under the shadow of St Peter's church, now Little St Mary's.[43] Twenty years later open conflict broke out between the secular clerks and the friars, whose separate way of life and

[40] Lawrence 1984, pp. 128–30.   [41] Roach 1959, pp. 151–5, etc.
[42] For what follows, Roach 1959, pp. 151–2.   [43] See below, p. 93.

29 *Cambridge: Little St Mary's formerly St Peter outside Trumpington Gate, fourteenth-century crypt; part of a group of oratories to provide altars for the fellows of Peterhouse*

privileges – enabling them to cut corners, to come and go, to finish their doctorates in less time than a secular master could aspire to – made the seculars bitterly jealous in every northern university. In 1303 the university passed statutes concentrating power in the hands of the masters of the faculty of arts – setting aside the friars, who reigned in theology – and making various restrictions as to where the friars could preach.[44] After three years of strife a compromise was agreed before papal judges delegate at Bordeaux – an unlikely place for university strife to be settled in the modern world, though many an argument has been mellowed by its wine. In 1318 the pope himself confirmed the university's basic status by declaring each of its faculties a *studium generale* and the community of masters and scholars a university – as it had been in effect for over a century – whose degrees carried licence to teach throughout Christendom, and also some measure of exemption from the bishop of Ely, which remained a theme of argument for centuries to come.[45]

The disputes underline certain permanent characters of the medieval university: its intimate relation with the bishop of Ely, its dependence on the friars, its relation of love and hate with the citizens. Above all, the arguments with the friars presuppose a situation peculiarly galling to the secular masters; for until well into the fifteenth century the friars' convents were the largest and most prestigious student hostels – or colleges, as we might call them – in Cambridge; and the reputation of the university as a home of learning, at least in theology, was mainly dependent on them. They included men like Thomas of

[44] Roach 1959, p. 153; Moorman 1952, pp. 35–7; Little 1935, esp. p. 687. [45] Hackett 1970, pp. 177–8.

Bungay, especially associated in later legend with Roger Bacon, who taught at Cambridge as well as at Oxford in the late thirteenth century; at the end of the century possibly Duns Scotus himself, whose career is exceedingly obscure; and in the early fourteenth century Henry of Costessy, a Biblical scholar of exceptional learning, so adept in Hebrew as to fall into suspicion of heresy. The friars had perhaps not founded the faculty of theology; but in the mid and late thirteenth century already they provided it with most of its conspicuous talent; numerically, they formed a large part of a tiny university, still in the mid fourteenth century perhaps no more than 400 to 700 students strong.[46]

When we contemplate the tiny university of the mid thirteenth century, we must wonder that it survived. The wonder is diminished by a unique record from this period – the earliest university statutes in Europe, composed in the mid thirteenth century and discovered and edited by Father Benedict Hackett, and published in 1970.[47] Whatever their precise status, which has been disputed, they reveal a brave, determined, self-governing community of secular masters rejoicing in their rights and duties and privileges. At its core are the active, teaching masters, mostly young, recently graduated scholars, the regents; and the regents formed the governing community until in the early fourteenth century they co-opted the non-regents – the rest of the graduate community still at work in or near Cambridge – to make a bolder presence in the face of the friars. There are many details of inception (entry to the master's or other degrees), dates of terms, meetings, courts, dress – and an emphatic insistence, common to most communities and societies of the late Middle Ages, on the duty to honour a dead king or benefactor and to attend the funeral of one of their own community. But the most striking theme is the democratic element: it is stated that the regents elect the chancellor by a majority vote and it is implied that a majority vote of the regents is the ultimate voice – then as now – in university decisions.[48] And it gives as the reason: 'Since it is difficult for a university (*universitatem*) to agree by common consent and unanimous will . . .' One of the most consistent elements in the history of the ancient universities, at once their genius and their bane – and an element greatly strengthened when they became confederations of colleges – is that, like the Swiss Confederation, they found it very difficult to agree. They could pursue common aims with fervour and clarity of vision; but always differing among themselves, rarely coming to a rapid or lucid decision. Such are academic communities.

[46] For the friars named, Moorman 1952, pp. 157–8, 173, 166; for the faculty of theology, Hackett 1970, pp. 131–2; Moorman 1952, p. 235; for the numbers, Aston, Duncan and Evans 1980, pp. 12–13.

[47] Hackett 1970; for discussion as to their precise status, see Walter Ullmann's review in *Journal of Ecclesiastical History*, XXII (1971), 134–9, who doubted that the statutes discovered by Father Hackett comprised an official collection.

[48] Hackett 1970, pp. 196–7.

4 *The first Oxford colleges*

A clerk ther was of Oxenford also,
That unto logyk hadde longe ygo.
As leene was his hors as is a rake,
And he nas nat right fat, I undertake,
But looked holwe and therto sobrely.

Chaucer, *Canterbury Tales*, Prologue, 285–9

That mutual charity between warden and fellows is not observed . . . Also that the fellows keep dogs, and that causes hindrance to the progress of their studies . . . Also that Wantyng has behaved irreverently towards the warden, when in the presence of all he called him Robert . . .

Complaints of fellows in Merton College meetings of 1338–9, Allen and Garrod 1928,
pp. 33–5

The oldest form of university establishment at Oxford was the academical hall, of which well over 150 are known to have existed in the late Middle Ages. It was amidst a sea of academical halls that the earliest colleges were to emerge in the thirteenth century.[1]

Big ecclesiastical landlords like Osney Abbey, St Frideswide's or the Hospital of St John the Baptist outside the East Gate owned many of the halls which rubbed shoulders with the lecture rooms and schools in which the courses were given. Since those in arts were mostly in Schools Street (which ran north from St Mary's to the city wall) halls for artists tended to be in the northern and eastern parts of the town.[2] The law schools were on the south of the High Street near St Edward's church. Thus halls for legists were situated in the vicinity of Vine Street, now Alfred Street. There were halls which specialised in Welsh or Irish tenants. Others owed all to the fame of the master who presided over them. There were large halls like Broadgates in the High Street and small ones like that of Geoffrey de Biham in St John the Baptist Street (now Merton Street). Most of their buildings have long since vanished. St Edmund Hall, the one independent hall to survive, if now with collegiate status, retains none of its original buildings. But Biham Hall, or to give it its modern name, Beam Hall, which now belongs to Corpus Christi College, although reconditioned and modernised, retains better than other fragmentary remains elsewhere the form of an academical hall in the medieval period.[3]

In the middle of the thirteenth century any would-be founder of a college had to feel his way. No one in England as yet knew exactly what an academic college was. It is true that

30

---

[1] Highfield 1984, p. 225.   [2] Highfield 1984, p. 226.
[3] Cf. Catto 1984, plate III, for another academic hall – Tackley's Inn.

30 *Oxford: St Edmund Hall, the Front Quad, north range, c. 1596*

no less than eleven different examples of colleges of different kinds existed at Paris. Some like the Hôtel Dieu had been founded as long ago as 1180. There a foundation of eighteen scholar-clerks was supported by an alms chest and linked to a hospital. At St Thomas in the Louvre there was a college for arts men only whose finances were put under the control of an ecclesiastic. More substantially endowed was the college founded by Robert de Sorbon, chaplain to St Louis. This extended to the secular clergy the concept of a college where those who had taken their B.A. degree might read for the M.A. and the higher degrees in theology. Its government was put under a mixed body, consisting of local clergy and university officials, 'the archdeacon and chancellor of Paris, the doctors of theology and the rector and proctors of the university', a complicated arrangement.[4] No direct connection can be established between these models and the earliest Oxford colleges, but contacts between Paris and Oxford were frequent and close. William of Durham, the founder of University College, was a doctor of theology of Paris and had left the French

[4] Highfield 1964, pp. 65–6.

60

university at the time of the diaspora of 1229. Robert Grosseteste, chancellor of Oxford and subsequently Bishop of Lincoln, is commonly thought to have studied at Paris.

Alan Basset, a member of a notable local south Midland family, set up a trust in 1243, originally intended to endow two chaplains. But at Grosseteste's suggestion this was converted into two scholarships for those who should also pray for Basset's soul.[5] In 1249 William of Durham left 310 marks in the care of the university to support ten, eleven, twelve or more masters at Oxford who should also pray for his soul.[6] The university authorities bought two houses near St Mary's in Schools Street, later known as the University's Hall, and a third which became Brazen Nose Hall, and other properties. By 1280 this loose arrangement was in need of investigation and overhaul[7] and examples of communities of scholars were already established to act as models.

The brother of another Parisian master, Giles of Bridport, Bishop of Salisbury, shortly before 1242 had set up De Vaux College at Salisbury, a substantial foundation, consisting of a warden, two chaplains and twenty scholars. Like all colleges it was also a chantry; and Bridport placed it under the care of an ecclesiastical authority, the dean and chapter of Salisbury. But Salisbury was not to become a university town and De Vaux College remained isolated.[8]

[5] Highfield 1964, p. 67.   [6] Carr 1902, p. 13.   [7] Carr 1902, pp. 12–15.   [8] Highfield 1964, pp. 67–8.

Sometime before 1260 Walter Kirkham, Bishop of Durham, after a violent attack on himself and his men, imposed a penance on his assailant, John de Balliol, a prominent northern landowner who had married a Scottish heiress from Galloway. Balliol was to maintain sixteen poor scholars at Oxford. The scholars who were thus supported became a group of pensioners, living together, sustained by an allowance, paid for by the founder's agents. When Balliol died in 1269 his widow, the Lady Dervorguilla, endowed the foundation. Under her statutes the agents or procurators were a Franciscan friar and a master of arts, and we know from later documents that Balliol College was to consist of sixteen scholars reading for arts degrees. They could not retain their scholarships if they went on to study theology or law.[9]

The first intention of Walter de Merton, a prominent king's clerk, and royal Chancellor to Henry III, was to set up at Oxford a foundation which should benefit his kinsmen. Since he planned to endow it with land in Surrey he asked the prior of Merton, his old employer, to act as guardian. His next step was hesitant, for in 1263 he thought that he was on the losing side in the civil war of Henry III's reign. He founded a college in two parts. The head of the college, who was called 'warden', presumably after the monastic official known as the 'warden of the grange' (*custos grangie*), was to reside with three priests at Malden in Surrey, the most important of the three manors which formed the college's first endowment. Meanwhile, twenty poor scholars were to be supported in Oxford by the output of the manors. The scholars were in the first place to include founder's kin, and members of the kin were to be educated from his bounty for the future.[10] The scholars were to share a common life on the Oxford site; and very soon, as the more senior scholars came to form a virtually self-governing community, they were known as companions or 'fellows, *socii*'.

In 1265–6 Merton's side in the civil war proved victorious, and in 1272–4 he was again Chancellor of England, one of a group of regents for Edward I as he slowly returned from his crusade to receive his kingdom. This meant that the college could be planned on a grander scale; and he also laid firmly on the scholars the responsibility for supervising and auditing their own financial accounts[11] – thus creating the model of the endowed, self-governing community central to the idea of a college. In 1289–94 the college was able to erect a chapel on a magnificent scale, replacing the old parish church of St John the Baptist, whose parishioners were found a modest place to worship inside the new chapel. As a college chapel the building has remarkable dimensions for its date: the seven bays of the choir are 102 feet long; and its size showed foresight, since by 1324–34 there were to be fifty fellows.[12]

The experimental nature of this early college is well reflected in the way in which the hall, the chapel and other buildings were grouped round the three original houses on Merton Street, forming what is now Front Quadrangle. More than anything else they represent the loose arrangement of buildings round a manor courtyard. The risk of fire was diminished by leaving space between them. When the warden moved to the college site he was placed in one of the original three houses, Flixthorp's, in the north-east corner, which was rebuilt and improved for the occasion. This enabled him to have a hall of his own in which to transact business and where his household could have its meals.[13] A stone

[9] Davis 1963, pp. 6–29.   [10] Allen and Garrod 1928, pp. 15–17.
[11] Allen and Garrod 1928, pp. 21–6.   [12] Aston 1984, p. 367.   [13] Highfield 1964, pp. 61–2.

32 *Merton College: the fifteenth-century chapel tower, the library and (on the left) Grove Building, from Christ Church Meadow*

muniment room and treasury was built to the west of the hall without any wood in it, to reduce the fire risk. The kitchen lay to the south of the hall and was separated from it for the same reason. Later ages tried to tidy up these loosely scattered buildings. The gatehouse was crenellated in the fifteenth century and the three houses on the street front were cased in Roman cement (from which they have since been freed), but the sense of the haphazard still lurks about the Front Quadrangle. The hall and chapel remain at different angles.

The early colleges were called indifferently college, hall or house: this ambiguity has never departed from them, but it is convenient to make a basic distinction between a college, which was an endowed academic chantry – a place where scholars were enjoined to pray for the founder's soul for ever – and a hall which might be as large and might have a

63

33   *Merton College: Mob Quad,
begun in the early fourteenth
century, completed 1378, with
the roof of the muniment room of
1288–91*

34 *(opposite) Merton College: the fifteenth-century north transept of the chapel (begun in the 1290s), the monument to Sir Thomas Bodley, died 1612 (p. 62)*

35 *The windows were given by Master Henry of Mamesfield, chancellor 1309–12, whose figure appears 24 times (c. 1296 to c. 1311)*

chapel, but had no permanent endowment, no everlasting chantry. The ambiguity remains; we talk of Merton College, Trinity Hall or Peterhouse: all are colleges. But we also talk of St Edmund Hall,[14] and this really was a hall until recent times. Since 1957 it too has become a college. But in the narrower sense the halls were really a part of the history of Oxford and Cambridge from the thirteenth century to the sixteenth, when most of them perished or were absorbed into colleges; some indeed had always been wholly owned

[14] For its early history cf. Emden 1968, pp. 60–1.

subsidiaries. Thus, from its foundation, Physwick Hostel at Cambridge was the property of its near neighbour, the college Gonville Hall. In the long run, if a hall had no endowment it was hard to maintain continuity; its rents became uneconomical; its existence was endangered.

Most early colleges were small communities of advanced students. Some were restricted to the study of arts, as Balliol was, while at others like University and Merton it was possible in addition to pursue courses in the superior sciences, notably in theology and canon and civil law. In Merton the study of medicine was forbidden in the thirteenth century though by the fourteenth this ban does not seem to have been enforced. The existence of the two types of college meant that there was an excellent reason for B.A.s of an arts college to wish to transfer to one where higher studies flourished. Thus for some eighty years several of the most distinguished members of Balliol, like Thomas Bradwardine, transferred to Merton to

38 *Merton College Library. The chained book is A. Desgodetz, Les Edifices Antiques de Rome (Paris, 1682); the book lying open is Conrad Gesner, Icones Animalium (Zürich, 1553)*

read theology. Then in 1340 a private benefaction made it possible for Balliol to change its statutes and to set up fellowships for those who wished to stay in Balliol to read theology. Parallel to these three foundations for the secular clergy the Benedictines of St Peter's, Gloucester, set up Gloucester College in 1283; in 1290 it was opened to monks from other Benedictine houses in the province of Canterbury. In 1337 it extended its range again to members of the whole order. The fifteenth-century buildings which survive (now in Worcester College) show that Glastonbury, Malmesbury, St Augustine's, Canterbury, and Pershore took advantage of the opportunity to send monks to Oxford. Durham College was founded similarly for the monks of Durham.

By contrast Exeter, Oriel and Queen's were all founded in the fourteenth century by men who, like Walter de Merton, had the closest relationship with the royal court. At

162

70

39 *The front entrance with its fifteenth-century sculpture. The Agnus Dei is shown on the left, the kneeling founder (Walter de Merton, Bishop of Rochester) and St John the Baptist on the right. In the foreground is the Book of Seven Seals*

Cambridge, meanwhile, Edward II himself, probably inspired by his treasurer, John Hotham, was founding the King's Hall, from about 1317 on; and three of his leading civil servants, Walter Stapeldon, the Treasurer, and Bishop of Exeter, Adam de Brome, chancery clerk, and Harvey de Stanton, Chancellor of the Exchequer, in a comparable way founded Stapeldon Hall (1314) and Oriel (1324) in Oxford and Michaelhouse in Cambridge (also in 1324).

Walter Stapeldon and his brother founded Stapeldon Hall, later known as Exeter College

40 *Exeter College chapel, 1854–60, in a quad of the seventeenth and eighteenth centuries*

after Walter's see, and they associated Edward II with their foundation.[15] It eventually occupied the sites of fourteen other halls. There were to be twelve fellows, eight from Devon and four from Cornwall, 'sophisters in arts', that is, they should study philosophy. Stapeldon chose the name of 'rector' for the head of his house to distinguish him from the warden of Merton, since the rector was to be subject to annual election. He placed the rather thin endowment in the hands of the dean and chapter of Exeter cathedral.

Adam de Brome in 1324 succeeded in associating Edward II with the foundation of Oriel, only to find that he had made a political mistake: in 1327 Edward was forced to abdicate. Oriel took its name from a house given to the foundation in 1327 and called 'La Oriole' (the origin of the name is unknown): it was to be a corporation consisting of a provost and ten fellows. They were to be in the first place theologians, although five or six of them had the option to proceed to the study of canon or civil law.[16] Brome preferred that the head of his college should take the title of provost, perhaps in imitation of the heads of some collegiate

[15] Buck 1983, pp. 99–114; Boase 1894, pp. v–viii.   [16] Rannie 1900, p. 7.

72

41 *Oriel College, Front Quadrangle, 1620–42*

churches like Wingham in Kent, which had been founded by Archbishop Peckham in 1287, and where the title provost was used as the equivalent of master.[17]

Robert Eglesfield, a member of the household of Queen Philippa, followed de Brome's example and in 1340 made a member of the royal family co-founder; he chose Queen Philippa, his immediate patron, rather than Edward III whose attention seems to have been fixed at this time on Cambridge.[18] Queen's College was to be for a provost and twelve

[17] Highfield 1984, p. 23.   [18] Cobban 1969, p. 12 and n. 4.

73

42   *New College, Great Quad and chapel, 1380–c. 1413*

fellows who had completed the M.A. course before election, since they were to study theology above all. One out of every seven fellows might read canon law, but all were to study superior sciences. In addition there were to be up to thirteen chaplains and a maximum of 72 poor boys, who were choristers. These were to have instructors in grammar, arts and chanting. Eglesfield's statutes were detailed and complicated and funds for carrying them out were far to seek. The founder had some success in attracting modest benefactors; the queen secured papal confirmation for the appropriation of three churches,[19] and Edward III added the advowson of a fourth, and the wardenship of St Julian's Hospital, Southampton.[20] But before the college had had much of a chance to get rooted it was hit by the plagues of 1348–9 and 1361, and only just survived. The 'poor

[19] Highfield 1984, pp. 238–9.   [20] Highfield 1984. p. 239.

74

boys' – or 'taberdars' as they were to become – rarely numbered more than three or four instead of anywhere near the number of 72 mentioned in the foundation statutes. Queen's certainly had vacant rooms to let and one of these was rented out to John Wyclif from 1363–4 to *c.* 1380.[21]

The series of Black Deaths which struck both town and university between 1348 and 1375 dealt them a number of heavy blows from which both took time to recover. Paradoxically the plagues made it easy for a founder in the last third of the century to buy up central sites for his college. The burgesses of Oxford (as of Cambridge) saw the multiplication of colleges as an 'objectionable symptom of their own decay'.[22]

William of Wykeham took advantage of these opportunities. This remarkable man from

[21] Magrath 1921, I, 112.   [22] Dobson 1977, p. 9.

44 *New College chapel. Artistic patronage did not cease in the fourteenth century : Epstein's Lazarus, 1951*

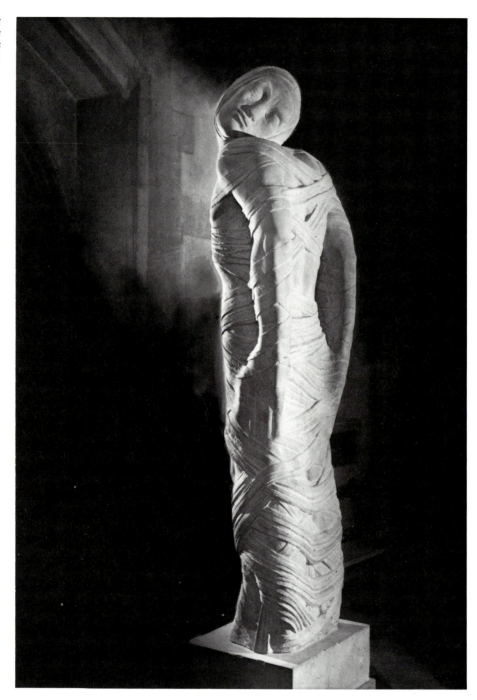

Hampshire had entered the royal service by 1356, and three years later was in charge of virtually all Edward III's major building works. In 1367 he was consecrated Bishop of Winchester and made royal chancellor.[23] Already by *c.* 1373 a group of boys was being instructed at Winchester in grammar – the germ of Winchester College – while the properties which were to make up the Oxford site of New College were being collected from 1369. The bishop had in mind a double foundation. The idea in itself was not a novelty. At

[23] Buxton and Williams 1979, p. 3; Partner 1982, pp. 1–8.

76

45 *The ante-chapel, interior, completed by 1386*

46 *A misericord in the chapel, late fourteenth century. A satire: three monkeys, presumably symbols of deceit – on the left one offers a sample of his water; in the centre another, in monk's cowl, emerges from a whelk-shell; on the right, a third in a cape, possibly a clerk (cf. G. L. Remnant,* A Catalogue of Misericords, *Oxford, 1969, p. 132, no. 15)*

Merton there had been teaching arrangements for the boys of the founder's kin and for a time for 'poor secondary scholars'; the poor boys at Queen's were to be chosen from the counties from which their endowment was drawn and brought to Oxford for their education. Wykeham's idea was to gather boys from a wide area to his foundation in Winchester, the seat of his bishopric and the county town of his own shire – to ground them in grammar there and send them on to Oxford.[24] The establishment was to be on a scale which dwarfed those of his predecessors. At Winchester there was to be a school for the 'seventy poor clerical scholars', while similarly in Oxford there was to be a college for a warden, seventy scholars, ten chaplains, three clerks and sixteen choristers. The scholars of under two years' standing were probationer fellows, after which they became full fellows. Thus he virtually doubled the number of fellowships available in Oxford. The bishop, it seems, had a clear concept of what a college should be in all its parts. His experience with royal buildings, especially at Windsor, had put him in touch with some of the best masons, carpenters and clerks of works in the country. Among them certainly were those whom he now recruited for the building of the Oxford college: William Wynford, mason, who had recently worked at Windsor, Hugh Herland, carpenter, and Simon Membury, clerk of works. With Wynford he had been associated at Windsor in the arrangement of a hall and chapel placed end-to-end to form one building, later St George's Hall. The college which the mason, carpenter and clerk of works were to build was to be both systematic and spectacular. The change in key between Walter de Merton and William of Wykeham is revealed by a comparison between Mob Quad at Merton and the Great Quadrangle at New College. Before Mob Quad was completed, the earliest surviving academic court had been built for Corpus Christi College, Cambridge, which dates from *c.* 1352–77.[25] But Mob Quadrangle is Oxford's earliest. The north and east sides had been built in 1304–11; the other two sides were only completed in 1378–9, when the beautiful library given by Bishop Read was attached with joints at the corners. By contrast Wykeham and his mason planned a great quadrangle with a chapel and hall back-to-back along the north side, a gate tower and warden's house over it in the west range and a library with eighteen traceried windows opposite the gateway on the eastern side. In the angle next to the hall was to be a muniment tower, and beyond the hall to the east the kitchen, standing apart to reduce the risk of fire. The great Henry Yevele is known to have been on hand to advise Wynford and his men.[26] A quadrangular college had been begun at Cobham in Kent in 1370: Sir John Cobham had led the two missions to the papal court which had resulted in Wykeham's appointment to the see of Winchester.[27] A letter from Wykeham to Cobham which survives at New College suggests that there was friendship between them. Yevele built the quadrangular college for Cobham and began another for the Earl of Arundel at Arundel in 1380. Whoever had the major responsibility for the New College plan – Wykeham, Wynford or Yevele, or a combination of all three – the result was magnificent; it was also influential. Ten years after the rest of the buildings the cloister was built to the west of the quadrangle for processions and burials, and scholarly contemplation, following the monastic example at Winchester which Wykeham knew well. The tower was placed to the north of the chapel to hold a peal of bells: seen from beyond the

[24] Buxton and Williams 1979, pp. 6–7.   [25] Willis and Clark 1886, I, 241–5, 250–1; *RCHM Oxford*, I, 48.
[26] Willis and Clark 1886, I, 156–62; on Wynford and Yevele, see Harvey 1984, pp. 352–6, 358–66.
[27] Highfield 1953, pp. 40–1.

city walls it looks like a fine supernumerary bastion. To the south of the quadrangle was the Long Room or Lavatory, used as such until the end of the nineteenth century. Its tiny windows like arrow slits still look narrowly down into New College Lane.

Wykeham placed the head of his college over the main gate whence he could supervise its life, and the example was quickly copied. The rectors of Lincoln (from *c.* 1430) and Exeter (from 1432), the president of Magdalen (from *c.* 1474–9) and even, as late as the early seventeenth century, the warden of Wadham, were all to live over the entrance gates of their colleges.[28] The economy of building chapel and hall back-to-back was copied at All Souls and Magdalen, whose founders had been Wykehamists. At All Souls the architecture of the ante-chapel with its 'slender columns . . . tapering to the roof' is directly reminiscent of the ante-chapel of New College; and the chapel at All Souls dominated the low penthouse roofs (as they then were) of the neighbouring chambers, just as New College Chapel towers over the chambers of the Great Quadrangle.[29] There were to be many conscious imitations of Wykeham's foundations. Henry VI planned to build a New College by the Cam – though only King's College chapel survives from his imaginative scheme. At Oxford All Souls and Magdalen are testimony to the growth of a Wykehamist tradition: quite quickly there were Wykehamists with a sense of belonging to a great family, well illustrated in the famous drawing of the founder and his *alumni* in the Chaundler Manuscript of the middle of the fifteenth century.[30] The link through Henry VI to the foundations of Eton and King's College, Cambridge, and the common dedication of all four foundations to the Virgin Mary led to the *Amicabilis Concordia* of 1444 between the four institutions who promised aid and counsel to each other, notably in litigation in all courts of law.

During the lifetime of the founder of New College the shadow of Lollardy fell over Oxford: if a Protestant metaphor is preferred, the morning star of the Reformation rose. Oxford bred not only the fount and origin of Lollardy, John Wyclif, but his leading disciples, who included Nicholas Hereford, who eventually recanted and died a Carthusian monk, and Philip Repingdon, who also returned to the Catholic fold and ended Bishop of Lincoln (1404/5–19). To most contemporaries at the university Lollardy was a disaster; it raised fears of more heresy to come and had a deeply inhibiting effect. As if to curb this danger the university bent its efforts to building the Divinity School, a major work of European architecture. Theology had produced some of Oxford's outstanding figures so far and it seemed that it might do so again, if they were suitably encouraged. The founder of Queen's had called theology 'a divine tree' with 'a sure faith in the root, a certain hope in its trunk, and widespread charity in its buds',[31] and there were far more theologians than legists or doctors. The monks and friars by the beginning of the fifteenth century all had their own buildings, but the leading secular clergy in 'The Grand Faculty of Theology – the queen and empress of the Faculties', as Bishop Fleming called it, were poorly provided for by lecture rooms in the old houses in Schools Street. The university could not pay for such a building. Archbishop Chichele of Canterbury and Thomas Langley, Bishop of Durham, were two of those who responded to its appeals.[32] A site was bought; but progress with the building proved very slow and in the process the taste of the fund-raisers and of some of the benefactors changed.[33] In an interesting indenture of 1440 between the university and its chief mason, Thomas Elkyn, as a result of aristocratic and other pressure, it was required that the over-elaborate style in which the building had been begun by Richard Winchcombe, mason, should be simplified. 'Since several magnates of the kingdom and other wise men', we are told, 'do not approve of, but object to, the excessive curiosity of this work, as it has been begun, therefore the university desires that Thomas should refrain as

[28] Green 1979, p. 9; Stride 1900, p. 187; Wilson 1899, pp. 23–4; Buxton and Williams 1979, p. 186.
[29] Even though heightened by the addition of a third storey in the seventeenth century. On All Souls, see Jacob 1967, p. 78.
[30] Buxton and Williams 1979, pl. 2 and p. 20. For the *Amicabilis Concordia*, see Buxton and Williams 1979, p. 20.
[31] Magrath 1921, I, 26 n. 1; Hodgkin 1949, p. 12.
[32] Legge 1923, p. 17.   [33] Colvin 1983, pp. 1–2.

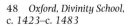

he has already begun to refrain from such superfluous curiosity, as in the niches for the statues . . . casements and fillets, and other frivolous curiosities which are irrelevant, but lead the said university to too great and sumptuous expense, and delay the progress of the work.'[34] The evidence of magnate pressure in the mid fifteenth century was also reflected in the early progress of Magdalen. The simplicity was more than a wish to save money; a version of perpendicular architecture of a conscious austerity prevailed from about 1430

[34] Anstey 1898, p. 192.

to the 1470s.[35] But by then taste had changed again, and the Divinity School was completed in a style as elaborate as Winchcombe's – almost certainly by William Orchard, whose monogram occurs in one of the bosses and who had worked as Waynflete's master mason at Magdalen. The length of time which it had taken to finish the building reflects growing economic difficulties as the century progressed; without the support of the executors of Cardinal Beaufort and Cardinal John Kempe it might never have been finished, and John's nephew, Thomas Kempe, Bishop of London (1450–89), gave no less than a thousand marks. His arms and those of a wide selection of the episcopal and noble friends of the university, including those of King Edward IV and his brother-in-law, Lionel Woodville, Bishop of Salisbury and chancellor of the university (1479–82), occur in the sculptured bosses of the vault.[36] Thus with the help of many workmen, Winchcombe, Elkyn and Orchard created what a Jacobean judge was to call 'the chiefest wonder in Oxford';[37] but neither the new Divinity School nor its doctors brought any effective revival of theology. For students of arts, meanwhile, Abbot Hooknorton of Osney had in 1439 built the 'new Schools' – a modest set of lecture rooms for renting out. But no new lecture rooms were provided for the other superior sciences, canon and civil law, still less for medicine. The university had quite exhausted its efforts.

Meanwhile Lollardy died hard. Philip Repingdon had sufficiently changed his ways to become Bishop of Lincoln. But one principal of St Edmund Hall, William Taylor, is almost certainly the priest of that name who was burned in 1423;[38] and another, Peter Payne, had to leave England, if he wished to avoid martyrdom. He made his way to Hussite Bohemia and died a sympathiser with the Taborites, at Prague in 1455.[39] A bishop who was in no way a Lollard, Reginald Pecock, Bishop of Chichester (1450–c. 1459), the author of the *New English Creed* and *The Repressor of Overmuch Blaming the Clergy*, found himself put on trial and forced to resign for uttering opinions which would probably have caused little alarm in the 1350s and 1360s.[40]

The founder of Lincoln College, Richard Fleming, was another theologian who found himself suspected of heresy. Archbishop Arundel had been recalled to favour by Henry IV after his disgrace by Richard II. The primate suspected Oxford of continuing to foster Lollardy. Shortly after Fleming had held the northern proctorship he found himself accused of Lollard opinions. At a disputation in the autumn of 1409 he put forward a proposition which was reported to the archbishop as having smacked of Wyclifism.[41] It had been vigorously opposed and then referred to a committee of twelve theologians appointed by the Convocation of Canterbury to keep an eye on the university which had bred the heresiarch. The committee was divided in its opinion and Fleming appealed to the congregation of the university and subsequently petitioned for redress to Henry IV himself. At first the king ordered the university to summon congregation to hear the appeal, but subsequently he ordered it to set up a committee of eight, four to be nominated by Fleming. The outcome of its deliberations is unknown, but Fleming seems to have escaped. The archbishop was fortified in his unfavourable view of the university by its unwillingness to accept the exercise of his jurisdiction as metropolitan (that is, as archbishop) at the visitation of 1411. Fleming very soon became, as Repingdon had done before him, a strong defender of orthodoxy. He was a member of the commission which drew up a list of 267

[35] Davis 1946–7, pp. 75–80.   [36] Legge 1923, p. 7 and pl. 20; p. 2 and pl. 38.   [37] Legge 1923, p. 1.
[38] Emden, *Oxford*, III, 1852.   [39] Emden, *Oxford*, III, 1441–2.   [40] Emden, *Oxford*, III, 1447–9.   [41] Green 1979, p. 3.

errors in Wyclif's writings and attended the Council of Constance. He followed Repingdon as Bishop of Lincoln (1419/20–31), and as such it fell to him (in 1427) to carry out the sentence passed by the Fathers of Constance whereby Wyclif's bones were dug up from Lutterworth churchyard, burned and cast into the river Swift.[42]

Fleming's college was to have as its main objective the training of men in theology to counteract heresy and, in the bishop's own words, 'to overcome those who with their swinish snouts imperil the pearls of true theology'.[43] Lincoln unlike New College was to be a little college, a *collegiolum*, consisting of a rector, after the manner of neighbouring Exeter, seven scholars or fellows, a number of deacons and two chaplains to serve the parishes of All Saints and St Michael's at the North Gate. These were two of the three parish churches which Fleming had secured permission from the king to 'unite, annexe and incorporate'. He founded his college in the churchyard of All Saints and some buildings adjoining the church.

Between the foundation of Lincoln in 1429 and of All Souls in 1438 there arose three small new colleges not destined to survive. Richard Clifford, Bishop of London, rented Burnell's Inn from Balliol in 1416 and clearly intended to found 'London College': he left a thousand marks for the support of scholars in his will. But his death in 1421 ended its chances of survival and when the money came to an end so did the college.[44] More successful was St Mary's College for Austin Canons licensed by Henry VI in 1435. It occupied the site of Frewen Hall.[45] Its gatehouse and part of its gateway survive. Its prior was to be the host of Erasmus. St Bernard's College was by contrast for Cistercians. It was inadequately funded by Rewley Abbey. Archbishop Chichele gave the licence for its foundation in 1437 although it was to be the Cistercians themselves who supported it.[46] Its site was beyond Balliol and its buildings were absorbed into St John's; those that survive form part of the Front Quadrangle. St Mary's and St Bernard's made no great stir and indicate that the university in the fifteenth century owed comparatively little to the monastic orders.

A notable development at the end of the fourteenth and beginning of the fifteenth century was the new interest shown in the old subject of civil law. Despite the failure of Vacarius and his successors to establish permanently an Oxford school of civilian commentators the study of civil law, as well as canon law, continued to be a useful asset for graduates who went on to become 'civil servant bishops' or to take up appointments in diocesan administration.[47] Well-known bishops and archbishops who read one of the Oxford courses in law and became bachelors or doctors in the fourteenth century were John Stratford, Archbishop of Canterbury, William Zouche, Archbishop of York, and Thomas Charlton, Bishop of Hereford. Some canonists found canon law a key to a career in the papal court before promotion to an English see. Such were Archbishop Sudbury of Canterbury and Bishops Bateman, Fastolf, Lynn and Ross. In his 1274 statutes Walter de Merton had made allowance for four or five of his fellows to study canon law, who might be dispensed in order to attend civil law lectures.[48] But the majority were to study arts and to proceed from arts to theology. Thus the number of canonists is never likely to have exceeded an eighth of the total. At Oriel by contrast five or six of Brome's ten fellows had the

---

[42] Green 1979, p. 4.   [43] Green 1979, p. 6, from the preface to the first statutes of Lincoln College.
[44] Emden, *Oxford*, I, 440.   [45] Knowles 1948–59, II, 27–8; *VCH Oxon*, II, 102–3.
[46] Knowles 1948–59, II, 26, 128; cf. *Calendar of Patent Rolls, 1436–1441*, London, 1907, pp. 45–6, printed in full in Stevenson and Salter 1939, pp. 67–9.   [47] Dunbabin 1984, pp. 573–4.   [48] Allen and Garrod 1928, p. 21.

option to proceed to canon or civil law. John of Winwick, a Lancastrian, and like Merton a king's clerk, who had been the architect of the Treaty of Brétigny and the keeper of the privy seal (1355–60), went much further. He proposed to set up a college entirely for lawyers, namely for poor scholars reading canon or civil law. On becoming bachelors or doctors his scholars were expected to lecture at Oxford. Winwick died before he could put his intentions into effect, and his brother and heir suggested giving an advowson to Oriel to maintain poor scholars, rather than setting up a new college. But the pope failed to approve of the idea and the whole project collapsed.[49] Nevertheless the English church courts were flourishing anew at the end of the fourteenth century and it was natural that founders should pay more attention to law. In 1379 Wykeham allotted ten places each to canonists and civil lawyers out of his total of seventy. At All Souls in 1438 they were to number sixteen out of forty and have a special dean allotted to them.[50] But this proportion clearly reflected the interests and experience of the founder, Henry Chichele, Archbishop of Canterbury.

Chichele was one of those fortunates who had benefited from Wykeham's foundation. In the famous mid-fifteenth-century picture of William of Wykeham among the distinguished 'alumni', Chichele is on the bishop's right as the Wykehamist who had attained the greatest eminence. Chichele demonstrated in his own person the importance of legal studies on the pathway to high office in the church and the royal service.[51] His foundation was to be the only one in medieval Oxford where the number of lawyers regularly exceeded that of the theologians. For although he wanted the arts students at All Souls on becoming M.A.s to proceed to theology, they did not always do so: thus 85 per cent of the recorded fellows before 1500 were lawyers and the majority of those were canonists. Given a choice between theology and legal studies most of the arts students chose law.[52]

Not surprisingly the Library at All Souls attracted gifts of law books: such were those given by Lyndfeld, a former fellow, who served Chichele as head of the archbishop's court, the dean of Arches, by Chichele himself, and King Henry VI, whom Chichele had associated with his foundation as co-founder.[53] All Souls soon bred up men as distinguished in civil law as Thomas Winterbourne, chancellor of Archbishop Bourgchier, John Porter, secretary to Cardinal Kempe, and John Goldwell, Bishop of Norwich – though no one, perhaps, quite so brilliant as William Lyndwood. Three of the archbishops of Canterbury in the fifteenth century were civil lawyers – Chichele, Stafford and Kempe – and lawyers formed 65 per cent of the large number of Oxford graduates who became deans of cathedrals or collegiate churches. The two faculties of law were much smaller than those of arts or theology, but canon law especially produced able administrators, officials and practical legists in large numbers and continued to do so until Henry VIII's Reformation closed the doors of the canon law school.

On 6 May 1448 William Waynflete, Bishop of Winchester, secured letters patent to set up Magdalen Hall on the site of two halls beside the city walls on the south side of High Street.[54] The founder was the son of Richard Patyn of Waynfleet in Lincolnshire, and had been for twelve years master of Wykeham's college at Winchester; he was, therefore,

---

49 Emden, *Oxford*, III, 2064: Oriel was perhaps chosen because of its founder's wish to encourage lawyers.
50 Jacob 1967, p. 79. It was especially the prerogative courts which flourished in the late fourteenth and fifteenth centuries.
51 See n. 30 above; for what follows, Jacob 1967, pp. 14–17.   52 Boyle 1984, p. 552.
53 Jacob 1967, pp. 83–4. For statistics of lawyers, see Aston 1977, pp. 9–16.
54 Wilson 1899, p. 6, between what is now Merton Street and Logic Lane.

50   *Magdalen College, Oxford:*
the cloisters, fifteenth century,
though much restored. The master
mason was William Orchard.
Unlike the cloisters at New College
they are part of the earliest
quadrangle

steeped in the Wykehamist tradition. He had also been recruited by Henry VI for his new school at Eton of which Waynflete had probably become headmaster and certainly provost (1442–7).[55] This patronage had brought him the special favour of Henry VI and the wealthy see of Winchester. When in 1456 he also became Chancellor of England he was already planning to acquire the site and buildings of the decaying Hospital of St John the Baptist outside the walls, beyond the East Gate. Success led to the refoundation of Magdalen in 1458 on the site of the hospital. Here was a new spaciousness: the extensive grounds of the hospital have given Magdalen one of the most beautiful collegiate sites anywhere to be found.

Waynflete naturally emulated Wykeham in his statutes; Magdalen like New College was to consist of seventy scholars, though its head was to be a president not a warden. The word occurs in English in the Lollard Bible for the governor of a province and it was also chosen

[55] Emden, *Oxford*, III, 2002.

86

51　*The hall, looking west, with sixteenth-century panelling*

for the head of Queens' College, Cambridge, founded in the same year as Magdalen Hall (1448).[56] There were to be other differences. Waynflete, less encouraging to jurists than Wykeham, allowed two or three of his scholars to study canon or civil law (and two or three might study medicine). But the chief difference was that thirty members of the foundation were half-fellows or demies. They only had half the allowance of a full fellow and their tenure was limited. They had to be more than twelve years old and might be not more than twenty-five. They proceeded from the study of grammar to that of logic and sophistry (advanced logic); two or three of them were to specialise in grammar, poetry and other arts of humanity so as to qualify to teach others.

Waynflete made it possible for students at Magdalen to receive instruction in every

[56] Murray 1888–1928, VII, 1310–11. For the whole story of the foundation of Magdalen, and the possible influence of Waynflete on Queens' see now J.F. Mills, 'The jurisdiction, endowment and early administration of Magdalen College, Oxford', Oxford B.Litt. thesis (1977). But this interesting account does not sufficiently allow for the independent initiative at Queens' of Andrew Doket.

52 *Magdalen College tower, 1492–c. 1509*

discipline save law or medicine throughout their university courses. This was hardly the origin of the tutorial system; earlier in the fifteenth century, at King's Hall, Cambridge, at least seventeen fellows acted as tutors to private pupils.[57] But the arrangement at Magdalen represents an important step towards a fully fledged collegiate tutorial system. The teaching staff at Magdalen consisted of a grammar master, an usher, lecturers in logic and sophistry and readers in natural philosophy, moral philosophy (or metaphysics) and

[57] Cobban 1969. p. 67.

theology. The philosophy and theology readers were to be well paid (£6 13s 4d and £10 annually) and, if necessary, chosen from outside the college, and the teaching was to be free.[58] In 1474 the founder secured the transfer to Magdalen of an endowment, which Sir John Fastolf had intended for a college of priests at Caister, Norfolk; from this he enlarged the fellowship and especially the number of chaplains.[59] At New College there had been ten priests and three clerks; at Magdalen there were to be four priests, eight clerks and sixteen choristers.

Following Wykeham's example and the model of Merton and Queen's, Waynflete provided grammar schools linked to his college, one at Waynfleet in Lincolnshire (1459) and the other in Oxford (*c.* 1478) – though no attempt was made to confine the choice of fellows to recruits from the two schools. One of Waynflete's statutes made it possible for not more than twenty commoners or 'non-foundationers' to be members of the college, living at the charge of their kin. They were to be the sons of noble and powerful friends of the college – thus was the need for good lordship to be recognised in an Oxford college. As early as the thirteenth century examples occurred of sons of noble families bound for an ecclesiastical career studying in Oxford. Such were Anthony and Thomas Bek, sons of Walter de Bek, who hired Halegod's house from Jacob the Jew in Merton Street in 1267.[60] In the fifteenth century a nobleman not destined for the church, Robert, son of Lord Hungerford, rented rooms in University College, as did his tutor, John Chedworth, a former fellow of Merton, for three terms in 1437–8.[61] The value of such an arrangement was indicated when the executors of Lord Hungerford himself contributed a large sum towards the cost of building Merton chapel tower between 1448 and 1450.[62] Chedworth was to help Waynflete with the revision of the statutes of Eton, and Waynflete himself, as headmaster of Winchester, was acquainted with Wykeham's provision for his school: 'We allow that the sons of noble and capable persons who are special friends of the said college be able to the number of ten to be instructed inside the college in grammar...'[63] From this Waynflete could easily deduce his concept of the nobleman or gentleman commoner which was to have such a lasting effect in the next three and a half centuries.

Waynflete followed Wykeham with a T-shaped chapel back-to-back with the hall; but the re-use of the hospital buildings led to a major rearrangement in the course of which he united the cloisters and the main quadrangle to the north of the hall and chapel. Between 1492 and *c.* 1509 the Bell Tower was added, with a singularly happy result, since it also stands as a sentinel watching all who come into the city over Magdalen Bridge. It is one of Oxford's most beautiful buildings and is ascribed to the mason, William Reynold.[64]

Andrew Doket had given Queens', Cambridge, the most formidable castle tower at its entry. Waynflete crenellated or embattled his whole complex, starting with an enclosing wall by William Orchard in 1467,[65] culminating in a president's lodgings appropriate for a man who might enjoy a secular status akin to noblemen and gentry. In the sixteenth century Magdalen was said 'to be crowned with battlements entire in the manner worthy of gentlemen'.[66] Other heads of colleges soon copied the lodgings of the president of Magdalen. Fitzjames's house as warden of Merton was embattled in 1497; that of William

[58] Wilson 1899, p. 39.
[59] Wilson 1899, p. 40. The transfer was made possible by the dubious circumstances surrounding Fastolf's will.
[60] Emden, *Oxford*, I, 151.   [61] Emden, *Oxford*, II, 985.   [62] Rogers 1866–1902, III, 720.
[63] Moberly 1887, p. 210.   [64] Wilson 1899, pp. 48–9; Harvey 1984, pp. 220–3.
[65] Wilson 1899, pp. 21–2.   [66] Buxton and Williams 1979, p. 199.

Broke, warden of All Souls, in 1510; those of the warden of New College and the dean of Christ Church had followed suit by 1543. At Magdalen the president's lodging in the Founder's Tower is 'like a little "castle" or "court" with its panelled bay window' looking outward, and the Bell Tower is 'frankly ornamental'.[67] In the main, New College, Lincoln and All Souls looked inward; Magdalen turned towards the world outside. In this it was to be copied by St Bernard's (1483–c. 1505), by the façade of Balliol (now departed) and by sixteenth-century colleges like Brasenose.

Meanwhile the university had been spurred to devise a new and larger library over the Divinity School by a series of gifts of books from Humphrey, Duke of Gloucester. The youngest son of Henry IV, he had formed a friendship with Zano Castiglione, Bishop of Bayeux, a Frenchman of Italian descent, who presented him with a collection of Cicero's *Letters*. The duke employed him to buy copies of the works of Guarino and Bruni for him in Italy. Bruni translated Aristotle's *Politics* at the duke's suggestion, and this was the beginning of the duke's contacts with several Italian humanists. He shared his academic interests with Oxford: between 1435 and 1444 he presented over 281 manuscripts to the University Library. In 1431 he wrote to suggest three reforms in the curriculum. As a result small changes were made and a 'new emphasis given to the study of rhetoric and classical literature'. In 1434 he initiated a lectureship in the seven liberal arts and three philosophies, but failed to endow it permanently.[68] The manuscripts he gave to the university were rich in classical and humanistic texts; the translations from Greek authors were especially appreciated. Unfortunately at his death in 1447 it proved impossible to collect all the Latin books which had been promised, and, more disastrously, the books in the Library which bore his name were dispersed in the sixteenth century. The duke's humanism was founded in Italy and nourished by Italian scholarship. There had been bibliophiles and scholars in the thirteenth and fourteenth centuries, like William Read, Bishop of Chichester, who had inherited the learning of the twelfth-century renaissance and developed it. But if the leading fifteenth-century scholars, Richard Fleming, founder of Lincoln, and his nephew Robert, William Gray, benefactor of Balliol Library, Thomas Linacre and William Grocyn, founding fathers of sixteenth-century scholarship, all owed much to the English medieval tradition of scholarship, they all went to Italy in order to absorb in Pavia, Florence, Padua, Ferrara or Rome the 'new' learning of the Renaissance.[69]

[67] Davis 1946–7, p. 81.   [68] Emden, *Oxford*, II, 983–5.
[69] Emden, *Oxford*, II, 697–700, 809–14, 827–30, 1147–9.

53   (*opposite*) Oxford, 'Duke Humfrey': the fifteenth-century library with seventeenth-century book-cases, the heart of the Bodleian

77

5 *The first Cambridge colleges*

We have determined and ordain that if any fellow . . . shall be incapable with a perpetual incapacity – or with one which in the judgement of the greater part of the fellows makes it hopeless to believe that he will profit further in study in the college in future, or attain the doctorate in any faculty – he shall forthwith be expelled by the master with the wise counsel and consent of the majority of the fellows, and another apt and capable to profit shall be elected . . . in his place.

> William Bateman's Statutes for Gonville Hall, 1355, Venn, III, 349

They advanced first to this College, against which they had a particular pique on account of the many Candle Rents with which it was endowed, . . . where they brake open the gates and fell with violence upon the Master and Fellows . . . Hence they proceeded to commit further violences . . . And no one knows what farther lengths this mad rabble might have gone, had not Henry Spenser, that warlike bishop of Norwich, casually come hither at that time with some forces, and fortunately suppressed them.

> R. Masters, *The History of the College of Corpus Christi and the Blessed Virgin Mary . . .*,
> Cambridge, 1753, I, 31–2 – on the riot of 1381

The idea of an academic college came to England from Paris; it settled first in Oxford, and if University College and Balliol had some shadow of existence first, Merton is the mother of all the colleges of Oxford and Cambridge. Yet it was at Cambridge that the colleges first came to be a large and significant element in the university; and although Oxford and Cambridge constantly influenced one another, and Oxford was always the senior partner down to about 1500, it may truly be said that the idea of a collegiate university was born in Cambridge.

It came very slowly. In early days the students lived mainly in lodgings and hostels approved by the university authorities, as at Oxford. The only permanent communities of scholars were the friars; they had settled in a modest way in the second quarter of the thirteenth century – tiny groups from young orders.[1] But they grew very fast and rapidly made their mark in the university. By the end of the thirteenth century no less than six houses had been founded; and although two faded away in the early fourteenth century, the major houses had by then become very large. By 1289 there were said to be 75 Franciscans and 75 Dominicans, and there were probably well over 200 friars in Cambridge in all. The numbers fluctuated; but the total was once again in the region of 200 in the late fourteenth century, at a time when the whole population of the university,

---

[1] Knowles and Hadcock 1971, pp. 222, 214–15, 224, 233–4, 239 (Franciscans, Dominicans, Carmelites), 241 (Austin Friars, perhaps later thirteenth century), 247–9 (Friars of the Sack, Pied Friars, third quarter of the thirteenth century); Moorman 1952; Brooke 1985a, pp. 73–4; *VCH Cambs*, II, 269–92.

masters and students, friars, monks, canons and seculars, lay perhaps between 400 and 700.[2] We cannot tell how many of the friars were actually students, and they undoubtedly had other practical and pastoral tasks to perform. They set an example which the colleges were to follow from the start of mingling pastoral and academic work. However we view them, they formed a major element in the university, and an increasingly prestigious one, for the friars travelled and some of the Cambridge friars came from Oxford and Paris and farther afield. After a remarkable ordinance made by Pope Benedict XII in 1336, every third year the lector appointed to read the *Sentences* – that is, to lecture in the Franciscan convent on the *Sentences* of Peter the Lombard, the fundamental text-book, after the Bible, of the medieval faculties of theology – was to come from more distant regions of the order, including Italy.[3] But the nature of their relationship with the university naturally bred an attitude of love and hate; and even if too much has been made of the hate, too little of the friendship and alliance – out of which Cambridge in truth became a university – one can readily understand why the seculars determined to form their own communities, to follow their own ways, to keep the government of the university in secular hands.

Peterhouse was founded by a bishop of Ely who was also a Benedictine monk.[4] His first thought was to impose a small community of scholars on the Hospital of St John where he had certain rights of supervision and patronage. The poor, the sick, the aged, and the religious consorted ill with the bright young scholars; and in 1284 the bishop, Hugh of Balsham, moved the students to lodgings under the shadow of St Peter beyond Trumpington Gate. Here a union of academic and pastoral was devised – with a certain monastic influence still visible in the Peterhouse statutes when they emerge into daylight a generation later.[5] The essential source of inspiration, however, was dramatically revealed when the church of St Peter – renamed Little St Mary's at this time to distinguish it from the college – was rebuilt, by some patron or patrons unknown, in the 1350s, on the exact model of Merton chapel.[6] What was built, as at Merton, was a large and splendid chancel, evidently meant for the college chapel; as at Merton, the nave was never completed, and from the first the parishioners and the college divided the chancel between them. In Peterhouse Bishop Hugh and his successors had fostered an imitation of Merton by the Cam. But there were two striking contrasts: Peterhouse was very indifferently endowed, and neither at first nor for many centuries to come were the fellows free to choose their master. Down to the nineteenth century they presented two nominees to the bishop of Ely, representative of their founder, and he chose, sometimes with admirable, sometimes with comical effect.[7]

Peterhouse hardly prepares us for the tide of fashion which followed. Between 1317 and 1352 seven new colleges were founded, and by patrons of widely differing background: the King's Hall by King Edward II in 1317; Michaelhouse by a civil servant, Harvey de Stanton, in 1324; University College by a Cambridge teacher and chancellor, Richard of Baddow in 1326 – later given permanent form by the Lady Elizabeth de Clare as Clare Hall in the

56–7 59

[2] See above, p. 58; Knowles and Hadcock 1971, *loc. cit.*
[3] Moorman 1952, p. 81.
[4] Hugh of Balsham, Bishop of Ely, 1257–86, had been a monk and sub-prior in his cathedral priory (Greenway 1971, pp. 46–7). On Peterhouse, *VCH Cambs*, III, 334; on St John's Hospital, Rubin 1987.
[5] This influence is studied in a forthcoming paper by H. Mayr-Harting; the statutes are in *Documents 1852*, II, 6–42.
[6] See above, p. 56 and plate 29; Brooke 1985a, pp. 71–2; *VCH Cambs*, III, 131; *RCHM Cambridge*, II, 280–3.
[7] See p. 262 below. For what follows, see Cobban 1969; *VCH Cambs*, III, 340–76, 456–61; Brooke 1985, chap. 1; Willis and Clark 1886, *passim*.

1330s; Pembroke in 1347 by another wealthy widow, the Countess of Pembroke, inspired by her Franciscan confessor; Gonville Hall by a country parson, turned land-agent, Edmund Gonville, in 1347–8; Trinity Hall by the Bishop of Norwich, William Bateman, in 1349–50; Corpus Christi by the two great civic guilds of Corpus Christi and St Mary in 1352. Then there was silence. The Black Death had come and gone, leaving many potential benefactors dead, or their rentals depleted; and the one great collegiate foundation of the late fourteenth century was New College in Oxford. This tide of colleges at

58   74

94

55 *The interior, though probably of the late sixteenth century, has lecterns on which to lay the chained books, and has the appearance of a library of the fifteenth or early sixteenth century*

Cambridge had begun with a foundation by Edward II, and the next followed with the foundation of King's by Henry VI in 1441.

Just as royal patronage had been decisive in deciding that Oxford and Cambridge – and not Northampton or Stamford or Lincoln or London – should be the homes of the ancient English universities, so royal patronage inaugurated the two movements of fashion which gave Cambridge its medieval colleges; and it was to be a queen-mother, Lady Margaret Beaufort, who presided over the third, creating Christ's and St John's in the opening

95

56 *Cambridge, the King's Hall: King Edward's tower, the clock tower, 1427–37, with the statue of Edward III, moved to its present site when the Great Court of Trinity was created by Thomas Nevile about 1600 (Willis and Clark 1886, II, 444–6)*

sixteenth century and making possible the ultimate take-over by the colleges of the university as a whole. Yet it would be a mistake to make too much of the royal initiative. Edward II seems to have been led by his advisers to provide a home and a school for the boys of the royal chapel in the King's Hall; and by similar means his son, Edward III, was induced to make a major college of it – and in the sixteenth century, great patroness as was the Lady Margaret, the form her patronage took owed much to St John Fisher.

Behind Edward II the historian of the King's Hall, Alan Cobban, has with great likelihood discerned the figure of John of Hotham, who had won Edward's affection and respect by notable service to his favourite Piers Gaveston, and was saved by Edward's personal favour from disgrace.[8] He rose from royal service to be Bishop of Ely in 1316, the year before the King's Hall was founded – and just as recent research has shown how important was his

---

[8] Cobban 1969, pp. 24–7. For what follows, see Buck 1983, chap. 5 (on Stapeldon Hall).

96

57 *The Great Gate, 1518–35, designed by John Wastell for Henry VIII. Below King Henry are the arms of England and France (for Edward III) and the coats of arms of Edward's sons*

alliance with the monks of Ely in making this a unique period in the cathedral's history – the era of the new choir and octagon and Lady chapel – so we may see his benign influence behind the King's Hall and the foundations which followed. Edward II's court has had a bad name with many historians, but his servants played a central part in the early patronage of colleges – witness also Harvey de Stanton, founder of Michaelhouse, and Walter Stapeldon, founder of Stapeldon Hall, later Exeter College, at Oxford.

59
40

The university itself was beginning to cast a friendly eye on such foundations, and the chancellor Richard of Baddow struggled hard to put together out of various university bequests and provisions, and his own modest resources, a University College.[9] When he was in difficulties the first of the princesses came to the rescue. Lady Elizabeth de Clare, granddaughter of Edward I and a widow of large resources, took over the foundation and

[9] Chibnall 1963.

58 *Corpus Christi College, Cambridge: the fourteenth-century horn believed to have been owned by John de Goldcorne of the Corpus Christi Guild, from which the scholars of the college still drink when they take their B.A.s. It is adorned with a little figure of St Cornelius, a third-century pope and patron of horns, copied from a Carolingian original (Oman 1972)*

endowed it, if not very adequately, at least much more effectively than Baddow had been able to do. Her close friend Marie de S. Pol, Countess of Pembroke, had been hitherto more involved with the second order of St Francis, the Franciscan women, or poor Clares or Minoresses, whom she transferred with a strong hand from Waterbeach to Denney.[10] Meanwhile, it may be, she was watching her friend the Lady Clare; and both may have discussed their pious aims with the old queen dowager, Isabella, the she-wolf, who in her disgraced old age – having betrayed her husband Edward II and seen her lover Roger Mortimer cut down by her son Edward III – may have remembered the King's Hall in which she had had some interest, not all of it benevolent.[11]

The other three foundations, Gonville Hall, Trinity Hall and Corpus, seem to have been closely linked. Edmund Gonville, though he held no office apart from his country rectories, consorted with great soldiers like Walter Manny, who helped him, and later himself founded the London Charterhouse; with William Bateman, his bishop, who completed his work; and with successive earls of Lancaster, for whom he probably acted as steward or agent in their East Anglian estates.[12] With Earl Henry the elder he founded the Dominican house at Thetford in 1335; and he may have had a hand in inspiring Henry the younger, the first duke, to join the citizens of Cambridge in founding Corpus. Gonville Hall was

[10] Bourdillon 1926, pp. 18–22.   [11] Cobban 1969, pp. 152–3, 247.   [12] Brooke 1985, pp. 2–12.

98

59 St Michael's church, rebuilt in the 1320s by Harvey de Stanton to be the chapel of Michaelhouse as well as a parish church. It is surrounded by St Michael's Court, Gonville and Caius College: to the north and east, beyond the church, the building of 1901–4 by Aston Webb and Ingress Bell; to the south-east the new building of 1934–6 by J. Murray Easton

founded, or became, an institution very like Stapeldon Hall, endowed with country rectories in the diocese of Norwich, engaged in rearing young men from the diocese, helping them complete their arts courses and embark on theology, or some other higher discipline. It was probably intended that they should return to the diocese, or to some higher sphere of usefulness, when the course was finished. Bateman had been a judge in the papal court at Avignon, who by diplomatic genius had become the pope's ambassador to Edward III and the king's ambassador to the pope and so won from both the bishopric of Norwich, where he was born.[13] His own college was dedicated to his cathedral, 'the Holy Trinity of Norwich', and to the study of his own science, canon law. But Corpus was a uniquely civic institution, founded by two guilds – even if Duke Henry was called in to be alderman of one to ensure the necessary patronal authority. It is characteristic of the history of town and gown in Cambridge that the town should show the values it set on the university in its midst, first by founding a college, then, in the Peasants' Revolt of 1381, by trying to destroy it.

All these colleges save the King's Hall were small communities mainly of graduate scholars or fellows aiming for, or completing, higher degrees. All had a close link with one

[13] Brooke 1985, pp. 5–6, 13–18; Thompson 1935; Emden, *Cambridge*, p. 44; Crawley 1976, pp. 1–15. For Corpus and the Peasants' Revolt, see *VCH Cambs*, III, 8–12, 371–3.

59 of the parish churches – so close that the founder of Michaelhouse rebuilt St Michael's church (150 yards from the rest of the college) to be college chapel and parish church combined, and Corpus, designed for close attachment to St Benet's, was often known as Benet College down to the nineteenth century.[14] The warden and fellows of the King's Hall had a link with All Saints, their parish church, and in 1342 became rectors of Great St Mary's itself, the university church; but in other respects this, outstandingly the most important of the early colleges, was different in composition and nature from its fellows. From quite early days it was far the largest, with over forty fellows. Its prime function was to educate the boys of the chapel royal, and to foster students who might grow into the royal service – or the wider services of church and kingdom. Thus it had from the start a large element of young arts students – of undergraduates, as we should say; and showed the way, which was taken up on a yet larger scale by William of Wykeham in New College, towards a large mixed community of older and younger students – an essential preliminary to the idea that the colleges could become the university itself.[15]

Cambridge in the fourteenth century was still a very modest place; and the student body, at most, by the latest estimate, 700 students or so, living in twenty or thirty hostels and eight colleges, was a poor relation to Oxford. The fifteenth century witnessed some decline by the Isis and a large increase by the Cam, so that by 1500 they were neck-and-neck; and from then on, though with many vicissitudes, they have prospered in more or less equal rivalry. The point of balance came after the foundation of King's and Queens' in the 1440s, and the intervention of Henry VI. Henry VI first impinged on Cambridge when the regency government acting in his name granted the licence to the abbot of Crowland in 1428, which led by slow stages to the formation of a modest college for Benedictine monks on the model of the Oxford monastic colleges. This eventually won patronage from the Duke of Buckingham, with whose help a fine court was built; but along with the other religious houses Buckingham College fell at the Dissolution – to be revived almost at once as Magdalene College (1542).[16]

63 Henry VI has been brilliantly revealed to us in recent years by Roger Lovatt as a schoolmaster *manqué* – strange, self-willed, pious, yet like many devout laymen possessed of a strong anti-clerical streak.[17] He had a profound suspicion, it seems, of the influence of Wyclif and his like in Oxford, and yet a great admiration for what William of Wykeham had wrought there, and he wanted to found a great college not dominated by its academic neighbours; and so he reckoned to have more room for manoeuvre in Cambridge. He set to work to erect a New College by the Cam while his favourite schoolmaster, William Waynflete, now Bishop of Winchester, was founding another in Magdalen College, Oxford. King's had been first conceived on a more restrained scale; and its first buildings are still represented by the western courtyard of the Old Schools.[18] But soon his ideas expanded, and he stripped away the streets and houses, the church of St John Zachary and the small new grammar college of God's House – moving the church a hundred yards to the north and the college to the place where Christ's now stands. Henry VI was a great founder, but

[14] Brooke 1985a, pp. 70–2.
[15] Cobban 1969; and see below, pp. 138–44. For what follows, see Aston, Duncan and Evans 1980.
[16] *VCH Cambs*, III, 450, 453; Willis and Clark 1886, II, 351–64; *RCHM Cambridge*, II, 137–45.
[17] Lovatt 1981.
[18] *VCH Cambs*, III, 376–89 (John Saltmarsh); Willis and Clark 1886, I, 313–497, *passim* (esp. pp. 321–33 for the first buildings); *RCHM Cambridge*, I, 17. For what follows, see now Woodman 1986.

60   *King's College chapel, begun by Henry VI, 1446–61, designed by Reginald Ely; continued in 1476–85, completed by Henry VII and Henry VIII 1508–15, the vault and decorations designed by John Wastell (VCH Cambs, III, 388–91. Woodman 1986 argues for some continuity between 1461 and 1477 and a larger involvement by Ely's successor, John Wolryche)*

he was a singularly inept king, and as his politics went astray so did the resources to build his college, and all that survived his fall and death was the shell of the mighty chapel which his successors, down to Henry VII and Henry VIII, were to complete – and a building site, now covered with a few fine buildings of the eighteenth and nineteenth centuries, and a vast acreage of grass.

   King's is justly famous for the marvellous beauty of its chapel, and for the spacious offering its site so ironically gave to the ample lawns of the riverside – the most familiar part

13

61 *(opposite) King's College chapel, interior, detail. The organ and case are seventeenth century, enlarged and altered at various dates, especially in the nineteenth century*

62 *The walls of the ante-chapel, like the vault, carry a massive display of royal emblems – here are the Tudor rose and the Beaufort portcullis*

of the university quarter. It is famed also as the largest of all the medieval colleges, with seventy scholars – even though as Henry VI's difficulties mounted the college's resources and its numbers declined; and it became notorious in later days for the regal independence which exempted King's men from university examinations till the mid nineteenth century – all that remained of Henry's grand scheme to separate his joint foundation of Eton and King's from all lordship save his own, all ecclesiastical interference save the pope's. It was a

63 *King's College chapel: Henry VI presides over the lectern, late fifteenth century*

64 *King's College chapel. The windows were designed by a succession of master glaziers between 1515 and 1547: their main themes are the birth, life and death of Jesus and the birth and death of the Blessed Virgin Mary. This is the Temptation of Christ – on the left, the messenger, in the centre Jesus, on the right Satan: by Thomas Reve, c. 1526 (Wayment 1972, p. 65)*

65 *Each window contains an Old Testament antitype, and a 'messenger' declaring a text to point the theme. Here is the messenger of the window on the north side of the screen, designed by Dierick Vellert, 1517, showing the Massacre of the Innocents (Wayment 1972, pp. 62–4)*

66 (opposite) King's College chapel. The screen and stalls are Renaissance work of 1533–6; the canopies and coats of arms were added in 1633, carefully designed to fit the early woodwork, and carved by William Fells

67 Great St Mary's church, rebuilt for the university between 1478 and 1519 by John Wastell: the tower, begun in 1491, was only completed in 1608; and the west portal was restored by Sir Gilbert Scott in 1850–1

splendid relic of a grandiose vision: a seminary of orthodox Catholic clergy worshipping in one of the most noble of medieval chantries. In the late fifteenth century the university itself began to rebuild Great St Mary's, and called in the notable master mason John Wastell to accomplish the task.[19] But fine symbol as Great St Mary's is of the university's function and purposes, it is totally overshadowed by its neighbour, King's chapel, completed by Wastell himself between 1508 and 1515, which records the soaring dreams of Henry VI and Henry VIII's yearning for a monument to his stature and an expiation of his sins.

167

[19] *VCH Cambs,* III, 130; Sandars 1869, pp. 10–22; Bushell 1948, pp. 33–51. On Wastell see Harvey 1984, pp. 316–25; Woodman 1986, pp. 155–205.

68   *Queens' College, Cambridge,
the first red-brick court, built
under the direction of the founder,
Andrew Doket, probably with the
help of Reginald Ely, in 1448–9;
the hall and (to the right) the
library*

But in its own day the sister foundation of Queens' had greater success and accomplished its founders' aims more completely; and the essential reason for this was that it was fostered by a local man who not only dedicated his life to its service, but was one of the most accomplished beggars in academic history.[20] Andrew Doket first comes into our view as

[20] Twigg 1987, chap. 1; Searle 1867–71, I, 1–104; *VCH Cambs*, III, 408–12; Emden, *Cambridge*, p. 190. For what follows see Brooke and Ortenberg, forthcoming, which dates the birth of Margaret of Anjou to 23 or 24 March 1430: her interest in Queens' must have been fostered well before 30 March 1448 when the college was formally entrusted to her.

108

69 *The library, 1448–9,*
interior: the lecterns (see plate
55) were converted to make
shelves for more books in the early
seventeenth century – and later
raised again still further: the
outlines of the lecterns can still be
seen

warden of the hostel of St Bernard in the 1440s; in 1446 he obtained a royal charter to erect it into a college; in 1448 he won the ear of Henry VI's young queen, Margaret of Anjou, who at the age of seventeen posed as a lively patron of the arts. While she was vainly trying to interest her husband in politics, he was securing her immortality by helping her to found a college. We may be sure that the wise entrepreneur Andrew Doket perceived something of this; and while her fortune was at the flood, took his share of it. With admirable taste and a remarkable efficiency in executing his schemes, he built the Old

70 *The lodge by the river (p. 112): it was identical in many features with the Old Court, and doubtless built soon after 1449. The 'geometrical bridge' spans the river*

71 *Queens' College. In the late sixteenth century the president's modest chambers were magnificently extended along cloister court to the lodge by the river*

Court of Queens' in 1448–9, probably with the help of the royal master mason, Reginald Ely, who was beginning King's chapel at this time.[21] Soon after, Doket built the charming
70 lodge by the river, which may well have been intended to house the noble and regal patrons he designed to interest in his foundation.

The Old Court of Corpus of the 1350s or a little later, and the Old Court of Queens' of the

21 *RCHM Cambridge*, I, 99–101; II, 167–8; Harvey 1984, pp. 94–9, at p. 97, and cf. pp. 95 ff.

72 *The central feature of the President's Lodge is the long gallery (cf. plates 1, 93) – the panelling is sixteenth century, the ceiling modern*

1440s, reveal most clearly the idea of a college as it developed in the late Middle Ages;[22] they are more modest versions of the great quad of New College, and the great court of King's that was never built. Wykeham provided a cloister and Waynflete incorporated it into his main design at Magdalen; but none of the more modest colleges attempted such an

[22] Plates 68–9, 73–4; *RCHM Cambridge*, I, 48–57, II, 167–74, and pls. 115, 221. For what follows, see above, pp. 75–80 (New College) and 62–3 (Merton).

73   *Queens' College, the great tower*

74   *(opposite) Corpus Christi College, Cambridge, Old Court, c. 1352–77, the earliest surviving complete college court*

imitation of so central a feature of a monastic or cathedral complex. Both Corpus and Queens' have domestic, enclosed courts. At Merton the original buildings had been rather scattered and not closely related to one another; only when the library was built in the late fourteenth century was Mob Quad completed: it is in the two Cambridge colleges that we see the earliest complete courts which survive. Corpus Old Court comprised library, master's chambers, kitchen and hall, and numerous staircases with fellows' and students' chambers. There is no chapel in the original conception, since St Benet's lay close at hand.

At Queens' there was kitchen, hall, lodge, library, chapel and many chambers – but also a mighty gate, identical in form to the castle gates of the period. The chambers at Corpus and Queens' followed the pattern established earlier in Oxford and very little altered till the mid seventeenth century. The early chambers allowed for two or three fellows or other students to live in a single room, with tiny studies in the corners and space for truckle beds in the centre; and the staircase allowed for a grouping of chambers with one or two fellows in charge – tutors, as they came to be called; and between the developing tutorial system and the design of these staircases of chambers, there was an evident and intimate link.

169

The design of these courts and the arrangement of the public rooms varied greatly from college to college; but one and all provided ample store of chambers, and most, from the late fourteenth century, had impressive gates.[23] But not even the Great Gate of the King's Hall – now of Trinity, of the early decades of the sixteenth century – wears so militant an aspect as that of Queens'. It was designed to emphasise, we may suppose, the notion of a college as a fortress of piety and learning, and defend Doket's flock from the rioters, the prostitutes and the heretics without. He may have foreseen unruly times ahead when he planned it; but when political disaster checked the growth of King's, Doket was more equal to the crisis than his royal master and mistress. He adroitly wooed the new regime of the Yorkists, and in the 1460s made Queen Elizabeth Woodville foundress beside Queen Margaret. If Elizabeth had an enemy more dangerous than Margaret it was to be King Richard III, her brother-in-law, who usurped her children's throne in 1483. But Doket, nothing abashed, sought higher patronage still – from the new king; and the final coup in a life of brilliantly successful fund-raising was the addition of a third queen to his foundresses – the short-lived Queen Anne, wife of Richard – and of much new endowment by King Richard himself.[24] Fortunate to the end, Doket died in 1484, and so never saw the ruin of his highest hopes at Bosworth Field the next year; Queen Anne was forgotten and the college survived on a more modest scale. John Fisher was to pay it the notable compliment of taking over the presidency for a while, and of imitating the colour and texture and design of the court for his own St John's. But the fellows of St John's in the eighteenth and nineteenth centuries unfortunately commanded resources which enabled them to destroy the beauty of the first court; this the fellows of Queens' have never been able to afford. To that extent – however much we may admire Andrew Doket as the type of academic founder, who, like Emily Davies many centuries later at Girton, worked both within and in the world outside to foster their great designs – we may be grateful that the battle of Bosworth helped to preserve one of the unique beauties of Cambridge.

57

Meanwhile the decline of Henry VI laid an infinite burden on those he had appointed to build and foster his college, and especially on Robert Wodelark, provost of King's from about 1452 to 1479, who was not only expected to gather the large estates and build the chapel, but was also put in charge of the King's Hall, and on two occasions had to do a spell as chancellor of the university.[25] When Henry fell, the endowments were confiscated, and

[23] The first to survive is New College (plate 42). Queens' gate bears some resemblance to Tattershall Castle of about the same epoch. It has been likened to the unfinished gate to the old court of King's; but the resemblance is not close, except that this would have been, if completed, a fairly formidable entrance (Willis and Clark 1886, I, 322–31, figs. 5–12). Queens' is a great deal more formidable than its successors of the late fifteenth–early sixteenth centuries – King's Hall, Jesus, Christ's and St John's (plates 9, 56–7, 91–2) – although the gate of St John's was evidently designed in imitation of it.
[24] Twigg 1987; Searle 1867–71, I, 87–101, esp. 95 ff.
[25] *VCH Cambs*, III, 408; A. Cobban in Rich 1973, esp. pp. 3–7.

although Wodelark won a respite and some measure even of restitution from Edward IV, he suffered continuous anxiety and for the rest of his life was hammered and crushed by penalties and disappointments. The agonies of trying to preserve a very large foundation seem to have inspired him to the idea of creating a tiny one of his own – the smallest ever founded, for two fellows only, though he anticipated some commoners as well. This community was to preserve the traditional orthodox theology, to which his life was dedicated, under the patronage of St Catharine, patroness of scholars and many others besides – whose image the ambitious young John Colton, first master of Gonville Hall, had stamped on his seal a century before.[26] But above all, St Catharine's was a chantry: the image in miniature of the medieval college, an academic chantry in which ceaseless prayer and masses for the founders and benefactors were inextricably united with academic study. Some founders had laid more, some less stress on the duties of fellows to sing for their souls; but the chantry element was always present in every college down to the Reformation,[27] and the splendour of King's chapel and the foundation of Trinity and Christ Church bear witness that though Henry VIII had broken the links with Rome he had no notion of ending this ceaseless round of prayer; he could ill afford to.

[26] A. Cobban and S.C. Aston in Rich 1973, pp. 1–32, 33–58; for Colton's seal, Brooke 1985, p. 18 and n. 42.

[27] This element seems little in evidence in the King's Hall, but this aspect of its history needs further investigation in relation to its intimate link with the Chapel Royal.

6   *1450–1550: the colleges take over*

> A beehive . . . whose scholars like clever bees will day and night make wax to the honour of God and sweet honey for their own profit and that of all Christians.
>
> Description of Corpus Christi College, Oxford, in the words of its Foundation Statutes, 1517

> I hear of no clerk that hath commen lately of [Gonville Hall] but savoureth of the frying pan, though he speak never so holily.
>
> Richard Nykke, Bishop of Norwich, 1530: see Brooke 1985, pp. 51–2 and n. 41; CC, p. 39

Oxford

The years 1450 to 1550 saw a rapid decline in the numbers of unendowed academical halls. The halls were at their height in the middle of the fifteenth century but by 1510 strain and decay were visible on every hand. The concern of the university authorities was reflected in the Aularian Statutes of *c.* 1483–1490, passed during the chancellorship of John Russell, Bishop of Lincoln.[1] They represented a serious attempt to impose a stricter discipline on the scholars of the halls through their principals. But the real trouble lay in the vulnerability of the halls during a period of depression as a result of their lack of endowment. An early sign of difficulty seems to have been the amalgamation taking place between grammar and arts halls. Thus White Hall and St Hugh's Hall were joined to St Edmund Hall under Principal Thamys (*c.* 1438–1459).[2] The unendowed grammar halls after 1480 may have felt keenly the competition caused by the establishment of Magdalen College School. At all events St Edmund Hall became a centre for the study of both grammar and other arts. The list which survives for the cautions made by the principals of halls in 1469 shows that there were then about fifty.[3] A rapid decline set in after 1505; by 1513 only eighteen were left. This catastrophic fall was mainly due to the fact that the halls had become unprofitable to their landlords. Regular expenses for repairs had to be met from rents which were becoming irregular. It is noticeable that in 1533 rooms at Hinxey Hall were said to be unoccupied and dilapidated.[4] In 1531–2 Osney Abbey relinquished the lease of St Edmund Hall which it had controlled for over 200 years to Queen's College and was doubtless glad to do so.[5] The regulation which compelled members of the university to become members of halls or colleges was putting pressure on the surviving halls and colleges to admit more students. In 1512 in addition an attempt was made to put an end to the remaining 'chamberdekyns', or unattached students. Colleges in some instances became willing to take over halls as additional accommodation. This seems to have been

---

[1] Emden 1968, pp. 198–200.   [2] Emden 1968, pp. 167–70.
[3] Emden 1968, pp. 2 and 186; Pantin 1964, p. 34.   [4] Pantin 1964, p. 82.   [5] Emden 1968, pp. 235–6.

118

the ground for the acquisition of St Edmund Hall by Queen's and for the similar use made by Merton of St Alban, Urban and Corner Halls.[6] Even so, W.A. Pantin has estimated that as late as 1550 nearly a third of the student body one way or another was still accommodated in halls.[7]

It had become clear by the beginning of the sixteenth century that existing arrangements were proving inadequate or undergoing change. Dispensations diminished the effectiveness of the regulations concerning the length of the courses: instances occur where the four-year course for the B.A. was completed in three or even less.[8] Dispensations were also helping to modify the system of lectures. The actual number of lectures heard in a term might be no more than sixteen or even as few as eight, while the lectures themselves instead of lasting for the greater part of an hour, as they had once been required to do, regularly took no longer than a quarter of an hour. As at Cambridge, instruction was being given quite often inside the walls of colleges and halls rather than through the necessary lectures of the regent masters.[9] Dispensation was also affecting the government of the university. It was tending to reduce the numbers attending convocation and congregation to a handful. On all these counts the statutes needed to be adjusted to take account of new practices. A lawyer chancellor like Archbishop Warham felt the matter keenly.[10] At the same time the Lady Margaret Beaufort by founding at Oxford and Cambridge, between 1497 and 1502, two endowed praelectorships in divinity, later to become professorships, had initiated a process by which the regent masters were to be replaced by a paid professoriate.[11]

If an account of the new foundations of Brasenose, Corpus Christi, Cardinal College and Christ Church needs to be set against this background, it must also include consideration of what was happening not only in Cambridge but in London, Paris, Orleans and above all in Italy in centres of learning such as Padua, Florence, Rome and Venice.

Already in the 1450s William Selling, a Benedictine, having studied Latin eloquence at Oxford under Surigone, had gone on to the universities of Padua and Bologna. When he returned to England he promoted the study of Greek from his post as prior of Christ Church, Canterbury, and took advantage of his diplomatic employments for Henry VII to meet French scholars with similar interests, such as Robert Gaguin.[12] A stronger influence at Oxford was William Grocyn. Having been a fellow of New College, the tutor of William Warham and divinity reader at Magdalen, Grocyn had gone to Italy in 1488 and had sat at the feet of Chalcondylas and Politian. On his return to Oxford he gave public lectures on Greek.[13] In 1487 Thomas Linacre, fellow of All Souls, had also visited Italy and stayed at Florence, Padua and Rome. He had helped Aldus Manutius for whom he had translated Proclus, *On the Sphere*.[14] Then John Colet and Richard Fox, the future founder of Corpus, both gained a university education abroad; and Colet, after studying in Orleans, Paris and Italy, came to Oxford in 1497 to lecture publicly on two of the Pauline Epistles. Here he met Erasmus and Richard Charnock, prior of St Mary's College.[15] R.W. Chambers has protested

---

[6] Salter 1923, p. xiv.   [7] Pantin 1972, p. 10.   [8] Mitchell 1980a, p. xxiv.
[9] Mitchell 1980a, p. xxv; cf. Leader, forthcoming.   [10] Mitchell 1980a, p. xxvii.
[11] Duncan 1986, pp. 347–8; Dowling 1986, p. 10. Edmund Wyllesford seems to have acted as 'lecturer' before Roper (Emden, *Oxford*, III, 2116); Duncan 1986, p. 350.
[12] Emden, *Oxford*, III, 1666–7.   [13] Emden, *Oxford*, I, 827; McConica 1965, pp. 44, 90.
[14] Emden, *Oxford*, II, 1148; McConica 1965, p. 44.
[15] Emden, *Oxford*, I, 462–4; Dowling 1986, pp. 112–18; Greenslade 1986, p. 313.

against the dubbing by Seebohm of Grocyn, Linacre and Colet as 'Three Oxford Reformers', since they would more properly be called 'Three London Reformers'.[16] Certainly their scholarly influence was greatest in the capital, where Colet was dean of St Paul's and refounded St Paul's School, and Linacre set up the College (later Royal College) of Physicians of London.[17] His point well reflects the interlocking between the ancient universities and the scholarly circles and households where graduates might find employment in London, not least in the royal household itself. The growing impact of a demand for the study of Greek at Oxford was not to be denied.

The story of the foundation of Brasenose is that of an unendowed hall which by acquiring endowment turned itself into a college. The history of the hall goes back to the thirteenth century. By 1435 a list of its principals begins. Then in the will of one of them, Edmund Croxton (1508), we are told that he left £6 13s 4d to Brasenose 'if such works as

75 (opposite) Oxford, Brasenose College. The brazen nose – a twelfth- or thirteenth-century knocker – relic of the thirteenth-century hall which preceded the college

76 The Old Quad, early sixteenth century, with the third storey of the early seventeenth century, and the Radcliffe Camera and the tower of St Mary's beyond

[16] Chambers 1948, p. 66.   [17] Dowling 1986, pp. 113–16; Emden, *Oxford*, II, 1148.

77   *Brasenose College façade, including the library, from St Mary's tower*

the Bishop of Lyncoln and Master Sotton intended there went on during their life or twelve years thereafter'. Brasenose was to have two founders, William Smyth, successively Bishop of Coventry and Lichfield, then of Lincoln, and Sir Richard Sutton.[18] In many ways the college which they founded was based on conservative principles. In study the emphasis was to be on scholastic philosophy and theology, and one of its aims, like that of Lincoln College where Smyth became visitor in 1495, was the refutation of heresy. It had a strong Lancashire and Cheshire connection. But two factors differentiated it from the foundations of the thirteenth and fourteenth centuries. Firstly it took over from Magdalen the idea that commoners of noble birth, to the number of six, might attend the college at their own expense providing they had incomes of £40 or more, or the expectation of such. Secondly one of the two founders – Sutton – was the first layman (or laywoman) to have initiated the process of founding an Oxford college.[19] Many founders had been anxious enough to

[18] Emden, *Oxford*, III, 1721–2; McConica 1986, p. 9.
[19] He came from Sutton (Cheshire), near Macclesfield. He was a barrister and member of the privy council.

122

CLARVS WYNTONIÆ PRÆSVL COGNOIE FOXVS
QVI PIVS HOC OLIM NOBILE STRVXIT OPVS
TALIS ERAT FORMA TALIS DVM VIXIT AMICTV
QVALEM SPECTANTI PICTA TABELLA REFERT ·

secure the co-operation of the laity, as Stapeldon and de Brome had been with Edward II at Exeter and Oriel or Eglesfield had been with Queen Philippa at Queen's; and even the Balliols would hardly have established Balliol if it had not been for the initial penance laid upon John by Bishop Kirkham. If the single most striking change of the sixteenth century was to be the addition to the clerical student body of growing numbers of laymen, then the existence of a lay co-founder at Brasenose who was also one of its initiators was a symbol of what was to follow. His colleague, Bishop Smyth, as chancellor of Oxford from 1500 to 1502, had been as closely associated with the university in the years before the foundation of Brasenose as with the wider world as president of the Council in the Marches of Wales, 1501–12. The two co-founders planned a college consisting of a principal and twelve fellows from the diocese of Coventry and Lichfield with a preference for those from Prescot, Lancashire, and Prestbury, Cheshire.[20]

The foundation of Corpus Christi College by Bishop Richard Fox in 1517 on the site of

[20] Emden, *Oxford*, III, 1721–2; McConica 1986, pp. 7–17.

79 *Corpus Christi College, Oxford, founded in 1517. The Front Quad, early sixteenth century, with sundial of 1581 and seventeenth-century additions*

three halls and two inns was to give Oxford its closest links with the New Learning.[21] It was specifically applauded by Erasmus. Of the three Oxford founders from the episcopal bench in this period – Smyth, Fox and Wolsey – Fox had by far the greatest continental experience. He had attended the university of Paris and was in the best position to appreciate the achievements of Waynflete at Magdalen and Magdalen College School. He

[21] Dowling 1986, pp. 27–33; Emden, *Oxford*, II, 715–19; McConica 1986, pp. 17–29.

124

certainly drew heavily on Magdalen for ideas and in particular recruited its president to be the first president of Corpus – John Claymond,[22] a remarkable scholar – and scholars of the quality of Reginald Pole and Edward Wotton. The three Magdalen praelectorships in theology and natural and moral philosophy were evidently the model for his own three lectureships in Greek, Latin and theology, even if he changed the subjects of two of them.

[22] Emden, *Oxford*, I, 428–30, cf. McConica 1975, pp. 153–4 and n. 6.

125

81 *Corpus Christi College, Oxford, the Library, with the chapel beyond*

Their lectures were to be open to the university. His college was founded for a president, twenty fellows, twenty 'disciples' or scholars, the three lecturers already mentioned, two chaplains and two clerks.[23] Fox instructed his 'disciples' to attend the lectures at Magdalen and he followed Waynflete's example by allowing from four to six noblemen to become members who should study under tutors. An alternative to noblemen might be men at law. He ensured a notable success for his new college's repute when he attracted to it Juan Luis Vives, the Spanish humanist, to lecture to the university.[24] Edward Wotton became lecturer in Greek, and Nicholas Udall, a 'disciple', fellow and future headmaster of Eton, lecturer in logic.[25] The lectures in Greek and Latin were to be additional to the existing arrangements for grammar and rhetoric in the trivium. The institution of lectureships freed these subjects from a strait-jacket which was becoming uncomfortable. In addition Corpus was able to give employment to notable humanist protégés of Cardinal Wolsey,

[23] Emden, *Oxford*, II, 717.
[24] Dowling 1986, pp. 149–50; Emden, *Oxford, 1501–40*, pp. 594–6; McConica 1986, pp. 26–7.
[25] Dowling 1986, p. 134; Emden, *Oxford, 1501–40*, pp. 639, 586–7; McConica 1986, pp. 25–7.

126

such as Thomas Lupset, praelector in humanity, and Thomas Mosgroff, reader in medicine, while Cardinal College was under construction.[26]

The emphasis put by Fox on the establishment of lectureships was echoed in the scheme devised by Linacre for the setting up of lectureships in medicine at Oxford and Cambridge. Mention begins to be made of them in the years following his foundation of the College of Physicians of London in 1518. By 1523 the university of Oxford was urging him to implement the plans for the establishment of lectureships, of which it had heard; but Linacre was unable to do this before he died in 1524.[27] Then the instructions which he left to his executors proved hard to implement. A lectureship at St John's College, Cambridge, seems to have been in operation in the mid 1520s. But at Oxford negotiations were long drawn out and Linacre's original intentions had to be redrafted by his surviving executor, Bishop Tunstall. It was not until 1559 that a Linacre lecturer was appointed at Merton College. Linacre had wanted to involve the Mercers' Company in the administration of the lectureships. Tunstall preferred to follow Fox and to entrust them to colleges.[28]

The most spectacular development in Oxford in the first half of the sixteenth century was the foundation of Cardinal College and its transformation into King Henry VIII's College and Christ Church. Thomas Wolsey was himself that rather rare phenomenon, an Oxford

[26] Emden, *Oxford, 1501–40*, pp. 366–7; 406–7; but for Mosgroff cf. Duncan 1986, p. 339.
[27] Emden, *Oxford*, II, 1149; Lewis 1986, pp. 221–8.
[28] Fletcher 1977, pp. 143–6.

East Anglian, and had been a fellow, bursar and dean of divinity at Magdalen. He visited Oxford in the same year that Linacre founded the College of Physicians in London, and caused a stir by announcing his wish to provide a number of lectureships at his own expense.[29] In 1523 he took matters further than either Waynflete or Fox when he set about the foundation of a college whose scale was to be truly magnificent. If completed it would have outshone New College and Magdalen and become, as the writer of the official university letter to the cardinal put it, 'a college which when finished, will equal the rest of Oxford put together'. He designed it for a dean, sixty canons, forty junior canons, forty-two servants of the chapel, including a teacher of music and six public professors. Twenty rich young commoners might join the foundation at their own expense. The subjects which the professors were to teach were medicine, philosophy, mathematics, Greek, rhetoric, humanity, theology and civil law. To support this grandiose body he obtained from the pope bulls to allow him to dissolve the priory of St Frideswide and 22 other monastic houses. He was thus doing on the grandest scale what Bishop Alcock of Ely had done when he turned St Radegund's nunnery into Jesus College, Cambridge, and Bishop Fisher when he changed St John's Hospital into St John's College, Cambridge (see pp. 150–1). Moreover if Fox had drawn on Magdalen, Oxford, Wolsey drew heavily on Cambridge. In 1527 he chose Dr Shorton, Master of Pembroke, Cambridge, to help with the recruitment of 'scholars of ripe wits and abilities to study and read there [in Cardinal College] with promise of great encouragement and reward'.[30] Three of his leading recruits – Gualter, Starkey and Morison – were already at Oxford. To them were now added no less than seventeen Cambridge men. They included one or two who in the following year showed that they had Lutheran contacts. Wolsey was as firmly anti-Lutheran as Henry VIII or Bishop Longland of Lincoln. But in his plan for public lectureships – to which high salaries should be attached in order to attract distinguished scholars – he showed that he was no mere conservative. His aspirations were warmly commended in the Oxford convocation of December 1528.[31] His great Dining Hall on the south side of Tom Quad demonstrates in its splendour what his chapel might have been on the north side if it had been completed. When he fell from power and his effects passed into the king's hands the college was allowed to receive its rents until Michaelmas 1530. There was some hope that through the influence of the Duke of Norfolk and Anne Boleyn's father, the Earl of Wiltshire, the college might yet be saved. But it was not to be. The wolves devoured the fatted lamb. The lands of Cardinal College were 'either sold to, or begged away by, hungry courtiers' and others, nor were any arrangements made for its existing members.[32]

Wolsey's household had itself been, in Strype's words, a 'university', and its break-up for those scholars who were members of it – Sampson, Pace, Tunstall, Gonell and Clement – was a disaster. But abroad in Italy the king supported the scholarly activity of his kinsman, Reginald Pole, in Padua and Venice, and continued to do so until Henry's divorce from Catherine of Aragon forced Pole to a decisive break with his royal patron.[33] Some members of Wolsey's household were able to transfer for a time to Pole's.

The vulnerability of the university to the attentions of the king was demonstrated in

[29] Emden, *Oxford*, II, 1149 (1524); Cross 1986, p. 121.

[30] Mitchell 1980a, pp. 210–12; Dowling 1986, pp. 119–20; Emden, *Cambridge*, pp. 525–6; Emden, *Oxford, 1501–40*, p. 516; Gray and Brittain 1960, pp. 21–36; Knowles 1948–59, III, 161–4; McConica 1986, pp. 29–32.

[31] Mitchell 1980a, pp. 234–7.   [32] Mallet 1924–7, II, 38.   [33] Emden, *Cambridge*, p. 454.

83   *Christ Church, the dining-hall of Cardinal College of 1525–9*

1530 when it proved slow in giving an answer to the royal question about the pope's power to dispense with the law against marrying a deceased brother's wife, the central issue in the divorce case. In March 1530 a terrified chancellor, Archbishop Warham, saw Oxford poised on the edge of a calamity. 'For the sake of your future', he wrote to the convocation, 'I urge you to reach a decision as soon as you can, and to make it conform to the law of God and the king's desires. Why can you not do as Paris and Cambridge have done? You would do well to delegate the business to a committee of thirty of your more learned members, as I have seen done on various occasions when I was in residence.'[34]

The king's interest in scholarship at Oxford was, however, sustained by the foundation of King Henry VIII's College in 1532.[35] This was to consist of a dean and twelve canons

[34] Mitchell 1980a, pp. 274–5; cf. Cross 1986, pp. 124–5.   [35] Dowling 1986, pp. 83–4; McConica 1986, pp. 32–3.

84   *Christ Church, the staircase to the hall by J. Wyatt (1801–4), with seventeenth-century fan vault*

directly subject to the king. Its first dean, John Higdon, had been dean of Cardinal College and two of Wolsey's canons were similarly appointed to King Henry's College. Here was a certain continuity. But the key feature – the lectureships – was for the moment dropped. The new canons included a head of house, Dr Cottisford, rector of Lincoln, an administrator who had been senior proctor, and Robert Wakefield, a Cambridge man, royal chaplain and a notable figure, since he had lectured at Louvain and Tübingen and knew Hebrew, Greek, Chaldaic and Latin.[36] Having been appointed regius praelector in Hebrew he gave his first public lecture in the hall of King Henry VIII's College. Subsequent canons were to include two other outstanding Cambridge men, Sir John Cheke, a future Provost of King's and tutor to Edward VI, and John Leland, the antiquary.[37] Henry saw the new foundation as a piece of patronage which he might exploit in the interests of learned members of the royal circle.

Meanwhile what might be gained or lost by royal interest was all too plainly shown when in 1535 Doctors Layton and Tregonwell arrived as royal visitors. Their main work concerned the reception of the university's submission to the oath of supremacy and the dissolution of Oxford's friaries and lesser monasteries. The university lost no less than twelve monastic halls of residence and friaries.[38] Thus the number of students was notably diminished. The visitors also made some positive contributions. The university was to be exempted from such major clerical taxes as first fruits and tenths. In exchange it was expected to help finance a new set of public lectureships. These were to be set up in Greek at Merton and Queen's, and in both Greek and Latin at New College and All Souls. Regular attendance at these public lectures was to be required.[39] However, it was at first a paper scheme: the first recorded Greek lecturer at Merton was Sir Thomas Bodley in 1565. Yet the king had recognised that instruction in new subjects was needed and that it might be attached to colleges – as a lecturer in astronomy had been briefly attached to Merton in 1517.[40]

However, it was in the old subjects that Oxford was to acquire regius praelectorships; already in March 1536 a former senior proctor, John Warner, was at the king's command put in charge of the conferment of degrees in medicine. Almost at once he became warden of All Souls, and seems to have become preoccupied by matters other than medicine.[41] His deputy in 1552, Thomas Fraunces, student of Christ Church, became his successor in 1554. He was a 'man of distinguished learning' who by 1561 had become a doctor to Queen Elizabeth and provost of Queen's. Later he was to win the approval of his London colleagues sufficiently to be elected president of the Royal College of Physicians of London.[42] Whether these first two 'regius professors' lectured is unclear. In the meantime John Story, principal of Broadgates Hall, had been appointed the first regius praelector in civil law.[43] These promotions were followed by the more spectacular foundations of three regius chairs at Oxford (*c.* 1540–2) in theology, Hebrew and Greek, and no less than five regius chairs at Cambridge in 1547. These were in physic, civil law, Greek, Hebrew and divinity. John Cheke was the learned first Oxford professor of Greek, while in 1549 Fagius became professor of Hebrew and, at Cranmer's suggestion, the chair of theology went to Martin Bucer.[44]

That Henry VIII was still ruminating the possibility of developing more colleges was shown in 1539 when Henry personally directed Sir Nicholas Bacon and others to draw up a scheme for the foundation of a college where Latin, French and civil law might be taught.

[36] Emden, *Oxford, 1501–40*, pp. 599–600; cf. Greenslade 1986, pp. 306–7.
[37] Emden, *Oxford, 1501–40*, pp. 114–15, 350–1.   [38] Knowles 1948–59, III, 362.
[39] Mallet 1924–7, II, 62–3; Cross 1986, p. 128.   [40] Salter 1923, p. 466.
[41] Emden, *Oxford, 1501–40*, pp. 215–16; Lewis 1986, pp. 229–31.
[42] Emden, *Oxford, 1501–40*, pp. 215–16; Lewis 1986, pp. 231–4.
[43] Emden, *Oxford, 1501–40*, pp. 544–5; Barton 1986, pp. 262–4, 285–6.
[44] Greenslade 1986, p. 316; Duncan 1986, pp. 352–4, 356–7; Logan 1977; Emden, *Oxford, 1501–40*, pp. 114–15; Porter 1958, p. 51.

85 *(opposite) Christ Church, Tom Quad, Mercury and Tom Tower. The southern range, from the left to the gate, is of the 1520s; the quad was completed in the late seventeenth century. Tom Tower, 1681–2, is by Wren (pp. 199–200)*

This proved abortive, but the idea of a collegiate solution to the need to train royal servants was clearly not lost to view.[45]

At Oxford the Dissolution of the Monasteries and the decision in 1542 to establish new dioceses ensured the further transformation of King Henry VIII's College. The king himself had at the time of the Dissolution followed up an idea of Wolsey that there should be thirteen new dioceses.[46] Bishops Gardiner and Tunstall seem also to have been interested in this proposition. They were thus anticipating similar suggestions for the reform of European dioceses which were to be made at the Council of Trent. But at the same time Henry was also susceptible to the pressure of those who were scrambling for loot and seeking to dissolve everything in sight. In 1539 a less radical scheme for diocesan reform had been put forward for reducing the number of new dioceses to six, of which Oxford should be one. In the original scheme the hand of Cromwell can doubtless be seen. Five of the six dioceses were to retain the buildings of monasteries in which the new cathedrals were sited. Thus to this day something of St Augustine's, Bristol, St Werburgh's, Chester, and St Peter's at Gloucester, Peterborough and Westminster survives. Less fortunate was the great abbey of Osney in which the new cathedral of Oxford was sited at first. Hardly one stone of the old abbey now stands upon another. Only the bells (and in particular Great Tom) were saved by being transferred to the new foundation of Christ Church, where they came to provide a material link with the Augustinian abbey. But Osney's loss was to prove the salvation of what Wolsey had left of St Frideswide's. Christ Church was to make use of the half-completed buildings of Cardinal College; and for the new joint foundation of college and cathedral the buildings of St Frideswide's Priory and Canterbury College were to be found more convenient than those of Osney.[47]

Before this happened the dangerous-looking Chantries Act of 1545 gave the king power to dissolve any college at either university; almost all colleges enjoyed chantry endowments and so their inclusion was logical enough. A commission was appointed to survey the college lands. The commissioners were all university men and included Matthew Parker, master of Corpus and vice-chancellor of Cambridge, John Redman, warden of King's Hall, and William May from Cambridge and Richard Cox, the royal almoner, from Oxford.

The king's serious interest in the university curriculum had recently been shown in the royal injunctions by which the teaching of scholastic theology and canon law had been forbidden. At the same time there also seem to have been many who, having importunately pursued him to have the lands and possessions of both universities surveyed, were meaning afterwards 'to enjoy the best of their lands and possessions by exchange of impropriated benefices and other improved lands'. These were the 'wolves' ready to devour the endowments of colleges, men like those who had already bought up the monastic lands sold off by the crown and who were to consume those of the chantries in the reign of Edward VI. But the king who had led the 'wolves' on in an attempt to solve his financial difficulties now abandoned the idea of exploiting the lands of the colleges. How had this result been achieved? There seems to have been a reform party to whom the universities could appeal. This included Queen Katherine Parr, Sir Anthony Denny of the king's privy

---

[45] Curtis 1959, p. 67. [46] Knowles 1948–59, III, 164, 358–9 and nn. 3 and 4.

[47] Thompson 1900, p. 11; Pantin 1985, p. 50; already by 9 June 1546 it had been decided that the site at Osney was inconvenient (Dawson 1984, p. 210). Canterbury College had been founded by Archbishop Islip between 1361 and 1363 as a house of study for seculars and for the monks of Christ Church, Canterbury (cf. Pantin 1985, pp. 1–50).

86 *A Christ Church servant –
perhaps William Forde, cook – by
John Riley (1646–91, active in
the 1680s)*

chamber and Richard Cox, the royal almoner, tutor to Prince Edward and himself a
university man; it also included John Redman's pupils from Cambridge, John Cheke and
Thomas Smith.[48] Cox was a former headmaster of Eton and fellow of King's College,
Cambridge, whom Wolsey had imported into Oxford. It was he who brought the first news
of the foundation of Christ Church to Oxford; and he was to become its first dean. For the
grandson of Lady Margaret Beaufort by 1546 had decided to make the twin foundations of
Christ Church, Oxford, and Trinity College, Cambridge, and thus to demonstrate the
crown's continuing interest in collegiate foundations at the universities. To replace King
Henry VIII College, Christ Church was founded by letters patent of 4 November on a
magnificent scale. It was to have an annual income of over £2,200, made up largely from
the lands of dissolved monasteries. Within it a cathedral chapter of the new foundation was
to incorporate a college. This made it a unique body in England. Its governing body was
made up of a dean and eight canons.[49] There were to be twenty students of theology, forty
of philosophy, and forty 'disciples' or scholars. Three professorships were set up in
theology, Greek and Hebrew. There was to be a generous provision of servants and
almsmen. Cox was made head of a corporation which was partly ecclesiastical, to serve the
new cathedral, and partly academic.

[48] See below, pp. 152–3; Dawson 1984, pp. 209–11; Emden, *Oxford, 1501–40*, pp. 146–7; Aylmer 1986, p. 531 n. 2; and
cf. Cross 1986, p. 133.
[49] Thompson 1900, p. 13 (where their names are given); and cf. now McConica 1986, p. 33 and especially n. 2.

87 *Trinity College, Cambridge. On the left, King Edward's tower of the King's Hall, 1427–37, moved to its present site beside the chapel (1555–67) when the Great Court was created about 1600. The fountain is of 1601–2, rebuilt in 1715–16; on the right, the Great Gate (plate 57)*

In the last week of October 1546, comparable royal action at Cambridge resulted in the foundation of Trinity College. Henry amalgamated Michaelhouse, King's Hall and Physwick Hostel to make a single college to produce a yearly income of £1,640[50] and endowed it with the revenues of 26 monasteries. The fact that he picked out King's Hall for particular attention was doubtless caused by its special contribution to the training of potential civil servants which it had sustained since the fourteenth century, though we may also see in it the hand of John Redman, last warden of King's Hall, first master of Trinity. His new college received its letters of foundation on 19 December 1546.

Before the foundation of Christ Church and Trinity College had been completed the king died on 28 January 1547. A draft set of statutes was drawn up for Christ Church but was never signed, and Christ Church was to manage without formal statutes until the middle of the nineteenth century.

[50] Dawson 1984, p. 211; Cobban 1969, p. 20 n. 1.

88 (opposite) Trinity College, the hall, looking north: it was built for Thomas Nevile by Ralph Symons, and completed in 1605

89 A detail of the screen at its south end with its 'barbaric profusion of strap-panels, caryatids, etc.' (Pevsner 1970, p. 170)

Edward VI's visitors at Oxford in 1549, like those at Cambridge, recognised the growing importance of the colleges. They attempted to make All Souls a centre for the specialised study of civil law, to make New College a centre for divinity and the arts, and to select another college for medicine.[51] The Cambridge visitors similarly wanted to join Trinity Hall, an existing college for civilians, with Clare Hall and to make of the united college one

[51] Mallet 1924–7, II, 83; Cross 1986, p. 137.

which would be entirely devoted to law.[52] A reason for this growing emphasis on colleges, whose endowments could support students of modest resources, is reflected in the protest by Bishop Latimer in the same year: he commented critically on a tendency for gentlemen's sons to be taking over the universities and extruding poor men's sons from training for the ministry.[53] However, the efforts of the Edwardians were soon to be swept away. Peter Martyr, the Florentine Protestant divine, who had found his position as regius professor of divinity at Christ Church precarious, eventually fled abroad and was lucky to escape. Soon after Mary's accession Oxford became the scene of the trials of Bishops Latimer and Ridley and Archbishop Cranmer, three of the leading Cambridge Protestant bishops. The government chose Oxford for the trials to demonstrate 'the heinousness of academic heresy'; it could also rely on the regius professor of divinity there, Richard Smyth, who conducted the government's case.[54] Certainly it secured the verdict it required and once the medieval heresy laws had been restored the three victims were burned in Broad Street.

Despite these convulsions, numbers had begun to pick up from about 1553; Queen Mary herself endowed the university with five rectories worth over £130 annually; and a certain confidence in the university on the part of the laity seems to have returned – including the gentry, as Latimer had perceived. This confidence was nowhere more clearly seen than in the foundation at Oxford of Trinity and St John's.

These two Marian foundations, of Trinity in 1555 and St John's in 1557, followed the example set by Sir Richard Sutton at Brasenose and demonstrated that pious Catholic laymen were now vying with bishops in their desire to extend the collegiate system. The founder of Trinity, Sir Thomas Pope, was the son of a yeoman, a civil servant who had made a fortune as the Treasurer of the Court of Augmentations.[55] Sir Thomas White, the founder of St John's, was a man of even larger fortune, Lord Mayor of London and a leading Merchant Taylor; and the appearance of a merchant founder is especially significant. The burgesses had joined the knights in recognising the value of a collegiate foundation in this striking way. Moreover there is a direct link between St John's and Corpus, since White borrowed directly from Fox's statutes. There were to be readerships in Greek and in Humanity, that is, in Latin. His college differed notably from all the others in that 37 of its places were to be reserved for the boys of Merchant Taylors' School, while beyond that he extended the range of recruitment to the merchant communities of Tonbridge, Coventry, Reading and Bristol.[56] Thus he was to ensure that a clothier's son from Reading, William Laud, should join his college, and ultimately become one of its most learned and famous sons.

Cambridge 1450–1550: the formation of the academic quarter

The great change which converted Cambridge, like Oxford, into a federation of colleges, and in the process brought Cambridge to something like parity with Oxford in numbers and repute – and witnessed the transformation of Cambridge between the High Street and the

[52] The scheme had the support of Protector Somerset (Curtis 1959, p. 159).
[53] Curtis 1959, pp. 69–70.
[54] Cross 1986, p. 142; Loach 1986, pp. 368–75; Emden, *Oxford 1501–40*, pp. 524–5; Duncan 1986, p. 353; for his early career see also McConica 1965, p. 266.
[55] Cross 1986, pp. 141–2; McConica 1986, pp. 43–5.
[56] Stevenson and Salter 1939, pp. 113–22; McConica 1986, pp. 45–8.

138

river into the academic quarter which gives it its fame and beauty to this day – was accomplished between 1450 and 1550.[57] In the second half of the fifteenth century and early in the sixteenth the chancellor, masters and scholars of the university of Cambridge united with some townsfolk and other generous benefactors to rebuild with lavish care the oldest and most central of the buildings of the university, the church of St Mary the Great.[58] Yet beyond the High Street, only a stone's throw away, lay King's chapel, completed at much the same time as the university church; and anyone who compares the chapel built for a single college with the church of the whole university must be struck by the contrast; for the chapel overwhelms the church by its greater size and splendour. This is a parable which may help us to understand the magical transformation of this hundred years.

No one set out to achieve the transformation; yet many took what we may reasonably call deliberate steps in that direction. By 1450 the university had a centre in the original quadrangle of the Old Schools and in Great St Mary's; and although the space between was a tumble of streets and houses, not the spacious lawn which has graced it since the eighteenth century, the university had already a recognisable centre.[59] But even in 1450 the spread of colleges to the west of the High Street far outstripped the university's own buildings. In the deep south lay Peterhouse, without the Trumpington Gate, modest in scale though graced by the fine church of Little St Mary's, which was also, and chiefly, Peterhouse chapel. Within the walls lay the new college of Queens', the earliest and perhaps the finest complete college court of brick in Cambridge, dominated by the massive gateway which proclaimed it a fortress of learning. North of Queens' lay the house of the Carmelites, a college of a kind, which was absorbed by Queens' at the Dissolution in the late 1530s, and beyond it the great open space, then presumably a pile of rubble, now mainly lawns, which marked the site of Henry VI's dream of a New College by the Cam, and the roofless chapel. Next came the university schools with Clare and Trinity Hall and Gonville Hall lapping round them; and away to the north the three colleges or halls which were to become Trinity: Michaelhouse and Physwick Hostel (then a subsidiary of Gonville Hall) and the King's Hall. The formation of Trinity and the founding of St John's were all that was needed to complete the academic quarter at its northern end.

Thus by 1450 the stage was set both for the making of the academic quarter as we know it, and for the conquest of the university by the colleges. Yet in many ways the concentration of academic life in west Cambridge was much less conspicuous then than now. First of all, the foundation of St John's at its northern end in the early sixteenth century, and the completion of Trinity and the building of Great Court in the mid and late sixteenth century, have given much of its character to the northern part of the quarter. Then the development of teaching within the colleges, of the tutorial system as it was in sixteenth- and seventeenth-century Cambridge, was essential to the nature of college dominance in later times; as was the decline of the hostels and the disappearance of all but a handful of students not members of a college.[60] The late fifteenth and early sixteenth centuries have often been called the age of Erasmus in Cambridge; and for all his sour

[57] For general surveys, see Brooke 1985, pp. 41–6; *RCHM Cambridge*, I, pp. xlix–liii.
[58] See p. 107 n. 19 above.
[59] Willis and Clark 1886, III, 1–97; *RCHM Cambridge*, I, 9–18. For what follows, see above, chap. 5.
[60] On the rise of the tutors and changes in teaching, see esp. Leader 1981 and forthcoming; Brooke 1985, pp. 41–4; Cobban 1969, pp. 66–85. On the hostels, Aston, Duncan and Evans 1980, pp. 14–15; Willis and Clark 1886, I, pp. xxv–xxviii; Stokes 1924: further enquiry is needed.

90 *Cambridge, the Old Schools from Great St Mary's tower, showing the main quadrangle of the fourteenth and fifteenth centuries with the new façade of the eighteenth century (plate 167), and the University Library of 1934 in the distance*

91 (opposite), 92 Cambridge, St John's College. The main gate, early sixteenth century, with the figure of St John the Evangelist and Tudor arms and emblems (cf. plate 62)

comments on the climate and living conditions of Cambridge and Queens', the great Dutch humanist and theologian chose out Cambridge because he admired John Fisher and saw in his university a real hope for the kind of studies he wished to enjoy and foster.[61] In both universities we can trace in this period the growth of tutorships and the development of serious teaching within the colleges. This came to render some of the former system of university teaching superfluous; in particular the lectures given by the 'necessary regents' – the recent M.A.s who had to justify their existence by lecturing – became increasingly unnecessary and faded away, though the regents continued to man the regent house, a major element in university government, until the nineteenth century. But their decline as lecturers did not spell the end of university teaching; rather the reformers of this age

[61] Thomson and Porter 1963.

93 *St John's College, the Senior Combination Room – formerly the master's long gallery. The structure, by Ralph Symons, was completed in 1599; the plaster ceiling was added in 1600, the panelling by 1603–4 (Willis and Clark 1886, II, 248–61)*

looked to make more permanent provision both in the university and in the colleges, and it is characteristic of the period that the Lady Margaret Beaufort was inspired to endow her preachers and her professors; that her grandson, Henry VIII, who aped her ways in a manner often erratic and inadvertent, founded the first regius professorships or 'praelectorships', or perhaps rather allowed them to be set up; and that the Lady Margaret was also engaged in founding and fostering colleges too.[62]

98   The central figure in this story is John Fisher. As student and fellow of Michaelhouse, he was one of many scholars engaged in making Cambridge the equal of Oxford in humanist study and in theology in the late fifteenth century. He early became chaplain of the Lady

97 Margaret, and it will be debated to the end of time whether it was he who inspired her to

[62] On the Lady Margaret see esp. Underwood 1979, 1982; also Brooke 1983; Roach 1959, pp. 166–8; on the regius chairs, Mullinger 1884, pp. 52–4; Logan 1977.

144

become a patron of Cambridge, or she who gave him a vision of what patronage could be, or what a devout presence in the royal court could achieve – for the Lady Margaret had to do her work for Cambridge 'as age crept on her, and she was wracked by rheumatic and arthritic pains – not eased by hearing four or five masses on her knees and kneeling for each of 63 Ave Marias a day'.[63] A fascinating calendar in a Book of Hours once hers, now in the British Library, records the vicissitudes of her fate through the anxious times in which she lived – from the moment, when she was aged thirteen, when her only son was born, through the dangers and chances of Yorkist rule, to the day of her son's unimaginable victory on Bosworth Field in 1485, to the sorrows of her old age, the death of her eldest grandson, Arthur, and of Henry VII himself.[64] But through all this she saw, and Fisher

[63] Brooke 1983, p. 17.
[64] Brooke 1983, p. 16 (the MS. is British Library Royal 2 A.xviii).

95 *(opposite) St John's College, the Old Library, 1623–8, the gift of John Williams, royal minister, Bishop of Lincoln, later Archbishop of York*

96 *Cambridge, Trinity Great Court (see plate 87)*

encouraged her to see, a deeper and more lasting hope for her foster sons in Cambridge. From her work in founding Christ's and St John's she has won a more lasting fame and earned a more heartfelt gratitude than the marriage treaties or political intrigues which filled her life could offer; and she rests beside her son in Westminster Abbey in a calmer sleep than her calendar presents to us, surmounted by the immortal effigy by Torrigiano.[65]

But John Fisher remains the dominant character in this story.[66] It would be foolish to attribute to him the whole glory of bringing humanism to Cambridge or of inspiring every stage in the Lady Margaret's patronage; but we may see his hand in every development, large and small – in the growing dominance of the colleges, in the splendour of the academic quarter, perhaps in her professorships, and in the minutiae of the quarters

[65] Plate 97; for her colleges see Underwood 1979, 1982, 1983; Lloyd 1934; Miller 1961, chap. 1.
[66] Bradshaw and Duffy, forthcoming; for what follows see *ibid.*, chapters by Brooke, and Underwood; see also Porter 1958, chap. 1.

147

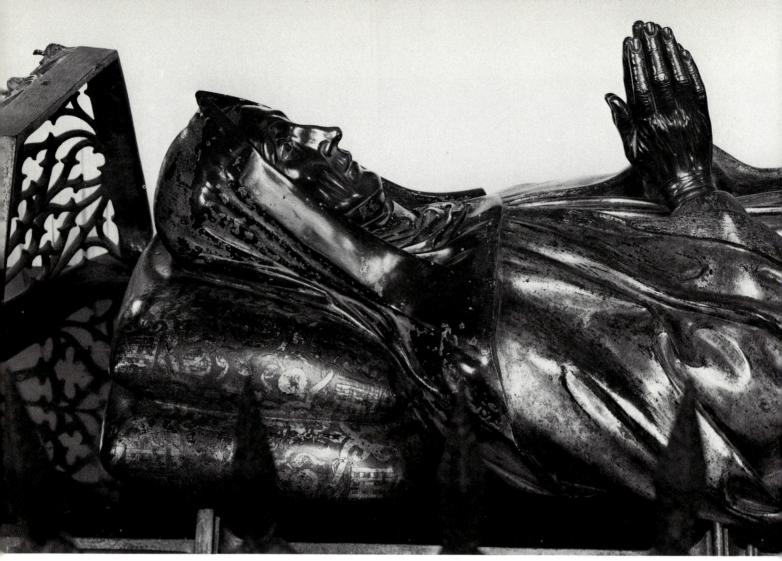

97 *The Lady Margaret Beaufort by Torrigiano; on her tomb in the Henry VII chapel, Westminster Abbey*

98 *St John Fisher, by Holbein: Royal Collection, Windsor Castle*

99 *Christ's College: Lady Margaret's coat of arms*

provided for foundress and chancellor in the Lodge at Christ's. Fisher was brought up in a Cambridge in which worldly values were very much in evidence, and he was for thirty years a bishop in a church and a courtly circle dedicated to worldly gain. Through all this, devout, ascetic, learned and imaginative, he passed unscathed; and in Cambridge indeed he rejoiced in the vision of a golden age in past and future – both equally imaginary – when men came there solely for the love of learning. He came in the footsteps of some of the most temporally minded men who have reigned in Cambridge. In imitation of Lawrence Booth, master of Pembroke for thirty years in the mid and late fifteenth century, he was for a while both Bishop of Rochester (1504–35) and president of Queens' (1505–8).[67] In imitation of Booth and Thomas Rotherham, Archbishops of York, he was for thirty years chancellor of the university (1504–35), holding what had been before the days of Booth and Rotherham a working office. But he used his pluralism in the cause of reform; he opened the paths of patronage, and kept them open till his own standing fell into doubt as Henry VIII prepared to break the links with Rome. There was above all a religious dimension to his vision of the university, which marks him off from Booth and Rotherham as surely as it sets him apart from the great chancellor who spanned the reign of Elizabeth I with a like devotion, William Cecil, Lord Burghley. The peace and prosperity of Cambridge owe much to both

[67] See Brooke 1985, pp. 39, 46; on Fisher in Queens', Twigg 1987, pp. 18–19.

149

100 *Christ's College, the Lady
Margaret's chamber, now the
master's drawing-room: restored
in the late seventeenth and early
twentieth centuries*

men; but Fisher was more closely involved in its life and himself an academic – yet he was an academic with a difference: for at the heart of his vision of academic life lay the college chapel, and it was this as much as the existing pattern of his own Michaelhouse and Queens' which inspired him to foster the founding of Christ's and St John's and the whole process whereby the colleges took over the university. In Oxford the process was more dramatic, for the colleges had counted for less, the halls had been far more numerous, in 1450; and yet the colleges conquered as swiftly as in Cambridge. So we must not attribute everything to Fisher.[68] Nor was he obsessed with the academic quarter, since his first foundation, Christ's, lay far outside it. But the victory of the colleges and the beauty of the academic quarter are monuments to him none the less surely for that. Even today the first court of St John's, mutilated in the eighteenth century and partly destroyed in the nineteenth, remains a moving testimony of the hold on his imagination of the lovely red-brick court of Queens' not very far away at the southern end of the quarter.

91

[68] See pp. 118–38 above.

150

101 *The Lady Margaret's oratory links her chamber and the college chapel. A window from it opens into the chapel, providing her with a pew: the splays are original, the window itself a replacement of the late nineteenth century. The panelling is partly sixteenth, partly seventeenth century, and the portraits are of John Fisher and Margaret herself*

These visions had a lasting quality; but his conviction that the university should remain a stronghold of Catholic theology and practice failed. 'What make you from Wittenberg?' said Hamlet to Horatio, espying his friend playing truant from Luther's university – and the same question could have been asked of many an idea and a proposition heard in the chambers and halls of Cambridge in the 1520s, to trouble the mind and conscience of the ageing chancellor. But it was another conscience, more strangely fashioned, which was to bring the dramatic conclusion to Fisher's rule: in the 1530s the conscience of the king, Henry VIII, coupled with anxiety for an heir and for Anne Boleyn, led him to the acts of savage tyranny which made John Fisher a martyr.[69]

On the day when St John Fisher was alive and dead the prospects of the university of Cambridge must have seemed grim indeed. The great chancellor, the gateway to the patronage which had created Lady Margaret's professorships, who had inspired and sustained the foundation of Christ's and St John's and had been the protector and prop of

[69] On Henry VIII's first divorce, Scarisbrick 1968, chaps. VII–VIII; Kelly 1976; corrected by Murphy 1984.

the whole university, had come to ruin, and with his fall much of his work was threatened. He had built up Cambridge on the same foundation which had led Henry VI to be its patron – as the home of securely orthodox, conservative theology; but also as the dawning hope of the new humanism.[70] It is true that in his last years the university had shown some signs of going its own way. The fellows of Gonville Hall had flocked to the court of Queen Anne – not one of them but 'savoureth of the frying pan', had observed the conservative Bishop of Norwich in 1531.[71] Cambridge had been the home, fleetingly, of Tyndale, more lastingly of Bilney, Ridley and Latimer; many in the university looked to the coming of Anne and the breach with Rome as a message of hope; almost all signed the oath of supremacy, acknowledging Henry VIII as the Supreme Head of the Church, with little apparent qualm. But the shifts and changes of the next few years profoundly threatened the traditional role of Cambridge as a seminary of Catholic clergy; the number of students of theology fell sharply away. It is true that Fisher's successor as chancellor, Thomas Cromwell, was for a short time the all-powerful minister who might be calculated to ensure that Cambridge survived, even if purged.[72] It is true that an uncountable number of laymen enjoyed its student life in this period, and they may have compensated for the loss of clergy. We cannot reckon their numbers, but we know something of their quality, for William Cecil and Walter Mildmay were later to be lifelong patrons and props of their old *alma mater* when they became the leading ministers of Elizabeth I.[73] But after Cromwell's fall, and in the obscure political manoeuvres of the early 1540s, the word went round that now the monasteries had fallen the colleges should come next; and in 1545 an Act was passed for the suppression of major chantries and of colleges.[74]

There are few passages more obscure in the history of Oxford and Cambridge than the tale of how they were saved from the rapacity of Henry VIII. It was not the Protestants but the cynical Catholic courtiers gathered round the Duke of Norfolk who tried to grab them; and it was, by a strange irony, the Protestant Queen Katherine Parr who was at the heart of the web of intrigue which issued in her own salvation and that of the colleges of which she can have known little. Her interest has long been attributed to two young Cantabs at court, Sir John Cheke of St John's, Greek professor and tutor of Prince Edward, and Sir Thomas Smith of Queens', humanist and Roman lawyer and twice later Secretary of State. The crucial step, as with the monasteries, lay in the appointment of the visitors, established by the Act of Parliament to investigate and report. For instead of Cromwell's hacks or other notorious enemies, it was Richard Cox, already dean of Osney and soon to be dean of Christ Church, who visited the Oxford colleges; the Cambridge colleges were visited by John Redman, Matthew Parker and William May. These men saved Oxford and Cambridge and their colleges from the royal grip. Of the Cambridge trio the oldest, the least known, and most probably the leader, was John Redman, a senior academic of great prestige, an accomplished theologian and the warden of the King's Hall, one of the largest colleges in Cambridge, the former teacher of both Smith and Cheke.[75] He avoided the limelight and is

---

[70] Fisher, however, was a moderate humanist: his educational programme at first was more conservative than, for example, Richard Fox's for Corpus, Oxford: see Underwood in Bradshaw and Duffy, forthcoming.

[71] Strype 1812, II, 696; cf. Brooke 1985, pp. 48–52 and 52 n.; Dowling 1984.

[72] Elton 1973, pp. 32–4.   [73] See pp. 155–6, 162–3 below.

[74] For the Act see *Statutes of the Realm*, III (1817), pp. 988–93 (37 Henry VIII, c.4); Mullinger 1884, pp. 76–7.

[75] Mullinger 1884, pp. 76–8. Mullinger attributed the successful intrigue in the royal court to Cheke and Smith; but it is noticeable that both were young men and at that time tutors in the royal family – and both were pupils of Redman, whom

little known; yet there is clearly a sense in which it is he rather than Henry VIII who should be honoured as the true founder of Trinity. The king had never shown much personal interest in Cambridge since the death of his grandmother who had brought him up to share a little of her zeal – enough to combine with his powerful, labyrinthine conscience to make him complete, in King's chapel, the greatest of all the chantries while he was preparing with his other hand for their abolition.[76] King's chapel was grandiose, and that suited Henry's ideas. But Wolsey had shown him a yet grander way, and in Cardinal College in Oxford lay the model of a foundation to outstrip even New College and King's, and paid for out of dissolved monastic property.[77] One of the ways in which Henry was cajoled to save the colleges was by the bribe of being offered, in each university, a monument of the most fashionable magnificence, splendid prayers, and a great academic community to honour his name when the changes and chances of his fleeting life were past. So far as Cambridge was concerned the bribe was offered by John Redman, who played, for yet larger stakes, the role which Andrew Doket had played in the fifteenth century in the foundation of Queens'. Whether Redman ever conceived the idea of Great Court – of a single quadrangle larger by far than the Tom Quad of Cardinal College, turned Henry VIII's College, then Christ Church – we cannot tell; it was not to be realised till the days of Dean Nevile, master at the end of the century, and such building as took place between suggests the contrary. But at least Redman conceived the idea that a trinity of colleges might be made into one.[78]

96
85

Parker and May are much better known, and were the two most able and effective Protestant heads of colleges in the Cambridge of Henry VIII's last years; after proscription under Mary they were to return to enjoy for a while Elizabeth's high favour – Parker to be Archbishop of Canterbury, the true creator of the Anglican *via media*, an achievement for which he won much hearty abuse from a capricious queen; and May to be Archbishop-elect of York, but to die before he could be consecrated.[79] May as president of Queens' led his college back into the forefront of Cambridge colleges; and when the Dissolution drew near, he looked with friendly eyes upon the prior of the Carmelites over the wall – to such good effect that he achieved a bargain by which the Carmelites surrendered their property to Queens' before the king could claim it – a coup which partly failed, for he and his college were made to surrender their gains and pay the market price for them.[80] However that may be, the Carmelite house is now buried under the northern segment of the college. Meanwhile Matthew Parker was laying the foundations of his reputation, both as a devout Cambridge man, and as a Protestant theologian of measured tones and doctrines, as master of Benet College, or Corpus Christi. His devotion to Corpus was such that in later years he gave it rich endowments and gifts of every kind, and above all his magnificent collection of manuscripts, the choicest plunder of the English monasteries – or, to put it another way, the best of the books he had managed to save from possible destruction by

we must infer to be the *éminence grise* so far as Cambridge is concerned. On him see Cobban 1969, pp. 289–90; Underwood (n. 66) in Bradshaw and Duffy, forthcoming. On the visitation, see Mullinger 1884, pp. 78–9; Roach 1959, p. 177; *Documents 1852*, I, 105–294.

[76] See p. 132 above.   [77] See p. 128 above.

[78] Cf. Fuller 1840 (1st edn 1655), p. 236 – 'of these three [Henry] compounded one fair college, dedicating it to the holy and undivided Trinity': the King's Hall, Michaelhouse and Physwick Hostel – which, though a hostel, was in size and buildings as substantial as its parent college, Gonville Hall (Brooke 1985, pp. 28–9).

[79] On Parker see esp. Strype 1711; Parker 1853; and the penetrating interpretation in Rupp 1977, chap. 6. On May, Searle 1867–71, I, 211–44, 285–94; Twigg 1987, pp. 32, 35, 38, 64 n., 65.

[80] Searle 1867–71, I, 216–33; Willis and Clark 1886, II, 3–6.

begging, borrowing and buying them from his own and other cathedral and monastic libraries.[81] But he knew the fellows of Corpus too well to trust them with his books, and in his will he laid down that the heads of Caius – home of his friend John Caius, a mighty conserver of old books and treasures – and Trinity Hall, were to make an annual inspection and if necessary confiscate them. Jealousy between the colleges has always been one of the great safeguards of the federation, and under this threat the fellows of Corpus have taken care of their books.

The troika of experienced heads and shrewd masters of academic politics conducted their visitation in 1546 and submitted a long roll of college accounts to the royal perusal. From these Henry was meant to deduce that the colleges were in such penury they were not worth the plucking; and Henry – and many a historian not brought up to the ways of college bursars – was duly deceived. Parker reported that Henry had said that 'he thought he had not in his realm so many persons so honestly maintained in living, by so little land and rent'.[82] But indeed the result was a foregone conclusion once the visitors were chosen. As part of the complex intrigue which saved the queen from following the example of some of her predecessors, and ensured a Protestant succession, the Cambridge colleges were left to enjoy their deficits and prosper as they might. Parker and May waited on the king to explain their findings; Redman meanwhile was awaiting a larger reward. The story is obscure; but we have glanced already at the role of the royal almoner, Richard Cox, in the founding of Christ Church and the salvation of Oxford (p. 134 above); and we need not doubt that John Redman played the same role in Cambridge and inspired the king with the idea that he might – if he spared the rest of the colleges – suppress Michaelhouse and the King's Hall and seize Physwick Hostel from Gonville Hall, thus rounding off nicely a great slice of the academic quarter to be appropriately dedicated to the Trinity.[83] The royal confiscators even made a token of compensation to the impoverished Gonville Hall, and the final act of confiscation was only made when this was wound up by a revolutionary act in 1983.[84] But for the advent of John Caius it is doubtful if Gonville Hall would have long survived the blow. Yet in spite of his rapacity John Redman was one of the saviours of Cambridge, and even a fellow of Gonville and Caius must acknowledge as much.

By such means the university, which must have seemed to some doomed on the scaffold on which John Fisher was executed, won through to enjoy royal favour once again. It did not emerge unscathed. We have seen how large a role the religious houses of Cambridge had played in the early history of the university, and of the city at large. The nuns had already been swept away to make place for Jesus College, and the Hospital of St John had given way to the college. It was the other houses, and especially the houses of friars, which had fostered the faculty of theology from the outset, which fell at the Dissolution.[85] But only for a time. The monks' college, Buckingham College, was revived very quickly and refounded by the courtier Lord Audley, a principal beneficiary of the Dissolution, who thus

7–9

[81] James 1912, 1, pp. xiii–xxii; for some revisions, see Dickins 1972; Page 1981.

[82] Parker 1853, pp. 35–6; the accounts are in *Documents 1852*, 1, 105–294. The queen's letter in Parker 1853, pp. 36–7, confirms that Thomas Smith had approached her.

[83] See n. 78 above; *VCH Cambs*, III, 462; Mullinger 1884, pp. 79–86; the account in Dawson 1984 has a very useful discussion of the king's end of the matter, but says little of initiatives in Cambridge itself – which are essential to any credible interpretation of the events.

[84] Brooke 1985, pp. 28–9.

[85] The houses of friars and Barnwell Priory surrendered in 1538; St Edmund's, the Gilbertine House, lingered into 1539 (Knowles and Hadcock 1971, pp. 138, 146, 197, 214–15, 222, 224, 233–4, 239, 241; Moorman 1952, pp. 127–41).

shared his gains with Magdalene College, Cambridge.[86] Later in the century Walter Mildmay, Puritan and Chancellor of the Exchequer, observed that the flow of godly preachers from Cambridge was inadequate, and in 1584 he revived the Dominican convent, the home of the Order of Preachers, as a college of preachers of another kind, Emmanuel College; and in his wake came Frances Sidney, Countess of Sussex, who

[86] *VCH Cambs*, III, 450–1; Willis and Clark 1886, II, 351–66; *RCHM Cambridge*, II, 137–8.

performed the same function in the space where the Franciscan house had been, founding there Sidney Sussex College.[87] The truth was that Oxford and Cambridge were never more necessary to governments than in the Tudor age – when the Tudor monarchs tried to disguise under a magnificent panoply of display and propaganda the endless insecurity they had inherited from the Wars of the Roses, and when religious change, to be effective, urgently demanded the steady recruitment of pastors and preachers well affected to the regime. Orthodoxy could hardly be guaranteed from a Cambridge bewildered by the pace of religious change, yet enjoying the new opportunities for choice and speculation. But while the devout Johnian Lord Burghley ruled in Westminster as Secretary of State and Lord Treasurer and in Cambridge as chancellor relations were close and as friendly as Burghley could make them; and while Matthew Parker and John Whitgift sat at Lambeth there was an intimacy between the archbishops and the university never witnessed before and hardly since.[88] In the short run the Reformation threatened disaster; in the long run it made the universities more necessary than ever.

[87] *VCH Cambs*, III, 474–5, 481; Willis and Clark 1886, II, 687–94, 723–36; *RCHM Cambridge*, I, 61–2, II, 203; Stubbings 1983; *Emmanuel Statutes*.

[88] Porter 1958, esp. pp. 102–19, 146–55, 169–80, 364–90; Roach 1959, pp. 180–9; Brooke 1985, pp. 60–1, 70–7, 87, 93, 96.

7 1550–1640: Cranmer to Laud – The Anglican establishment at Cambridge and Oxford

If learning decay, which of wild men maketh civil; of blockish and rakish persons, wise and goodly counsellors; and of evil men, good and godly Christians; what shall we look for else but barbarism and tumult? For when the lands of colleges be gone, it shall be hard to say whose staff shall stand next the door.

> The Duke of Somerset, chancellor of Cambridge, 1547–52, quoted in *CC*, p. 21, from William Harrison, *Description of England*, 1577

I concluded at the last, to set up my staff at the Library Door in Oxon . . .

> Sir Thomas Bodley, quoted in Philip 1983, p. 1

It is widely believed that the universities of Oxford and Cambridge were fundamentally transformed in the second half of the sixteenth century. Seminaries of clergy they remained, but in an utterly new sense, for the old theology, the old canon law, the old chantry duties, and the masses which had been a large part of their *raison d'être*, had vanished. The accounts of Merton College record in fascinating detail the refurnishing of the college chapel at every crisis of the Reformation. First of all, in the late 1540s, the joiners and carpenters were handsomely paid for dismantling the medieval furnishings and replacing them with plain wood. In 1553–4 the same team of carpenters made further profit from reassembling and renewing Catholic furnishings; and in 1559 they were at work again, restoring the old communion table, clearing away the relics of popery.[1] The external change was very visible; the changes of doctrine dramatic. But much remained. The fellows were no less pious; and it is not at all clear that because they spent less money on the chapel and spent less time within it that they valued it less or regarded its place in their life as less central.

Alongside the religious changes went a marked increase in numbers in the late sixteenth century, which is usually attributed to a new interest shown by sons of gentlemen and of the middling sort from many kinds of home who were seeking a grounding in the ancient universities.[2] Their academic careers are difficult to trace in detail, for only a few colleges have full matriculation registers for this era, and many young men came without any idea of taking a degree – but for a year or two of higher education, before passing on to the Inns of Court or other vocations. If we are to understand this we must first grasp the evidence offered by the three new colleges of the late sixteenth century in Cambridge.

---

[1] Fletcher and Upton 1983, pp. 119–30.
[2] For current doctrines and discussions, see Curtis 1959; Simon 1963; Cressy 1970, 1972; Kearney 1970; Morgan 1975, 1984; Russell 1977; Brooke 1985, pp. 80–4; McConica 1986, pp. 672–80, 689–92.

103   Cambridge, Gonville and Caius College: The Gate of Virtue, 1567–9, a peaceful Renaissance gate, planned by John Caius to be the main gate of his college – note the contrast with Queens', plate 73

104   (opposite) The Gate of Honour, 1575: completed after Caius's death, but reflecting his eclectic taste: over a four-centred Gothic arch rises a miniature triumphal gateway of the Renaissance

The new colleges in Cambridge: Caius, Emmanuel and Sidney Sussex

At first sight the three new colleges at Cambridge between 1557 and 1596 seem to do little more than repair some of the losses of the Dissolution and its aftermath. The friars had departed and Trinity had swallowed Physwick Hostel. The refoundation of Gonville Hall as Gonville and Caius College in 1557–8 led to the building of Caius Court, one of the fairest of

105 *The tomb of John Caius in the college chapel. Under skull and book, 'Vivit post funera virtus' – '"Virtue" lives on after death' – 'Fui Caius' – 'I was Caius'. The work of Theodore Haveus of Cleves, 1575 (see plate 169)*

that age in Cambridge; but in number of chambers this did little more than restore what Trinity had taken with Physwick Hostel.[3] The new colleges of Emmanuel and Sidney were laid out on the sites of the two most important academic communities of the university's early days, the Dominican and Franciscan convents, which had significantly been left unoccupied. But each of these colleges made its own mark. John Caius, though an eccentric of hasty temper, was a man of great vision and wide learning: a humanist who

[3] Brooke 1985, chap. 4, esp. pp. 65–7, and cf. *ibid.*, pp. 28–9 (on Physwick Hostel).

106 *College silver. On the right, the silver-gilt ceremonial cup given by Archbishop Matthew Parker (1559–75), who was a friend of John Caius; on the left the silver-gilt flagon given by Richard Branthwaite and William Webb, who joined the college in 1608–9 (Cambridge Plate, p. 55, no. TJ4; cf. Venn, I, 198–200)*

107 *On the left, Lord Hopton's 'little kitchen of plate', mid seventeenth century – three out of four beakers used on his travels, and given to the college by his chaplain, Richard Watson. On the right, the bowl and cover given by Francis Glisson, the celebrated physician, regius professor of physic, who died in 1677 (Cambridge Plate, pp. 38, 41, 52, nos. B4, 2 H3)*

planned his college on a pattern of Christian humanism in which the students entered the college by the Gate of Humility, dwelt there under Virtue, a lovely Renaissance gateway in marked contrast to the castle tower of Andrew Doket at Queens', and departed – as their successors do to this day – through the Gate of Honour to receive their degrees.[4] The

[4] Brooke 1985, pp. 65–7.

charming mixture of Gothic and Renaissance, of plain and ornate, of pagan and Christian, culminating in the exquisite beauty of Caius's own tomb – in which the taste of Caius and of his mason, Theodore Haveus of Cleves, were mingled – reflects the eclectic, personal taste of a man of singular originality. It was combined with a profound conservatism: his troubles with his colleagues in Caius were much exacerbated by his constant tendency to compare the present, seen through jaundiced eyes, with a rosy vision of the past. But he was a really notable scholar and physician, who had scoured Italy for manuscripts of Galen, and sat at the feet of several of the best continental masters of physic.[5] Such was his reputation that in a relatively short span of years he earned enough to double the college's endowment, and in a few more almost to double its buildings. His college became the first to have a somewhat secular image, as the home of physicians and religious tolerance.

The young fellows accused Caius indeed of a popish tendency, on the specious ground that he had carefully preserved the college's old vestments and Catholic books; and although it is unlikely that he was a recusant in doctrine he was undoubtedly conservative, a lover of the old ways. The insurgents called in the vice-chancellor and the master of Trinity – John Whitgift, the future archbishop – and they made a bonfire of Dr Caius's treasures. The old master, now sickening for his final illness, was driven to resign. His final task was to commission Theodore Haveus to create the beautiful and splendid tomb which still adorns the college chapel – a reminder that here at least more money, not less, was spent on adorning the chapel after the Reformation than before.[6]

Far different was Sir Walter Mildmay's Emmanuel and the Sidney Sussex of Lady Frances Sidney, Countess of Sussex; both were Puritan foundations, to further education of godly pastors – and good preachers.[7] Emmanuel was founded 'for the education of young men in all piety and good letters and especially in Holy Writ and Theology, that being thus instructed they may hereafter teach true and pure religion, refute all errors and heresies, and by the shining example of a blameless life excite all men to virtue'[8] – and Sidney was conceived in very much the same spirit, and grew up to foster Oliver Cromwell and his comrade-in-arms, the Earl of Manchester. But for two generations Emmanuel had the greatest success of all, rearing under its first master, Laurence Chaderton, the very model of a fervent preacher and a moderate Puritan, a generation of divines who spread about the land just as Mildmay had hoped. For a time Emmanuel had so high a reputation as to be the largest college in Cambridge. Its fame was not confined to England; for just as Trinity inspired Trinity College, Dublin, founded in 1591 – and presided over by five Cambridge provosts in succession – so the great college founded in Cambridge, Massachusetts, in the late 1630s came to be based on Emmanuel and on Cambridge; and when a young minister from Emmanuel called John Harvard died in 1638 and bequeathed to the new college a large share of his modest estate, the founding fathers attached his name to it.[9] As for Emmanuel itself, in the oft-repeated tale first told in print by Thomas Fuller, when Elizabeth I challenged the founder, 'Sir Walter, I hear you have erected a Puritan foundation' – 'No, Madam, saith he, far be it from me to countenance anything contrary to your established laws, but I have set an acorn, which when it becomes an oak, God alone knows what will be the fruit thereof.'[10]

---

[5] Brooke 1985, pp. 55–60; V. Nutton 1979, and his *John Caius and the Manuscripts of Galen* (Cambridge, 1987).
[6] Brooke 1985, pp. 75–8, and pl. 6 (for Theodore Haveus also p. 66 and n. 54, and pl. 15).
[7] See pp. 155–6 above, and n. 87.   [8] *Emmanuel Statutes*, preface, p. 25 (Dr F. Stubbings's translation).
[9] Morison 1935.   [10] Fuller 1840 (1st edn 1655), p. 278, cited *Emmanuel Statutes*, p. v; CC, p. 49; etc.

Cambridge: the statutes of 1570

The changes of the Reformation and the Elizabethan settlement made Oxford and Cambridge both more necessary to government, and more at its mercy. In Cambridge eleven heads of houses departed in 1553 at Mary's accession, and a like eleven died, resigned or were removed in 1558–60, at Elizabeth's.[11] Dr Perne, a man of tolerance who has hardly deserved his reputation as a vicar of Bray, survived from 1554 to 1589 as master of Peterhouse, and Dr Caius survived the changes of 1559 as master of Caius, because he enjoyed the prestige of founder, because he was close to Cecil, and even closer to Matthew Parker, ex-master of Corpus, Archbishop of Canterbury from 1559.[12] It is often said that the new statutes for Cambridge university drafted by John Whitgift and approved by Cecil and Elizabeth I in 1570 were marked by important progress in the authority attributed to the vice-chancellor and heads; and contemporary objections to them stressed as much. But they did not come out of a clear sky: they consecrated authority already long claimed, and it was custom rather than the statutes which made the heads supreme in university affairs. Conflict between the democratic senate and oligarchic authority had produced already in the 1550s Cardinal Pole's statutes, which gave the heads first voice in choice of the vice-chancellor.[13] The statutes of 1570 went further in giving them a major say in all university appointments. It had long been the practice for legislation to be prepared by a small caucus of representatives of the faculties called the *Caput Senatus*, a characteristic late-medieval device linking faculties and regents on the one hand, and vice-chancellor and heads on the other. From 1570 its nomination lay primarily with the vice-chancellor, assisted by the heads, and its members each had a right of veto on any proposal to submit a grace to the senate. Thus it was in theory a very powerful body and likely to be subservient to the vice-chancellor; and remained so till the mid nineteenth century, when it was abolished.[14] But the veto was rarely applied; and much more power was exercised by custom than by statute. In practice from the late sixteenth century the vice-chancellor came regularly, then invariably, to be one of the heads, increasingly appointed by rota; and it became the practice at some date not precisely known – but it is well recorded in the 1620s and 1630s – for the heads to meet in the vestry of Great St Mary's week by week after the university sermon. They met at first, perhaps, to discuss the sermon, for religious censorship was one of the prime functions they tried to undertake or usurp; but in due course they came to discuss all matters of business. These weekly meetings were never statutory, but they were for two centuries the centre of university government, and they were imitated in the 1630s in Oxford in the formation of the hebdomadal board.[15] In this as in other ways William Laud was to pick up Whitgift's wand in the 1630s and use it to conjure the statutes under which Oxford lived till the 1850s.

[11] Mullinger 1884, pp. 150–2; Porter 1958, pp. 92–5, 101–6.

[12] Brooke 1985, pp. 60–1, 70–7.

[13] On the draft statutes made under Pole's direction and their place in the sequence of statutes, see Hackett 1970, pp. 303–4; the statutes of 1570 are in *Documents 1852*, I, 454–95. For commentary, see Hackett 1970, p. 304; Mullinger 1884, pp. 222–34; Porter 1958, pp. 163–8.

[14] For the obscure early history of the *Caput* see Mullinger 1884, p. 217; for its later history see esp. Winstanley 1935, pp. 24–7.

[15] The best early record of these meetings is in British Library Harleian MS. 7019, fos. 52–93 (a reference we owe to David Hoyle: see Hoyle 1986; Brooke 1985, pp. 122–3, and esp. 122 n. 71): this contains returns of 1641, but referring back over quite a long period of time. For the hebdomadal board, see p. 185 below.

Religious change: recusants and Puritans

In Oxford, as in Cambridge, 1559 saw the departure of a group of heads. William Tresham, the 'cancellarius natus', Richard Martial, dean of Christ Church, and Thomas Reynolds, warden of Merton, refused the oath of supremacy and were deprived; so was William Allen of All Souls, a future cardinal.[16] Richard Smyth, the regius praelector in divinity, prevaricated and slipped away to Louvain: he was to become in due course professor of theology and chancellor of Douai.[17] Generally the change does not seem to have affected the universities as traumatically as the changes under the earlier Tudors. In 1570 a new urgency entered the religious conflicts with the excommunication of the queen by Pope Pius V – followed by the arrival of the Jesuits and the exaction of the oath to the Thirty-Nine Articles in 1581. Then Oxford produced its Catholic martyrs, Edmund Campion, Cuthbert Mayne and George Napper. Campion had been a fellow of St John's in the 1550s and 1560s, and it was not till 1569 that he left, nor till 1573 that he joined the Jesuits; in 1580 he returned to England – and to Oxford – and died a martyr's death in 1581.[18] Meanwhile, in 1576 Allen had written to the Jesuit General that Oxford 'was more responsive to the ancient faith, and from thence we mostly recruit our seminary at Douai'.[19] But the recusants found a home for a time in both universities, especially at Gloucester Hall in Oxford and at Peterhouse and Caius in Cambridge. From Peterhouse came Henry Walpole, who was inspired partly by Campion's example to join the Jesuits in the 1580s, and followed him to a martyr's death in 1595. But the largest nest was in Caius, whose successive masters, John Caius and Thomas Legge, were laymen and evidently cared little for religious controversy, for all Caius's devotion to vestments; Legge in particular enjoyed having a lively, rumbustious community under his friendly eye, but paid for it when the Protestant majority among his fellows rebelled sourly against the powerful recusant influence in their midst. Legge was an ecclesiastical lawyer who became a pillar of that branch of the Anglican establishment; he was tolerant of recusancy rather than a supporter of it. But that there stirred a fervent recusant devotion among the young men we cannot doubt. We know the names of about eighteen Caians of Legge's time who passed into the Society of Jesus or the secular Catholic priesthood, ranging from Christopher Walpole, Henry's brother, through John Fingley, hanged and quartered in York in 1586, to Richard Holtby, who came, like many of the recusants, from Yorkshire, and survived into extreme old age, though Provincial of the Jesuits, to die in 1640.[20]

The new statutes at Cambridge in 1570 were stimulated by controversy roused from another wing of the church, the Puritans, led by the celebrated Thomas Cartwright, Lady Margaret professor of divinity, who was expelled from his chair in that year.[21] The vast majority of the recusants and the Puritans were loyal subjects of Queen Elizabeth; but for both, obedience to a 'prince' who insisted on Anglican uniformity, however widely drawn, brought serious scruples of conscience. It was to take several generations for them to

[16] Emden, *Oxford 1501–40*, pp. 576–7; Thompson 1900, p. 22; Duncan 1980, p. 231; *DNB*; Russell 1985, pp. 224–5.

[17] Emden, *Oxford 1501–40*, pp. 524–6; cf. p. 138 above.

[18] Mallet 1924–7, II, 136–7; for Mayne, Rowse 1950, pp. 443–4, and *DNB*; for Napper, Falkner 1899, p. 203, and for Campion, Falkner 1899, pp. 200–3 and *DNB*.

[19] Rowse 1950, p. 514; cf. Loach 1986, pp. 378–9.

[20] Venn 1913, chap. VII; Brooke 1985, pp. 87–92. On Caius and Legge, Brooke 1985, chaps. 4, 5; on Henry Walpole, *DNB* (A. Jessopp).

[21] Porter 1958, chap. 8, esp. pp. 174–7; Collinson 1967, esp. pp. 122–5, 139–41.

108 *Peterhouse chapel, from the east, built by Matthew Wren, 1628–32, encased in ashlar by John Cosin in the 1660s and 1670s – with seventeenth-century brick to the left, eighteenth-century stone to the right (by Sir James Burrough)*

realise that they could neither win over nor find a home within the fold of the established church; and a large proportion of the leading Cambridge theologians were at least moderate Puritans at the turn of the sixteenth and seventeenth centuries. Archbishop Whitgift himself was a moderate Calvinist, but all the more determined to check the spread of extreme views, and especially of practices which threatened the authority of the bishops and the queen. Meanwhile a moderate Puritanism solidly based on Calvin was fostered above all in Christ's and transferred with Laurence Chaderton and others to Emmanuel when it was founded in 1584.[22] Such Christ's men as George Downham had introduced the teaching of the great French humanist Ramus, who had revised Aristotle to make him conform with Calvin.[23] A powerful and influential figure at the head of a smaller group was the eminent Swiss divine, Peter Baro; French by origin, he had been raised to orders by Calvin at Geneva, but became none the less Calvin's most trenchant critic in Cambridge, and Lady Margaret professor of divinity.[24] His statements against Calvinist predestination and other fashionable doctrines led him to something like a trial before Whitgift. The

[22] Stubbings 1983: *Emmanuel Statutes* and commentary: by Dr Stubbings's kindness we have also seen Ibish 1985. The fascinating first library inventory has also recently been published: Bush and Rasmussen 1985.

[23] Kearney 1970, chap. III, esp. pp. 61–2. For Ramus's comparatively slight influence at Oxford cf. McConica 1986, p. 713.

[24] Porter 1958, pp. 376–90.

109   *Peterhouse chapel from the west*

seventeenth century opened with recusants within the university relatively few and growing fewer, but with every sign that the confrontation would continue and grow between high and low churchmen. At first there were many shades of opinion and much collaboration; though tempers soared at times, there were plenty of moderate men to cool the argument. But in the 1620s and 1630s opinion polarised; and in both Oxford and Cambridge the polarisation was enhanced by the arguments in Westminster. First of all, a party was formed in Cambridge in the 1630s in support of the high church policies of Archbishop Laud, led by John Cosin, master of Peterhouse; and he or a friend sent reports on the observances of college chapels which give a fascinating picture of diversity of practice.[25] They observed that fellows and fellow commoners of colleges preferred the tavern to the college chapel, and that most colleges neglected traditional academic dress and followed the fashion of the day – including 'long frizzled hair'; they noted that there

[25] Cooper, *Annals*, III, 280–3, from Thomas Baker's transcript in British Library Harleian MS. 7033, fos. 161–5 (formerly 152–5): Baker thought they had been written either by Cosin or by Sterne of Jesus. Cf. Brooke 1985, p. 113 and n.

166

110 *Gonville and Caius College chapel: the ceiling and cherubs, 1637, restored after 1660. The organ is by Johannes Klais of Bonn, 1981*

was disorder in the schools and feasting on Fridays. Most of the report gives vivid details of the practices in the university church, Great St Mary's, and the college chapels. In St Mary's there was a confusion of town and gown – while it was 'a theatre' at commencement time, since the university ceremonies were performed there till the Senate House was built in the eighteenth century, it was always partly occupied with lumber and surrounded by shops; and at the university sermon the chancel was full of 'boys and townsmen'. It was a prime concern of the high churchmen to provide secluded college

108–9 chapels, such as Matthew Wren had built for Peterhouse, separate from the congregation in Little St Mary's, just before Cosin became master; and also to move the communion table to the east end, make an altar of it, and set it about with rails. Some chapels already met these requirements; some showed features both low and high; others retained the practices of the previous generation, and we are not surprised to find the Puritan colleges of Emmanuel and Sidney Sussex among them. At Benet College – Corpus Christi – the altar was 'poorly furnished. In performance of service they skip the exhortation for haste, and to make amends, instead of the hymns appointed between the lessons, they used to sing long psalms of their own appointing.' Most of this criticism reflects the divergences of low and high church practice; but at Trinity there is an interesting variant. 'They have long been noted to be very negligent of their chapel . . . the best come but seldom . . . In some tutor's chambers . . . the private prayers are longer and louder by far at night than they are at chapel in the evening.'[26] Thus Laud watched over Cambridge from afar; in Oxford he had long reigned directly as chancellor of the university. But in the early 1640s came the Long Parliament and the fall of Laud; then the Cambridge Puritans sent a rival set of reports, equally fascinating, to the dominant Puritans in Parliament. They expressed disapproval

110 of the influence of Cosin and his friends. They had filled college chapels with cherubs and ritual; and at the meetings of the heads they had, so the reporters believed, defended sermons of evidently popish tendency.[27]

The changing pattern of entry

It is an open question how many commoners there were at Oxford and Cambridge in the first half of the sixteenth century.[28] In Elizabeth's reign the improvement in the evidence is spasmodic. The best-preserved of all the students' records of the age are the matriculation books of Gonville and Caius, which start in 1559 when Dr Caius became master of the college, which he had recently refounded.[29] As master, he was a very indifferent success: crabbed and cantankerous, he dealt with his young fellows by expelling some and putting others in the stocks. But as a benefactor and record-keeper he was incomparable. From 1559 we know the name and age and parentage of every entrant to the college, the tutor to whom he was assigned and his room – though some of this information fades away after a time, and the efforts to reconstruct the social history of Cambridge from the statements of parents' occupation have had to be modified as the traps have been detected.[30] None the less, it is a good record; and we have nothing like it for any other college so early, nor for most for a while to come; and yet to compare the situation after 1559 with the fifty years before is like comparing light with darkness. We know that the college had contained some notable commoners, including William Butts, the royal physician who fostered both Dr

[26] Cooper, *Annals*, III, 281.   [27] See n. 15 above; Hoyle 1986; Brooke 1985, pp. 122–3.

[28] For discussion, see Russell 1977; Brooke 1985, pp. 83–4; McConica 1986, pp. 689–92. A high proportion of the commoners of Elizabeth's reign of whom we have evidence came for relatively short periods and left without taking degrees: but for the matriculation registers we should have almost no trace of them. Scholars commonly impinge on college accounts, where they survive: the accounts of commoners could lie wholly with their tutors, not with the college, and so leave no record in the college accounts – and see below.

[29] Venn 1887; also the basis of Venn, I; see Brooke 1985, pp. 80–4 and references, esp. to Cressy 1970, correcting earlier interpretations.

[30] See esp. Cressy 1970; cf. Brooke 1985, p. 81 and n. 8. For William Butts (below), see Brooke 1985, pp. 49–50, 56–7 and pl. 13a; Dowling 1984, esp. pp. 35, 38. For Physwick Hostel, Brooke 1985, pp. 28–9, and p. 139 above.

Caius's medical interests and the early Protestant reformers in the college, and Sir Thomas Gresham, one of the greatest financiers of the century. Yet the only way we can assess their numbers is by counting the space in the chambers. But the great difficulty is that Gonville Hall (as it was before 1558) owned two large hostels, Physwick and St Margaret's Hostels, which were attached to the college; and Dr Caius himself, who had once presided over Physwick Hostel, estimated their student accommodation as at least thirty or forty. They were appropriated by Henry VIII when he created Trinity; and in due course Caius himself built his own new court which could house up to about fifty fellows and students. So here there was an increase, but a modest one – even allowing that the hostels were now part of a greater increase in Trinity; and until much closer work has been done on the Cambridge hostels we are very much in the dark how great the increase was, or how different the commoners of Elizabeth's reign were from those of Henry VIII's.[31] But William Cecil, Lord Burghley, chancellor of the university from 1559 to 1598, and Sir Walter Mildmay, founder of Emmanuel College in 1584, testify that two able commoners of the 1530s and 1540s from St John's and Christ's retained the liveliest interest in their place of education even at the peak of royal government.[32]

None the less, there are copious indications that opportunities for commoners were widening, and that they were coming in greater numbers to both universities. In Oxford from the early sixteenth century they formed a leaven in Magdalen, in Brasenose and notably at Corpus Christi; but it was in the second half of the sixteenth century and early in the seventeenth that commoners entered into their own, in three grades reflecting their wealth and status in the world outside: noblemen, gentlemen and ordinary commoners.[33] The gentleman commoner or fellow commoner spread through many societies in both universities – in some, simply as a well-to-do presence with ampler privileges, such as feeding at the fellows' table. In Christ Church, Oxford, and Trinity, Cambridge, especially, they were to acquire a bad name as idle, extravagant lay-abouts; but not all misbehaved or led their less fortunate colleagues astray, and some became important patrons and benefactors. Below them socially, but still at no cost to the college, were ordinary commoners; and below them again were battelers, poor scholars, semi-commoners (the three terms seem to have been synonymous), and on the bottom rung servitors or sizars – who served the commoners and fellows, and enjoyed much-reduced fees.[34] By the various means of earning open to them, including, as time went on, some modest teaching, servitors and sizars could earn their keep. But the term 'sizar' is indeed confusing; for service in college had no necessary social degradation in it, any more than fagging in a public school. It has been estimated that out of a 100 students in Caius in the late sixteenth century, 13 were fellow commoners, 50 pensioners, 37 sizars; but many of the sizars were younger brothers of pensioners, many went on to be scholars; four out of the eight masters between 1573 and the early eighteenth century had begun as sizars.[35] It was only in the

[31] See pp. 139, 152 above.

[32] See p. 156 above, nn. 87–8; *Emmanuel Statutes*, esp. pp. 7–9, 16–17 – Mildmay's statutes for Emmanuel were very closely modelled on Fisher's for Christ's: see notes in *ibid.*, pp. 29–88.

[33] For gentlemen commoners see Mallet 1924–7, II, 13; Stone 1975, I, 24–8; Aylmer 1986, p. 529; for ordinary commoners McConica 1975, pp. 151–81; Russell 1977, pp. 721–45; McConica 1986, pp. 47–8 and n. 1, cf. *ibid.*, pp. 671–80, 689–91.

[34] For battelers and semi-commoners see Mallet 1924–7, II, 13; for servitors Stone 1975, p. 11. For sizars in Cambridge, see Brooke 1985, pp. 117–18, 121, 128, 140, 248; Venn 1913, pp. 131–5; for Oxford, McConica 1986, pp. 668, 724.

[35] Venn 1913, p. 131 (cf. *ibid.*, pp. 128–31). For Corpus Christi, Oxford, cf. McConica 1986, pp. 666–93.

eighteenth century that the sizars were given a mark of permanent social inferiority – and after a while rebelled against it, and eventually disappeared.

In other ways opportunity opened, as old restrictions which tied scholars to particular counties or regions fell into disuse. John Jewel, nominated to a postmastership, almost certainly by Henry Parkhurst, fellow of Merton, whose pupil he became, was born in Devon where Merton had no land. Some old moulds were thus slowly softening.[36] But at the same time new ones were being made, since new scholarships and fellowships tied to localities were established, and old ones – for example the East Anglian links of Caius and Corpus or the north country links of St John's at Cambridge – often survived or were renewed. It remains clear that between 1560 and 1640 Oxford and Cambridge greatly increased in size.

Average matriculations at Oxford increased from just over 190 a year in the decade 1571–80 to 340 between 1581 and 1590; overall numbers rose by contemporary estimates to between 2,000 and 3,000 in the early seventeenth century.[37] In Cambridge overall numbers increased from about 1,630 in 1570 to about 3,000 in the 1620s and 1630s. Whatever the case before, the commoners now greatly affected the balance.[38]

A very substantial element still came intent on a clerical career, and the majority of fellowships, by law or custom, fell to clergy. Other professions, law and medicine, continued to attract their adherents. This is the age of William Harvey, the founder of the science of physiology and a great royal physician, who was a scholar of Caius in the 1590s and warden of Merton in the 1640s.[39] A wide range of disciplines was studied and some sciences, and especially mathematics, saw a new leap forward. But above all it was the first golden age of the universities as places of general education. A remarkable symptom of their place in society at large is the number of Oxford and Cambridge graduates in the House of Commons: 67 in 1563, 160 only thirty years later.[40] Many sons of gentlemen and yeomen, and of the middling sort, came for one or two or three years and went on to the Inns of Court or back to their estates or professions. Training in disputation and declamation was found valuable for those seeking a general education; and many an ambitious young man met his future patron at university, or was set on the path which led to promotion. The Earl of Bath carried his tutor off to Devon in the 1570s, and the two of them sent many a Devonian to leaven the East Anglian mixture in Caius in the next fifty years.[41] There must have been a more conspicuous element of the rich and the comfortably off in both universities in this age than before, and there may have been some validity in the complaints of William Harrison and Sir Humphrey Gilbert that the university of Oxford was being encroached upon by the rich at the expense of the poor; but it has been shown that during Elizabeth's reign, in a fair sample of colleges, there was not much infiltration by gentry or aristocracy, and the poor, or at least the poorer gentry, retained their place: Exeter, University and Magdalen colleges at Oxford were hardly affected by the

[36] Emden, *Oxford 1501–40*, pp. 317–18, 433; McConica 1986, pp. 670–1.
[37] Aylmer 1986, p. 522; Curtis 1959, p. 3 and n. 1; and cf. Mallet 1924–7, II, 389 n. 2; Stone 1975, I, graph 1, p. 6, and table I A, p. 91 (annual freshmen admissions).
[38] For Cambridge see Curtis 1959, p. 3; *VCH Cambs*, III, 188, 203. Alternative figures of 1,267 for 1564 and 1,813 for 1573 are quoted in Cooper, *Annals*, II, 206–7, 315–16. For Oxford in 1566 cf. McConica 1986, pp. 154–5, where some 2,000 for *c*. 1580–1600 is suggested. For the commoners see McConica 1975, pp. 151–81; and see above, p. 157 and n. 2.
[39] Keynes 1966; Brooke 1985, pp. 93–5. For what follows, see esp. Feingold 1984 (on mathematics).
[40] Curtis 1959, p. 59.
[41] Venn, I, p. xiii; Brooke 1985, pp. 115–16 and references.

aristocracy.[42] Yet in the long run the growing numbers of rich commoners influenced the style of living of the rest; and in 1600 the first sets of rooms specifically for gentlemen commoners were built at Christ Church.[43]

One important role the commoners performed was to help support the colleges in times of inflation – which was especially rapid in the second half of the sixteenth century. It became increasingly common for tutors to look after scholars and commoners alike: this happened at Trinity, Oxford, from its foundation in 1555; at Exeter in 1564, Balliol in 1572, at Brasenose in 1576 and at University College in 1583.[44] In 1626 it was observed that 'for a man to live in College without a tutor is as much disgrace as for one of your servants when you have turned him away to hang still about your house'.[45] The tutorial group of students was thus the unit and basis of education in both universities, and a part of their economy; for the young fellows in great numbers earned a living wage from teaching.

Meanwhile the colleges had been finding ways to improve their incomes. The great difficulty was that their endowment lay almost entirely in land, and their estates were let out for customary rents, which never altered, and on leases sometimes for long periods of years. In the late sixteenth century this was largely offset by the system, which became virtually universal in Oxford and Cambridge, of entry fines: rents stayed stable but fines at the renewal of leases were exacted more in accord with current values. In 1576, on the inspiration of two eminent Cambridge men, Sir Thomas Smith and Andrew Perne, the master of Peterhouse, an act was passed which is the earliest known case of index-linking.[46] One third of the rents from the estates of the colleges of Oxford and Cambridge, Winchester and Eton were to be taken in kind, in corn rents. In practice these were in part or as a whole commuted into money from an early date – but they were regularly assessed at the current price, which rose in years of bad harvest and fell when harvests were good, thus ironically improving the lot of colleges in bad times. The effect of this on college finances was variable; but these changes – and friends and benefactors – helped to preserve colleges in varying degrees of prosperity over the generations ahead. Meanwhile the practice had already arisen in some – and was eventually to spread to them all – by which a substantial dividend was declared at the year's end to be distributed among the master and fellows of a college; and in some it was the best pickings – the corn rents and fines – which were divided in this way, and not among all the fellows, but among the privileged seniors.[47] Thus in the late seventeenth and eighteenth centuries heads and senior fellows received a very tolerable stipend, while the juniors languished on a fixed pittance which did not grow as prices rose.

Yet with all the vicissitudes of social and economic change, and the dramatic shifts of the Reformation, an extraordinary continuity persisted. The medieval colleges survived; new ones joined them; the basic nature of the college, though shorn of its function as a chantry, retained most of its other features. If the fellows had looked forward to a greater liberty, to freedom to marry, for example, they were quickly disabused by an edict of Elizabeth I of

---

[42] McConica 1975, pp. 168–71; McConica 1986, p. 729.

[43] Thompson 1900, p. 41; cf. McConica 1986, pp. 679 and n. 2, 729.

[44] Stone 1975, I, 25.

[45] Stone 1975, I, 26.

[46] The clearest account of how the system of entry fines and corn rents worked is in Venn, IV, *Estates Record*, pp. i–x (E.J. Gross); cf. Brooke 1985, pp. 102–3. For the Act of 1576, see Cooper, *Annals*, II, 342–3; Mullinger 1884, pp. 374–80; Roach 1959, pp. 188–9; Aylmer 1986, pp. 535–7, 541–3.

[47] So Caius: Brooke 1985, pp. 96–8.

111 *Oxford, Jesus College hall, portrait of Queen Elizabeth I*

1561 which enjoined celibacy on the fellows of colleges – an injunction generally observed until the 1860s, though equally generally ignored by the heads of houses whom Elizabeth assuredly had not intended to absolve.[48] In the early years of the century the Lady Margaret and John Fisher had planned a college whose prime function was to provide pastors and preachers.[49] When Sir Walter Mildmay founded Emmanuel in the 1580s he furnished it with statutes at many points identical with those of Christ's.[50]

[48] Parker 1853, p. 151; Brooke 1985, pp. 68–9, 223–6.

[49] Though the statutes are not specific on these aims, but emphasise the significance of theological study: Rackham 1927, esp. pp. 42–3, 86–9; Rackham also prints the statutes of Godshouse, from which Christ's sprang, and Lloyd 1934, pp. 12–13, 298–302, showed that many provisions in Fisher's statutes were closely based on these. But the Emmanuel statutes are verbally closer to Fisher's than are either to the Godshouse statutes.

[50] *Emmanuel Statutes*, p. 17, and Dr Stubbings's notes, *ibid.*, pp. 29–88, *passim*.

112 *Oxford, Wadham College, entrance to hall and chapel, 1610–13, with statues of King James I and the founders, Nicholas and Dorothy Wadham*

Oxford: Jesus, Wadham and Pembroke

The townsmen of Cambridge who filled the chancel of Great St Mary's, and a large part of the nave as well, represented a modestly increased urban population; the population of Oxford (it is estimated) doubled between the 1580s and the 1630s, when a great number of thatched cottages or 'squab houses' were run up 'unseemlie to look too' and 'verie dangerous to casualties of fire', as they were to demonstrate only too plainly in the great fire at Oxford of 1644.[51] This growth was matched by a similar increase in the academic throng; and to provide it with shelter old colleges expanded, and new ones were founded.

The earliest of the three new colleges is especially interesting, since, though the nominal founder was Queen Elizabeth, its real founder was Hugh Price, a Welsh clergyman and

[51] Porter 1984, p. 290.

113 *(opposite) Oxford, Wadham College, the hall, interior, c. 1612–13*

114 *Oxford, Pembroke College hall, 1848, by John Hayward*

lawyer.[52] Oxford was the nearest university to Wales, and until the foundation of the Welsh colleges had few rivals to the claims of an ambitious Welshman. Jesus College was never specifically restricted to Welshmen, but within twenty years of its foundation it was drawing heavily on the principality.

The two new colleges of the early seventeenth century, Wadham and Pembroke, founded in 1612 and 1624, both followed the pattern set by Trinity and St John's: both were founded by laymen, and Wadham jointly by a layman and his wife. Nicholas Wadham, an Oxford graduate and a west country gentleman who had married a wealthy widow, was said to have been worth £14,000 and to be possessed of lands to the value of £800 per annum. He had no children and bought up the site of the Austin Friars where he and his wife founded a college for a warden, fifteen fellows, fifteen scholars and some commoners. Lectures were to be provided inside the college by a praelector in humanities

52 Baker 1971, pp. 1–4.

175

and a moderator in philosophy. Since Wadham's links were with the west country, it is not surprising to find that four of his first fellows came from Exeter College and that many of the early fellows were west countrymen.[53]

By contrast the fortune of the lay-founder of Pembroke seems to have been made in the course of a career in which he had been maltster, grazier, corn-grower, wool-dealer and the largest trader in woad in England. He was one of the most important citizens of Abingdon; he was elected mayor in 1585, but declined the office. He explored the idea of making a substantial benefaction to Balliol, but, when this fell through, set up a college to be named after the chancellor, William Herbert, Earl of Pembroke, for seven fellows and six scholars and with a close connection with Abingdon School, of which he had himself been a scholar. His co-founder was a clergyman, Richard Wightwick, rector of East Ilsley, an old Oxford man and chaplain of a local magnate, Lord Henry Norris of Rycote. Wightwick gave £500 for building new chambers, a very long lease of five manors and £200 in cash. This endowment enabled the college to bring its numbers up to a master, ten fellows and ten scholars. As at Wadham there were to be commoners living at their own charge; as at Jesus an existing hall was taken over. In this case it was Broadgates Hall, which had for some time provided lodgings for wealthy commoners from Christ Church. Broadgates now became part of Pembroke.[54] By this date at Oxford, as at Cambridge, most of the older colleges had admitted commoners. Thus Merton, which accepted gentlemen commoners between 1607 and 1616 but then desisted, renewed the experiment in 1650.[55] New College had taken steps by 1679 to secure the visitor's agreement to the acceptance of gentlemen commoners, contrary to the founder's statutes, but does not seem to have taken much advantage of the permission thus gained until the nineteenth century.[56] Only All Souls was to pursue its way without gentlemen commoners and the financial assistance that they brought. Naturally the colleges and halls which had not been designed for large numbers of commoners came under pressure to put up new buildings. New blocks of accommodation were built at Oriel, St John's and University Colleges and additional chambers were constructed at St Edmund and Magdalen Halls.[57] At Merton in 1608–10 the first three-storey building, the Great Quadrangle, was put up by Sir Henry Savile.[58] It seems that it was designed to hold the nine senior M.A. fellows on the first floor and the postmasters whom they had nominated on the ground floor – they had recently been brought in from Postmasters Hall outside the college. Another three-storey building was soon to appear at Wadham.[59]

Sir Henry Savile (1549–1622), 'courtier, scholar, mathematician, founder of the Oxford professorships of Astronomy and Geometry, for four years a scholar of Brasenose, for thirty-seven years Warden of Merton, and for five-and-twenty years Provost of Eton, a friend of Bodley and of the Bodleian', was, as George Hakewell wrote, a 'Heroical Spirit'.[60] From the notes of his lectures on Ptolemy's *Almagest* in Latin it can be shown that he used the ancient author as a framework within which to set the views of Copernicus, Regiomontanus and other modern cosmologers. He regarded Copernicus as 'prince of

41
118
30

[53] Wells 1898, pp. 20–34.   [54] Macleane 1900, pp. 49–94.
[55] Henderson 1899, pp. 182–90.   [56] Buxton and Williams 1979, pp. 45, 212.
[57] Cf. Aylmer 1986, p. 548 n. 2; for the use of cocklofts, cf. Newman 1986, pp. 630–1.
[58] *VCH Oxon*, III, 102. Four or five B.A. fellows could be accommodated on the second floor, and servants in the cocklofts. Thus over half the governing body (about 24) could be fitted into the new quadrangle.
[59] *VCH Oxon*, III, 283–4 (1610–13).   [60] Garrod 1963, pp. 102, 118.

modern mathematicians'.[61] After he had lectured steadily in the early 1570s he asked for leave to go abroad in 1578 on what was a version of the Grand Tour with a member of the Sidney family.[62] But it was much more, since he seems to have been given letters of introduction to leading students of mathematics and astronomy in a variety of European centres – Breslau, Vienna, Padua and Venice. In Venice he began to employ agents to search for 'undiscoverable books in Patmos', an indication that he was perhaps already engaged on patristic studies which would lead to his *editio princeps* of St John Chrysostom.[63] On his return to England he became Greek tutor to Queen Elizabeth. As 'an extraordinary handsome man, no lady having a finer complexion', he proved a successful courtier. Three years later he was elected warden of Merton with the active support of the queen and Lord Burghley.[64] His main achievements for Oxford came in the reign of her successor, James I. Savile seems to have had a special penchant for building. During the construction of the Arts End of the library Bodley said of his approval of a change, 'it is to me as the judgement of a mason'. On Bodley's death in 1613 Savile was to see that his friend's wishes were fulfilled. If Aubrey reports Hobbes correctly Savile 'would fain have been thought as great a scholar as Joseph Scaliger'. This he was not. But he was a remarkable polymath – 'the magasine of all learning', as Richard Montague said. Sometimes this grated, as when he drove Isaac Casaubon over in his coach from Eton to Oxford to introduce him to the university and to lionise him.[65] But he had the broad vision and never more so than when he founded chairs in geometry and astronomy in 1619. These acted as an example and a powerful stimulus to the foundation of other chairs and lectureships as well as to the development of the scientific revolution in England.[66]

Libraries and printing presses: Sir Thomas Bodley

When Nicholas Wadham was thinking of founding a college he was advised by a neighbour to imitate Sir Thomas Bodley, the founder in 1598 of the Bodleian Library.[67] The comparison was apt from several points of view. Both were west countrymen, and Bodley, like Wadham, had married a rich widow by whom he had no children. Her fortune was not in land, like Wadham's, but had been built up, it was said, from the trade in pilchards between Devon and Catholic Europe. The fifteenth-century University Library of Humphrey, Duke of Gloucester, had been dispersed. The room built to house it over the Divinity School lay desolate. Bodley was to spend on the repair and extension of the library not less than £8,000, while to fit it out he and his friends laid out a further £11,000. He had added to the existing buildings of 'Duke Humfrey' the construction of Arts End by 1612. At this time a public library was a rare phenomenon in Europe, and Bodley engendered a great deal of interest and support. Already by the time of the first catalogue (1605) it contained about 5,600 volumes, and by 1620 the number had reached 16,000.[68] To the east the Schools Quadrangle soon provided rooms for lecturers expounding not only the old

34

53

115

[61] Feingold 1984, pp. 47–8; McConica 1986, pp. 716–21.   [62] Feingold 1984, p. 125.
[63] Highfield 1963, p. 80; Greenslade 1986, p. 321.   [64] Brodrick 1885, pp. 60–1; Fletcher 1976, pp. 188–9.
[65] Pattison 1875, pp. 398–402. On the Bodleian, Gibson 1931, pp. 528–37; Craster 1981, pp. 183–4.
[66] Philip 1983, p. 23; Craster 1981, pp. 183–4; Feingold 1984, p. 32; McConica 1986, pp. 716–17; for the foundation statutes, Gibson 1931, pp. 528–37.
[67] Wood 1891–1900, I, 259; the neighbour's name was N. Ovang.
[68] Philip 1983, p. 14; Macray 1890, p. 58.

traditional subjects but also Greek, moral philosophy and history, and for the two new Savilian professors, while above the lecture rooms were the university archives, an observatory and a public picture gallery – the first in England.[69]

The library had an excellent librarian, the indefatigable Thomas James, chosen by Bodley himself. Under his care the Bodleian soon became a repository rich in manuscript materials especially on patristic writings and orientalia. This made it an object of special interest to Archbishop Laud, who added notably to its holdings. First he persuaded the chancellor, the Earl of Pembroke, to give to it the outstanding Barocci Collection of 200 Greek manuscripts from Venice. Later he gave to it himself, in four separate donations, some 1,250 manuscripts of his own, thus nearly doubling the Bodleian manuscript holdings.[70] This was especially valuable as the library had as yet no money for new purchases and remained largely dependent on gifts of books and manuscripts. Some of these were handsome indeed, like the collection of Sir Kenelm Digby, or the 8,000 volumes given by John Selden.[71] Meanwhile the first steps had been taken by an agreement with the Stationers' Company to bring to the library free copies of all London publications; this eventually led to the establishment of a copyright library, even if endless efforts were to be needed for the system of deposit to become effective.[72] For the moment the Bodleian served almost as a national library. It at once attracted the attention of foreign scholars especially from Germany and Protestant Europe.[73] Plans were discussed in Cambridge for a Bodleian in the fens, and some hoped that the Duke of Buckingham, elected chancellor in 1626, would provide the needed bounty – but an assassin's hand reserved that role for a later age and for the Rockefeller Foundation.[74] Meanwhile the University Library at Cambridge flourished as best it could, inadequately housed, under two remarkable scholars and bibliophiles – Abraham Whelock and William Moore.

There had been printing in Cambridge since the early sixteenth century, but in spite of a royal charter of 1534 licensing the university to appoint printers and stationers, the jealous eyes of the Stationers' Company in London had kept the growth of serious provincial printing in check. In 1584, after long negotiation with Lord Burghley, the chancellor, and noisy argument with the Stationers, Thomas Thomas, ex-fellow of King's, was licensed to print books, and issued a miscellany in which the influence of the moderate Puritan divines was evident, and especially of William Whitaker, master of St John's. In spite of rumbles from Lambeth, Thomas survived as printer; and after his death in 1588 he was succeeded by John Legate and a line of printers which included Thomas Buck, who was to print in 1629 and 1636 two of the best editions of the Authorised Version of the Bible.[75] An attempt to revive printing at Oxford had inspired convocation to lend £100 to an inn-keeper and bookseller, Joseph Barnes, 'that he might have a press in the University for printing books the more easily'. At the same time the chancellor was asked to plead with the queen for her leave to print in Oxford. She must have agreed to the request for Barnes began to print in 1585. He then managed to survive as a printer contracted to the university until 1617 and thus was on hand to print the first catalogue of the Bodleian in 1605.[76] Both university presses were much strengthened when they were empowered by

[69] Mallet 1924–7, II, 227–9.   [70] Philip 1983, pp. 37, 39–41.   [71] Philip 1983, pp. 41, 47–9.

[72] Philip 1983, pp. 27–8; but cf. *ibid.*, p. 52; Oates 1986.   [73] Philip 1983, p. 35.

[74] Oates 1975, esp. p. 9; for what follows, *ibid.*, pp. 9–11. And see now Oates 1986.

[75] Black 1984, chaps. 3–5, esp. pp. 38–64. For what follows, Johnson and Gibson 1946, p. 5.

[76] Johnson and Gibson 1946, p. 6; Hammer 1986, p. 77.

Charles I to appoint three printers who might have two presses and two apprentices apiece, and by confirmation of their privileges in a charter of 1636 which also allowed them to print all types of book including the Bible.[77] When Laud became chancellor he wished to advance much further beyond these modest beginnings. He gave himself as one of his objectives 'to set up a Greek Press in London and Oxford for Printing of the Library Manuscripts; and to get Letters and Matrices . . .'[78] In the section of the Laudian statutes on printing he envisaged an 'Architypographus' or controller who should oversee the university's public printing-office to which he attached the office of Superior Bedel of Civil Law when that should next fall vacant.[79] But this chance did not offer itself until 1656 and a building in which to house the press was not found until 1669. In default of funds of its own the university in 1637 came to terms with the Stationers' Company in a 'Covenant of Forbearance' by which it agreed to forbear from printing Bibles, and certain other books named, in exchange for an annual income of £200. With this income it set about buying Hebrew and Arabic types.[80] It was already able to print in Greek type which Sir Henry Savile had given in 1615.[81] But even so a university press properly speaking was not yet in being when Laud fell from power in 1641.

New subjects to study

If Greek was the most striking new subject to find its way on to the Oxford syllabus (and into a lecture room in the New Schools), moral philosophy was similarly successful, and there were others which looked as if they might break in. Such was Hebrew which had secured the recognition of a chair, attached to a canonry at Christ Church. Teachers of Hebrew also appeared within the colleges, such as the Fleming, John Drusius, and Bensarius, a French exile, who both taught the language at Merton.[82]

Mathematics, already taught for the B.A. course at Oxford in the form of arithmetic, was developed in 1619 to include geometry for all those of two years' standing, while in addition astronomy was now needed for the M.A. course.[83] Mathematics was given a great boost by the foundation of the Savilian chairs. The first Savilian professor of geometry, Henry Briggs, was recruited from Cambridge; he was the inventor of Briggsian logarithms. In 1621 he could write cheerfully to the Master of Sidney Sussex about the situation of mathematics at Oxford and compare it favourably with what he already knew at Cambridge. The professor of geometry taught not only Euclid, Apollonius's conics, Archimedes' mathematical principles, descriptive geometry and calculus, but also the practical application of arithmetic in land measurement, practical geometry, mechanics and surveying.[84]

Natural philosophy benefited from a public lectureship, provided by Sir William Sedley, while chairs in history, music and moral philosophy were founded by William Camden (a friend of Savile), William Heather (a friend of Camden) and Sir John White.[85] Under the influence of the teaching of anatomy at Padua and other medical schools abroad a

---

[77] Macray 1890, p. 34.   [78] Carter 1975, pp. 26, 32; Trevor-Roper 1962, pp. 274–5.

[79] Johnson and Gibson 1946, p. 15.   [80] Johnson and Gibson 1946, p. 19; Carter 1975, pp. 33–4.

[81] Johnson and Gibson, p. 14 and n. 1; the Oxford press was using Hebrew type as early as *c.* 1588 (Greenslade 1986, p. 317).

[82] Fletcher 1976, pp. 43, 75, 247; since Drusius was teaching in 1572–4 he could have taught Sir Thomas Bodley. Cf. C. Roth 1966, pp. 242–51; cf. Greenslade 1986, pp. 316–18.

[83] Feingold 1984, p. 28.   [84] Curtis 1959, pp. 116–18.   [85] Feingold 1984, p. 32.

lectureship was founded by Richard Tomlins in 1624 and attached to the chair of medicine, which had been strengthened financially by associating with it the mastership of Ewelme Hospital (1617).[86] Despite this and the instruction of the existing Linacre lecturers – not to mention the setting up of the Physick Garden after 1622 – the teaching of medicine remained largely literary, tied to the texts of Galen and Hippocrates.[87] Finally Archbishop Laud when chancellor, following the example of Cambridge, established the Oxford lectureship in Arabic in 1636 with a salary of £40 per annum; and the distinguished Arabist Edward Pococke became its first holder.[88]

Cambridge, rejoicing in the regius chairs of the 1540s, rested on its oars: only one new chair was founded between 1542 and 1663. In 1632 Thomas Adams, draper of London, endowed the lectureship which became the Sir Thomas Adams's professorship of Arabic – which the founder regarded as tending 'not only to the advancement of good literature by bringing to light much knowledge which as yet is locked up in that learned tongue; but also to the good service of the King and State in our commerce with those Eastern nations, and in God's good time to the enlarging of the borders of the Church, and propagation of Christian religion to them who now sit in darkness'.[89] At the same time Sir Henry Spelman was encouraged to endow teaching in Anglo-Saxon; and to these joint ends the celebrated scholar Abraham Whelock, university librarian, was harnessed; he was an assiduous scholar in Arabic and Persian and began to write a refutation of the Koran – but (so the story goes) was dissuaded by a missionary who knew better the temper of Islam than he. Not till 1663 was another chair founded – but that was to be the greatest ornament of all, the Lucasian chair of mathematics, adorned by many eminent names from Isaac Barrow and Isaac Newton to Stephen Hawking.[90] Meanwhile, if the Cambridge of the 1620s heard the voices of few professors, it rejoiced in the most mellifluous of its Orators, George Herbert (1619–27); and the unregenerate Herbert delighted to flatter the king and the court – the chief function of the Orator in that age – before he betook himself 'to a study of divinity' and left Cambridge for his final years of pastoral care and poetry.[91]

Subjects which were not statutory also flourished if they were thought to contribute to a gentleman's education. Thus several modern languages were taught. At Oxford the Italian professor of civil law, Alberico Gentili, taught his native tongue as well as civil law.[92] Italian and French were taught after 1581 by John Florio, the son of an Italian Protestant refugee; Spanish by an Italian in 1595.[93] Spanish also benefited by the arrival of Protestant refugees.[94] These developments reflected clearly the influence exercised on the university by the well-born undergraduates. Although many of them never completed the courses, those who did and who wished to follow a career in church or state were increasing in numbers to such an extent that the question was asked, Was the university beginning to produce too many graduates? Puritan critics of clerical pluralists alleged that there were nearly 200 graduates at Oxford without livings and 140 at Cambridge, a problem which they sought to alleviate by confining pluralist clergy to a single living.[95] Some superfluous graduates who did not enter the professions seem to have become 'the penurious writers

[86] Mallet 1924–7, II, 245; Curtis 1959, p. 153; Gibson 1931, pp. 551–5.
[87] Feingold 1984, p. 32; Mallet 1924–7, II, 245; and cf. Lewis 1986, pp. 213–56.
[88] Trevor-Roper 1962, p. 282.   [89] Tanner 1917, pp. 81–2.   [90] Tanner 1917, pp. 82–3.
[91] Tanner 1917, p. 49; on Herbert see *DNB*; Tuve 1952.   [92] Curtis 1959, p. 140; Fletcher 1976, p. 168.
[93] Curtis 1959, pp. 139–40.   [94] Fletcher 1976, pp. 128, 168, 317.   [95] Cf. Curtis 1962, pp. 32–4.

of Elizabethan London', the capital's 'first Grub Street', while in the countryside those members of the gentry who went down from Oxford and Cambridge to their lands and country houses helped to establish a learned magistracy.[96]

Links with Parliament and the crown

The wider interests of the universities were seen when at least as early as 1570 they began to petition for representation in Parliament. According to a later petition from Oxford (1603) it was important that the statutes and regulations of the university should not be infringed by Acts of Parliament.[97] But it is certain that the request also reflected the determination of the university not to be worsted in its 300-year-old contest with the city. In 1563 Elizabeth had issued a charter granting the university extensive privileges: its members were to be solely under the jurisdiction of the university and at the same time could trade as if they were burgesses. Moreover the chancellor and his court had been enabled to make statutes which (as stated in 1649) required 'a civil man to go to the vice-chancellor for leave to be out of his home after 9 o'clock at night or before 4 o'clock in the morning'.[98] This was thought to be 'a greater tyranny than is fit for any freeman to bear'. Parliamentary representation would offer a safeguard of privilege in the face of a resentful city. Naturally the city opposed the proposition, led by Thomas Wentworth, son of that Peter Wentworth who was so vociferous in Elizabethan Parliaments. He was himself the member for the city from 1604 to 1628 and City Recorder, 1607–27.[99] His efforts were unavailing. Towards the end of her reign Elizabeth tried to stabilise the numbers of the House of Commons, which had grown greatly as a result of petitions. The university members whom James I added a week before the opening of his first Parliament were among the last additions made by the crown. Each university was to have the right to elect two Members of Parliament. The king may have expected such members to be well affected to the monarchy. If so, he was not mistaken. The first members, Daniel Dunne and Thomas Crompton, had belonged to the group whom Whitgift had built up to oppose the Puritans in the Commons.[100] Equally amenable were to be Sir Thomas Edmondes and (under Charles I) Sir Francis Windebanke, the king's Secretary of State. That it was not impossible for the university and the city to co-operate was demonstrated when they combined their efforts to persuade the crown to improve the navigation of the Thames between Burcot and Oxford. Following an Act of Parliament of 1624 locks were built which eventually enabled the first barges to reach Oxford from London in 1635.[101]

Royal visits both under Elizabeth and the early Stuarts were frequent enough to show that, if in England the universities were not exactly 'for Kings', as the royal foundation of Salamanca was for the king of Castile, nevertheless relations were close and cordial even if at times too close for comfort. Ever since the reigns of Henry III and Edward I the crown had looked to the universities as a source of loyal churchmen and statesmen and this expectation was enhanced by the Reformation. Since the links were closest with Trinity College, Cambridge, and Cecil himself came from its neighbour St John's, it is not sur-

[96] For the overproduction of graduates and pluralists, see Hill 1956, pp. 239–40.   [97] Porritt 1909, I, 99–100.
[98] Fasnacht 1954, p. 76, and cf. *ibid.*, pp. 183–5.   [99] *DNB.*
[100] Cf. Neale 1957, pp. 406–7; Mallet 1924–7, II, 238–9.   [101] Thacker 1909, I, 72.

prising that Elizabeth visited Cambridge first, in 1564, when she was guided round by Cecil. But at Oxford Leicester and Hatton were chancellors in succession and there too were royal foundations to be visited, notably Christ Church. Twice the queen visited Oxford and on each occasion she was greeted by the Public Orator outside the gates of Christ Church.[102] She had already secured the election of her old Greek tutor, Henry Savile, as warden of Merton, and in a characteristic manner also gave her name to a scheme whereby a lease of that college's best manor, Malden in Surrey, was made to the Earl of Arundel for 5,000 years to help him in his financial difficulties.[103]

Oxford, the Stuarts and William Laud

The links between Oxford and James I became still closer. His love of learning led him to observe that if he were to be a prisoner he would wish the Bodleian Library to be his prison. Aptly his statue presides over the Tower of the Five Orders in its Schools Quadrangle.[104] Soon after the Hampton Court conference the president of Corpus Christi College, Oxford, John Rainolds, initiated a project which became dear to James's heart, the revision of the Bible which resulted in the Authorised Version of 1611.[105] The revisers included the professors of Hebrew and Greek from Oxford and Cambridge as well as other leading scholars, more than fifty in all. There were six groups who set to work, two each at Oxford and Cambridge and two at Westminster. The Oxford scholars included the master of University College, the warden of Merton, the rectors of Lincoln and Exeter and many others. Those at Cambridge also included many leading divines, with Lancelot Andrewes to the fore; and among the *savants* who struggled with the Apocrypha were Andrew Downes, regius professor of Greek, William Branthwaite, master of Caius, and John Bois. The notes left by Bois give some illumination to the obscure story of the Apocrypha's making.[106]

When James visited Oxford in 1605 he was fulsomely received. He sent his eldest son to Magdalen and may be said to have established a special link with the university which lasted through the seventeenth century. He was to call Oxford 'the holiest temple of Mnemosyne' and his 'eldest daughter'.[107] When he presented a copy of his works to both universities he found that Oxford valued them the more since it placed them in its archives 'with great solemnity, as was fit for a relic and work of that worth'.[108] Oxford certainly knew how to touch the royal vanity. Moreover, while Cambridge had given offence by entertaining the Elector Palatine in 1613 with a disputation as to whether succession in kingdoms should be by heredity or election, Oxford had been quicker to adopt the king's 'three darling articles', namely his demand that students taking degrees should take a new oath of uniformity to the Church of England, as well as the oaths of supremacy and of obedience to the Thirty-Nine Articles.[109]

[102] Mallet 1924–7, II, 150–4; Falkner 1899, pp. 189–92; Williams 1986, pp. 397–400.
[103] Cf. Brodrick 1885, pp. 265–6; Fletcher 1976, p. 112; Williams 1986, pp. 430–1.
[104] Macray 1890, p. 33 and n. 1.
[105] On the Authorised Version, see Cross and Livingstone 1974, pp. 170–1; Allen 1969–70; Brooke 1985, p. 104, and references.
[106] Allen 1969–70; Macray 1890, pp. 33–4; Brooke 1985, p. 104; and on Branthwaite and his library, *ibid.*, pp. 104–10.
[107] Macray 1890, p. 59.
[108] Macray 1890, pp. 58–62; but cf. *ibid.*, p. 62 n. 1. We are grateful to Miss B. Kemp for the references in nn. 107–8.
[109] Cf. Mallet 1924–7, II, 235.

In Oxford as at Cambridge the growing separation of the 'Puritan' and Arminian sections of the Church of England had not yet produced a fatal break. Thus the colleges and halls offered to an intending student and his parents a wide choice of possibilities. Magdalen Hall, for instance, under John Wilkinson, flourished as a 'Puritan' academy. This was the period when it was attended by both Thomas Hobbes and Clarendon. Quite opposite was the flavour of St John's, where Buckeridge and Laud were developing a very different Arminian tradition. For the moment, variety produced an efflorescence. So it was

183

116 *The Convocation House under Selden End in the Bodleian Library, 1634–7, showing the vice-chancellor's throne*

too at Cambridge. The root and source of Puritan tradition had been in Christ's, which received, however, a high church master in Valentine Carey in 1609 – 'Woe is me for Christ's College!' cried a fellow of Emmanuel; but his own college may have benefited from the change in Christ's, for Emmanuel and Sidney, the latest foundations, remained the secure strongholds of Puritanism; and Emmanuel was for two generations the most flourishing college in Cambridge.[110] At the other extreme lay Jesus and especially Peterhouse, where Matthew Wren and John Cosin held sway in the Laudian interest in the 1620s and 1630s, adorning their new chapel with a ceiling of heavenly cherubs, now departed to another world. Most colleges enjoyed a mixture of two or many shades. Thus Caius, which had fostered Cosin and Jeremy Taylor, another notable protégé of Laud, and filled its chapel ceiling with cherubs who (after a spell of exile in the 1640s and 1650s) are still witnesses to this epoch in the history of Cambridge, yet had a low church element too, led by the cautious and careful master, Thomas Batchcroft.[111]

108–9

110

[110] Brooke 1985, p. 110; for all this see Porter 1958, esp. pp. 238–42; Stubbings 1983 and *Emmanuel Statutes*; a major study of early Emmanuel is contained in Ibish 1985.

[111] For Cosin, Taylor and Batchcroft, see Brooke 1985, pp. 110–17, 121–6; and for the church parties, esp. Hoyle 1986 and his unpublished studies of Cambridge religion in the 1620s and 1630s.

117 *King Charles I in the fifteenth-century bay window of Magdalen College hall, Oxford: glass of c. 1633*

Early in Charles's reign two important royal statutes were promulgated for Oxford. In 1628, in imitation of Cambridge, a proctorial cycle was introduced to put an end to the abuses of canvassing and treating at proctorial elections.[112] The offices were now to be circulated according to a careful system. More significantly in 1631 a royal decree brought about what had already been customary at Cambridge for some time: a weekly meeting of the heads of houses in what was to become known as the hebdomadal board. This development followed Laud's appointment as chancellor and was probably inspired by him with the Cambridge model in mind. It put university affairs into the hands of the heads for a long time to come. These changes were known as *Statuta Carolina*, and Charles had visited Oxford as prince in 1616, as king for the Parliament of 1625, and again on a visit in 1629; yet it was only when the hand of Laud began to be felt that the king acquired more than a ceremonial association with the university. Thus in 1630 Charles proposed to abolish the Calvinistic discipline in Guernsey. It was then pointed out to him that there were no Anglican ministers to replace the Presbyterians. So when some property escheated to the crown in the following year he set it aside to found a fellowship apiece at Exeter, Jesus and

[112] Gibson 1931, pp. 561–5.

118   *Oxford, St John's College,*
Canterbury Quadrangle,
completed 1636, the gift of
William Laud

119 *The bust of William Laud in St John's College Library, 1633, by Hubert Le Sueur (c. 1595–c. 1650)*

Pembroke Colleges in order to produce some reliable clergy for the Channel Islands. In the same year he gave the advowson of St Aldate's to Pembroke College.[113] In all this ecclesiastical business the hand of Laud seems to be writ large.

Since the Earl of Leicester in Elizabeth's reign had introduced as chancellor the practice of nominating the vice-chancellor, the procedure had offered chancellors an opportunity of choosing their friends among the academic community. In 1634 and again in 1636 Laud thus nominated respectively the sympathetic Warden Pinke of New College and the archbishop's own kinsman, Dr Bailey, the president of St John's, as his vice-chancellors. Their accounts show how a New Convocation House was built at the west end of the Bodleian on land bought from Exeter, with a vestry (or Apodyterium) where the Chancellor's Court could be held. Over both was constructed the notable westward extension of the Bodleian which was to house the Selden Collection and to become known as Selden End.[114] The New Convocation House went some way towards freeing St Mary's, where convocation had hitherto normally met, from secular business, though the process was not complete until the building of the Sheldonian Theatre.

When in 1636 the king and queen decided to pay an unsolicited visit to the university, Laud did not hesitate to use the occasion to symbolise the close association between the monarchs and the university of which he was chancellor. As former junior proctor and president of St John's, the chancellor built up the occasion. He was able to show them Oxford's most graceful quadrangle completed: the Canterbury Quadrangle of St John's. It

116

118

[113] Macleane 1900, pp. 123–5. This was at Laud's suggestion.
[114] Wood 1891–1900, IV, 53–5; Macray 1890, pp. 81–2.

120   *St John's, Beehive Building, 1958–60, by Architects Co-Partnership*

revealed 'sweet harmony in every part' and has proved his most lasting achievement. With lavish generosity he paid for the whole cost of the visit, over £3,000.[115] This year marked the climacteric of early Stuart Oxford, for it also saw the promulgation of the Laudian Code, a conscientious attempt to amalgamate the old with the new. The statutes had been crying out to be reconciled and revised since the days of Wolsey and Warham. But late-sixteenth-century chancellors of Oxford, like Leicester and Hatton, were no lawyers and did not possess that feeling for detailed legislation which Cecil, with Whitgift's help, had so notably inspired at Cambridge.

William Herbert, Earl of Pembroke, Laud's predecessor as chancellor, had been *121* persuaded to press forward towards the long-desired codification. But it took the legalistic mind of the archbishop coupled with his determination to push things through to secure its

---

[115] Hutton 1898, p. 137, quoting Abraham Wright; also Taylor 1936, pp. 545–7. See now H.M. Colvin, *The Canterbury Quadrangle, St John's College, Oxford*, Oxford, 1988.

completion. Not that Laud effected this achievement single-handed. Herbert had appointed delegates to investigate and scrutinise the existing confusion. They were to be helped by a team of four wise men as sub-delegates: Bodley's Librarian, Thomas James, the professor of civil law, Richard Zouche, the Savilian professor of geometry, Peter Turner, and above all the antiquary, Brian Twyne.[116] There were regular Monday meetings of the four in the tower of the New Schools when Twyne propounded parts of the statutes to his colleagues.

[116] Mallet 1924–7, II, 314–15; Trevor-Roper 1962, p. 278.

How much of the resulting code was their work and how much Laud's, it is hard to say. But it is certain that without the archbishop's driving force the great codification would never have been completed as early as 1636. The mere act of compiling the new code was notable. For the university had never had such a piece of legislation before. Now the statutes in 21 titles were signed by the king and the archbishop and confirmed at convocation as its written constitution. They covered every branch of academic administration down to the minutest details of dress. The most important single feature was the substitution of examination for degrees for the series of attendances at and participation in Latin debates, to which had been added the submission of theses, declamations and testimonials. The *Statuta Carolina* were incorporated and in a valuable appendix a set of revised rules for the halls was drawn up. The Laudian Code was to remain unaltered for more than a hundred years and in large measure lasted until the nineteenth century.

Thus Laud had contributed to every aspect of university life, as builder, patron of learning and administrator; and if his statutes did eventually suffer radical change, the porch of St Mary's, the chair of Arabic, above all the Canterbury Quadrangle of St John's, *28 118* with Le Sueur's statues of Charles and Henrietta Maria opposite one another, looking demurely down, remain to remind his critics as well as his admirers of his effective devotion to his university.

8 *From the age of Cromwell to the age of Newton*

The 1650s – Cambridge
Be diligent and constant at chapel . . .
Play not at chess or very seldom, for though it be an ingenious play, yet too tedious and
    time-devouring.
Refraine football, it being as it is commonly used a rude, boisterous exercise, and fitter for
    clowns than for scholars.

The rules of James Duport of Trinity, CC, p. 94

The 1660s – Oxford
An age given over to all vice – whores and harlots, pimps and panders, bawds and buffoons,
lechery and treachery, atheists and papists, rogues and rascals, reason and treason,
playmakers and stageplayers, officers debauch[ed] and corrupters . . . aggravated and
promoted by presbyters.

A. Wood in Wood 1891–1900, II, 125, Dec. 1667

Oxford

From the autumn of 1642 to the summer of 1646 Oxford became the royalist capital and a major garrison town. In December 1642 no less than three troops of horse and four regiments of foot were quartered there and parts of nine other regiments were to be stationed at Oxford before the siege was raised. This meant not only that quarters had to be found for a garrison of over 2,000 in the little country town, but also for another army of courtiers and members of the government and their hangers-on. No wonder Oxford nearly burst. The colleges and university buildings were naturally invaded. The king's headquarters were at Christ Church, the queen's at Merton. When the royalist Parliament met in January 1644 the Lords were housed in the New Schools, the Commons in the Convocation House. The Court of Requests did its business in the Philosophy School and Chancery took over the Convocation House when Parliament was not sitting. The chief magazine was placed in New College which was judged more defensible than the castle. A complicated series of fortifications was constructed, to whose cost the colleges had to contribute.[1] Heavy taxation was also resorted to in order to meet the pay of the garrison and other expenses. Most dramatically in 1643 the college silver was requisitioned to be melted down at the mint in New Inn Hall Street and turned into Oxford silver pounds and wages for the royalist troops.[2] In the midst of the siege a disastrous fire occurred which

[1] Toynbee and Young 1973, pp. 9–12, 36–43; Varley 1932, pp. 28, 47–56, 63–9, 106–21.
[2] Varley 1932, pp. 35–47.

swept away 800 houses in five parishes between what is now George Street and St Ebbe's.[3] Although a formal appearance of university life continued many of the students left to join the University Militia. Indeed, the disruption was very great. The number of admissions dropped in the decade 1640–9 to less than half what they had been in the previous ten years. At Wadham they fell from over seven in 1643 to three in 1644 and none the year after.[4] V.H.H. Green has shown that the admission fees that could be exacted at Lincoln fell from over £7 in 1640 and over £8 in 1641 to 13s 4d in 1643 and even to 6s in 1646.[5] The land revenues of many colleges seem to have held up better than might have been expected. Those of New College, which had averaged £2,970 per annum in the five years before the war fell to £1,059 in 1643–4; but Lincoln College, despite losses from battels, room rents and fines, managed to make a surplus in 1643 and 1645–6 and only fell into deficit in 1647–8.[6]

Oxford was lucky in having been besieged by Fairfax, since he was anxious to avoid unnecessary casualties and damage. In his summons to the royalist commander on 11 May 1646 to deliver up the city he stated 'I very much desire the preservation of that place, so famous for learning, from ruin which inevitably is like to fall upon it unless you concur.'[7] He could easily have let fly with his artillery but generally refrained from doing so and was rewarded by the city's surrender on terms. When the siege was raised there was a sudden rush back towards more normal conditions. Admission fees rose to over £11 at Lincoln in 1647. But before normality could be achieved three visitations by three commissions had to be undergone. The abolition of bishops in 1641 had swept away the existing visitors of many colleges.

With the coming of the Parliamentary visitations came also the return of members who had backed Parliament, and the extrusion of those royalists who refused to submit to the new authorities. The split which had existed since the beginning of the war now widened, even if the authorities moved quite slowly. They proved liable to fall out among themselves and also with the Parliamentary committee in London under whom they operated. The first set of commissioners worked fairly harmoniously under the chairmanship of Sir Nathaniel Brent, the warden of Merton. Having abandoned Oxford for the capital nearly three years earlier, he had been dismissed by Charles I in 1645. Now he was reinstated. Between April 1648 and January 1650 the visitors made 400 appointments, in the main replacing those who had refused to submit.[8] Subsequently a little under 90 appointments were made although these were mostly the result of normal vacancies. Thus Walker's estimate of about 400 fellows, scholars and chaplains expelled may be close to the truth. Some colleges, however, suffered much more severely than others, especially New College and All Souls which were particularly hostile to the new regime. At New College at least fifty fellows were expelled.

There can be no doubt that the upheaval brought in some outstanding men. One of these was Warden Wilkins of Wadham, the 'greatest curio of his time', under whom that college flourished as never before (1648–59). It became the headquarters of a brilliant group of men, the members of a club for experimental science which had begun to meet in 1648 in the lodgings of William Petty over an apothecary's shop. The club included men like John Wallis, mathematician and Savilian professor of geometry (who introduced the use of

[3] Porter 1984, pp. 289–300.   [4] Wells 1898, p. 56.   [5] Green 1979, p. 244.   [6] Green 1979, p. 246 n. 2.
[7] Falkner 1899, p. 247.   [8] Burrows 1881, pp. lxxxix–xc. For what follows see Matthews 1948, pp. xiii–xiv.

122 *Sir Christopher Wren, by Edward Pierce (Ashmolean Museum)*

infinite series as an ordinary part of analysis), Thomas Willis, physician and future Sedleian professor of natural philosophy, Lawrence Rooke, fellow commoner and professor of astronomy, Goddard, warden of Merton, and Bathurst, physicians (Bathurst was to become president of Trinity), Hooke, experimental philosopher, and William Petty himself, professor of anatomy and political philosopher.[9] Under Wilkins, moreover, the young Christopher Wren was recruited into Wadham as a gentleman commoner, perhaps the most outstanding member of that order. Already at the time of his admission (1649) he had made a mechanical weather-recorder, a device for writing in the dark, a deaf-and-dumb alphabet and a treatise on spherical trigonometry.[10] Evelyn has a good account of meeting him at the warden's house when an exhibition of scientific specimens and models was displayed to which Wren had contributed much. It included transparent apiaries, a speaking statue, a variety of shadows, dials, perspectives, and many other artificial, mathematical and magical curiosities, a way-wiser, a thermometer, a monstrous magnet, conic and other sections, and a balance on a demi-circle.[11] Under the aegis of Wilkins the young genius flowered.

For a short time scientific Oxford burgeoned and displayed its resilience. It is true that Wilkins migrated to become master of Trinity, Cambridge, in 1659 (a sad end, for he was

[9] Wren 1750, p. 196; Wood 1813–20, IV, 215–19, 627–31.
[10] Wren 1750, pp. 182, 185, 181 and 239.   [11] Evelyn 1955, III, 110–11.

ejected next year); and the club moved first to Boyle's lodgings in the High Street and then to London where Wilkins and his friends were to found the Royal Society in 1662.

Wren, however, remained as a fellow of All Souls, from 1653 to 1661, almost certainly designed the sundial there and steadily pursued his mathematical and astronomical studies and his scientific experiments.[12] He was especially good at geometrical demonstrations. But in 1657 he was called away to London to become professor of astronomy at Gresham College. His rooms there quickly became a rendezvous for some of the men of science who were to found the Royal Society. But he did not for long enjoy peace since in 1658 the college became garrisoned by troops. Soon after the Restoration he was lured back to Oxford on being appointed Savilian professor of astronomy in 1661. He was to hold the post for twelve years and during that period the Sheldonian was to be built (1664–9), not to mention other commissions at Oxford, Cambridge and in the capital, culminating in the construction of St Paul's. Not surprisingly his work as professor of astronomy was liable to be set aside.[13]

The numbers attending the university under the Commonwealth and Protectorate soon picked up. The estimated annual admissions in the decade 1650–9 at *c.* 438 were well on their way to matching pre-war figures.[14] Most colleges had been allowed to regain control over their elections by 1653. The quarrel between the 'Presbyterians' and the 'Independents' had brought about the the resignation of the vice-chancellor – Reynolds – who found (1650) that he could not take the 'Engagement' to be faithful to the Commonwealth, without king or House of Lords, and a second set of visitors began to operate in June 1652.[15] Cromwell himself took a personal interest in higher education and encouraged the possibility of founding new universities at Durham and Dublin. He visited Oxford in 1649 with Fairfax and allowed himself to be elected chancellor in 1651, even if he put most of his powers virtually into commission in the following year.[16] When Reynolds resigned, his successor John Owen, a graduate of Queen's, was a former chaplain of Cromwell and also an 'Independent'. Cromwell and Fairfax both treated the university sympathetically, considering the support which it had given to the king during the Civil War. Cromwell gave manuscripts to the Bodleian Library and £100 a year for a divinity lecturer.[17] They both showed themselves to be as conservative as Laud when they insisted that Latin should remain the language of conversation in hall and of instruction. Cromwell defended the universities against schemes for radical reform put forward at the Barebones Parliament. Yet one of Cromwell's protégés, William Sprigg, fellow of Lincoln, thought that universities should have a wider educational programme and in his view 'should stoop more to a more honest civil notion of Schooles of Education and humane literature, for the training up the youth of the Gentry in learning and good manners'.[18]

A third set of visitors was appointed in 1654 and, pursuing individual reforms among the colleges, functioned until April 1658.[19] Their powers remained a topic for debate and unease. Owen, who thought that convocation should be remodelled, fell from power in 1657 to be replaced as vice-chancellor by Conant, rector of Exeter. Despite the desire to regain normality it was taking the university a long time to become stable again after the war.

[12] Wren 1750, p. 195; Sherwood and Pevsner 1974, p. 95.
[13] Wren 1750, pp. 195–6, 260; Downes 1982a, p. 7 and n. 23.   [14] Stone 1975, I, 91, Appendix IV, table IA.
[15] Mallet 1924–7, II, 386, 390–1.   [16] Carlyle and Lomas 1904, II, 179–81; Mallet 1924–7, II, 390–1.
[17] Abbott 1937–47, III, 427.   [18] Green 1979, pp. 254–5.   [19] Mallet 1924–7, II, 392.

123 *The Sheldonian Theatre, designed by Christopher Wren for Archbishop Sheldon 1663–9 – see also* front endpaper*: on the left, the Clarendon Building, 1711–15; in the centre, the Bodleian*

124 *(opposite) The interior: the organ case is by T. G. Jackson (1876)*

Good research work was being done notably by Robert Boyle, son of the Earl of Cork. After studying on the Continent he settled at Deep Hall, next to University College and set up a laboratory. Here he worked towards the publication of his *New Experiments Physico-Mechanical*. As an experimental alchemist he could as yet not expect to hold a university position.[20] Oxford was only slowly moving towards new academic studies. No new colleges were founded under the Commonwealth and Protectorate. If a little building started up again, such as the construction of Brasenose chapel, the truth was that the university had lost the religious variety which it had offered to Presbyterian and Arminian alike under James I and had not yet found the flexibility which it needed in its courses to adapt itself to the scientific revolution. Nor was its lost religious diversity to be restored by the Restoration.

[20] *DNB*; Wood 1813–20, IV (Fasti), 286–7 and n. 6; Simcock 1984, p. 7.

The Restoration brought back besides the king the leading royalists who had been excluded from Oxford university for fourteen years. The chief figures were Clarendon, Sheldon and John Fell. It inherited from the Cromwellian regime Sir Christopher Wren. Gilbert Sheldon, who had taken his B.A. from Trinity as long ago as 1617 and had been warden of All Souls for 22 years before his deprivation, was already over sixty in 1660 and very busy as the new Bishop of London: he was to be translated to Canterbury in 1665. But he was not so busy that he could not take an interest in the building of the theatre which bears his name. Until this date the university's full-dress ceremonial occasions, notably the Act (at which until 1733 theses were publicly maintained and sermons preached by new doctors), had taken place in St Mary's church. There annually, benefactors were commemorated and honorary degrees conferred. Now churchmen increasingly felt this to be anomalous and the commission which was secured by the youthful Wren was for the construction of an entirely secular building which should also house the University Press. A Roman theatre was the prototype. Its construction was a symbolic act in which the increasing secularisation of the university was recognised. Charles II, the Duke of Ormonde (the chancellor of Oxford) and Archbishop Sheldon himself were all displayed on the building in Roman dress. In recognition of the realities of the climate the theatre was roofed in with a ceiling showing 'Truth descending upon the Arts and Sciences' painted by the king's serjeant painter, Robert Streater. The university was deep in Sheldon's debt; the archbishop paid £12,000 for the building and also distributed cups and fees. It is a pity that in the nineteenth century Edward Blore was commissioned to repair and alter the top, including the cupola.[21]

Edward Hyde, first Earl of Clarendon, was like Sheldon a giant, if unlike him a layman. A student of a lively Magdalen Hall in the 1630s, he was one of Charles II's closest advisers in 1660, chancellor of England, and virtually head of the government until his dismissal in 1667. Aware of the defects of Oxford as a place of general education, in his *Dialogue concerning Education* he proposed to found an academy at which riding, dancing and fencing should be taught as well as logic, disputations and Latin speeches. He wanted plays in Latin and English to be performed. His proposal was never carried into effect, but the fact that it was made shows the dissatisfaction of a member of the élite with the existing courses for those who were not going into the church. Despite his failure to implement his ideas, his interest in and influence on his university were considerable in his lifetime and greater after his death, since he generously left it residually the profits from the sales of his *History of the Rebellion*; and although these were slow to be harvested they were substantial enough in the next century to enable the Clarendon Building to be erected and the University Press *123* to be moved there from the Sheldonian when the latter proved an unsuitable home for it. The Clarendon Press imprint was first used in 1713 for a selection of verses in honour of Queen Anne, but 'At the Sheldonian Theatre' continued to be more common for many years.[22]

With Wren's appointment as Surveyor General to Charles II he was naturally drawn away to the capital, where an extraordinary opportunity was to come his way with the need to make good the damage wrought by the Great Fire of London. However, commitments in London did not prevent him from carrying out important commissions both at Oxford and Cambridge. Apart from the Sheldonian, already mentioned, he built the Garden Quad at Trinity, Oxford (1668), and screens for the chapels of Merton and St John's. At Cambridge both Pembroke and Emmanuel benefited from his skills before, in a crescendo, he proffered a design for a new Senate House and University Library (which was declined) and the great new library at Trinity College (1676) for Isaac Barrow.[23] He was thus an obvious man to turn to when the dean of Christ Church, John Fell, wished to pursue the completion of Wolsey's buildings.

John Fell had been bred in the scarlet, since his father, in the years before the Civil War, had been dean of Christ Church and vice-chancellor before him. This may help to explain his autocratic temper which made him disliked in the university. But he knew how to make himself agreeable at the court of Charles II and among the noblemen and gentlemen to be found there, many of whose sons came up to Christ Church during his time as dean. One notable result of this policy soon became evident. From them and from others he was able to raise over £9,400 to help pay for the major architectural scheme which he had for improving his college. In the first place this amounted to the completion of Wolsey's great quadrangle, left untidy and incomplete at the time of the cardinal's downfall. When this had been done his outstanding deed was to commission Wren to finish Wolsey's *85* gatehouse. This Wren did by 1682 with the construction of the gigantic domed tower in which Great Tom, formerly 'Mary', the recast bell of Osney Abbey, was to hang and to give

[21] Downes 1982b, pp. 18–20; Sherwood and Pevsner 1974, pp. 255–6; Colvin 1983, pp. 13–20.
[22] Sutcliffe 1978, pp. xxiv–xxv.   [23] Downes 1982a, pp. 72–7; cf. Pevsner 1970, pp. 172–3.

its name to the tower itself – Tom Tower – and to the quadrangle. This is Wren's masterpiece in Oxford. It gives coherence to what would otherwise be an incoherent quadrangle and it makes of the west front of Christ Church what has been called 'one of the finest façades in the world'.[24] Fell did not confine himself to Christ Church. He had already helped Sheldon with the Sheldonian. In addition, in Wood's words, 'He . . . advanced the learned press, and improv'd the manufacture of printing in Oxford in such manner as it had been designed before by that public-spirited person Dr Laud archb. of Canterbury . . .' A learned man and the author of a critical work on St Cyprian (1682), he lived long enough to agree to the king's demand for the expulsion from Christ Church of its most distinguished student in his time – John Locke the philosopher;[25] though it is true that Locke had probably brought his fate on himself through his association with the Whig circle of Shaftesbury – the leader among those who wished to exclude the king's Catholic brother from succeeding to the throne.[26] Yet though Fell became Bishop of Oxford and held the see for ten years Locke lived to see the world of the Stuart court, which Fell had served so assiduously, swept away.

After the enthusiasm with which Charles II had been welcomed on his visit in 1663, this development was entirely unforeseen. Charles had followed his father and grandfather in holding Parliaments occasionally at Oxford, once in 1665 to avoid the Plague, and again in 1681 to sidestep the mob in the Whig-dominated capital, though on that occasion the move did not result in a subservient meeting, and Parliament, insisting on an exclusion bill, was dismissed after a bare week. His brother James, who had been warmly welcomed as Duke of York in 1683, clearly overreached himself in 1687, when he came in person as king to enforce the appointment of a Roman Catholic president of Magdalen in place of President Hough, whom the fellows had elected according to their statutes but in defiance of a royal instruction.[27] This famous case for the most part turned loyal Oxford against James II – a striking testimony to his tactlessness, given the support which he might easily have retained had he been more sensitive.

The antiquarianism of the seventeenth century was well represented in Restoration Oxford by Elias Ashmole and Anthony Wood. Ashmole, Windsor Herald, after a varied life as a collector of 'rarities' and a founder member of the Royal Society, had acquired the natural historical and anthropological collections of John Tradescant the elder through the kin of his son, the younger John Tradescant. Both father and son had been keepers of the royal gardens to Charles I and Henrietta Maria. Their collections, known as Tradescant's Ark, were housed in their home in South Lambeth where they constituted England's first museum open to the public.[28] Adding something of his own, Ashmole gave these collections to Oxford university on the sensible condition that it made proper arrangements for their preservation. This it did in 1678–83 by the construction of the (Old) Ashmolean Museum to the west of the Sheldonian.[29] This beautiful building, whose architect was almost certainly Thomas Wood, master mason and 'stone-cutter', not only housed the Ark, it also provided lecture rooms for the professor of natural philosophy, a room for a professor of chemistry and the first 'purpose-built teaching laboratory' in

[24] Trevor-Roper 1950, p. 14, and for Wren's letter to Fell of 9 September 1682, cf. Downes 1982b, pp. 56–7.
[25] Wood 1813–20, IV, 196–7.   [26] Wood 1891–1900, III, 117.
[27] Wilson 1899, pp. 192–210; Ogg 1955, pp. 183–5.   [28] Macgregor 1983, pp. 8–11, and 24–39.
[29] Simcock 1985, pp. 25–6 and esp. n. 67; cf. Sherwood and Pevsner 1974, pp. 254–5.

126 *Elias Ashmole (1617–92), by John Riley (1646–91) (Ashmolean Museum)*

127 *John Tradescant Junior (1608–62), perhaps by Thomas de Critz (Ashmolean Museum)*

England. It seems that Wood 'not only built but also designed the building'. He was subject to the influence of Wren but no direct link between Wren and the Ashmolean has yet been established, though it is likely that he designed the continuation of the screen of Roman heads in front of the façade. Ashmole was more than an antiquary. For the preamble to his statutes 'provides one of the most perfect expressions of "Baconianism", establishing inductive method and utilitarian aims as the guiding principles of his Museum'.[30] Chemistry had been prominent under the Protectorate when Willis and Boyle each had their laboratories. Now university provision for it had been made. The first Keeper of the (Old) Ashmolean, Robert Plot, like Clarendon and Wilkins, a former member of Magdalen Hall, gave the first university chemistry lectures there and the Philosophical Society met there on Tuesday afternoons.[31]

Anthony Wood, in his own words 'historiographer and antiquarie of the most famous University of Oxford', had a Boswellian gift for recording precise information, as well as describing leading Oxford figures in trenchant if not caustic vein. He tells us of the first coffee house in Oxford, for instance, opened in *c*. 1654–6 opposite the Angel in the High Street between Queen's and St Edmund Hall.[32] He records the arrival of coaches from London bringing the news and newspapers which could be read or read out over coffee. As early as 1667 he had travelled to London in a stage coach, which he tells us took two days. Two years later flying coaches were covering the 54 miles in one day and brought the price down to 12s.[33] Thus closer links with the capital were pulling the university nearer to the centre of political life. As to his character sketches here is his comment on Fell at Christ Church:

strikt in holding up the college discipline; 4 times in a day at public service in the cathedral, twice at home; loved to have tales brought to him and be flatterd, and therefore the most obnoxious in his house would choose to please him that way to save themselves. These persons he favoured more; allowed them the chambers that they desired, allowed them pupills, [gave them] his countenance – while the sober partie that could not or [would] not tell tales and flatter were browbeaten. The college was so much at his beck that he flew further and endeavoured to govern the University.[34]

Restoration Oxford began also to be affected by more luxurious standards of accommodation. One small influence in this respect was the need felt to set up common rooms. In the tradition of the medieval parlour or solar off the hall, these had already been established as combination rooms at Cambridge.[35] In the sixteenth century fellows had paid for their own fruit and spices beyond what the college supplied as the common college meal. Payments for these extras had been entered up in spice books or their equivalents. Now the fellows wanted rooms to which they could withdraw from the smelly atmosphere of hall in order to drink wine and eat fruit at their own expense elsewhere. In 1661 Merton had a common room fitted up over the kitchen, which acted like a hypocaust.[36] Trinity and Wadham followed suit. At New College when the Law Library had been moved William Byrd constructed a senior common room in its place, opening up the flue of a chimney to provide a hearth.[37] Comfort was further enhanced by panelling, much of it of the finest craftsmanship. Additional and more comfortable rooms were also needed in New College

[30] Simcock 1984, pp. 1–2.   [31] Simcock 1984, p. 2; Simcock 1985, p. 7.
[32] Wood 1891–1900, I, 188–9.   [33] Wood 1891–1900, II, 109, 153 and n. 10.
[34] Wood 1891–1900, I, 348–9; cf. Bennett 1986a, pp. 10–12.   [35] Willis and Clark 1886, III, 376–86.
[36] Buxton and Williams 1979, p. 210.   [37] Buxton and Williams 1979, p. 210.

128 *(opposite) Oxford, the Old Ashmolean, 1678–83, now the Museum of the History of Science, almost certainly designed by Thomas Wood*

129 *New College, Oxford,
Garden Quadrangle, 1682–4,
1700–7, with screens of 1711*

130 *Queen's College, Oxford:*
the Library, rebuilt 1692–5

to free the very large number of fellows from the necessity of sleeping four to a room. The first step was to add another storey to the Great Quadrangle. This had been accomplished under Warden Nicholas by William Byrd in 1674–5. Then New College followed the common pattern (if modestly) by planning to add sixteen noblemen or gentlemen commoners who should pay their own fees. Buildings were erected for them in Garden Quadrangle, also to Byrd's design, in 1682–4.[38] Interestingly Byrd followed Caius and Wren in the comparative novelty for Oxford of abandoning the four-sided quadrangle by opening up one of its sides 'like a three-legged table' as Wren did for Charles II's palace at Winchester and had begun to do at Trinity, Oxford, in 1668. (At Cambridge, Caius Court was already

[38] Buxton and Williams 1979, pp. 208, 212–16 (part of the north range of Garden Buildings, which also housed a senior fellow and two chaplains).

131 *The interior, south end, showing the stucco figures of Arts and Science, and, above, the arms of Provost Timothy Halton (died 1704)*

open to the south and St Catharine's was in 1674 building a court open to the east.) This plan was to give to New College the splendid buildings opening on to its garden and the city wall. Many of these buildings were paid for in part by levies on the members of the college.[39]

The last decade of the century saw the erection of two outstandingly beautiful buildings by unknown architects. The Library of Queen's has been rightly said to be 'worthy of Wren

138

[39] Buxton and Williams 1979, p. 208; cf. Willis and Clark 1886, III, 274–81.

132 (opposite) Queen's College Library, woodcarving on one of a pair of cupboards by Thomas Minns, and a seat in the library

133 The façade of Queen's, 1709–35

or Hawksmoor'.[40] It represented the beginning of a great building programme at Queen's which stretched into the eighteenth century and was to destroy that college's medieval buildings. Of the same date (1691–4) is Trinity chapel, the first to free itself completely from the Gothic style. Its altarpiece of inlay work must be the finest in Oxford even if its tone is entirely secular.[41]

134

Yet against the spectacular architectural achievements of Wren, Thomas Wood and William Byrd and the architects of Queen's Library and Trinity chapel, a disturbing tendency for admissions to fall away was gradually making itself felt. In the 1660s freshmen enrolments had run at *c.* 460 per annum. By the 1690s the number had fallen to *c.* 303.[42] Professor Stone suggests that it was the poor students of plebeian origin who were the hardest hit. The practice of bishops and wealthy clergymen paying for the education of poor children seems to have dropped away in this period.[43] There was also a decline in the numbers of noblemen and gentry. Pre-university schooling became more expensive to

40 Heyworth 1981, p. 107; Sherwood and Pevsner 1974, pp. 186–7; cf. Colvin 1983, pp. 32–4; Colvin 1986, pp. 833–4.
41 Heyworth, 1981, p. 136; Sherwood and Pevsner 1974, pp. 205–6; cf. Colvin 1983, pp. 29–32; Colvin 1986, p. 833.
42 Stone 1975, I, 91, Appendix IV, table 1A.
43 Stone 1975, I, 40.

acquire. The real value of scholarships of fixed amounts fell as at Wadham. Job prospects seem to have deteriorated. The courses themselves rose in cost more than the cost of living to between £40 and £50 per annum by 1700. Since one might end up with an appointment worth no more than £40 per annum it became doubtful whether it was worth spending four years in order to obtain such a position. Moreover the university acquired a reputation for hard drinking and sottishness which put parents off.[44] The nobility and gentry seem increasingly to have sent their sons to schools like Westminster and Eton and then to have engaged private tutors or to have sent their children on the Grand Tour which became more accessible than it had ever been before. With its intense devotion to church and king the university became more and more of a seminary for the Anglican Church, but it failed to offer the same attractions to 'Presbyterians', for instance,

[44] Stone 1975, I, 52–3.

136 *Trinity College, Oxford, the*
gate-tower, 1691–4

as the university in the early seventeenth century had done. Indeed from 1673 the Test Act
excluded from offices and places of trust under the crown anyone who refused to take the
oaths of allegiance and supremacy and receive the sacrament according to the Church of
England; thus Dissenters and Catholics were formally excluded.[45] The position of the state
religion was reiterated in 1678 and the invocation of the Virgin Mary and the saints was
explicitly denounced, as was the Sacrifice of the Mass. This 'rock of rigid dogma' made the
university both intolerant and exclusive. After 1689, moreover, Oxford's strong whiff of
Jacobitism made it suspect to the supporters of the Glorious Revolution.

[45] Ogg 1934, I, 369.

212

Cambridge

In Cambridge, William Laud's reign was short. In 1635 his faithful henchman John Cosin was made master of Peterhouse, and in 1636 Cosin or another sent his reports on Cambridge, its chapels and its worship, to the archbishop. By 1641 the tide had turned and it was Puritan divines who were reporting to the Long Parliament on the deeds of Cosin and his like.[46] In December 1643 William Dowsing set to work to dismantle the Laudian ornaments and dispose of the images which had survived the Reformation in the chapels and churches of Cambridge. Saints and cherubs and popish inscriptions rapidly disappeared under his inquisition. By a mysterious providence the glass of King's chapel escaped, but much else departed – some of it for ever, some of it (like the cherubs of Caius) to return at the Restoration, some of it even to be reconstructed by later antiquaries from Dowsing's Journal.[47]

64–5
110

Dowsing seems to us a philistine and a vandal; but he represented a genuine sentiment deeply felt and thought out by better minds than his; and, as in the sixteenth century, his radical measures accompanied others of a much more conservative kind. Cambridge was politically sensitive: by 1643 it was firmly in the hands of the Earl of Manchester, later to be chancellor, and the local M.P., Oliver Cromwell.[48] But there had been stirrings of royalism before and they were not extinct; Cromwell's efforts to prevent silver being sent to the king had been only partially successful. On grounds partly political, partly religious, as in the 1550s, masters departed and fellows followed them. In March 1644 Manchester formally ejected five heads, and it was said that 200 other scholars and fellows went too in that year.[49] In 1645 three more heads were removed, and after the execution of Charles I in 1649 and the enforcement of the 'Engagement', the oath to support the new regime in state and church, Batchcroft of Caius, a timid but respected conformer, and four other heads, went into exile. Thus eleven of the sixteen colleges had lost a head, three of them twice, and other changes followed; Manchester, now chancellor, himself refused the Engagement, which involved the abolition of the Lords as well as the monarchy, and he too was replaced.[50]

For the most part, the Civil War and the Commonwealth marked a caesura in the building programmes of the colleges. In the late 1630s Clare had embarked on a complete rebuilding of its single court on one of the most confined college sites.[51] The court had already been rebuilt in the sixteenth century and the thinking behind the campaign of 1638–42 is not recorded. But its date coincides with the highest student figures in the university at large before 1850; and it is noticeable that it began with the two ranges containing most of the chambers – and that unlike its predecessor, or the Great Court of Trinity, it is in four storeys. Its early stages were most efficiently organised by the bursar, Barnabas Oley, with John Westley as mason and architect. They started with the bridge, an

---

[46] See pp. 166–8 above.

[47] Mullinger 1911, pp. 267–72, gives a summary: for this use of Dowsing's journal, see *ibid.*, p. 271 n. 1.

[48] For all that relates to Cambridge in this epoch, see esp. Twigg 1983. Mullinger 1911 is still useful; so is the account in Roach 1959, pp. 199–203.

[49] Mullinger 1911, pp. 273–5; H.C. Porter in Rich 1973, p. 104.

[50] Roach 1959, pp. 200, 202.

[51] Willis and Clark 1886, I, 93–116; *VCH Cambs*, III, 342; Pevsner 1970, pp. 56–9. On Westley and Grumbold, see Colvin 1978, pp. 879, 367–8.

2

137 *Cambridge, Clare College: the east front and entrance, 1638–41 – see also the* final *endpaper. The south front was* finished *in 1642 and the court was completed between 1669 and 1676 (Willis and Clark 1886, I, 95–100, 102)*

object of great beauty and commodious for bringing stone for the masons; and the east and south wings were complete by 1642. Then came the Civil War, and a pause; after the Restoration, the college went on to finish the court – blending a charming, modest Baroque designed by Wren's mason Robert Grumbold with the Jacobean of the first campaign.

With all the comings and goings, the committees, the enquiries, the oaths and the purges, there was a strong wish in many circles for the life of the university to continue. Many of the new heads were local men of learning; and several of them came from the great home of Puritan theologians, Emmanuel. These included the eminent Cambridge Platonists, Benjamin Whichcote, who became provost of King's, and Ralph Cudworth, who was master of Clare for a time.[52] Also an Emmanuel man was the one fire-eating Puritan preacher in the list, William Dell, who was master of Caius from 1649 to 1660. Dell was a man of ideas, fecund in schemes (not perfectly thought out, but inspired in their way) to spread universities about the land. Yet he had a strong conservative streak, as John Twigg has recently shown: even before he became master of Caius his writings show some appreciation of traditional university methods and values; and once he was master he showed little inclination to upset the normal tenor of college life.[53] He stayed much of the time in London on Parliamentary business or in his Bedfordshire home, where he had a living in plurality with his headship; and in the mid 1650s he handed the running of the college over for a time to an able, intelligent, diplomatic young physician, William Bagge. By good fortune a cache of Bagge's correspondence has survived, which shows the routines of teaching and student life and estate administration going steadily on, though strains were evidently felt by the older members of the community; but Bagge was able to keep on friendly terms with the ex-master, Batchcroft, whom he sometimes consulted, and the ex-fellow, William Moore, university librarian and notable benefactor (in spite of his ejection) to the college library.

Among Bagge's patients was one Mrs Lightfoot, whose husband, the master of St Catharine's, is perhaps the best symbol of this element of continuity through the alarms and excursions of the Commonwealth.[54] Most colleges had declining numbers: as at the Reformation, the religious changes bred many uncertainties and anxieties, and it seems that it was the element of clergy-to-be and theologians which first declined; contrary to what one might suppose, the sons of the gentry held steady.[55] But in the late seventeenth and eighteenth centuries a general decline took over, so that between its peak in the 1630s and its nadir in the 1770s the university as a whole fell to roughly a third of its student numbers.[56] But in the mid and late seventeenth century there was one conspicuous exception: St Catharine's held steady and even increased its population for a time. Its golden years started with John Lightfoot, who became master at the most unpropitious time, after the second ejection his college had suffered, in 1650. He was a Hebrew scholar of prodigious learning, who sailed before the winds that blew; but he was not a trimmer. He honestly believed in 1650 in a Church of England without bishops; but the doctrinal chaos of the 1650s led him to welcome the Restoration, though not the penal code by which the restored church was bolstered. A genial man, his first act in 1660 was to offer the mastership to his predecessor, and when this pleasant gesture was rejected, he hastened to seek confirmation from the king – and the fellows of St Catharine's rode out to greet him on his triumphant return.[57] Meanwhile he was preparing for a new world by announcing his intention 'to beat down enthusiasm . . . to maintain the honour of learning and a regular clergy'; and by adroitly changing the dedication of one of his books from Oliver to

[52] On the Cambridge Platonists, see Cragg 1968, Patrides 1969.
[53] Twigg 1984, esp. pp. 104–5; Walker 1970; Brooke 1985, pp. 127–31. For what follows, Brooke 1985, pp. 131–40.
[54] Brooke 1985, p. 138; for Lightfoot see Luckett 1973, pp. 114–19.
[55] See esp. the evidence deployed in Cressy 1972, chap. 7, esp. table 31, p. 257.
[56] Venn summarised the evidence, as far as was then known, in the chart attached to Venn, III, 392.
[57] Luckett 1973, p. 115.

138 *Cambridge, St Catharine's College, late seventeenth century (mainly built 1674–87; the chapel completed 1699–1704)*

139 *(opposite) Cambridge, Trinity College Library, designed by Wren for Isaac Barrow, 1676–90, from Nevile's Court*

Charles.[58] He was also breeding up the lively and witty John Eachard, fellow from 1659, master from 1675. Eachard was already, before he became master, collecting money for rebuilding the college to house the numerous students the reputation of Lightfoot and Eachard and their colleagues had gathered. The fine red-brick court, still the heart and core of St Catharine's, is a monument to Eachard and to the exceptionally flourishing state of the college in his time: when he died in 1697 the new buildings were nearing completion, and the college counted among its members both Thomas Sherlock and Benjamin Hoadly, who were to be the leading Tory and the leading Whig among the bishops of the age of Walpole and Newcastle.[59]

The late seventeenth century was a great age of building in Cambridge, culminating in the new Library of Trinity. It is a very fitting monument to a college whose master, the

[58] Luckett 1973, p. 119; cf. *ibid.*, pp. 114–19 on Lightfoot and pp. 119–22 on Eachard.
[59] Luckett 1973, pp. 121–3 and references; Willis and Clark 1886, II, 98–106; *RCHM Cambridge*, II, 179–85; on Sherlock and Hoadly, Luckett 1973, pp. 110–14, 131–3.

eminent mathematician and divine Isaac Barrow, had handed over the Lucasian chair to a younger Trinity man called Isaac Newton a few years before summoning his good friend the Savilian professor of astronomy at Oxford, Christopher Wren, to design the library for him: for this was the age of Newton and Wren.[60] The towering genius of Newton seems

[60] On Newton, see Westfall 1980; Manuel 1974; Jacob 1976; *DSB*, x, 42–101 (I.B. Cohen); on Wren, Colvin 1978, pp. 917–31 and references; Willis and Clark 1886, II, 531–47 (Trinity Library); cf. *ibid.*, I, 146–9 (Pembroke chapel); II, 703–9 (Emmanuel chapel and gallery); *RCHM Cambridge*, I, 62–6 (Emmanuel); II, 148, 153–4 (Pembroke); II, 213–14, 236–41 (Trinity); and Pevsner 1970, pp. 72–3 (Emmanuel), 125–7 (Pembroke), 172–4 (Trinity).

141–2 *Woodcarving on the bookcases, by Grinling Gibbons, 1690–3. The acorns and grasshopper probably commemorate Dr William Lynnet, who paid for the carpentry of one classis, or bay of book-shelves (Willis and Clark 1886,* II, *545 nn., 685)*

143 *Cambridge, Pembroke College chapel, designed by Christopher Wren for Bishop Matthew Wren, 1663–5*

144 *(opposite) Interior. The east end was added in 1880 by George Gilbert Scott (son of Sir G. G. Scott)*

now too large for the modest academic pretensions of his university; yet he was far from isolated: it was the age of the scientific revolution and he was one of a group of brilliant mathematicians; he had many pupils and disciples, including a few theologians, like Samuel Clarke and William Whiston, who (more daring than Newton) came near to founding eighteenth-century Unitarianism. Other disciplines flourished which owed nothing to him: the master of Caius, Robert Brady (1660–1700), was not only a notable physician but one of the greatest medieval historians of the age of Mabillon.[61]

When called in to design the Trinity Library in the 1670s, Christopher Wren was no

[61] On Clarke and Whiston, see Ferguson 1976; on Brady, Pocock 1950–2; Brooke 1985, chap. 8. Jean Mabillon, O.S.B., was the most eminent of the Benedictine scholars of the reformed Congregation of Saint-Maur – the Maurists – who were the central characters in the transformation of medieval and patristic scholarship in the seventeenth and eighteenth centuries: see Knowles 1963a, pp. 213–39; 1963b, pp. 33–62.

220

145 *Matthew Wren's communion plate, bequeathed to Pembroke College: mitre, chalice, paten. The mitre (and a crozier not illustrated here) may have been fashioned to sit on the bishop's hearse at his funeral. The chalice and paten are of c. 1663, the mitre is undated, probably of the 1660s (Cambridge Plate, pp. 14–15, nos. ECC 6–7)*

stranger to Cambridge. In 1663 old Matthew Wren, Bishop of Ely and former master of Peterhouse, sent for his nephew to design for him a new chapel in the college of his youth, which was Pembroke, to be his monument and to enshrine his image of all that such a chapel should be, restored to life after the years of darkness which the bishop had spent in the Tower.[62] It is the perfect image of the enclosed Anglican community of a college, as the Trinity Library symbolises the larger world of learning. It is a gem, and if it seems not quite so confined in its taste and its genius as the Wrens designed it to be, that is because of its eastward extension – most sympathetically contrived by George Gilbert Scott in 1880. The west end still smiles across Trumpington Street at the uncle's chapel at Peterhouse; and a

143–4

108–9

[62] See n. 60 above.

quarter of a mile to the east the other notable chapel of this generation, also Wren's, lends charm and grace to the main court of Emmanuel.[63]

Many of the most brilliant and original of Newton's ideas were bred in Cambridge; but in his later life he lived mostly in London; and that powerful London club the Royal Society became the main forum of his influence. There are many reasons why the golden promise of Restoration Cambridge was not kept, so that the university came in the course of the eighteenth century to be a backwater – more so, perhaps, than Oxford. In the Hanoverian dominions governed by the Georges both were effectively eclipsed by Edinburgh – and even more, from the mid eighteenth century, by Göttingen, founded by George II, and destined to lead the revival of the German academic world.[64]

[63] See n. 60 above.   [64] Turner 1975.

9 Oxford and Cambridge in the eighteenth century

I found myself received with a sort of respect, which this idle part of mankind, the Learned, pay to their own species, who are as considerable here, as the Busy, the Gay and the Ambitious are in your World.

> Alexander Pope to Teresa and Martha Blount, about Oxford, September 1717, quoted in Sutherland and Mitchell 1986, pp. 779–80 and n. 1

Oxford

It took a long time for the university of Oxford to exorcise the Stuarts. The emergence of Whigs and Tories during the reign of Charles II left a legacy of faction to the succeeding century and, after the death of Anne, Jacobites persisted among the Tory ranks. Oxford for the most part remained Tory and factious, when during the long regime of Walpole and Newcastle the government was Whig. The Tory chancellor, Ormonde, who turned Jacobite, was followed in that office by his brother, Arran.[1] Though the university continued to resent any interference in its elections by the chancellor, the latter's office retained sufficient powers and patronage to make it attractive to leading politicians. For instance the chancellor still chose the vice-chancellor and appointed the heads of halls. There was thus to be a long period in which Arran (who only died in 1758) never chose a vice-chancellor from the Whig colleges. These were Christ Church (after 1730), Merton, and in due course Jesus, Wadham and Exeter. Given Ormonde's flight it is not surprising that at Westminster a strong suspicion remained that Oxford was treacherous. This view was sedulously encouraged by Whig members of the university. They fostered the oft-repeated suggestion that there should be a Hanoverian visitation such as those which the university had endured under the Commonwealth and the Protectorate. This would not so much have been aimed at the overhaul of the curriculum, though this was sometimes mentioned, as at the overthrow of the political opponents of the Whigs.[2]

Whig and Tory struggles for power tended to preoccupy the governing bodies of colleges regularly during the first half of the eighteenth century. But by the time the cause of the Young Pretender was lost beyond recall at Culloden and the Hanoverian dynasty had dug itself in, the difference between Whig and Tory was gradually evaporating. By 1760 Oxford had freed itself sufficiently from the past to send the warmest addresses to George III.[3] By

---

[1] Ward 1958, pp. 57–8.
[2] Ward 1958, pp. 74–5, 79–80, 87; Langford 1986, pp. 106–8; for the chancellor's powers see Sutherland in Sutherland and Mitchell 1986, pp. 212–13.
[3] Ward 1958, pp. 213–14.

the time of the election of Lord North as chancellor in 1772 and of Sir William Dolbern as burgess in 1780[4] it had reconciled itself to the Hanoverian court.

The eighteenth century at Oxford has frequently been condemned for its torpor. But if it was the university of Parson Woodforde it was also that of John Wesley, Samuel Johnson, William Blackstone, Edward Gibbon and Jeremy Bentham, however little gratitude Gibbon

---

[4] Ward 1958, pp. 278–9. One of the chief architects of the change was Nathaniel Wetherell, master of University College, vice-chancellor (1768–1772), cf. Mitchell 1986b, pp. 164–5.

147 *All Saints: the interior. The conversion into a library is by Robert Potter*

and Bentham showed for what it gave them. Paradoxically the eighteenth century also saw the erection of some of Oxford's finest buildings. The series of heads of houses and fellows who were also amateur architects of distinction and in some cases expert draughtsmen, begun by Fell, continued with Henry Aldrich, dean of Christ Church. He was, it seems, in large measure the architect of the beautiful church of All Saints, now Lincoln College Library.[5] Dr George Clarke, fellow of All Souls, was a notable benefactor of

[5] Colvin 1983, pp. 24–7; Bennett 1986b, p. 41.

Christ Church, University College and Worcester, to whom he left his valuable personal library.[6] But his most distinctive architectural contribution was to the design of Christ Church Library.[7]

153

By the eighteenth century, donations of books such as Clarke gave to Worcester were forcing the hands of the colleges who were their recipients to improve their library

---

[6] He also left £3,000 to help pay for the new buildings at Worcester; Colvin 1986, pp. 834–5; Daniel and Barker 1900, pp. 204–7.   [7] Colvin 1983, p. 34.

accommodation. It had been the gift of Bishop Barlow of Lincoln which had made it necessary for Provost Halton of Queen's to construct a new library to hold them.[8] The enlargement of the Bodleian Library itself at one time occupied the mind of a former member of University College, the fashionable court physician, Dr John Radcliffe. He had himself perceived the needs of the library and, according to Hearne, was very 'ambitious for glory'.[9] But when he made his will in 1714 he had changed his mind. He negotiated with Hawksmoor over the design of a new, separate library, but it was the Tory James Gibbs who was selected by Radcliffe's Tory trustees to construct it after Hawksmoor had died.[10] The choice was singularly fortunate for Gibbs's building is more elegant than Hawksmoor's

8 Hodgkin 1949, p. 130.
9 Hearne 1885–1921, v, 2; cf. Philip 1986, pp. 732–3.
10 Friedman 1984, p. 241; cf. Colvin 1983, pp. 64–73; Colvin 1986, pp. 845–7. The Radcliffe Trustees offered the Radcliffe Camera to the Bodleian as a reading room in 1860.

150 *The Radcliffe Camera,
1737–49, designed by James
Gibbs: it is flanked by Brasenose
on the left, by the Bodleian and All
Souls on the right*

would have been. When completed, the Radcliffe Camera had cost (together with the buying up of the site) over £40,000.[11] Edward Gibbon and Jeremy Bentham came not to believe in the education to be gained at Oxford, but John Radcliffe did. It was lucky for Oxford that this was so. The University Library was, of course, conceived of as a library chiefly for the dons and learned and not for the ordinary undergraduates. The same was true of the spate of other college libraries to which the century bore witness. This was naturally the case at All Souls which had virtually no undergraduates. There it was a quondam fellow, Christopher Codrington, who had acquired a West Indian fortune, who unlocked the door with a gift of £6,000 for a library and a further £4,000 to buy books.[12]   151

Dr Clarke had given All Souls its Warden's House and had commissioned William Talman

[11] Friedman 1984, p. 252; Colvin 1986, p. 835. He also paid for an important extension to University College (built by Townsend under Clarke's direction, Colvin 1986, p. 839).   [12] Colvin 1983, p. 40; Philip 1986, pp. 746–7.

151 All Souls College, the Codrington Library, designed by Nicholas Hawksmoor, 1716 and later: on the left, the statue of Christopher Codrington

and Hawksmoor to erect twelve sets of rooms in Great Quadrangle in 1709. So it was natural that Hawksmoor should also be employed to build the library which was to form the north range of the quadrangle. He did this in a most ingenious way so that the library, if Classical within, should be Gothic on the exterior and match a pair of romantic Gothic towers on the eastern side which should embrace an entrance to the new senior common room. His scheme, unfinished when he died, was completed to his plans and greatly enhances the east side of Radcliffe Square. Hawksmoor knew that a great library was

230

152 *The Great Quadrangle, looking towards the Codrington Library, with New College tower beyond*

proposed for the centre of the square and had the good sense to close the western side of his quadrangle with an arcade low enough for the new library to be seen over the top of it and his towers to be seen from the square.[13]

153

Christ Church Library like Queen's bears witness to the generosity of donors of books, manuscripts and pamphlets which could only be accepted if new room was found in which

[13] Downes 1979, pp. 3, 43, 48, 101, 129, 132–47; cf. Colvin 1986, pp. 837–8. He also designed the beautiful High Street screen and entrance of Queen's (Downes 1979, p. 107).

153 *Christ Church Library,*
1717–72, designed by Dr George
Clarke, fellow of All Souls, with
Tom Tower beyond

to house them. At Christ Church Dean Aldrich left his college a library of 3,000 books and pamphlets and a first plan for a building on the south side of what was to become Peckwater Quadrangle.[14] The library was begun in 1717 to the designs of Dr Clarke. During the 55 years that it was building more gifts poured in – 3,500 pamphlets from Lewis Atterbury in 1722, 12,500 books from Canon Stratford, Lord Orrery and Archbishop Wake. The design was adapted so that the open arcade (like that at Trinity, Cambridge) on the ground floor could be closed in to take the magnificent collection of pictures given by General Guise in 1760–3.[15] Magdalen too would have had a new library if Edward Holdsworth's design for a great quadrangle and library had been put into effect. In fact, with modifications by William Townsend and advice from others, only the north range of New Building was started in 1733 and left unfinished, as it remains (with its

155

[14] Philip 1986, p. 748; Trevor-Roper 1950, p. 18.
[15] Colvin 1986, pp. 839–40; Trevor-Roper 1950, p. 19.

232

154 *Christ Church, Robert Freind, canon of Christ Church, 1737, headmaster of Westminster School; by J. M. Rysbrack, 1738*

returns tidied up) to this day. Worcester and Oriel Libraries were completely rebuilt in *156–7*
the second half of the century. The basic design of Worcester seems to have been begun by
Dr Clarke before he died in 1736. It was to house his own great collection, mostly inherited from his father who had been secretary at war in the Commonwealth and under
Charles II.[16] A gift of books from Lord Leigh stimulated the erection of Oriel Library which
was built to the designs of James Wyatt in 1788–9.[17]

[16] Daniel and Barker 1900, p. 204.   [17] Philip 1986, p. 748; Colvin 1986, p. 851.

155 *Magdalen College, Oxford, the New Buildings, 1733 (pp. 232–3)*

156 *Worcester College,
Provost's Lodgings and library,
second half of the eighteenth
century (p. 233)*

The tendency to build special rooms for noblemen and gentlemen commoners continued during the most aristocratic of centuries. Since they paid the highest room rents and often double fees there was profit in this development as well as patronage. Christ Church had initiated the custom and, though Corpus Christi provides a good example of a Gentlemen Commoners' Building (begun in 1737),[18] it was Christ Church which most notably continued the habit. The replacement of Peckwater Inn and neighbouring buildings involved the provision of rooms for gentlemen commoners. Dean Aldrich devised the superb Palladian plan for Peckwater in 1705. But when Richard Robinson, Archbishop of Armagh, gave £4,000 for a new Canterbury Quadrangle on the site of Canterbury College (which had been suppressed at the Dissolution of the Monasteries) he did so on the under-

158

---

[18] Fowler 1898, p. 45.

236

157   *Oriel College Library*
1788, designed by James Wyatt

standing that it was to be kept exclusively for noblemen and gentlemen commoners.[19] The donation of this lordly prelate is also a testimony to the fact that the university remained above all a training ground for the Anglican clergy and that its clerical old members like Archbishops Sheldon and Robinson were mindful of their debt when they reached the top of the ladder of ecclesiastical preferment. Since Christ Church was the college most open to government intervention through appointments to its deanery and canonries, it developed a strong Whig connection and bred many members of the episcopal bench. By contrast, at the lowest level of curates and clerical assistants, life in the eighteenth century could be very hard and there was not much hope of influence or benefactions from them.

[19] Trevor-Roper 1950, p. 20; for noblemen and gentlemen commoners generally, cf. Doolittle 1986, pp. 261–3; Green 1986a, pp. 318–21; for the building cf. Colvin 1986, pp. 832–3, 850.

158 *Christn Church, Peckwater*
Quadrangle, by Dean Aldrich,
1705–14

Accommodation for Bible clerks and servitors from whom they might be recruited was often very cramped, since they naturally sought the cheapest rooms.

Dr Johnson sharply criticised the custom at Oxford and Cambridge of using poor scholars or sizars to wait on the rest. 'He thought that the scholar's, like the Christian life, levelled all distinctions of rank and worldly pre-eminence.'[20] Paradoxically the habit of serving did act as a leveller of a kind, but for some it was a sign of social inferiority. One of the servitor's tasks was to knock up the other undergraduates first thing in the morning. 'If he was working early Johnson did not like to be interrupted and it is recorded of him that despite his sympathy for their cause he once joined in what was a common practice – "hunting the servitor".'[21] At Hart Hall there were four servitors, one to every eight undergraduates. At Queen's a servitor's place was worth £6 a year. This included 5s each a quarter for calling

[20] Bate 1978, p. 104.   [21] Bate 1978, p. 98.

159 *Dr Johnson at Pembroke College, Oxford: the teapot said to be Dr Johnson's*

160 *The bust of Johnson in Pembroke College Library by John Bacon (1740–99)*

three commoners at 6 a.m., and 10s also a quarter for calling a gentleman commoner in residence.[22] In addition at every meal the servitors brought commons of beer and food from the kitchen for the other undergraduates and kept a list of absentees. They were not usually on the foundation and thus had little chance of preferment. George Whitefield, the Methodist, had been a drawer at the Bell Inn in Gloucester before becoming a servitor at Pembroke, where he performed comparable activities. It is true that William Lancaster, provost of Queen's (1704–17), a village schoolmaster, showed that even a servitor could prosper greatly.[23] He had been a servitor to a member of the Cumbrian Lowther family when he first came up. He owed his success to the backing of three powerful patrons – Sir John Lowther in the first place, but subsequently to Joseph Williamson, a notable benefactor of Queen's, and to Bishop Compton of London, himself a former Queen's man, who made him his chaplain and presented him to the valuable living of St Martin-in-the-Fields. He married a kinswoman of the bishop and finished up Provost of Queen's. Again, John Baron at Balliol who came up in 1686 and took his B.A. in 1690 was elected fellow in 1691, master in 1705 and vice-chancellor. But for servitors these were exceptional examples.

At a variety of colleges, for example in Queen's, the Laudian statutes had continued to be conscientiously observed during the second half of the seventeenth century. It was only in 1760 that the university was advised by counsel that it had the power to alter or repeal the statutes.[24] In theory the statutes continued in the eighteenth century also to provide a syllabus for a general education in Latin, Greek, rhetoric, grammar, ethics, logic, chemistry, anatomy and law. But only a proportion of these subjects would be taught in college; reliable evidence on readings at Christ Church is provided by its unique surviving Collections Books; but though the tutors might see their pupils as frequently as once or twice a day, their lectures too often provided dull and unimaginative fare. This was true of those given on logic by Johnson's tutor, Jorden, at Pembroke[25] or of those experienced by Bentham at Queen's. Since in addition the cost of an Oxford education had risen faster than the cost of living to reach some £80 to £100 a year by 1750,[26] it is not surprising to find that the numbers of undergraduates matriculating continued to fall away to reach their lowest ebb in the decade 1750–9.[27] Thereafter they began very slowly to recover, though by the end of the century they had still not reached the level of 1700, still less that of 1660 or the early seventeenth century.

Around the middle of the century indeed there seems to have occurred a general breakdown of discipline in several colleges which coincided with an increasing sense of the inadequacy of the courses. Gibbon at Magdalen, Bentham at Queen's, Harris at Merton all testified to their dissatisfaction with their treatment.[28] The tutorials might consist in no more than going over translations from Cicero or other classical authors or Sanderson's *Logic* in classes which tended to be routine. Despite the efforts of the professors of geometry

---

[22] Magrath 1921, II, 87–8; Bennett 1986d, pp. 375–6; for servitors generally see Doolittle 1986, p. 265, Green 1986a, pp. 322–3.

[23] Hodgkin 1949, pp. 117, 132; for Whitefield cf. Bennett 1986d, p. 373.

[24] Ward 1958, pp. 210–11; Sutherland in Sutherland and Mitchell 1986, chap. 7.

[25] Bate 1978, p. 90; for the Christ Church Collection Books see Quarrie 1986, pp. 493–506.

[26] Stone 1975, I, 43. For other estimates cf. Green 1986a, pp. 328–30; Bennett 1986d, pp. 372–3.

[27] Stone 1975, I, 100 (table 8); cf. Green 1986a, p. 309.

[28] Gibbon, in Murray 1896, pp. 62–95 and esp. p. 67; Malmesbury 1844–5, I, p. xi; Bentham 1843, X, 35–45.

(and especially of Edmund Halley of Queen's)[29] and astronomy, science was largely neglected chiefly for lack of funds at the university level and for the absence of lecturers in those subjects in the colleges. In some colleges gentlemen commoners were expected to pass the different stages of their courses like anyone else. But this was not universal, and where they were not so obliged they could idle their time away and set a bad example to the scholars and ordinary commoners.

Nor was the university in a position to supply what the colleges failed to produce. The brave initiative of the Ashmolean Museum in part came to grief because the founder had only provided a salary for the first keeper for the first two years of its existence. The second keeper, Edward Llwyd, drew up a catalogue of the fossils in his collection and managed to secure the publication of the first work on British palaeontology.[30] But he was left to survive for the remaining nineteen years of his life without a salary. Not surprisingly his immediate successors were comparatively unimportant. Chemistry, physics and astronomy were lectured on with more success than natural history. Chemistry lectures were given by a general practitioner, Dr Freind, and another doctor, Frewin, and anatomy lectures by Dr Alcock (*c.* 1737). There were important links between Alcock's pupil and successor, Dr John Smith, Savilian professor of geometry, and the Radcliffe Infirmary, whose physician he became when it opened in 1770.[31] It also seems that Dr Wall, the founder of the Worcester porcelain factory, had learned his furnace chemistry at the Oxford chemistry lectures. Wall also pursued an interest in mineral waters which had been a subject of special interest to the first keeper of the Ashmolean Museum, Dr Plot, and opened up the spa at Malvern as a result. Dr Smith made a special point of testing mineral waters. But the laboratory at the museum, despite its 'furnaces, stills, and sand baths, a great alembic with barrel and worm, an Athanor and a great Reverbatory' was a primitive and hampering affair and there was little room or opportunity to experiment.[32]

The Radcliffe trustees, who had contributed £5,000 to the building of the Radcliffe Quad of University College in the early eighteenth century and had built the Radcliffe Infirmary in 1759–70, in 1772–4 encouraged astronomy by the construction of a fine observatory and a house for the professor who had already been provided with a salary by Savile.[33] Indeed it was a Savilian professor of astronomy, Dr Gregory, who had been struck before 1700 by the need to teach natural philosophy with experiments. As a result lectures on experimental philosophy had been given in Hart Hall in that year by John Keill and later by Desaguliers.[34] The keeper of the Ashmolean, John Whiteside (1680–1729), gave lectures on physics illustrated by experiments. He charged each person attending the course a guinea and a half. On his death James Bradley, the astronomer, and Savilian professor of geometry, bought his equipment and lectured with it at the museum on experimental philosophy until 1760.[35] In the last two decades of the century a return was made to chemistry. Dr Martin Wall, son of Dr Wall of Worcester, as an unpaid reader, lectured on

[29] Turner 1986, pp. 676–7; Halley's papers on terrestrial magnetism were to hold the field for the next 200 years. He persuaded Newton to write the *Principia* and paid for the publication out of his own pocket (Busbridge 1974, pp. 21, 23).

[30] Simcock 1985, p. 7; MacGregor and Turner 1986, pp. 645–7.   [31] Simcock 1984, p. 9.

[32] Simcock 1985, p. 9; an athanor is a furnace in which a constant heat is maintained by means of a self-feeding apparatus. A reverbatory is one whose flames are forced back on to the substance which is exposed to it.

[33] Webster 1986, pp. 707–8; Colvin 1983, p. 77; Turner 1986, pp. 680–1. The Observatory was chiefly by James Wyatt, the house by Keene (cf. Colvin 1986, pp. 849–50).

[34] Turner 1986, pp. 670–2; Simcock 1984, p. 11; Sutherland in Sutherland and Mitchell 1986, pp. 472–3.

[35] Turner 1986, pp. 672–3; Simcock 1984, p. 12.

161 *(opposite) Oxford, the Radcliffe Observatory, 1772–94, designed mainly by James Wyatt, now part of Green College (p. 241)*

162 *Worcester College: the fifteenth-century 'cottages' of Gloucester College or Hall, built by various Benedictine abbeys to house their monks while studying in Oxford: in 1714 they became the nucleus of Worcester College*

the chemical needs of medical students with great success. His laboratory assistant, James Sadler, and Thomas Beddoes gave experimental courses.[36] Those of Beddoes in 1788–92 were especially popular. Sadler distinguished himself by becoming the leading British astronaut and making the first English ascent in a hot air balloon in 1784.[37] But endowment was needed desperately in order to give continuity and hope and this was only achieved with the appointment of the first Aldrichian professor, John Kidd, in 1803.

The University Press found a new home in the Clarendon Building, built to a design by Hawksmoor and named after the author of the *History of the Rebellion*. The Bodleian Library like the Ashmolean continued to show signs of life especially in the closing decades of the century when increasing funds enabled it to make some daring purchases of rare books. But it was the combined attacks on the syllabus and the subscription oaths which showed that the days of the *ancien régime* were numbered. *123*

Two attempts were made to found new colleges in the eighteenth century; Gloucester Hall was refounded as Worcester College and acquired enough endowments to enable it to

---

[36] Turner 1986, pp. 666–7; Simcock 1984 pp. 8–9; Simcock 1985, p. 11.
[37] Turner 1986, pp. 674–5; Simcock 1984, p. 8 and esp. n. 80.

flourish,[38] and Hart Hall under Dr Richard Newton as principal was incorporated as Hertford College in 1739. But the absolute necessity of endowments for halls and colleges if they were to have a reasonable chance of survival was shown by the reconstituted Hertford College, for it expired for lack of them in 1805.[39] Its principal had been convinced of the need for university reform as early as 1720 and tried to put his scheme for it into operation at Hart Hall with weekly disputations twice a week, public lectures on Thursdays and declamations on Saturdays. There were comparable regulations at Lincoln in 1770.

It was the importance of college examinations which convinced Cyril Jackson, dean of Christ Church (1782–1809), that the existing arrangements must be changed. Since Christ Church had never had any statutes it had not been hampered by archaic regulations: it was able to maintain a high standard of college examinations at the end of term, or 'Collections' as they were called. Moreover it could afford five or six tutors, readers and a lecturer in mathematics. It had thus succeeded in spreading the work load and in providing some specialised teaching. Other colleges had often had difficulty in keeping one or two tutors. The existing regulations on celibacy for fellows and the poverty of tutors' stipends tended to ensure that tutors were tempted away when livings fell vacant and offered them the chance of matrimony as well as better pay.

Dissatisfaction was also showing itself over subscription to the Thirty-Nine Articles required of all undergraduates and graduates on admission to the university. The protestant non-conformists who, as well as the Roman Catholics and Jews, were thus excluded were growing increasingly restive. They had many sympathisers within the Church of England. In 1771 an association was formed to petition Parliament for relief.[40] The following year a debate took place in the House on a clerical petition which sought relief. This coincided with agitation against academic subscription in Cambridge and a public campaign in the press. The debate at Oxford swung back to convocation in 1773 when a group supported a proposal that subscription to the Articles at matriculation (that is, on admission) should be abolished. The fact that Cambridge partly got round the difficulty by agreeing that graduates in arts instead of subscribing to the Articles should declare themselves 'bona fide members of the Church of England as by law established' suggested that Oxford despite the support of its chancellor and of the king and a string of powerful Tory M.P.s would not indefinitely be able to maintain its Anglican clerical monopoly.

Cambridge from Bentley to Wordsworth

From 1700 to 1742 Trinity was presided over by Richard Bentley, the most brilliant and original classical scholar of his day – a man of the widest international reputation, who delighted above all in improving the texts of Latin poets and quarrelling with the fellows of Trinity.[41] He lived for war, whether it be with false quantities in Horace, or with his colleagues; and he set such an example that it is scarcely wonderful that Trinity became the notorious home of gentleman layabouts. The Trinity Library had exceptionally liberal

---

[38] Dunbabin 1986, pp. 298–9; Daniel and Barker 1900, pp. 154–81; for the buildings cf. Colvin 1986, pp. 841–2.
[39] Hamilton 1903, pp. 63–96; Green 1986c, pp. 611–13.
[40] Ward 1958, p. 246.   [41] Monk 1830; Brink 1986, chaps. 2–4.

163 *Cambridge, Trinity College.
Richard Bentley: the bust by L.-F.
Roubiliac in the library, 1756*

rules for student readers[42] – but they may have needed it (as other societies did not) to escape from the fellow commoners who haunted the courts.

Dean Nevile, the master of Trinity who created Great Court, had combined to the full the roles of master and dean of Canterbury. In eighteenth-century style, Bentley united many roles in his capacious character. He was royal librarian; he was regius professor of divinity; he was archdeacon of Ely; he was master of Trinity. In his guise as master, he inaugurated forty years of strife by spending large sums of money the fellows had hoped to receive in dividends in refurbishing the Master's Lodge, the last major work of Robert Grumbold.[43] It is overlaid now by what Whewell and Salvin attempted 150 years later, but Bentley's great staircase still records his presence. The Cambridge colleges claimed to share in the exemption of the university from control by the bishop of Ely – a claim securely founded on forged papal bulls – and so the archdeacon had no function to perform in Trinity, nor (for

164

[42] Gaskell and Robson 1971, pp. 33, 36.
[43] Monk 1830, pp. 115–17; Willis and Clark 1886, ii, 610–16.

164 *The staircase in the Master's Lodge, a part of Bentley's improvements, c. 1705 – with portraits of two masters of Trinity, Christopher Wordsworth (William's brother, 1820–41) and William Whewell (1841–66)*

the most part) anywhere else.[44] He won the regius chair by a most ingenious intrigue; he certainly knew more of the textual history of the New Testament than any of his line before Westcott; and the story is told that in the great fire in the Cotton Library in 1731, Bentley personally saved the Codex Alexandrinus.[45] But his most notable exploit as regius was to present 58 candidates simultaneously for the degree of doctor of divinity in celebration of George II's visit to Cambridge in 1728.[46] No one has done more to raise – or to lower – the academic reputation of Cambridge than Bentley; but in his arrogance he regarded all other scholars as men of straw, and in any case what really mattered in early-eighteenth-century Cambridge was the political struggle of Whig and Tory, and this grand gesture added 58 Whig voters to the senate.

They were sorely needed. Outside his own fellowship, Bentley's chief opponents had

[44] On the disreputable origins of the university's exemption, see Hackett 1970, p. 42 n. 2.
[45] Monk 1830, pp. 311–13, 342–8, 577; Winstanley 1935, pp. 111–12.
[46] Monk 1830, pp. 542–3.

165 *The Senate House from the south, mainly of the 1720s (p. 249), designed by James Gibbs with the help of James Burrough*

been the Tory master of St Catharine's, Thomas Sherlock, and Sherlock's brother-in-law the master of Caius, Thomas Gooch.[47] The Tories kept Gooch in office as vice-chancellor for three years, from 1717 to 1720. Among the Tories, Sherlock seems to have been the most intelligent, and he made his name in the wider world for his celebrated attack on Benjamin

[47] Brooke 1985, pp. 163–70 and references cited; on Sherlock, see Carpenter 1936; on their friendship, Curtis 1966.

Hoadly in the Bangorian controversy of the 1710s.[48] From 1715 Sherlock was dean of Chichester and in 1719 he left Cambridge, on the first step in a progress which was to carry him eventually to the bishoprics of Bangor, Salisbury and London (1748–61), and Gooch to Bristol, Norwich and Ely (1748–54). Meanwhile, in the early 1720s, Gooch as vice-chancellor had summoned Bentley to his court for a minor misdemeanour, and on the master of Trinity proving contumacious, had pronounced him stripped of all his degrees. In the end, after almost innumerable delays, Bentley had a judgement in the King's Bench – his favourite forum – declaring Gooch's sentence contrary to natural justice and void; but in the interval he had used it as an excuse for not attending college chapel, and the story is told that when his degrees and his hoods were restored he returned to chapel only to find his pew locked against him.[49] Thus Bentley added lustre to his chair, his college and his university, and reduced the whole academic process to a farce.

It is characteristic of the ironies of academic history that while Gooch and Bentley were bringing the university procedures into disrepute, Gooch and his colleagues were preparing a fine architectural setting for the university itself.[50] The Senate House was begun in the early 1720s to a design worked out by James Gibbs in collaboration with a young colleague of Gooch in Caius called James Burrough. It was originally intended to form one wing of a three-sided court, open to the university church at the east, and Senate House yard (as we now call it) was cleared of a clutter of buildings to prepare for it. But as the shadow of the Senate House moved slowly across the south side of Caius Court, the fellows rebelled, and in 1727 reminded the master of the statute of Dr Caius that the south side of his court should never be closed. Dr Gooch had long since ceased to be vice-chancellor, and took the precaution of retiring to the safe distance of his canonry in Chichester; from there he wrote a stern remonstrance to the university, and threatened – and brought – an action in Chancery to stop the Senate House entirely closing the view. This must have been extremely embarrassing to Burrough, but he was a genial and resourceful man; and years later devised another plan, aided by his disciple James Essex, first a builder, then, under Burrough's tuition, the chief architect of Cambridge in the third quarter of the century. Between them they designed a new eastern range and east front to the Old Schools, intended to harmonise with the still unfinished Senate House. But when they produced this scheme in the early 1750s the Whig Duke of Newcastle was in the first flush of authority as chancellor, and he pushed a rival plan by his favoured architect, James Wright. It was Palladian like the Senate House, but markedly less severe in idiom and adorned with dainty fruit and garlands of leaves. The contrast is a monument to the political battles of the age, for Newcastle was the prince of Whigs, and Burrough a lifelong Tory.[51]

In due course the Senate House was finished by the addition solely of an east front, partly paid for by a legacy from Burrough, and designed by the faithful Essex. The foundation stone for it was laid by Burrough's successor as master of Caius, John Smith, when he was

166 *(opposite) The Senate House, interior, the dais and the vice-chancellor's chair*

168

[48] Carpenter 1936, esp. chap. IV; on Hoadly, see esp. Luckett 1973, pp. 110–14, 131–3. For Sherlock as dean of Chichester see Horn 1971, p. 8.
[49] Monk 1830, pp. 555–6 and 556 n.
[50] For what follows, Willis and Clark 1886, III, 43–71; *RCHM Cambridge*, II, 9–14; Pevsner 1970, pp. 199–203; Brooke 1985, pp. 170–2.
[51] On Newcastle and Cambridge, Winstanley 1922; on Burrough, Brooke 1985, pp. 170–4; Venn, I, 517–18, III, 126–9; Colvin 1978, pp. 168–70; Cocke 1984 (esp. on his relation to Essex).

167 *The Old Schools, east front, by James Wright, 1754–8 (Willis and Clark 1886, III, 66–7), with King's chapel*

168 *The view from Caius Court,*
Gonville and Caius College

vice-chancellor in 1767.[52] The other wing was never built, and the university buildings were already inadequate for their major function, which was to house the University Library. Between 1837 and 1842 C.R. Cockerell built the last major extension before the Library moved in 1934, an inventive neo-Classical building admirable in conception but crowding its neighbours and crushing the Gate of Honour.[53] Still, the view from Caius Court to this day is a curious and fascinating palimpsest of the history of Cambridge. In the middle distance a fragment of the fourteenth-century Regent House still shows, with King's chapel, the greatest of all monuments to the fifteenth and sixteenth, beyond. In the foreground, Dr Caius's Gate of Honour, and his court, link the Renaissance with the Gothic world. To left and right, Senate House and East Front remain a fascinating memorial of the battles of Senate House Yard of the 1720s and the 1750s, with the space between secured

[52] Willis and Clark 1886, III, 69–71.
[53] Willis and Clark 1886, III, 120–1; Pevsner 1970, pp. 203–4.

169 *A chamber in Caius Court: built 1565–9 – the portrait in the recess is of John Caius's mason, Theodore Haveus (p. 162) – probably wainscoted in 1697 (Brooke 1985, p. 156)*

by Dr Gooch and the Court of Chancery. And in the foreground, to the west, Cockerell's library, now the Squire Law Library, a reminder of a victory of academic needs over politics and planning, characteristic of the nineteenth century.

Meanwhile the university prepared in various ways for a life of growing comfort and elegance, and while some became prodigiously idle, for others new opportunities for work and scholarship appeared. Many a college chamber in this age was elegantly wainscoted; and even the tiny community of Magdalene, only taking in five or six students a year, contrived to give its hall the charming panelling and the unusual and elegant stair in 1714; and in 1724 was enriched by the library of Samuel Pepys.[54] In spite of this the reputation of the college did not stand very high; and there is a charming letter from a Caius freshman to Thomas Kerrich, anxiously preparing for his own début in 1767: 'Your opinion that Magdalen[e] is the worst College in the University seems founded upon

170–1

[54] Willis and Clark 1886, II, 366–75; cf. Pevsner 1970, pp. 118–21.

170 (above) Magdalene College, Cambridge, the hall, panelled in 1714, looking north

171 The hall staircase, looking south; the pilasters on the balcony survive from the earlier woodwork of 1585 (Willis and Clarke 1886, II, 381)

172 *Magdalene College, the*
Pepys Library. The building seems
mainly late seventeenth century,
but partly of the sixteenth, partly
of the eighteenth century: the
library came to the college in
1724

prejudice, rather than on reasonable ground. The College is but badly situated, and I think, not overstocked with Undergraduates, but it has one ornament . . . by which it outshines not only all the Colleges here, but perhaps all the Universities of the world' – he is referring to the mathematician, Professor Edward Waring.[55] And indeed, later in the century again, Magdalene was by no means ill-regarded by Henry Gunning. Describing an unusual festivity laid on by a fellow commoner of another college, he observed: 'The evening was passed in a convivial manner, perfectly new to the undergraduates of Magdalene, whose temperate habits and devotion to tea were quite proverbial.'[56]

In extreme old age Henry Gunning, a genial old radical with a caustic pen who had presided over university ceremonial and administration (such as it was) as Esquire Bedell from the year of the French Revolution, 1789, to his death in 1854, sat down to write his *Reminiscences*.[57] By the time when he wrote, the university had passed into a new world; Prince Albert was chancellor, the first royal commission had met and reported, and the

[55] Venn 1913, p. 244. Waring was Lucasian professor 1760–98, and fellow of Magdalene, 1758–76 (*DNB*; *DSB*, XIV, 179–81 (J.F. Scott)).   [56] Gunning 1854, I, 39.
[57] Gunning 1854; on its genesis see Bartholomew 1912.

173 *Two of the three Esquire Bedells' maces given by the Duke of Buckingham when he was chancellor, 1626–8 (Cambridge Plate, p. 11, no. M2). One or other was carried for many years by Henry Gunning*

dedication of his book to George Peacock and Adam Sedgwick is a reminder of how great some of the changes had been. Gunning himself stated firmly at the outset that he was no *laudator temporis acti*: 'On the contrary, I believe the time I came to College [1784] to have been (with the exception of six or seven years preceding) the very worst part of our history. Drunkenness being the besetting sin of that period, I need scarcely add that many other vices followed in its train' – but more incredible to his readers, he reckoned, was the unscrupulous behaviour of examiners, who 'for the sake of making money' assigned 'the highest honours . . . not on *the most deserving*, but upon those who had been fortunate enough to avail themselves of their instruction as *Private Tutors*!'[58] And he goes on to describe his own arrival at Christ's, where 'The number of admissions . . . in my year was only three; two of the men professed not to read, and I was ignorant of the first Proposition in Euclid.' His tutor Parkinson was entangled in an unlucky engagement, and having missed the mastership was not free to marry; and this made him elusive and abrupt. But after Gunning had lost heart altogether and given up the intention of serious reading,

[58] Gunning 1854, I, pp. xix–xx.

Parkinson suddenly invited him to breakfast, gave him kindly advice and helped him on the way to reform. Characteristically, however, it was much more the company that he kept than his tutor who helped him to serious reading and a tolerable degree.[59]

Gunning's denunciation of the 1780s as 'the very worst part of our history' was for nearly a century a commonplace; and although some efforts have been made in recent years to rehabilitate the eighteenth-century universities – and although it has long been known that serious study was possible – it is hard to understand why Cambridge could attract such a number of able and remarkable young men as it did in the 1780s. Gunning himself became a hard-reading man and sixth Wrangler, and he made friends, not only with other reading men in Christ's and among the better set in Trinity, but also with the Senior Wrangler of 1788, now a fellow of Caius, John Brinkley, who was shortly to leave for Ireland where he became professor of astronomy in Dublin and, many years later, Bishop of Cloyne – one of the most eminent astronomers of his day and Copley Medallist of the Royal Society.[60] Brinkley was a man who combined the mathematical-scientific bent which formed the chief character of such academic life as flourished in Cambridge at this time, with the clerical bent which gave the university its main vocation. For the paradox was that as the university became increasingly clerical in the late seventeenth and eighteenth centuries, so theology ceased to be its most flourishing subject – and eventually a serious subject at all – and was overtaken by mathematics; and the one major academic reform of the eighteenth century was the establishment of the mathematical tripos as a seriously competitive enterprise: from the middle of the century the hard-reading men competed with ever growing zeal for the position of Senior Wrangler.[61] The tests were still by public disputation and argument more than by examination (hence 'wrangler'), and relatively few competed seriously; but the examination gradually took on a leading role and for the hard-reading men there was a strenuous course in many subjects, literary and scientific, with mathematics as the crown, and an ample supply of private tutors and private rivals. Meanwhile, though theology languished, there were genuine clerical influences too, of which the most conspicuous to us is the evangelical, which flourished first in Magdalene, then in Queens' under Isaac Milner, president from 1788 to 1820, Lucasian professor and dean of Carlisle, and the leading evangelical in Cambridge.[62] Gunning had a great dislike of Tories and low churchmen, yet he reluctantly admits that Queens' increased in numbers under Milner:

but the majority of them were men who, in those days, were termed *Methodists*, afterwards *Calvinists*, and then *Serious Christians*. Previously . . . these Low-Church doctrines had been entirely confined to Magdalene College. I have heard Dr Gretton . . . [master of Magdalene 1797–1813] declare, he thought there must be something in the air of Magdalene that made men Methodists; 'for', said he, 'we have elected Fellows from Clare Hall, from Trinity, and other Colleges, whom we have considered to be most Anti-methodistical, but in a short time they all became Methodists'.[63]

Gunning's prejudices thinly disguise one of the powerful forces working in Cambridge at the turn of the eighteenth and nineteenth centuries.

[59] Gunning 1854, I, 6–12, etc.
[60] Gunning 1854, I, 17, 87–91; cf. Brooke 1985, pp. 185–6; Venn, II, 107–8; *DNB*; *DSB*, II, 468–9 (Susan M.P. McKenna).
[61] Gascoigne 1983; *VCH Cambs*, III, 227–9; Winstanley 1935, pp. 49–57; Wordsworth 1877.
[62] On Milner see Twigg 1987, pp. 159, 161, 170–8, 181–3 and colour plate 5B.
[63] Gunning 1854, I, 262–3. Gunning uses 'methodist' in its unspecific sense – as we should say, evangelical – not of a denomination: only Anglicans could be full senior members of the university.

To Cambridge in the 1780s, besides Brinkley and Gunning, came also William Wordsworth. It had long been the home of poets, and Thomas Gray had died fellow of Pembroke and professor of history not long before. Wordsworth came to St John's, a college noted for its north countrymen, where his uncle was a fellow; it was one of the few colleges which had grown and flourished since 1760, under the reforming master W.S. Powell (1765–75).[64] And Wordsworth had been exceedingly well grounded in mathematics at Hawkshead. But he cared little for the clerical life of Cambridge – though he was to be a fervent Anglican in later years – and nothing for the fellows, save his uncle, who departed to a country living in 1788; and he rapidly lost interest in mathematics. By a curious logic he determined that, if he was not to be a mathematician, to follow any other serious course of reading would displease his family – and so he read for pleasure only, discursively but deeply, in English literature and Italian and a little Latin; he discovered that a devout lover of nature – even as he sighed for the hills – could find much of delight to him in the flat meadows and fens of Cambridgeshire.[65] The vision of Cambridge in *The Prelude* is a distillation of eccentric genius out of a thousand commonplace impressions, and so tells more than any journeyman could of the excitement and anxiety that so many thousands have known at their first coming. As the carriage rolled down Castle Hill and dropped him at the Hoop Inn by St John's he looked with intense imagination at the folk about him, sought out his friends, set himself energetically to join the throng:

> I was the Dreamer, they the Dream; I roamed
> Delighted through the motley spectacle;
> Gowns grave, or gaudy, doctors, students, streets,
> Courts, cloisters, flocks of churches, gateways, towers:
> Migration strange for a stripling of the hills,
> A northern villager.
> As if the change
> Had waited on some Fairy's wand, at once
> Behold me rich in moneys, and attired
> In splendid garb, with hose of silk, and hair
> Powdered like rimy trees, when frost is keen.
> My lordly dressing gown, I pass it by,
> With other signs of manhood that supplied
> The lack of beard.[66] – The weeks went roundly on,
> With invitations, suppers, wine and fruit,
> Smooth housekeeping within, and all without
> Liberal, and suiting gentleman's array.
> The Evangelist St John my patron was:
> Three Gothic courts are his, and in the first
> Was my abiding-place, a nook obscure;
> Right underneath, the College kitchens made
> A humming sound, less tuneable than bees,
> But hardly less industrious; with shrill notes
> Of sharp command and scolding intermixed.
> Near me hung Trinity's loquacious clock,
> Who never let the quarters, night or day,

---

[64] Miller 1961, pp. 64–8.   [65] Moorman 1957, chap. IV.

[66] Wordsworth in fact lived – quite comfortably it seems – on a Foundress's scholarship and the allowances his uncles gave him: see Moorman 1957, pp. 92, 124.

174   *Cambridge, Trinity College, ante-chapel, statue of Isaac Newton by L.-F. Roubiliac, 1755 (Willis and Clark 1886, II, 600)*

Slip by him unproclaimed, and told the hours
Twice over with a male and female voice.
Her pealing organ was my neighbour too;
And from my pillow, looking forth by light
Of moon or favouring stars, I could behold
The antechapel where the statue stood
Of Newton with his prism and silent face,
The marble index of a mind for ever
Voyaging through strange seas of Thought, alone.
   Of College labours, of the Lecturer's room
All studded round, as thick as chairs could stand,
With loyal students faithful to their books,
Half-and-half idlers, hardy recusants,
And honest dunces – of important days,
Examinations, when the man was weighed
As in a balance! of excessive hopes,
Tremblings withal and commendable fears,
Small jealousies, and triumphs good or bad,
Let others that know more speak as they know.
Such glory was but little sought by me,
And little won . . .[67]

[67] Wordsworth, *Prelude* (1850 edn). III, 30–75.

10 Cambridge and Oxford 1800–1920

Upon beholding the masses of buildings at Oxford, devoted to what they call '*learning*', I could not help reflecting on the drones that they contain and the wasps they send forth.

William Cobbett, *Rural Rides* (1830), quoted in the *Oxford Literary Guide to the British Isles*, ed. D. Eagle and H. Carnell, Oxford, 1977, p. 259

A father to his son's tutor in Cambridge
I do not understand the tenour of your communication. When I was an undergraduate at Queens' [c. 1808–11] it would have been accounted a disgrace to the college if any man had been present in hall on a Newmarket day.

CC, p. 173, quoting A. G. Bradley, *Our Centenarian Grandfather*, London, 1922, p. 48

The Cambridge of Hopkins and Whewell

On 11 February 1766 William Cole wrote to Horace Walpole: 'At Cambridge they seem to be going mad. Last week a grace was actually prepared in the Senate House in order to petition the Parliament for leave that the Fellows of colleges might marry' – and he went on to suggest that the scheme would reduce the fellows to beggary, the colleges to hospitals for the poor, the university to discredit.[1] He need not have worried. The rule that fellows might not marry, based on an edict of Elizabeth I of 1561, enshrined in the university statutes of 1570 and in many college statutes too, was not breached until 1860, and not finally swept away till the 1880s. These dates are a paradigm of reform in Cambridge. There were many schemes for reform, many reformers, even a few reforms. Cambridge in 1880 was a very different place from Cambridge in 1780. Yet if we look at the profound changes which have created the university and colleges we know today, most of them began in the late nineteenth century, few of them before 1870.

Four seem to us especially fundamental. The admission of women in a formal sense came to Cambridge in 1948 – extraordinary as it now seems that even Cambridge could stand against the tide of events and movements and reasonable opinion so long. But Girton was founded in 1869 and moved to Cambridge in 1873, and Newnham was already established in 1871: in both cases the name came later – but the seed was sown.[2] In 1871 by Act of Parliament the Test Act was abolished for Oxford and Cambridge: all degrees and fellowships – save those tied by special provision to clerical posts, as deans of chapel and the

---

[1] CC, p. 151. For what follows see Brooke 1985, pp. 68–9, 223–7 and references. The statute of 1570 (*Documents* 1852, 1, 493) strictly applied to *fellows*, and heads of houses reckoned themselves exempt from it; though some heads were bidden to celibacy by college statutes which were gradually amended or abandoned.

[2] Bradbrook 1969; Hamilton 1936.

like – were thrown open to non-Anglicans.[3] In 1871 the chancellor, William Cavendish, seventh Duke of Devonshire, made a gift which enabled the Cavendish Laboratory to be built, and the provision by the university of central facilities for research and teaching in the natural sciences was under way.[4] In the late 1870s and early 1880s the second of the great royal commissions compelled the colleges to make provision for this central teaching, a compulsion more happily received in some colleges than others. The master and fellows of Emmanuel, seizing time by the forelock, endowed the Dixie professorship of ecclesiastical history.[5] The master of Caius, preaching in Great St Mary's on Easter Day, 1882, denounced the commission: 'I am constrained to say that in my judgement . . . the changes of which we shall shortly be spectators may take as their motto, "I am not come to fulfil but to destroy".'[6] But in the same college, as in many by this date, a fresh wind of change was blowing, and moves were afoot not only to aid the university but to restore the almost moribund teaching function of the college – and this change has made the colleges great centres of teaching and learning once again.

None of the changes is yet complete. Great university laboratories and central facilities of all kinds now abound, far beyond the wildest dreams of the seventh Duke and his Cambridge advisers; but there is still a sprinkling of faculties with a very modest share in them. The colleges notionally contribute to the university, but in fact a greater divide separates the two than is readily grasped by those outside Cambridge, greater far than in Oxford. And the Cambridge tutor still does not teach: he has a pastoral, moral, administrative function; he makes a merit of not teaching. Cambridge has had to devise a new word for what the rest of the British universities call the 'tutorial' – the supervision; for individual tuition has in fact come to Cambridge as much as to Oxford and is the most notable contribution of the nineteenth century to its teaching methods. But the role of the Cambridge tutor – however much or however little it may be defended and admired – is a reminder that it was not in the colleges that the new traditions of personal tuition were born. And as for women, no one who contemplates the high tables or the faculty boards of Cambridge in the 1980s could suppose for a moment that they have achieved equality of opportunity.

Still, great changes have occurred, and it is the business of this chapter to discern and explain them. The resistance of the colleges to change has been powerful – not universal, not continuous, for they have contained many enlightened and radical folk, though it has often been observed that a man can be radical in principle and in politics, and deeply conservative in the affairs of his club or his college. But the story is naturally full of false alarms and false starts; full of ironies and absurdities; and yet within the colleges we may discern the seeds of change.

The whole story has been obscured by the tendency to concentrate on the large colleges and ignore the small.[7] Trinity and St John's down to the middle of the nineteenth century recruited half the freshmen in Cambridge between them; and even if we allow for a liberal

---

[3] Winstanley 1947, chap. III.
[4] Winstanley 1947, pp. 194–8.
[5] Winstanley 1947, pp. 328–9; cf. Chadwick 1984.
[6] Winstanley 1947, pp. 358–9; for what follows, Brooke 1985, chap. 12.
[7] This tendency was already visible in Winstanley's later books – see Winstanley 1940, esp. pp. 384–5, and comments in Brooke 1985, p. 189 and n. 4, on Winstanley's influence on, for example, Garland 1980. The variety of the colleges, and (until recently at least) the inaccessibilty of many of their archives, have tempted students to concentrate on the few.

sprinkling of well-to-do layabouts in both, and especially among the fellow commoners of Trinity, the eminence and distinction of these two colleges are also undeniable. But let us spread our view a little more widely.

Peterhouse in the early nineteenth century languished under the mastership of Dr Barnes. He had been chosen in 1787, and he remained Master till his death at the age of 95 in 1838.[8] Peterhouse was one of the colleges where free election was not yet known: the fellows put up two candidates to the bishop of Ely, their founder's successor, who chose between them. The fellows ingeniously offered Dr Barnes as a man of straw, hoping the bishop would appoint their favoured candidate, George Borlase. The bishop, who had been thwarted in his original design of appointing a protégé, after a wrangle in the courts, appointed Barnes. Why he was reckoned so unsuitable a candidate is not now quite clear: he was instrumental in the election of his defeated rival to the Knightbridge professorship of moral theology in 1788 and himself succeeded to the chair in 1813; neither of them gave any lectures that we know of – but that was not the custom. None the less the college tradition has it that he was a mere abuse. Yet the society in his later years contained two of the central figures in the revival of teaching in the university in the early and mid nineteenth century, William Hopkins and Charles Babbage.

Henry Gunning recorded with pleasure in his *Reminiscences* the appointment as Esquire Bedells in 1826–7 of George Leapingwell and William Hopkins, who between them generously performed his own share of the office after he became incapacitated. And he went on with pride to talk of Hopkins.

Soon after [his] election he commenced taking pupils, and his success as a private tutor has, probably, been unparalleled. Being desirous of learning precisely the number of his pupils who had obtained distinguished honours on the Mathematical Tripos, he sent, at my particular request, the following reply to my inquiry: –

    'Dear Gunning.

From January 1828 to January 1849, inclusive, i.e. in twenty-two years, I have had among my pupils 175 Wranglers. Of these, 108 have been in the *first ten*, 44 in the *first three*, and 17 have been *Senior Wranglers*.

Yours very truly,

Dec.4, 1849   W. Hopkins.'[9]

Hopkins was a brilliant teacher, though not to every man's taste – John Venn in the 1850s complained that his classes were too large for effective tuition.[10] But he certainly did more than any man to raise the standards of mathematical teaching in Cambridge and he passed on the baton to his pupil Isaac Todhunter, who lived till 1884. The importance of Hopkins's work becomes clear when we contemplate Venn's account of college teaching as it was in Caius in the 1850s. There were college lectures, 'but then we had none but these. The inter-collegiate system was as yet unknown; in fact I am in the habit of priding myself on the claim of having been the first to introduce it in the University, some fifty years ago, in my own department of the Moral Sciences . . . The elder Mr Weller, you may remember, rather prided himself on the educational advantages which he had conferred upon his

---

[8] Winstanley 1935, pp. 283–95 – also for what follows; and cf. Walker 1935, pp. 99 ff. It seems likely, however, that Barnes's reputation has suffered excessively owing to the manner of his appointment.

[9] Gunning 1854, II, 358–9.

[10] *Caian*, XXXI (1922–3), 110–11; Brooke 1985, p. 220. On the private tutors and coaches, see Winstanley 1940, pp. 411–12.

better-known son; he had, he said, just let him run about the streets and pick up information for himself. The College authorities of my day adopted a somewhat similar plan.' The tutor did not lecture, and the college lectures were fairly perfunctory. 'We selected our coaches by mutual advice and comparison; we decided for ourselves what line of studies we would follow.'[11] This seems to have been pretty generally the practice. Thus even in Trinity, where the tutors sometimes took a quite different view of their tasks from Venn's tutor in Caius, there is a significant contrast between the record of the young William Whewell as a very ardent and assiduous private coach in 1817–18, and his later reputation as an impatient and neglectful tutor of Trinity.[12] Unlike the Oxford tutors, the official tutors of Cambridge failed to preserve or restore their character as the foremost teachers in the university; and it was Hopkins and his like who created the tradition of Cambridge supervision.

William Hopkins was also a scientist of some distinction, who wrote on the motions of glaciers – a theoretical investigation, not, as one might suppose, a satire on the university he served. But the real content of the mathematics he taught – and the movement which brought the English universities back into the main stream of continental development in mathematics – was provided by Woodhouse, Babbage and Peacock; Whewell and Herschel were among the eminent men who opened the wider vistas of natural science in their generation.[13] Robert Woodhouse was a fellow of Caius and the founder of nineteenth-century mathematics in Cambridge; as Lucasian and Plumian professor in the 1820s he taught and handed on the mantle to many younger teachers. As an original scientist and teacher, he was perhaps less brilliant than Charles Babbage, Hopkins's colleague in Peterhouse, founder of nineteenth-century mechanics and inventor, in effect, of the calculating machine. Thus far, Peterhouse and Caius; but their achievement cannot be understood – nor anything of nineteenth-century Cambridge – without a visit to Trinity and St John's. In Trinity we find George Peacock, a man of many parts.[14] In 1812 he had formed with Woodhouse, Babbage and John Herschel – the great hereditary astronomer who was perhaps the most brilliant of all these mathematicians and scientists – an analytical society which was the forum for their discussions and investigations, which were to provide new content for the mathematical tripos. In 1815 he became lecturer in mathematics in Trinity and for a while genuinely taught the subject. In the 1830s he became in rapid succession Lowndean professor of astronomy and dean of Ely; and it is an interesting comment on the problems of reform that while his *Observations on the Statutes of the University of Cambridge* of 1841 were remarkably astute and enlightened – and earned him his place on the first royal commission on the university – he felt no need to resign his chair when he became dean and was roundly accused of treating it in his last years as a sinecure.[15] As dean he wisely sought the advice of Robert Willis of Caius, now Jacksonian professor of natural philosophy, which had meant to Jackson the study of gout and meant to Willis mechanical engineering: Willis was the foremost architectural historian of his day

---

[11] Venn 1913, p. 263.

[12] Clark 1900, pp. 22–4.

[13] Winstanley 1940, pp. 157–60; Garland 1980, chap. 3; *DSB*, I, 354–6 (N.T. Gridgeman on Babbage); XIV, 500 (E. Koppelman on Woodhouse); Brooke 1985, pp. 194–5; Ball 1889, chap. vii.

[14] See *DSB*, X, 437–8 (E. Koppelman); *DNB* and references in n. 13 above. See also Peacock's *Observations on the Statutes* (Cambridge, 1841).

[15] Winstanley 1940, p. 177.

175 *William Wilkins in Cambridge: Downing College, designed in 1805: the hall, built 1818–21*

– and Peacock will be remembered by all who contemplate the octagon and the lantern of Ely cathedral as the dean who called in George Gilbert Scott to restore them.[16]

Most of Sir John Herschel's work was done outside Cambridge; not so that of his fellow Johnian J.S. Henslow, who joined the great geologist Adam Sedgwick in founding the Cambridge Philosophical Society, and was professor of botany from 1827 to 1861.[17] In 1828 Charles Darwin embarked on a career of idleness as an undergraduate at Christ's. But although by his own account 'my time was sadly wasted there', he made some acquaintance with Sedgwick and friendship with Henslow, who imparted his own enthusiasm for natural history and botany, set him on a course of serious reading, and recommended him for appointment to the *Beagle*. Both professors lived to see the apotheosis of their young protégé with the publication of *The Origin of Species* in 1859 – and Sedgwick characteristically to welcome it in a series of letters to the author as the work of a promising pupil who had not turned out too well.[18]

In 1823 Robert Woodhouse was compelled to relinquish his fellowship at Caius when he married Harriet Wilkins, sister of his friend William Wilkins, who had also been a fellow of Caius from 1803 till 1811.[19] In his own way Wilkins is as significant a figure as

[16] On Willis see Brooke 1985, pp. 203–5 and references, especially to Willis and Clark 1886, and Clark's *DNB* article on him; on Willis and Clark see the centenary article by David Watkin in the *Cambridge Review*, CVII (1986), 68–70. On the restoration of Ely, see Pevsner 1970, pp. 342, 347, and the detailed studies of Phillip Lindley, esp. '"Carpenter's Gothic" and Gothic carpentry: contrasting attitudes to the restoration of the Octagon and removals of the Choir at Ely Cathedral', *Architectural History*, XXX (1987), pp. 83–112.

[17] Winstanley, 1940, pp. 32–40 (Henslow) and index, s.v. Sedgwick; for Henslow also *DSB*, VI, 288–9 (M.V. Mathew); for Sedgwick *DSB*, XII, 275–9 (M.J.S. Rudwick), Clark and Hughes 1890.   [18] Garland 1980, pp. 105–12.

[19] Brooke 1985, p. 194, cf. pp. 192–3; on Wilkins see Liscombe 1980; Colvin 1978, pp. 893–6.

Woodhouse, and his work is certainly a great deal more visible today. In early life he was both fellow of Caius and headmaster of the Perse School; and meanwhile he was travelling round the Mediterranean engaged in the architectural, archaeological studies which inspired his later work. In 1805 his work as junior dean of Caius and master of the Perse was overwhelmed by his appointment as architect to Downing and Haileybury. He rapidly became the most successful architect in Cambridge; and although his later years saw many disappointments, no other single architect has laid his hand so firmly on the city: he designed Downing in the Classical taste, the screens of King's and the chapel of Corpus in

177

177 *Corpus Christi College, Cambridge, the New Court, designed in 1822–7, and the chapel, where Wilkins is buried*

the Gothic – and the main buildings of King's, and the new courts of Corpus and Trinity, in his characteristic adaptation of a Gothic taste to the collegiate needs of Cambridge. Nor was he the only architect who flourished in this era: for in the 1830s Rickman and Hutchinson filled one end of the Backs with the Gothic fantasy of St John's new building; and between 1821 and 1832 Sidney was almost completely remodelled by Wyatville.[20]

This explosion of building reflects the first great surge in numbers in the university: between 1800 and 1825 numbers rose almost threefold.[21] Then they were steadier for a while: the next steep climb in the 1860s and 1870s ushered in the age of Alfred Waterhouse. On both occasions it is very noticeable that the steep increase in demand for places in Cambridge was well under way before the serious reforms in university and

[20] Pevsner 1970, pp. 151–2, 158–60; Willis and Clark 1886, II, 746–9. On the architects, Colvin 1978, pp. 442, 688–93, 959–63.
[21] Venn, III, chart following p. 392. For Porson (later in this paragraph), see esp. Brink 1986, chap. 6.

college teaching of these epochs. It was only in the 1820s that professors began seriously to lecture, or were commonly of the eminence of Woodhouse, Babbage, Henslow or Sedgwick. Richard Porson had conferred lustre on Cambridge as regius professor of Greek between 1792 and 1808, but he did so from the safe distance of London. It was only in the 1870s that intercollegiate teaching, and widespread effective college teaching, got under way. The charts of rising numbers strongly suggest that the pressure for reform came largely from below: that the undergraduates demanded teaching, and the university was shocked into compliance.

We must not exaggerate the matter. Of the motives of most of the entrants to Cambridge in the early nineteenth century we know little – and it would be quite contrary to much of what we do know to suppose that most of them came to study. A competitive tripos had existed since the mid eighteenth century.[22] But if we ask, When did it become an almost universal ambition to do tolerably well in the tripos? the answer lies after 1950. Nor can pressure from below explain the genius of Herschel, the enthusiasm of Henslow, the massive influence of Sedgwick – or, still less, the scientific revolution of the later nineteenth century. But there is something in it none the less. There was an extraordinary concentration of young talent in Cambridge in the period 1800–30, and it needed to be satisfied. The two central events of the 1820s were the formation of the Apostles and of the University Boat Club.[23] At first the Apostles was only one among a group of discussion and debating societies; it was the generation of Frederick Denison Maurice in the 1830s, and the apostolic succession of Henry Sidgwick in the 1850s and 1860s, which made it a major element for a time in the intellectual history of Cambridge – a meeting-place indeed of older as well as younger Apostles; but generally governed by undergraduates, however powerful the influence of their elders. Sidgwick defined its central quality as 'a belief that we *can* learn, and a determination that we *will* learn, from people of the most opposite opinions'.[24] Though it has sometimes been given the opposite character – of a forcing house of a particular model of student opinion – the characteristics Sidgwick named have certainly dominated it in many periods of its history, and explain something of the influence wielded by a notoriously secret society. We must not exaggerate this: the Apostles are exceptionally well documented; but their society was one among many – one characteristic way in which the young have lived up to their vocation of teaching their elders. The young sought out William Hopkins if they wanted to shine in the tripos; they met in intellectual societies if they wanted to improve the world or only their own minds. Frederick Denison Maurice preached within the Society and later from many rostrums and pulpits the intellectual earnestness which was one of the major impulses of the Victorian age. But his was not the only impulse of the Cambridge of the 1820s and 1830s: the well-to-do, like young Darwin, hunted and shot; and organised sport made its first appearance in the boat clubs.

The age of reform impinged on Cambridge in so many ways – in the political interests of young and old, in the themes discussed, in the proposals for change and improvement of every kind, in the growing habit among professors of lecturing – that it is difficult for us to grasp how conservative Cambridge remained. The university and most of the colleges lived under statutes of the sixteenth century or earlier, some of them treated with fundamentalist respect, some totally ignored, many not at all understood. The men who presided over

[22] See p. 257 above.   [23] Allen 1978; cf. Brooke 1985, p. 190.   [24] Allen 1978, p. 4.

178 *William Whewell: the bust by T. Woolner, 1872, in the ante-chapel, Trinity College, Cambridge (Willis and Clark 1886, II, 602)*

major projects for university reform, like Dr Whewell, the master of Trinity, or Dr Philpott, the master of St Catharine's, saw no reason for change within the walls of their colleges.[25] Whewell was master of Trinity through the first royal commission and general revision of statutes in the 1850s, and saw to it that Trinity emerged virtually unmoved. The college was recruiting men of the most varied and original talent, who organised a movement for reform after his death which emerged in the draft statutes of 1872 – draft and abortive, since the new royal commission was in the wind and the Privy Council refused to ratify them.[26] But the movement is a remarkable revelation of what Whewell had kept in check. St Catharine's in the late nineteenth century was to be a backwater presided over by the unfortunate C.K. Robinson, who became master in 1861 by voting for himself.[27] This had been normal practice – Dr Philpott had done the same. But in 1861 new standards in such matters prevailed: Mr Robinson became the victim of conflict between the atmosphere of the 1860s and an archaic constitution Dr Philpott had failed to reform, and his defeated rival was able to raise a fearful scandal. The mingling of new movements and ideas with an extreme conservatism explains some of the paradoxes. One 'infamous slanderer', as J.W. Clark called him, wrote a letter to the press in 1836 suggesting that Cambridge was sluggish, and inspired Adam Sedgwick to a characteristic reply:

It is most strange that in a letter on the present state of Cambridge no notice should be taken of the noble institutions which have of late years risen up within it; of the glories of its Observatory; of the

[25] Winstanley 1940, pp. 190–6, 344–72, *passim*; Rich 1973, pp. 168–86.
[26] Winstanley 1947, chap. VI.   [27] Winstanley 1947, chap. I; cf. Rich 1973, pp. 164–7, 204 ff.

179 *The Fitzwilliam Museum, façade, by George Basevi, 1835–45, with the pediment designed by Charles Eastlake; the sculpture executed by W. G. Nicholl. The museum was completed by C. R. Cockerell and E. M. Barry: substantial additions have been made in the twentieth century*

newly-chartered body, the Philosophical Society . . .; of the new Collections in Natural History; of the magnificent new Press [the Pitt building]; of the new School and Museum of Comparative Anatomy; of the noble extension of the collegiate buildings . . .; of the general spirit of inquiry pervading the members of the academic body, young and old; . . . of the general activity of the professors, and of their correspondence with foreign establishments organized for objects like their own, whereby Cambridge is now, at least, an integral part of the vast republic of literature and science . . .[28]

Yet John Venn, looking back at the 1850s, could say that the provision for natural science – outside the medical schools, outside the Geological Museum called after Sedgwick himself – 'was a small table, such as two people might take their tea at'. With its help Professor Stokes, the Lucasian professor – later Sir George – lectured on optics.[29] But at least there was from 1849 a natural sciences tripos.

If Sedgwick had written his catalogue of marvels twenty years later, a conspicuous item would have been the Fitzwilliam Museum: founded by bequest of Lord Fitzwilliam in 1816,

[28] Clark 1900, p. 16.   [29] Venn 1913, pp. 263–4.

housed at first in the Perse School in Free School Lane, then virtually redundant, rehoused in the 1840s and 1850s in a palatial building begun to the designs of George Basevi (1834–7) and completed by C.R. Cockerell and E.M. Barry.[30] Here the collection of pictures and artefacts was arranged by Thomas Worsley, master of Downing, in 1848–9. In 1855 William Whewell, as vice-chancellor, presided over a modest scheme of redecoration, and took it on himself to rearrange the pictures to his taste, partly to do more justice (as he thought) to the schools of painting best represented, partly so that he could hide behind decorous curtains in the remotest gallery the Fitzwilliam's fine series of Venetian nudes. It was a characteristic act of tactless self-assertion; always impulsive and energetic, he could engage in radical activity without warning, while resisting all reforms except his own.

178   William Whewell united in a single massive personality most of the impulses of this world. In his later years he was celebrated for his stern aloofness, a withdrawn figure who hardly knew the younger fellows of Trinity, and despised those he did; who as a tutor had been brusque in manner and perfunctory in his duty to the students.[31] It is not surprising that he was unpopular, though it is strange to learn that a Victorian vice-chancellor could be persistently hooted at in the Senate House. As J.W. Clark observed in his perceptive memoir, 'He was not naturally a reformer.'[32] Yet he was at the centre of many of the new movements of his day.

He was a man of intense intellectual curiosity, and his interests spread from theology through the history and philosophy of science (to which his contributions have lasting value), to mineralogy, of which he was for a time professor, to branches of natural science almost beyond counting, and the history of medieval art. One of his most characteristic monuments is Whewell's Court at Trinity, in exquisite Tudor Gothic executed by Anthony Salvin, reflecting the romantic, medieval Whewell who had enjoyed many visits and discussions with Robert Willis. His scientific treatises show something of the mixture of self-will and prodigious intellectual energy which marked him. He sped from science to science propounding daring and original ideas in each. His books tended to have large and glaring faults, but they were a powerful stimulus. We should naturally expect to find him in the forefront of the plans to introduce natural sciences into the Cambridge curriculum; and he was indeed at the head of the final charge, the syndicate which promoted the triposes in moral and natural sciences in the late 1840s; but only after years of resistance and counter-suggestion, and bewildering changes of view.[33]

He had been bred in the mathematical tripos and accepted it as the best of all educations. He joined in measures to improve it, and convert the old rhetorical exercises into nineteenth-century written examinations. He was prepared to see other disciplines infiltrated into it a certain distance. He accepted the classical tripos, which came at last in 1822, and the modest and voluntary theological examination, which followed twenty years later.[34] But when other triposes were mooted his first instinct was to insist that candidates for honours in them should have a grounding in mathematics first. In his heart

[30] Willis and Clark 1886, III, 198–229; *RCHM Cambridge*, I, 18–22; Pevsner 1970, pp. 210–11. On Basevi, Colvin 1978, pp. 93–5.

[31] The best general account of Whewell is still Clark 1900, pp. 1–76; for very valuable studies of him as master and as a scientist see Robson 1967, Robson and Cannon, 1964; see also Winstanley 1940, index.

[32] Clark 1900, p. 17; cf. Winstanley 1940, chap. IX.

[33] See n. 31 above; Winstanley 1940, pp. 208–13; Clark 1900, pp. 66–8.

[34] Winstanley 1940, pp. 65–71, 169–74, 208–13; Clark 1900, pp. 66–8.

he regarded the Trinity Wrangler as the summit of creation – much as many of the best minds groomed in Oxford up to a century later viewed the products of Greats.

A devout piety towards the traditions of Cambridge and Trinity and a deep respect for German professors were characteristically mingled in Whewell's mind. This may, a little, have reflected his respect for authority and hierarchy in academic affairs, but it was a genuine perception of the prestige and achievement of the German universities from one who had some first-hand knowledge of them. In 1847 he had the inspired idea of nominating Prince Albert, the Prince Consort, as chancellor – a most unlikely candidate in many ways, for he had studied education in Germany as well as in England, and knew far more of the German universities than most British academics. In the event he was only elected by a narrow majority.[35] In alliance with his Cambridge friends he set to work to play more than the purely ceremonial role which the office had gradually been acquiring. His strength lay in his serious interest in university reform and his friendly relations with Whewell and Philpott and other leading figures. His weakness was an excessive reverence for Cambridge traditions, which prevented him pushing his friends into making the university reform itself. With his encouragement the university embarked on triposes for moral and natural sciences – philosophy and natural science as we should say; but Whewell and his like, in Cambridge as in Oxford, were quite unprepared for the more serious reform on which enlightened opinion in the country at large was determined. So Parliament, led by Lord John Russell, insisted on the setting up of the first royal commission in 1849–50. But it included George Peacock, Adam Sedgwick and Sir John Herschel, and Goldwin Smith of Oxford, and the commissioners still sought a method of reform inspired from within, and regarded their aims as modest.[36]

This was not at all the view taken of it by many in Cambridge. The vice-chancellor, Dr Corrie, master of Jesus, opposed innovation in every sphere of life, and reckoned the commission unconstitutional – claiming high legal authority for his stand, and refusing to answer any of the commissioners' questions. The answers were quietly furnished by less recalcitrant colleagues. The master of Caius, Dr Chapman, answered their enquiries 'under a strong and earnest protest', and refused to let the commissioners see the statutes of Dr Caius which governed the college. Caius himself had taken a less secretive view and had furnished an official copy to Archbishop Parker, so the commissioners were able to study and print the statutes from the copy at Lambeth. Whewell, who had tried to place himself at the head of every major syndicate planning university reform, took a stern view of interference with his college – offering indeed 'every assistance in my power' – but only so far as 'is consistent with my duty to the College and the University' – which he made clear was distinctly limiting.[37] By slow and painful stages the commission did its work. From its report in 1852 stemmed new statutes for the university, and statutory commissioners were appointed to discuss with every college the revision of its statutes. By 1860–1 the process was complete, and it is fascinating to observe how much had changed in some directions, how little in others. The central bodies were remodelled, and the Council of the Senate replaced the Caput; committees gradually formed to handle every area of university

[35] Winstanley 1940, pp. 106–21.

[36] Winstanley 1940, chap. XI.

[37] Winstanley 1940, pp. 234–6; see *Documents 1852* for the remarkable scholarly research undertaken on behalf of the commission, including editions of the Caius statutes from the Lambeth MS., and of a draft by Caius in the University Library (MS. Mm.4.20: cf. Brooke 1985, p. 67, n. 58).

business – though Faculty Boards were not fully established till the 1920s. Within the colleges the old scholarship and fellowship funds with their antique restrictions were almost entirely swept away, and with them in many cases almost all memory of their early benefactors. Mr Wortley, benefactor of Caius in the mid eighteenth century, had stipulated that one of his fellows should bear the name of Wortley (but not Wortley Montague or Montague Wortley). Such provisions could now be forgotten. Much useless clutter was removed – though much genuine tradition and sentiment needlessly went with it. But much of the old world remained. An Act of 1856 opened most university degrees to those who were not of the Established Church – but not any university office or fellowship. The statutory commissioners were prepared to take a favourable view of proposals to abolish or limit celibacy; but very little happened. Leslie Stephen has left a hilarious record of how the junior fellows of Trinity Hall held the seniors and the commissioners to ransom.[38] They could not command the two-thirds majority needed to pass a statute; but they could prevent any rival statute passing – and they made it clear to the commissioners that if some at least of their demands were not met, their work would never be done. The result was a limited removal of the marriage bar: in Caius alone (so far as we know) it was at this date totally abolished.[39]

The Oxford of Newman

Oxford university emerged from the eighteenth century with its teaching function less impaired than its sister's at Cambridge, and the fame of a few of its tutors, and especially John Henry Newman – though only a tutor for six of his 89 years – was to give it a prestige which has lasted to this day. In general esteem Newman has no rival in the Cambridge of his day save Charles Darwin, and he was a characteristic Cambridge student only in his idleness. Yet in 1800 neither Oxford nor Cambridge was a major force in the international world of thought or letters; even within the dominions of King George III they were outshone by Göttingen and Edinburgh, and some of the characteristics of Cambridge were closely paralleled in Oxford: in particular, the unexplained surge of recruits, including men of a wide and varied talent; and the extreme and notorious conservatism of the colleges, a mode of thought and attitude all the more powerful at Oxford since college life and teaching still had some vigour in it.

There were four different areas in which reform began to change the university of Oxford in the early decades of the nineteenth century: in fellowships, scholarships, professorial lectures and the examination system. The opening of fellowships to candidates from other colleges, and from shires not named by their founders, proceeded quite slowly. There had been spasmodic examples before the end of the eighteenth century, as at Balliol in 1783 and at Oriel in 1795, when Copleston, a classicist from Devon and a Corpus man, was elected to a Wiltshire fellowship.[40] Oriel played an important role since by 1821 all its fellowships had been opened to the whole university. The vindication of this development was made clear by the elections of Keble and Whately in 1811, of Arnold in 1815, Newman in 1822, and Hurrell Froude and Robert Wilberforce in 1826, all men of first-rate

---

[38] Stephen 1885, pp. 108–10 (cf. Crawley 1976, p. 161). For Wortley (earlier in this paragraph) see Brooke 1985, p. 151; for the 1856 Act, Winstanley 1947, pp. 37–9.

[39] Brooke 1985, pp. 224–6.

[40] Doolittle 1986, p. 235; Mallet 1924–7, III, 183 and n. 5.

quality. Even so, the speed of the change must not be exaggerated. As late as 1850 there were only 22 fellowships open to general competition, out of a total of well over 500.

The competitive scholarship was a Balliol contribution. That came in 1827,[41] and Jowett called it a 'turning point in the fortunes of the college'. It was impressive that it was brought about by the unanimous wish of the Balliol tutors, and that the master, Richard Jenkyns, supported the change though unconvinced of its virtues.

In 1813 the Prime Minister, Lord Liverpool, wrote to the newly appointed professor of modern history and political economy,[42] Edward Nares, advising him that the professor's lectures should be revived and delivered in person.[43] This Nares subsequently did, thus setting a fashion which spread. The writing was on the wall: in 1829 convocation voted that all professors be required to lecture in person.

The new examination statutes of 1800 and 1807 were supported by Cyril Jackson, dean of Christ Church – a prelate high in royal favour who refused to leave Oxford for a bishopric – John Eveleigh, provost of Oriel and John Parsons, master of Balliol.[44] They initiated a B.A.

[41] Jones 1982, pp. 100–1.
[42] Merton College, E.2.42, pp. 161–2 (letter of 12 Dec. 1813).
[43] For earlier attempts by George III and Lord Bute to encourage regius professors to be more vigorous, cf. Sutherland in Sutherland and Mitchell 1986, pp. 474–5 and p. 475 n. 1. A separate chair in political economy was established in 1825. Thanks to its endowment by Mr Drummond of Albury the first professor was Nassau Senior. Its most distinguished holder has probably been Professor Sir John Hicks. Between 1825 and 1912 no less than 25 new professorships were established. For details see *VCH Oxon*, III, 30–5.
[44] Green 1986c, pp. 623–8; Mallet 1924–7, III, 166–70.

degree – a Pass School – in a variety of subjects: Latin and Greek literature, grammar, rhetoric, logic, mathematics, physics, philosophy, the elements of religion and the Thirty-Nine Articles. For a B.C.L. history and jurisprudence were added. The M.A. consisted of mathematics, physics, metaphysics and history. The concept of Honours derived from the fact that up to twelve candidates could be given an Extraordinary Examination and be placed in order on a list. A separate Honours School of mathematics and physics followed in 1807,[45] and candidates for the Extraordinary Examination were to be classified in the First or Second Class. Peel was thus able to take a 'Double First' in Literae Humaniores and mathematics in 1808.[46] In the same year Responsions appeared as a first examination to be taken usually in the second year; they consisted of Latin, Greek, logic and geometry.[47] The standard was not exacting. To start with, the examinations were chiefly oral, but they had become for the most part written by 1830. 'Honours' clearly were not obligatory and for a long time the vast majority of undergraduates took instead the much less rigorous Pass School.[48] For example at Lincoln College out of its 208 undergraduates between 1815 and 1834 only 32 took 'Honours'.[49] In the early decades of the century Christ Church,

[45] *Oxford University Calendar* (1828), p. 100; Green 1986c, pp. 627–8.
[46] *Oxford University Calendar* (1828), pp. 101–3.
[47] Green 1986c, p. 628; Mallet 1924–7, III, 169.
[48] Mallet 1924–7, III, 168. This had a separate examination from 1830.
[49] Green 1979, p. 384.

which had a long and effective tradition of regular examinations on undergraduate reading – the early 'Collections' – shone especially.[50] But gradually a small group of colleges began to send their men in for Honours regularly. As at Cambridge, this encouraged the growth of professional coaches, and – earlier than at Cambridge – of college tutors who took their task seriously. By the late nineteenth century the old examination rooms in the Schools Quadrangle were totally inadequate. After seven years of discussion T.G. Jackson was chosen as the architect of the new Examination Schools (1877–82).[51] Remarkably, over a hundred years after their construction they still fulfil the purpose for which they were built.

It seemed as if the university was going to be slow to recognise that reform of the Church of England was overdue. In its religious policies, despite the appearance of Wesley in Lincoln and the subsequent formation of the Holy Club, the impact of Methodism on Oxford was short-lived. Indeed the expulsion by the vice-chancellor of six Calvinistic Methodists from St Edmund Hall in 1768 marked its end.[52] But though not so strong as at Cambridge, the evangelical movement would not let matters rest.[53] Then lightning flashed from a different direction.

Three elections at Oriel – of John Keble in 1811, of 'that clever young gentleman', Mr Newman in 1822, and of Edward Pusey in 1823 – brought together as fellows of one college three key members of a group who were going to rock the Anglican Church in general and Oxford in particular.[54] They were to form part of what came to be known as the Oxford Movement, the Tractarians. Although deep divisions eventually separated its adherents, some common features were outstanding: an interest in primitive Christianity and the apostolic succession of the Church of England, which they strenuously defended, an attempt to revive the Anglican ideals of the seventeenth century and a determination to stem the spread of liberalism in theology, as manifested by German Protestant scholars. Their issue of controversial books and pamphlets culminated in a series of tracts of which the first – *Thoughts on the Ministerial Commission respectfully addressed to the Clergy* – was written by Newman in 1833.[55] Newman's religion was always dogmatic and un-sentimental. That was why Jowett later nominated him 'the most artificial man of our generation. . . His conscience had been taken out and the [Catholic] Church put in its place.' In 1841, stimulated by the ecclesiastical policy of Whig governments, Newman had reached that point in his thinking which issued in Tract 90, *Remarks on Certain Passages in the Thirty-Nine Articles*, which led him no longer to defend the Church of England but to transfer his allegiance to Rome. A further decision of the Judicial Committee of the Privy Council, affecting a matter of doctrine, caused others to defect, most notably the future

---

[50] For Christ Church Collections cf. Quarrie 1986. These were college examinations held towards the end of term when all junior members were examined orally by the dean and tutors. For 'Collections' at Balliol see Jones 1982, p. 97. They have evolved on the one hand into 'informal College written examinations which are still known as "Collections"', and on the other into the interviews which undergraduates have with the master and their tutors (known as hand shaking) at the end of term. These practices remain widespread among colleges today. See now E.G.W. Bill, *Education at Christ Church, Oxford, 1660–1880* (1987).

[51] Colvin 1983, pp. 143–7.   [52] Mitchell 1986b, pp. 165–6; Green 1986b, pp. 457–64.

[53] Later important evangelicals included Dr Seymour, warden of Wadham (1831–7), Henry B. Bulteel, fellow of Exeter (1823–9) and John Hill, vice-principal of St Edmund Hall (1812–51), cf. Reynolds 1975, pp. 36–118. The evangelicals formed an increasing undercurrent which was in due course to help bring about the refoundation of Magdalen Hall as Hertford College (see p. 293 below) and the foundation of St Peter's Hall, now St Peter's College (see p. 319 below).

[54] Mallet 1924–7, III, 185–214.

[55] Cross and Livingstone 1974, p. 1019.

Cardinal Manning.[56] This was the celebrated Gorham case, which arose in 1847 because Henry Phillpotts, Bishop of Exeter (1830–69), a former fellow of Magdalen, strove to condemn the Calvinist views of the elderly, respected divine and antiquary, George Gorham – a characteristic product of Queens', Cambridge, of the age of the evangelical president Isaac Milner – on infant baptism, and failed. What was scandalous to the Tractarians was that a Judicial Committee in which the archbishops were outnumbered by eminent judges should appear to determine an issue of doctrine, and in a Calvinist sense. That the judgement was drafted by an ex-fellow of Caius, Lord Langdale – who interpreted the matter in terms of law and formularies, not of doctrine – if noticed at all, did not increase its favour among the Oxford divines.

In Oxford itself, some of the movement's most interesting features sprang from the attitude of those who remained Anglican, and who linked the cause of reform in the church with reform in the university. Charles Marriott offers the example of a man who declared that 'Oxford has became exclusively a university for the rich'. He resented with 'holy indignation' the exclusion of poor men from the university. He wished to found a college or hall for poor students and others. He pointed out that it was not enough to open scholarships to competition; those who had been educated at expensive schools should not be put at an immense advantage in competition with those who had not. Since the expenditure of undergraduates had been fixed by the 'tyranny of custom and fashion' at the extravagant rate of £100 to £250 a year, a way must also be found to lessen the cost of university education.[57] By 1848 the questions of 'University Extension' and of the poor scholar had been fairly put and had interested many who were not necessarily supporters of the Oxford Movement. Methodical instruction in different subjects by university lecturers, it was argued, should be placed within the reach of students in urban centres at moderate cost.

Meanwhile schools like Eton, Winchester and Westminster were influencing the university in quite a different way. The playing of cricket had been growing steadily since the beginning of the century, with matches taking place between Eton and Westminster and Eton and Harrow. Rowing followed suit in the 1820s at Eton and Westminster, encouraged by their ready access to the Thames. The first boat-race between Oxford and Cambridge was rowed in 1829, an event which was to make the two universities more widely known to the general public than anything else. Later, in the second half of the century 'The Rugby Game' or rugger and 'The Association Game' or soccer were to be enthusiastically played and required the appropriate playing-fields. Demand for sporting facilities where games could be played ensured that a patchwork of green open spaces would be preserved close to the buildings of the university and colleges, and incidentally equip an increasingly crowded city with precious lungs.

[56] This was a case in which Bishop Phillpotts of Exeter examined a Cambridge graduate evangelical, G.C. Gorham (who was suspect to the high church party), when he was presented to the living of Brampford Speke in Exeter diocese. Although Gorham was over sixty and had been ordained for many years and the incumbent of St Just-in-Penwith in the same diocese, the bishop's examination occupied 38 hours and was distinctly inquisitorial. The key question was the nature of baptism. Gorham held that spiritual regeneration is not given or conferred at baptism – a Calvinist viewpoint. The superior ecclesiastical court (the Court of Arches) upheld the bishop's view that Gorham had failed the test. But this judgement was reversed by the Judicial Committee of the Privy Council with both the archbishops and the Bishop of London as assessors. If the Bishop of Exeter had had his way a wedge could have been driven into the position of the evangelicals within the Church of England (cf. Cornish 1910, I, 319–34; Brooke 1985, p. 201 and n. 51 for other references).

[57] Cf. Burgon 1891, pp. 185–7.

The desire of three Oriel tutors, headed by Newman, to introduce new books and to reorganise instruction for the better undergraduates proved an opening shot in a battle over the need to provide better and more specialised tuition.[58] As increasing burdens were laid on the colleges' tutorial arrangements, their inadequacy became ever more apparent. In 1832 the provost of Oriel, Edward Hawkins, scion of a family of distinguished surgeons, removed his three tutors from their tutorships in order to keep matters in his own hands. But the debate had only just begun. From outside in 1836 came the threat of a bill in Parliament to establish a commission for the reform of college and university statutes, though this did not survive a second reading.[59] From inside a demand was made for a new school of law and history, and it was now recognised that the introduction of Honours Schools had led to a higher rate of failure than at Durham or Cambridge. Again the university was failing to provide the professional men required by the Home Civil Service. It could not even produce enough clergymen for the Church of England.

When the findings of the royal commission of 1850–2[60] were enshrined in the Act of 1854 it was the responsibility of W.E. Gladstone as M.P. for Oxford university and Chancellor of the Exchequer in Aberdeen's ministry to steer through the necessary legislation. At the centre of the commissioners' discussions had lain the question whether to put power into the hands of the professors or to remodel the tutorial structure in the colleges. This might be done by encouraging tutors to specialise and by paying them better stipends. Otherwise they tended to leave when vacant livings came up. Then there was the question whether the university was to remain clerical or to become secular. Could numbers be increased and costs lowered by allowing men to live for part of the time in lodgings? A tutors' association was formed and proved a powerful lobby.[61] The publication of *Oxford Reform and Oxford Professors* by one of the most radical reformers – Henry Halford Vaughan, the regius professor of modern history – hardened opposition to the adoption of a system dominated by professors. Gladstone came down on the side of the tutors; the strengthening of the university at the centre had to wait for the Cleveland Commission which Gladstone himself appointed in 1871 when he was Prime Minister. But the old hebdomadal board, dominated by the heads of houses, was replaced by a new hebdomadal council whose members were elected by congregation.[62]

In the Examination Statute of 1850 (originally put to convocation in 1849) a First Public Examination was established in classics and mathematics. For their second and final examination all candidates had to take two schools. One of these had to be classics and the other might be mathematics, natural science or 'history and cognate sciences'. It took a little time before the last-named emerged as the school of jurisprudence and history. This examination became known as 'Great-go' or 'Greats'. Since the First Public Examination was examined by moderators it soon turned into 'Mods.' Although 'Greats' to begin with included some political economy and study of scripture, its most important component was philosophy, to be joined later by ancient history. The Latin and Greek needed for Moderations were intended to provide a standard in Greek and Latin literature

---

[58] Engel 1983, p. 25.   [59] Engel 1983, p. 34.
[60] Engel 1983, p. 34; Winstanley 1940, chap. xi.   [61] Engel 1983, pp. 43–9.
[62] For the original distinction between convocation (the old greater congregation) and congregation (the old lesser congregation) see p. 54 above. Congregation was now redefined. It was to consist of all professors, certain other university officials and all members of convocation resident for 20 weeks within $1\frac{1}{2}$ miles of Carfax (i.e. the centre of the city of Oxford; cf. Engel 1983, p. 61).

*182 (opposite) The University
Museum at Oxford, 1855–60,
designed by Sir Thomas Deane,
Son, and B. Woodward*

independent of philosophy. These developments underlined the need for specialised teachers.[63] In pressing for a school of natural science Henry Acland, reader in anatomy (from 1851 Aldrichian professor of clinical medicine) was the chief inspiration. He was the son of a Devonian graduate of Christ Church, Sir Thomas Dyke Acland, and had been elected to a fellowship at All Souls in 1840. But fate had fortunately ensured that he had gone to learn his medicine in a London hospital and at Edinburgh.[64] Another spur to the new school had been the inauguration of the natural sciences tripos at Cambridge in 1849. Time and again in the modern period action at Cambridge has provoked counteraction in Oxford and vice versa, as each university vied for the premier place in the English world of learning.

That the Old Ashmolean was much too small to act as a centre for Oxford science was realised by Charles Daubeny, a Wykehamist, professor of chemistry and subsequently of botany and rural economy as well. He too had attended Edinburgh university before his Oxford appointment. He had the dream of a new home for Oxford science.[65] But the key figure was Acland. He led the demand for 'a great museum for all aspects of Physical Science', and the result was the University Museum, built between 1855 and 1860. Coming under the aesthetic influence of his friend, John Ruskin, Acland determined that it should be constructed in a Rhenish Gothic style and, more absurdly, decided that the chemistry laboratory should imitate the Abbot's Kitchen at Glastonbury Abbey, a piece of self-conscious medievalism which was not appreciated by many who subsequently had to work there.[66] Nevertheless buildings had been constructed with facilities for chemistry, experimental philosophy, mineralogy, geology, medicine and anatomy (which included biology), in short a centre for science, long before anything of the kind existed at Cambridge. Almost at once a great debate on the merits of Darwinism took place beneath its roof at a meeting of the British Association held at Oxford in 1860.[67] The Bishop of Oxford, Samuel Wilberforce, an amateur scientist and a vice-president of the association, denounced Darwinian evolution as a 'theory founded upon fancy, instead of upon facts'. The bishop spoke flippantly and expressed the 'disquietude' he should feel were a 'venerable ape' to be shown to him 'as his ancestress at the Zoo'. T.H. Huxley sprang to the defence of Darwin. As legendary accounts proliferated, their debate came to signify the victory of natural science over antique cosmologies, although at Oxford 'for a time after this science was tolerated sceptically rather than cordially welcomed'. Ironically in 1868 the Clarendon endowment, originally intended for a riding school and carefully harboured since the eighteenth century, enabled the Clarendon Laboratory for Physics to be established.[68] Gradually the modern Science Area has grown up around the Museum and the different scientific schools have branched off from the old tree. Yet despite the achievements generated there, especially since the First World War, many of them of international importance, it was not until the Second World War that a natural scientist was elected as head of an Oxford college. By 1939 a Nobel laureate, J.J. Thomson, had been

[63] By a statute of 1849 candidates for Honours were to take 'Greats' and a second Honours school, either modern history and law or mathematics (Prest 1982, p. 188). In February 1849 a delegacy was established for the appointment of examiners in mechanical philosophy, chemistry and physiology (Sinclair and Robb-Smith 1950, p. 55).

[64] Sinclair and Robb-Smith 1950, pp. 48–9 and 55.

[65] Simcock 1984, p. 17; Simcock 1985, p. 54.

[66] Simcock 1984, pp. 14, 16.

[67] Simcock 1984, p. 13; for the myths surrounding the Wilberforce–Huxley debate, see Lucas 1979.

[68] In 1870 (Simcock 1984, p. 15 and n. 160). See p. 199 above.

master of Trinity at Cambridge for over twenty years – and he was not Cambridge's first scientific head.

Not only the Old Ashmolean but also the Bodleian experienced an *embarras de richesses* by 1850. Its curators needed to find a new home for the Arundel Marbles and other works of art hitherto housed in the Schools Quadrangle. Moreover a handsome benefaction from Sir Robert Taylor for the encouragement of the study of modern languages in Oxford was coming to fruition after long delays. As a result it was decided to erect a new building on the corner of St Giles and Beaumont Street to combine two objectives. It was to consist both of the Taylorian Institute and the University Galleries. A competition for the design in the 'Grecian character' was won by C.R. Cockerell and the Galleries and Institute were opened in 1845.[69] The Galleries have become the Ashmolean Museum while the Taylorian has indeed encouraged the study of modern languages; and in 1904 a school of them was to take its place beside those which promoted the study of Latin and Greek.[70]

[69] Colvin 1983, pp. 122–3, Mallet 1924–7, III, 296–7. [70] In 1904. A school of English had been set up in 1895.

280

Cambridge and Oxford in the age of Pattison and Jowett

We have taken William Whewell to represent the mingling of innovation and reaction so characteristic of early Victorian Cambridge – a man remarkably compounded of immovable tradition and dazzling readiness to innovate. For originality in others he was not always so well prepared, and 'we are not sure', wrote J.W. Clark, 'that he ever allowed the *Origin of Species* to be admitted into the College Library'.[71] Yet Whewell was among the giants. More characteristic of the rank and file of good Cambridge fellows of the next generation was Henry Richards Luard (1825–91).[72] He was a fellow of Trinity from 1849 till his death in 1891; from 1860 he was also vicar of Great St Mary's, and from 1862 registrary of the university. He thus combined three roles in the story we are unfolding. A.J. Engel has taught us to see the great transition of nineteenth-century Oxford as *From Clergyman to Don*.[73] Luard was an extremely conscientious vicar according to his lights, a good pastor to his parishioners in a fairly formal, old-fashioned way; a regular and valued preacher, nearer in conviction to Harvey Goodwin of St Edward's, fellow of Caius and high churchman, than to Charles Clayton, tutor of Caius and vicar of Holy Trinity, the noted evangelical successor to Charles Simeon, of Holy Trinity and King's.[74] The combination of clerical office in Cambridge with a fellowship was a great deal more natural then than now, and harked back to the medieval tradition that parish churches and college chapels should be under the same roof. Furthermore, Great St Mary's is the university church, and where more natural for the university registrary to spend his Sundays? In that office he succeeded the celebrated diarist Joseph Romilly, and governed the university administration, a remarkably unexacting task by modern standards. But Luard was also a lifelong scholar, and in that sense a bridge between what had been occasional in the *ancien régime* and became the norm in much more recent times. He was anything but the idle fellow of legend, as anyone who has handled his catalogues of manuscripts or the numerous volumes in the Rolls Series must testify. He was as prolific as William Stubbs, the great regius professor of modern history at Oxford (1866–84), though not his equal as a scholar; and his eighteen volumes – with the major chronicle of Matthew Paris at their centre – are a monument to his industry and thoroughly justify J.W. Clark's claim that he was 'the very prince of index-makers',[75] while making it a wonder that he had time to cure the souls of Great St Mary's. Yet his scholarship was conservative: he loved the classics and hated to see footnotes in English – his comments on those who print English translations opposite their Latin were unprintable.[76] If he had treated Matthew's Latin with more respect, if he had paused to translate him, his scholarship would have been more correct – but he would never have finished. Meanwhile, in his attitude to Trinity, he joined Whewell in ensuring that the statutes of the 1850s made minimal changes; and he hated the changes in those of 1882, foreseeing only ruin from the abolition of celibacy. Yet it enabled Luard himself to marry and retain his wife with his fellowship, both of which he dearly loved.[77]

In 1870 the colleges of Oxford and Cambridge excluded from the vast majority of their offices and fellowships all women, all men who were married, all free churchmen, Jews and agnostics. There were exceptions: heads of house might marry and cynics and hypocrites

---

[71] Clark 1900, p. 75 n.   [72] On him see esp. Clark 1900, pp. 328–43; also *DNB*.   [73] Engel 1983.
[74] Brooke 1985, pp. 218–21, 231; on Simeon, esp. Smyth 1940.   [75] Clark 1900, p. 338.   [76] Clark 1900, p. 332.
[77] Clark 1900, pp. 329–30, 342–3. Clark tells us (pp. 329–30) that Luard was the first fellow of Trinity to marry and retain his fellowship.

could subscribe religious tests without serious anxiety. But the anomalies were striking; and the notion was abroad that universities were academic institutions, not ivory towers of privilege; they should lead in the van of enlightenment, not rest motionless as bastions of reaction. As in many confederations, the capacity of the colleges for free and independent action has been at once the genius and bane of the constitution of Cambridge. On a longer view it is undoubtedly the case that many of the major changes of the last hundred years have been fostered and advanced by, indeed have been scarcely conceivable without, this tradition of independence; but many changes which we would hardly question were retarded by it. It is small wonder that Henry Sidgwick came to see the power of the colleges as the barrier to reform, and resigned his fellowship at Trinity in 1869.[78] This was fundamentally a protest not only against the surviving tests – the law which confined membership of the senate and all offices in college and university to Anglicans, which was tottering to its fall and was abolished in 1871 – but also against the many privileges which *de facto* survived. Sidgwick was the centre of a group of enlightened men – some had first met in the Apostles, others gathered in the Grote Society in his middle years – who shared a profound belief in religious tolerance, though some were still believing Christians, others, like Sidgwick, reverent agnostics. Their point of view has won the day so fully that it is now almost incredible to many of us that it took so long – indeed, it is only credible at all if we contemplate the ironical consequences over the last hundred years of the tradition of college and university government and college teaching.

The medieval university had been like a medieval city, freedom-loving, noisy and factious; and from the first, for reasons far from clear, many colleges had been founded with some measure of self-government by the fellows. Down to the mid nineteenth century a scholar of New College, Oxford, at the age of eighteen or less might become a fellow and a member of the governing body – and if in practice his rights and his authority were circumscribed, he had some genuine foretaste of the lot of the modern democratic voter.[79] From the sixteenth century the heads were often grave and usually reverend but always powerful seniors; in Oxford they determined the pattern of university business; in Cambridge the regents and the senate could only vote on motions put before them by the tiny oligarchy of the Caput, which represented the faculties indeed, but had been nominated by the vice-chancellor (in effect with the approval of other heads). But when a vote took place it was the majority which won; the tradition of democracy in some form survived and was fostered in the creaky old federal constitution of colleges and university until it could be reborn in a world much more congenial to democratic notions. Many of the new and civic universities of the nineteenth and twentieth centuries were established in plain reaction against Oxford and Cambridge. They tended to foster religious freedom from the start, and they came (sometimes a little slowly) to open their doors to women. The civic universities were invariably under the tutelage of councils predominantly non-academic who regarded the professors as their employees, however much they respected them; and the pattern of government much more resembled continental than English universities. Within the civic universities, in the academic sphere, the professor and head of department was commonly an autocrat; and so little understanding had his overlords of his work that he could have a degree of independent authority no Oxbridge professor has ever dreamed

---

[78] Sidgwick 1906, pp. 198–9; Winstanley 1947, pp. 67–8; Wormell 1980, p. 73; Brooke 1985, p. 231.
[79] Buxton and Williams 1979, esp. pp. 11, 76–82.

of. Something of this still survives here and there; and the structure of partly lay councils, of departments with professorial heads, is by no means a thing of the past. But it has been modified profoundly in the modern and new universities by two movements of opinion – by the view that academic interests should prevail in university decisions and academics be strongly represented even on councils; and by a progressive democratisation of departments so that in many the head (or chairman) is democratically elected and rotates; in many more the professors have to listen to their younger colleagues; and in most, serious academic business proceeds from the rank and file up to the higher committees. All of this greatly disturbs those who believe in oligarchy or efficiency narrowly conceived; but those who have lived with these changes also know that the immensely increased sense of involvement of junior staff which has often resulted has made for an increase in educational efficiency worth many tedious committees. The causes of these very fundamental changes in British universities are complex – and some of them really belong to the world of the new universities and the student power struggle of the 1960s. But there can be no question that one of the most powerful factors has been the steady flow of men – and in recent decades of women too – and ideas and infections from Oxford and Cambridge into the modern universities. By this means the ancient tradition of independence and self-determination so deeply embedded in Oxbridge has infiltrated the other universities, to a degree sometimes surprising to natives of Cambridge or Oxford who scarcely regarded their own as democratic at all. Needless to say, the influence has flowed in the other direction too. Oxford and Cambridge can be very parochial and scarcely acknowledge the existence of other universities. In the 1920s the head of an Oxford college, congratulating a graduate from a provincial university who had just become an assistant at Newcastle, none the less expressed surprise: 'I thought they would want a man with a degree' – and the formal attitude of Cambridge to the degrees of all other universities save Oxford still shows that the consequences of this peculiar doctrine have not wholly disappeared.[80] Yet with this ostrich-like quality goes a cosmopolitanism, a readiness to listen, to absorb, to pilfer the best from elsewhere and build it into the local fabric, which sits in bewildering fashion beside the inward-looking qualities, the myopia, so characteristic too.

By the same token the professors in the provincial universities – as in the more ancient Scottish universities – in a measure lived up to their vocations from the first: they lectured and examined and many of them engaged in scholarship. The weakness of the lecturing system in Oxford and Cambridge meanwhile had led to the formation of a different system of tuition, whose heart and core is the Oxford tutorial. The word covers a much wider range of human activity than is always realised; but at its centre lies a tradition of personal attention and individual teaching which is seen in the world at large as the special mark of the British universities. In the late nineteenth century it came to be the fact that tutors and college lecturers, when they taught at all, often did so extremely effectively and usurped the tradition of the private coaches. It is true that the tutorial is not universally admired – that a wide variety of teaching methods, classes, seminars, and lectures, flourish in all universities today; but in so far as the tutorial or something like it is a feature common to all

---

[80] Only degrees from Oxford and Trinity College, Dublin, can be 'incorporated' – that is, converted by grace into Cambridge degrees – and under recent ordinances only in virtue of university offices or other special causes. The story of the provost of Oriel used to be told by the late Sir James Mountford, who had come to Oxford with a first degree from Birmingham, and in later life, as vice-chancellor of Liverpool university, used to reminisce of the Oxford prejudices of his youth.

184 *Benjamin Jowett (1817–93), by G. F. Watts, in Balliol College hall*

184 *Benjamin Jowett (1817–93), by G. F. Watts, in Balliol College hall*

the universities of Britain this is a mark of the influence of Oxford and Cambridge upon them.

The great debate in mid-Victorian Oxford on teaching methods, and on the purposes of the university, was polarised in the rival opinions of Mark Pattison, rector of Lincoln (1861–84), and Benjamin Jowett, master of Balliol (1870–93). Pattison was cruelly portrayed in his own lifetime by his friend George Eliot as Dr Casaubon in *Middlemarch*, and can now be contemplated in truer colours in the recent books of V.H.H. Green.[81] He believed passionately in a university where 'culture for culture's sake' should be pursued. Much influenced by his knowledge of developments in German universities, he wanted the professoriate to predominate and to make the university a centre of scholarship and learning. Other characteristics were to strike the wife of a fellow of Oriel when Newman and he came to dine together at Oriel for the first time since Newman became a Roman Catholic. Mrs Butler had already noted Pattison as being a 'peculiar-looking man supposed to be peculiarly pleasing to ladies'. Now she noted 'such a contrast between his dry cynical face, and Newman's genial smile'.[82] It was to be Benjamin Jowett of Balliol, however, the friend of Florence Nightingale, who was to dominate the epoch which followed 1854 and to lead those who pressed forward towards the second royal commission.

[81] Green 1957, 1979.   [82] C. Colvin 1985, pp. 270, 275.

185 *Balliol College Library, fifteenth century, and chapel, by William Butterfield, 1856–7, with the building by Alfred Waterhouse, 1867–8, on the right*

In contrast to Pattison, who had been deeply impressed by the achievements of German professors in research and who emphasised the importance of culture for culture's sake, Jowett stood for professionalism and the prime position of teaching. Or to put it in Pattison's own words, 'The separation between Jowett and myself consists in a difference upon the fundamental question of University politics – viz Science and Learning v. School-keeping.'[82a] Cutting across this controversy lay another great debate – that between the clericals and the seculars who wished to raid the endowments of clerical fellowships in order to create new professorships in a wide range of subjects. The parallel demand for more tutorships also worked against the number of fellowships reserved for the clergy. In spite of the Tractarian Movement the influence of the church was everywhere under attack.

Jowett had been elected a fellow of Balliol in 1838. Although he had been implicated in

[82a] Cf. Green 1979, p. 503.

the moves which had brought about the University Reform Act of 1854, he had then played a subordinate role. In his college he had subsequently been held back from developing his full influence by his opponents, who elected Scott as master in that same year. But in 1870 the party of reform gained a majority on the governing body and Jowett became master. 'I am where I wish to be', he replied in a letter which answered congratulations from his old tutor, A.C. Tait, recently appointed Archbishop of Canterbury (1868–82). 'My desire here is not to be a leader of a party, but to educate the young men or get them educated.'[83] There followed a strengthening of tutorial effectiveness through the institution of weekly 'conclaves' at which the work and conduct of every undergraduate was put under review. Through tutors who specialised in mathematics, history and political science as well as classics, Jowett and a group of his colleagues steadily raised the standards. Already in 1848, when himself a tutor, Jowett had developed the habit of the vacation reading party. Something similar had been initiated at Cambridge, it seems, as early as 1817 when Fanny Burney's son, Alexander, had attended a party at Ilfracombe, organised by Mr Jacob of Caius in the form of paid coaching.[84] The reading party extended tutorial advice beyond the bounds of term. After Jowett's election as master the tutorial system at Balliol was sustained, among others, by the idealist philosopher T.H. Green (1836–82), and by Green's disciple, the economist and social reformer Arnold Toynbee (1852–83).

Like Jowett they believed that the aim of education must be to prepare a man for a life of action. This might be in politics. Christ Church, that nursery of 'crowded statesmen and ceaseless bishops', had already established a tradition of educating future prime ministers and governors general of India.[85] The dean of Christ Church had written to Robert Peel, when newly elected to Parliament, 'Be assured that I shall pursue you, as long as I live, with a jealous and watchful eye. Woe be to you if you fail me.'[86] This training was enhanced when the Oxford United Debating Society (the future Oxford Union) was founded in 1823. It reached its height in the nineteenth century when three future prime ministers began their political careers at the Union.[87] But now at Balliol another tradition was added, that of public administration and imperial service.

Jowett had sat on the Committee on the Indian Civil Service under the chairmanship of Macaulay. As a result Jowett took a deep interest in the future of the service and at one stage wrote to all successful candidates in the I.C.S. examination inviting them to join Balliol for the probationary two years which it became necessary for them to serve at one of eight British universities. Arnold Toynbee was appointed specifically to lecture to these I.C.S. candidates. In 1879 more than half the probationers were studying there. Nine years later Jowett is found writing to his former pupil, the viceroy, Lord Lansdowne, 'There is more opportunity of doing great and permanent good in India than in any department of

[83] Tait Papers, personal letters vol. 88, fo. 163, 1 October 1870, quoted in Prest 1982, p. 150 and n. 50.

[84] For Jowett's reading parties cf. Faber 1957, pp. 186–7; and for that run by Mr Jacob of Caius at Ilfracombe in 1817 see Burney 1972–84, and especially x, 517–18 and n. 13. In this case Mr Jacob was paid as a coach (Edward Jacob (c. 1796–1841) was a junior fellow of Caius 1816–24, senior fellow 1824–41, and an equity draftsman: see Venn, II, 160).

[85] Trevor-Roper 1973, p. 36. Christ Church prime ministers before 1870 were George Grenville, Shelburne, Portland, Liverpool, Canning, Peel and Gladstone; governors general of India before the Mutiny were Wellesley, Minto, Amherst, Bentinck, Auckland, and George and Charles Canning.

[86] Parker, *Life of Peel*, I, 27–9, quoted in Mallet 1924–7, III, 172.

[87] Gladstone, Salisbury and Asquith.

186 *Oxford, St Catherine's College, 1960–4, by Arne Jacobsen*

administration in England.' Between 1892 and 1896 52 per cent of successful candidates for the I.C.S. were Oxford graduates.[88]

But the Home Civil Service was not neglected. One of the most striking examples of the Jowett tradition in a later age must be that of Sir William Beveridge, who after taking three first classes at Balliol and serving as the sub-warden of Toynbee Hall (founded in Whitechapel in London for working men, as a memorial to Toynbee) joined the Home Civil Service, in the Board of Trade, and through the Beveridge Plan of Insurance for All laid the foundation of the welfare state after the Second World War.

The interest expressed by the first reform commission in increasing numbers while holding down costs by allowing undergraduates to live outside college in lodgings led to the institution in 1868 of non-collegiate or unattached students. They were to make very slow progress. By 1877, it seems, there were only two tutors to deal with 275 of them. When

[88] Symonds 1982, pp. 57–8. The eight universities were Cambridge, London, Oxford, Aberdeen, Edinburgh, Glasgow, St Andrews and Trinity College, Dublin. See now Symonds 1986.

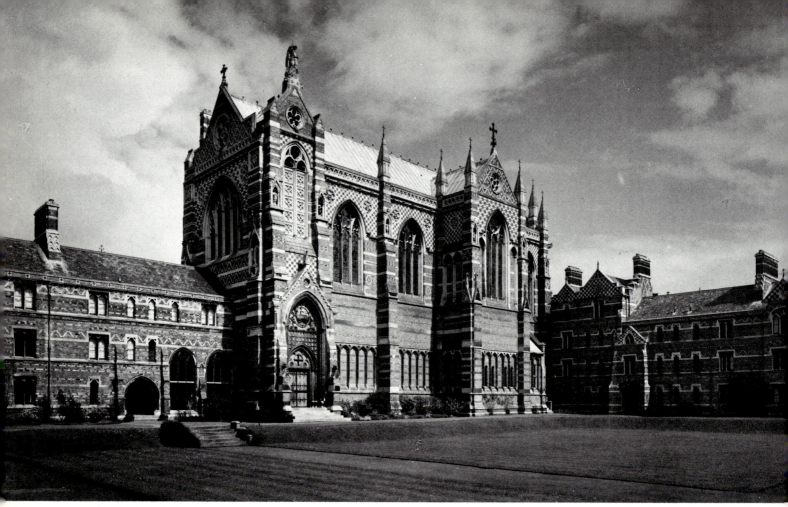

187 Keble College, the chapel,
by William Butterfield, 1873–6

188 (opposite) A detail of the
chapel, showing the sacrifice of
Isaac by Abraham

reorganised in 1930 these students became St Catherine's Society, the ancestor of St Catherine's College into which the society was transformed in 1963.[89]

That the two universities would reach out to England as well as to the Empire was shown by a Cambridge don, James Stuart of Trinity, who asked his university for the recognition of extra-mural work in the early 1870s. He had been 'specially impressed with the needs of the two classes which had sought his help – the working men of Crewe and an association for the higher education of women in the north of England'. Cambridge agreed in 1873 and Oxford and London followed its example.[90] The idea was taken a step further when in 1899 Mr and Mrs Walter Vroosman founded a hall – in Oxford but outside the university – to which working men might be brought to enjoy a higher education. It became Ruskin College and thus commemorated a man whose ideas had so much influenced the building of the museum and whose lectures on art and architecture and radical views on political economy had stimulated Oxford for half a century.[91]

Meanwhile, in the mid 1860s, early steps were being taken to bring about the foundation of Keble College, the first completely new foundation since that of Wadham in 1610. The attempt to provide adequate endowment for impoverished halls had led to the rise of Pembroke College on the site of Broadgates Hall (1624), and of Worcester College on the site of Gloucester Hall (1716). Hertford was to spring up out of Magdalen Hall (1875);

[89] *Oxford University Calendar* (1984–5), p. 263.
[90] Mallet 1924–7, III, 466 n. 3. The Oxford Department was founded in 1878 (*Oxford University Calendar* (1984–5), p. 130).
[91] Cf. Mallet 1924–7, III, 473 and n. 2, Chester 1986, pp. 20–1, *VCH Oxon*, III, 34–5.

288

189 William Morris in Cambridge: Jesus College chapel, the north-west corner of the nave ceiling by Morris and Co., 1864–7, with the college arms (note Alcock's cocks) and emblem, the crowned IHS (Jesus); and in the border, angels holding a scroll, containing the Passion hymn Vexilla Regis by Venantius Fortunatus (sixth century): 'Fulfilled is now what David told . . .'

190 (opposite) William Morris and G. F. Bodley: Queens' College hall roof, detail, c. 1449, painted in the 1870s

while the halls of New Inn, St Mary and St Alban were amalgamated with Balliol, Oriel and Merton respectively. But the foundation of Keble, which was opened in 1870, represented a fresh departure. A committee formed by W.W. Shirley became, after Keble's death in 1866, the promoters of a memorial college.[92] They breathed the very spirit of the Tractarians.

The promoters stated in their appeal for funds that they 'do not intend to establish an Institution which would be sought only by persons of inferior social position, or of attainments and intellect below the ordinary level of the University, but rather to found one in which men of liberal education may find all the advantages of a College combined with economy and simplicity of living'.[93] The current movement in architecture favoured Gothic prototypes as shown by Pembroke College hall and Exeter College chapel. The architect employed in the construction of Keble, William Butterfield, had already gained a

114 40

[92] Cf. *DNB* and Mallet 1924–7, III, 427 and n. 1.   [93] *Keble Record* (1960), p. 22.

191 *William Morris in Oxford: St Cecilia by Morris and Burne-Jones, Christ Church, the cathedral, north aisle, 1874–5*

185   reputation in Oxford by the rebuilding of Balliol chapel and the Grove Building of Merton.
187–8 Now he conceived an extensive set of buildings, which were erected between 1868 and
       1883 in an elaborate Decorated style. The great height of the chapel gave it a Romantic air,
       even if its critics accused it of being stylistically 'holy zebra'. The cost of the chapel was
       borne by a single benefactor, William Gibbs, who was able to contribute a princely sum
       from a fortune made in the import of guano and in banking. The three main buildings were
       paid for by the Gibbs family at a cost of £80,000.[94] Nevertheless a tight budget for the rest of
       the college, and the recognition that its members should not be served breakfast and lunch
       privately in their rooms, as was normal at other colleges, led the architect to design two-
       room sets strung along both sides of a central corridor with a provision of servants' rooms
       distinctly meagre by Oxford standards. The first, northern, range was built between 1868
       and 1870, when it was ready for occupation. The corridors of Keble anticipated those of

[94] Thompson 1971, p. 394, Mallet 1924–7, III, 429.

192 *Exeter College chapel, tapestry by Morris and Burne-Jones, 1890*

Girton by a short head. Keble was only one of many colleges which showed an alert awareness of current trends in Gothic fashion. Thus at Jesus College, Cambridge, Pugin himself did outstanding work in the chapel in the 1840s, and Bodley, William Morris, Burne-Jones and their colleagues in the 1860s and 1870s. In Queens' Bodley built the new chapel in 1858–61 and he and the Morris firm adorned the old hall. In Oxford they established their reputation by their stained glass, especially in the cathedral; and their tapestry was hung in the chapel of Morris's own college, Exeter (1890).

In sharp contrast to the Anglicanism of Keble, the abolition of all religious tests in the Act of 1871 opened both universities fully to Dissenters and Jews.[95] The test at matriculation for undergraduates had already been removed in 1854. It showed that in future the Anglicans were not going to have it all their own way. Yet the refoundation of Hertford in place of Magdalen Hall in 1875 was the result of the benefaction of a banker, Thomas

---

[95] Mallet 1924–7, III, 332.

193 *Hertford College, Oxford, and the Bridge, by T. G. Jackson, 1913–14, with New College beyond*

Baring, M.P. for South Essex, who was a devoted adherent of the Established Church, and the son of Dr Charles Baring, an Oxford evangelical and Bishop of Durham. A former fellow of Brasenose, he had wanted to set up scholarships open only to members of the Church of England, and five fellowships with an endowment of £30,000, to which he should have the first nominations. When his endowment was offered to his old college, Brasenose, under the shadow of the recent Act it demurred. Hertford, however, by arguing that since their establishment came later than the Act of 1871, they stood outside it, with the aid of a further carefully worded Act of Parliament, managed to absorb this substantial benefaction.[96]

[96] Hamilton 1903, pp. 142–9.

294

1880–1920

In Cambridge the modern teaching tradition, in general terms, is a product of the generation which opened in 1870, and one of the solvents of change was the abolition of celibacy. The connection is not at first sight obvious, since a fundamental element in the college tradition, for centuries before 1870 and increasingly after, has been the nucleus of resident bachelor fellows who have provided a core of the tutorial and teaching strength, a permanent senior presence, sometimes hardly felt by the students, sometimes very closely and deeply and effectively in touch and in tune with them. Those who opposed the abolition of celibacy held that the resident don would disappear, that the community of the fellowship would be destroyed. The problem they perceived was a real one. In the sixteenth and early seventeenth centuries most resident senior fellows had also been tutors and involved in teaching; the link had become less and less marked, until it was invisible to the young Venn in the 1850s.[97] The majority of fellows were non-resident; most held their fellowships till one or other of the great accidents of life – death or marriage – overtook them. To convert the fellowship into a teaching cadre meant that the idle life fellow had to disappear and the notion of a career, of a whole life, of teaching within a college, be reborn. This is one of the greatest revolutions wrought in Cambridge in the late nineteenth and early twentieth centuries, and it happened slowly, unevenly, by fits and starts. If the teaching fellows had all married, no doubt the common life of colleges would have suffered, the tutorial traditions would have been in many cases broken. But if the teaching fellows had not been free to marry, the formation within Cambridge of the academic profession, based equally in college and university, could not have happened.

In the present state of knowledge the revival of college teaching is a story which can hardly be told.[98] Most existing college histories were written about 1900 for the splendid series of college histories published by F.E. Robinson in London. The series itself is a remarkable and significant event – no commercial publisher had attempted such before, and none would dream of it now. The late-Victorian era which saw the first blossoming of the old school tie – in public schools and grammar schools alike – saw the same spirit at work in the colleges. College clubs, college magazines, annual gatherings of alumni – all manner of expressions of a community spirit – flourished in the late nineteenth and early twentieth centuries. The authors of these histories were only slightly aware of it. John Buchan's history of Brasenose – his first published book, the work of a moderately mature undergraduate – is a notable piece of historical fiction with little perception of recent change. In E.S. Shuckburgh's *Emmanuel College* (1904), where reform and enlightenment had proceeded apace under Samuel Phear as master and William Chawner as senior tutor, much of this is readily apparent in the account of the new statutes of 1882 and the foundation of the Dixie chair which accompanied them. But Shuckburgh then proceeds to a rather tedious catalogue of 'other measures that fell' under the mastership of Dr Phear. 'In 1884 an entrance examination was established; in 1885 a slight increase was made in the tuition fee, in order that the Lecturers might do for their men what had formerly been done at much greater cost by private tutors' – and he goes on to detail important and impressive developments in the college library, which made it more useful both for fellows

---

[97] Venn 1913, pp. 262–3.
[98] For individual colleges, see for example Bury 1952; Brooke 1985, pp. 232–47; and next note.

and for undergraduates.[99] This deadpan treatment of so fundamental a reform is characteristic: great changes were carried through in this period because the most enlightened had a blinding vision of what university education could be; because ordinary practical men saw sense and economy in making college lecturers teach; because the most conservative hardly noticed anything was happening. And it happened in its own way and at its own pace. David Newsome has described how he was taught history in Emmanuel in the 1950s by Bertram Goulding Brown and Edward Welbourne.[100] Goulding Brown was one of the last of the coaches, a private tutor who was none the less an institution in the college. He took the history tripos in 1902–3 and was a contemporary of the original 'Junior Historians' who reformed the teaching of history in the 1910s and 1920s, men like Sir John Clapham of King's, E.A. Benians of St John's and Z.N. Brooke of Caius. In his room 'neither furniture nor furnishings had changed since he first took root there during the 1914 War'.[101] He seemed immensely old, but was still very much alive. Edward Welbourne was the professional college tutor and director of studies, and in that sense a new man of the twentieth century; but he preserved with loving care the curious antipathy to professional scholarship – to professors, footnotes and Ph.D.s – which was commonly found in Cambridge in his generation. Warm-hearted, tactless, ingenious and absurd, he was none the less elected master of Emmanuel in 1951 in what was alleged to be the most rapid election in the history of the college – but it was also said to have been the first after the appearance of C.P. Snow's *The Masters*.

Equally telling is the evidence from Caius. The most important of all the college histories of this period is the *Biographical History of Gonville and Caius College* by John Venn, of which volumes I–III, Venn's own, appeared in 1897–1901, accompanied by a short history by Venn in the Robinson series (1901).[102] Venn came of a celebrated evangelical family and so went to Caius in the 1850s when the well-known evangelical, Charles Clayton, was tutor. He became a Wrangler, a fellow and a clergyman; but he also became a deeply versed logician and a central figure in the development of moral sciences in the 1860s and 1870s. His influence was greatly enhanced by the circle in which he moved – Leslie Stephen was his cousin, Henry Sidgwick and J.P. Seeley were among his friends, A.J. Balfour and F.W. Maitland – later to be supreme among Cambridge legal historians – were among his private pupils. He passed through the various phases appropriate to the avant-garde young don: he married in 1867 – though in Caius this meant no loss of the fellowship, which he held till his death as president of the college in 1923; he became increasingly liberal in theology and eventually renounced his orders; he taught for the moral sciences in Caius for 25 years and organised inter-collegiate teaching; he was a steadfast supporter of every liberal cause, and his wife was one of the committee of ladies who assisted Miss Clough in the running of the hostel which was to grow into Newnham.[103] In middle life he became passionately devoted to the study of college history – in particular to collecting detailed biographies of Caians, to which he added an introduction in which the old Wrangler – and inventor of Venn's diagrams – laid the foundation of the statistical study of university alumni of earlier centuries. He went on (in imitation of Joseph Foster's *Alumni Oxonienses*)

99 Shuckburgh 1904, p. 183; cf. also *ibid.*, p. 184.
100 Newsome 1984.
101 Newsome 1984, p. 104.
102 Venn, and Venn 1901: see Brooke 1985, pp. xiii–xiv, 218–22, 231–2.
103 Hamilton 1936, p. 104; and see above, n. 55.

194   *Caius in the nineteenth and twentieth centuries. The building by Alfred Waterhouse, 1868–70 – with statues of the founders, John Caius (died 1573) and William Bateman (died 1355) over the first founder, Edmund Gonville (died 1351). To the left, the Senate House; in the background, Trinity and St John's*

to a catalogue of all Cambridge alumni, which was completed under the patronage of J.A. Venn, his son, president of Queens', in the 1950s.[104] Study of the details he and his colleagues collected about the Caians of the 1880s and 1890s shows how closely the college kept in touch with its alumni in that era: Caius has a good record in this respect, and has kept the *Biographical History* going steadily over the years – but the material in it for the later lives of Caians grows steadily less complete as the decades pass. The 1890s and the 1900s, the decades when the college song was written and E.S. Roberts elected master, were the high-water mark of college loyalty – and, not surprisingly, a great age of benefactions.[105] But fine as Venn's work was there is a notable lacuna in his histories: he

[104]   *Alumni Cantabrigienses*, ed. J. and J.A. Venn (1922–54). For what follows, cf. Brooke 1985, Appendix 3, esp. p. 314, showing percentages of Caians whose later professions were unknown: under 5 per cent for the years 1886–90 and 1907–11, 32.2 per cent for 1951–5, in spite of many efforts.

[105]   Brooke 1985, p. 257.

tells us almost nothing of the inner story of the college in these years of dramatic change – neither of the passage of the celibacy statute, when he was first a fellow in the late 1850s, nor of anything but the bones of the educational revolution in which he played a leading part.

The central figure was undoubtedly E.S. Roberts, who was tutor from 1876, later senior tutor and president and virtually master in the 1890s, when Norman Ferrers was a cripple; actually master from 1903 to his death in 1912.[106] In a quite literal way he was married both to the old world and the new – and when he married Mary Harper in 1886 he insisted on an extremely inconvenient tutor's house being formed within the college so that marriage to her did not separate him from his first love. In the tutor's house and the Master's Lodge Mrs Roberts began to form her own circle in the new community of fellows' wives, and her children played in the courts as a reminder that a new age had dawned.

E.S. Roberts was extremely active in gathering college lecturers about him – classicists like himself, scientists of various disciplines, lawyers, physicians (no novelty in Caius), and in his later years a historian and a modern linguist or two. He was also extremely active in promoting inter-collegiate collaboration in his own and similar fields – out of which, after a long interval, the structure of faculty libraries and faculty boards was to emerge, and much more recently, of faculty buildings even for the humanities. But the most significant developments in university teaching and in the relations of the college and the university came from another direction.

The second royal commission of the 1870s, which produced its crop of new college statutes in the early 1880s for both Cambridge and Oxford, was primarily destined to shift the balance of college and university finance so that the university could resume its role in teaching and research.[107] In the process it tidied up many anomalies left over by the earlier commissioners, including the surviving pockets of celibacy. But its efforts were especially bent to the problem of finance and the endowment of professors. Thus in Oxford, by the ordinances for individual colleges which followed the Act of 1877,[108] a number of professorships were founded by the suppression of fellowships, and of those remaining a specific proportion could now be held by laymen. One professor, however, was overlooked by the reformers: the chair of poetry, dating from 1708, whose incumbent was, and still is, elected by the members of convocation. It symbolises a lyrical side of life at the university which has little to do with academic courses. Although never held by Shelley, Gerard Manley Hopkins or Swinburne, one of its holders – Matthew Arnold (quoting Byron) – expressed his feeling for Oxford in the well-known lines from the preface to his *Essays in Criticism* (1865):

Beautiful City! so venerable, so lovely, so unravaged by the fierce intellectual life of our century, so serene! 'There are our young barbarians, all at play!'

And yet steeped in sentiment as she lies, spreading her gardens to the moonlight, and whispering from her towers the last enchantments of the Middle Age, who will deny that Oxford, by her ineffable charm, keeps ever calling us nearer to the true goal of all of us, to the ideal, to perfection, – to beauty, in a word, which is only truth seen from another side?[109]

---

[106] Brooke 1985, chap. 12, esp. pp. 223, 226–7, 234–6; and for what follows, *ibid.*, pp. 249–50.
[107] Winstanley 1947, chaps. VII–VIII; *Royal Commission 1874*.
[108] Engel 1983, pp. 156–201.
[109] Arnold 1865, pp. x–xi; cf. *Childe Harold*, canto IV, stanza 141.

Although of her most outstanding twentieth-century poets – T.S. Eliot, Louis MacNeice and W.H. Auden – only the last held the chair, and none attempted such an apostrophe as Arnold, nevertheless a poetic tradition outside the academic courses has continued to be a regular feature of the place, fit companion for the life of fantasy epitomised by Lewis Carroll in *Alice's Adventures in Wonderland* and by J.R.R. Tolkien in the *Lord of the Rings*. Both Carroll (a pseudonym for the Reverend C.L. Dodgson) and Tolkien held regular academic appointments but gave free rein to their imagination in their off-duty writings. Dodgson was mathematical lecturer of Christ Church for over 25 years (1855–81) and wrote more than a dozen new books on mathematics, but his masterpieces remain *Alice's Adventures in Wonderland* and *Through the Looking-Glass*, children's books written for Alice Liddell, the daughter of the dean of Christ Church. J.R.R. Tolkien, who held successively the chairs of Anglo-Saxon and of English language and literature, used his imagination and linguistic skills to create a story in the *Lord of the Rings* which, if strongly influenced by Nordic mythology, is notably original and compelling.

Cambridge has had its share of poets, and has contributed through the novels of C.P. Snow to the literature which keeps before the public eye the less endearing side of university life. But its professors have been dedicated to sterner tasks than poetry, at least since the reforms of the 1870s and 1880s. As at Oxford, the endowments of Cambridge lay mainly with the colleges: they always had a greater appeal to their alumni and to outside benefactors than the university, until the days of scientific laboratories in the late nineteenth and twentieth centuries, or of the new University Library of 1934, which was made possible by the Rockefeller benefaction. In the 1870s the university was poor, some of the colleges rich; it stood to reason that their funds should be mobilised to redress the balance and open the windows of opportunity to the rapid multiplication of disciplines. So the colleges were to be taxed to support the university, and professors to be lodged in colleges as professorial fellows, with the idea that they should be partly paid by the colleges on which they were quartered.[110] A small number of the more enlightened colleges went straight ahead: Emmanuel founded the Dixie chair of ecclesiastical history and gathered Mandell Creighton to give lustre to its fellowship and to the circle of Cambridge historians.[111] All the colleges were compelled in some measure to join the scheme. As soon as Caius got wind of it they elected the regius professor of physic, Sir George Paget, then 72 but still very active in the revival of the medical school. Thirty years before, he had nearly become master, and a memorial window in the college chapel records the memory of George Paget, 'the beloved physician', who was re-elected to the fellowship in 1881.[112] In 1882 the college completed its tale of professorial fellows for the time by electing J.R. Seeley. As a friend of Sidgwick, Seeley had rejoiced when he became regius professor of modern history in 1869 to be without a college tie or fellowship. But he was also a friend of at least two fellows of Caius; and his particular forte – the liberal Protestantism of *Ecce Homo* and the study of the moral and political lessons of history as set forth in his *Expansion of England*, the classic statement of a moderate Victorian imperialism – was very congenial to some at least of the fellows of his day. History had been part of a tripos for a generation, at

---

[110] Brooke 1985, pp. 245–7; cf. Winstanley 1947, pp. 328–31. For the wider setting, Rothblatt 1981.
[111] Winstanley 1947, p. 328; cf. Chadwick 1984.
[112] Brooke 1985, pp. 206–7, 246, and references in p. 206 n. 63. On Seeley, see Wormell 1980; Rothblatt 1981, chap. 5; Brooke 1985, pp. 222, 231, 246–7.

195 *Cambridge, Downing Site, the Mond Laboratory 1933, now the Department of Aerial Photography. The building was designed by H. C. Hughes, the Crocodile by Eric Gill*

first unequally yoked to moral sciences, then (from 1870–4) to law; ultimately its own mistress.[113] In the late 1880s nearly a third of the undergraduates in the college were studying medicine or natural sciences already; a significant number were still in mathematics and a growing number in classics and law; moral sciences, modern languages, history, theology (a tripos from 1874), oriental languages and music made a showing; a substantial number still took pass degrees and over one in ten left with no degree at all.[114] Soon after, mechanical sciences were to join them, later still economics and English and archaeology and anthropology and geography; and in the mid twentieth century, social and political sciences. Between them, the natural and medical and mechanical sciences have in the last twenty years captured well over half the under-graduates in Caius – though several other disciplines, including history, make a distinguished showing; but this is not a typical pattern. Much more generally characteristic is the decline of the ordinary degree almost to extinction, and the much slower decline –

[113] Winstanley 1947, pp. 188–9, 206–8; McLachlan 1947–9; Roach 1959, p. 261. The marriage with law was authorised in 1868, first examined in 1870; the history tripos was approved in 1873, examined from 1875.
[114] Brooke 1985, p. 310; for these and for what follows, Tanner 1917, pp. 443–971, 972–86, and the *Cambridge University Calendar*.

though also in the end to a tiny proportion – in the number who take no degree.[115] In a word, the faculties have taken over and standards have steadily risen.

The report of the second royal commission, and the appointment of statutory commissioners which followed, were unfortunately timed. The royal commission pronounced in 1874; the Oxford and Cambridge Act of 1877 set new statutes in motion; the statutory commissioners began to draft them in 1877–8, the very year in which the great agricultural depression began to strike deep into the resources of the colleges, removing in a series of blows more than had ever been envisaged as the university tax. This gave the colleges a golden excuse to drag their feet in their support of the university.[116] The recovery in college finances has been very uneven, partly owing to inequality of endowment, probably almost as much owing to the quality of college administration and investment, especially in the palmy days when Maynard Keynes was bursar of King's, in the 1920s and 1930s. The financial weakness of the colleges between 1880 and 1930 had

---

[115] Due to failure or withdrawal: the days have long since passed when any students (except those specially affiliated or seconded) came to Cambridge not aiming for a degree. In Caius the percentage taking the Ordinary Degree was 15 per cent of the entry of 1886–90, 27.4 per cent of that of 1907–11; still 12.2 per cent of that of 1951–5, but 1 per cent of that of 1967–71. Meanwhile those who took no degree had fallen from 11.6 per cent (1886–90) or 14 per cent (1907–11) to 5.2 per cent (both 1951–5 and 1967–71) – it would be lower still now. See Brooke 1985, p. 310.

[116] Winstanley 1947, chaps. VII–VIII; and for what follows, Howard 1935; Brooke 1985, pp. 251–2, 257. On the expansion of university buildings, Pevsner 1970, pp. 204–18.

the consequence, probably very beneficial, that they were not tempted seriously to compete with the university in the provision of laboratories and materials of research. The urgent need to provide effective endowment, especially in the natural sciences, stimulated a flow of funds into university research and building; and the one table on which Venn saw Professor Stokes demonstrating optics in the 1850s had already grown to seven or eight acres of laboratories by 1913, and was to grow out of all imagining in the 1920s and 1930s – and even more in the 1950s and 1960s. Then chemistry obliterated Lensfield House, which William Wilkins had built so that he could contemplate Downing as he breakfasted; the fields of north Cambridge were filled with veterinary buildings and a university farm; a new Cavendish Laboratory arose on a scale comparable to the Chatsworth of the seventh Duke of Devonshire; and further out still appeared the legendary Mullard Radio-telescope Observatory which has brought Nobel prizes in the late twentieth century to Sir Martin Ryle (an Oxford man in exile) and Professor Anthony Hewish.

196

Meanwhile, the most powerful stimulus towards the provision of effective university departments came partly from the succession of eminent scholars and scientists who led them, partly from the growing numbers of students of high quality who expected to be led. Lord Annan's celebrated and amusing scamper through the intellectual aristocracy of nineteenth- and twentieth-century Britain has revealed the great dynasty which started with the marriage of the Darwins and the Wedgwoods far from Cambridge, but spread out in a great tree including such names as Keynes and Adrian, many of whose branches have flourished in Cambridge in the last hundred years – even to the present, when they include the Anglo-Saxon scholar Simon Keynes of Trinity, in whose veins flow the blood of Darwins, Wedgwoods, Adrians and Keyneses.[117] Gwen Raverat's enchanting *Period Piece* has made familiar the story of how the Darwins settled in Cambridge – linked in blood and academic distinction to many others of their day – and how they and their large families were able to stay there owing to the timely abolition of celibacy. In due course they intermarried with many local families, and joined the younger tree formed by the alliances of the descendants of J.N. Keynes, celebrated as a notable university registrary, and even more as the father of J.M. Keynes the economist, who was childless, and Sir Geoffrey Keynes, surgeon and bibliographer, whose son, himself a Cambridge professor, married the daughter of Lord Adrian, most celebrated of Cambridge physiologists in the twentieth century and ultimately master of Trinity and chancellor of the university. These academic dynasties have contributed much to Cambridge. But in truth the vast majority of the men and women who have played any notable role in Cambridge have been recruits of the first generation – the first of their families to study there. The apostolic succession of great scientists who have won Nobel prizes from the Cavendish laboratory illustrates this. J.J. Thomson came from Manchester, where he had been a student at Owens College, the nucleus of the future university, and he came because he won a scholarship at Trinity in 1876, though he very soon attracted attention in the laboratory and by 1884 he was an F.R.S. He died master of Trinity in 1940; but meanwhile he had handed over the Cavendish chair in 1919 to Ernest Rutherford.[118] Thomson's fame rests on his work in the physics of electricity and the discovery of the electron; Rutherford is perhaps the most famous of all Cambridge's atomic scientists. He came first from New Zealand, and also owed his arrival

---

[117] Annan 1955, esp. pp. 260–5, and references; for what follows, Raverat 1952; Harrod 1951.
[118] *DSB*, XIII, 362–7 (J.L. Heilbron on Thomson); XII, 25–36 (L. Badash on Rutherford).

197 *Joseph Needham in Chinese costume, carrying the scientist's slide rule, by James Wood, Gonville and Caius College*

in Cambridge to a scholarship; he served his apprenticeship under Thomson, then had a spell as professor in Thomson's old home in Manchester – returning to the Cavendish chair in 1919, bringing with him as research student the young James Chadwick.[119] Chadwick was later to be professor at Liverpool and master of Caius, but it was while he was still Rutherford's lieutenant that he discovered the neutron, the basis of his scientific fame – though he is perhaps most widely known as the British scientist who carried the miraculous skills of the Cavendish to America in the 1940s to join the team who devised the atomic bomb. Whatever our attitude to the holocaust of 1945, it blew away for ever Belloc's legend of the remote and ineffectual don. The towering figure among the Cambridge biochemists, Sir Frederick Gowland Hopkins, came even more slowly and by a more devious route: he became a medical student at the age of 27 when he had earned enough by his own savings; in 1898, aged 37, he arrived in Cambridge to work in the group of medical and physiological laboratories developed by the organising genius of Sir Michael Foster – and slowly and painfully, with some aid from Emmanuel, and more from Trinity, earned enough to feed himself and his family; in the end he fed the whole world with the vitamin.[120] Under his aegis grew another generation of scientists – not only biochemists but men of wider views, such as Sir Vincent Wigglesworth, who passed from biochemistry to the study of parasites and then became one of the world's most original insect physiologists; and Joseph Needham, the biochemist turned historian of *Science and Civilisation in China*.[121] It was said of Whewell that omniscience was his foible; Needham is omniscient by a freak of nature, modestly borne, and unites in his capacious frame an

[119] On Chadwick, Massey and Feather 1976; J.B. Skemp in Venn, VII, 485–502; Brooke 1985, pp. 269–75.
[120] On Gowland Hopkins, *DSB*, VI, 498–502 (E. Baldwin); on Sir Michael Foster, Geison 1978.
[121] Wigglesworth 1976; Brooke 1985, pp. 276–81, 296, 300–1, and refs.

exceptional range of scientific learning with a warm romantic Anglo-Catholicism he learned in Cambridge and Thaxted in the 1920s and 1930s, and a devotion to socialism and China which also dates him to the 1930s. The flood of able students demanding nourishment met a rapidly growing cadre of university teachers of exceptional talent. This is part of the story of Cambridge in the last hundred years: it is not the whole story, for there have been very many students with no vocation to serious study and teachers of lesser genius or none. But by the mid twentieth century, however the proportions were drawn, it had become an academic community of the highest international fame – such as it had not enjoyed a hundred years before. Nor does it signify whether in surveying this progress one first remembers John Maynard Keynes, the most glamorous of its great economists, who came from the heart of the Cambridge establishment, or Rutherford or Hopkins, who came from New Zealand and from Eastbourne.[122] The achievement is unthinkable without a powerful native base and an immense and constant recruitment of talent from a wider world.

Cambridge, like the rest of the world, has changed very much since the 1870s and 1880s, most obviously perhaps in the role of religion in its constitution, and in the entry of women. Since Cambridge had been at the end of the eighteenth century in large measure a seminary of Anglican clergy, it might be supposed that the transition from clergyman to don in the late nineteenth century would spell a decline in religious faith and in the study of theology. But the story is full of ironies. First of all, the main character of its studies and its life has become secular, sure enough. Even (or especially) among those who still admit to membership of a conventional religious communion, freedom from religious tests of every kind has become an article of faith as fervently held as its opposite was by the founders of the university and of most of the colleges. The keynote of many statements and statutes of the late nineteenth century and later, 'education, religion, learning and research', sounds hollow in many ears today since religion means nothing to them. But there are still many to whom it means much, and it is far from clear that even attendance in college chapels has suffered in the way that is commonly assumed. Until 1860 daily attendance at chapel was incumbent on all the fellows of all the colleges – but as a majority were absent for much of the year, it must have been largely a dead letter. Compulsory chapel remained common for undergraduates until the end of the First World War, and, in a few, still longer; but how it was enforced is a mystery, since most college chapels in Cambridge could never have held anything like the whole population of a college at a single service. In some there was an elaborate ritual of name-taking; in some it was probably more honoured in the breach than the observance; and such evidence as has so far been sifted suggests that regular communicants in some college chapels were much more numerous in the 1950s than in the early twentieth century – though doubtless changes of religious fashion were also involved.[123] The chapel of Sidney Sussex College was entirely rebuilt and much enlarged between 1911 and 1923: the enlargement perhaps reflects the urgent needs of a growing college when compulsory chapel was still the rule; but its completion and refitting after the First War also shows the tastes and aspirations of a college in which clerical and Anglican influence remained strong, emulating the Wren chapels of Pembroke and Emmanuel.

In theology the matter is much clearer. Cambridge had no Oxford Movement, no Newman, to look back to; it had Frederick Denison Maurice at intervals; but the first golden age of Cambridge theology since the seventeenth century was at its height in the twenty years which followed the abolition of the tests, in the great days of Professors Lightfoot and Westcott and Hort and the building of the Selwyn Divinity School.[124] The abolition of tests

---

[122] For Keynes, Harrod 1951; for Rutherford and Hopkins, see nn. 118 and 120 above.

[123] Brooke 1985, p. 293 n.; cf. *ibid.*, pp. 230–2, 290–4 (290 n. for the end of compulsory chapel in Caius). For the wider context, Green 1964. For what follows (Sidney chapel), *VCH Cambs*, III, 485; Pevsner, 1970, pp. 160–1.

[124] For Westcott, Lightfoot and Hort, see the useful short accounts with bibliography in Cross and Livingstone 1974, pp. 171, 667–8, 823, 1470. On the Selwyn Divinity School see Rupp 1981.

199 *Cambridge, Selwyn College, court and chapel, 1881–95, designed by Sir Arthur Blomfield*

led to much anxiety, and Selwyn College was founded by those who feared that Anglican education would die in Cambridge.[125] In the sense in which they meant, it probably has; but as a centre of theological learning Cambridge never stood so high in its history as in the generations which separate the heyday of the triumvirs, and especially of Westcott and Hort, who presided over the Revised Version of the Bible, from that of the brothers Chadwick – Henry, regius professor of divinity in both Oxford and Cambridge, and his elder brother Owen, ecclesiastical historian and doctor of divinity, and also regius professor of modern history, president of the British Academy, and the master who led Selwyn into a new and wider world.[126]

Meanwhile at Oxford the tutorial system had received a powerful stimulus when it became possible to recruit married tutors. Thus at Balliol, Jowett was able in 1879 to deflect a

[125] *VCH Cambs*, III, 495–6.   [126] See *Who's Who*.

306

former Balliol exhibitioner called A.L. Smith from going to the Bar and to offer him a post as tutor and lecturer in modern history.[127] That subject had broken off from law six years previously and looked like becoming popular. Smith was the son of a civil engineer who had died when his son was very young. The boy had been helped to go to Christ's Hospital, where he had a hard upbringing in the days when that school was still in London and had not yet moved out to the green fields of Horsham. At Oxford he gained first classes in Mods. and Greats and a second in modern history. In choosing A.L. Smith as a tutor Jowett showed the sharp eye which he had for a good man. Smith was to prove one of the best tutors of the late nineteenth and early twentieth centuries. The master of Balliol in the last years of his life turned especially to him to carry out and share his aspirations. Jowett offered him a heavy load. Smith was at times to be given as many as forty pupils.[128] Often this involved taking them into his home where they were looked after by his wife – herself a remarkable woman. In addition he was asked to prepare likely schoolboys for matriculation in order that they might subsequently enter Balliol. They included scions of the aristocracy, like Viscount Weymouth, or sons of eastern potentates like the son of the Sultan of Perak;[129] 'A.L.' needed to be the man of great vitality which he was. He was also an excellent lecturer and the series of lectures which he gave on political science and another on Aristotle's *Politics* were particularly memorable. He was also to lecture on what was to become a famous text of the Oxford history school – Stubbs's *Select Charters and other illustrations of English Constitutional History*. As one of his pupils put it, 'Stubbs's Charters were turned from a valley of bones into a host of jolly bustling humanity.' 'He had a Maitlandian grip on the Middle Ages. If he were explaining Domesday Book you realized that he had put his hands between King William's. If it was the Crusade, he had ridden with Richard south from Acre and had been uneasy about his left flank.'[130] The university was served as generously as the college. Among many commitments to it he acted as proctor, curator of the Bodleian Library and member of the hebdomadal council. On his monument in Balliol chapel when he died in 1924 it was recorded that he stimulated his pupils 'to the strenuous life' (*ad strenuam vitam*).[131] He certainly set them a vigorous example. Another pupil wrote when he had gone down, 'He made me feel, as I still feel, and as I know many others feel, that he was thinking of and planning my well-being; that I could always rely on the best that was in his power. That, I take it, is the supreme achievement of the teacher – to leave with his pupils the sense that he is always present with them, always guiding them, always part of them.'[132] Before Jowett died in 1893 he had arranged for a tutorial house to be built (by T.G. Jackson) on the edge of the college cricket field, or 'The Master's Field' as it was known, so that this exceptional married tutor could live conveniently a family life in a house which was close to Balliol. It was called the King's Mound after the fortifications of Charles I which were situated in the garden. 'A.L.' outside his college commitments proved a ceaseless examiner – as awarder for the Oxford and Cambridge Joint Board Examinations and as a final schools examiner at many civic universities as well as at Oxford and Cambridge. He was a keen supporter of the Workers' Educational Association and one of

[127] Smith 1928, pp. 82–4.
[128] Smith 1928, p. 139. This was not unique. A.H. Johnson (fellow of All Souls and lecturer in modern history at Merton (1884–1923)) was given help by Merton, it was said, when he had more than forty pupils.
[129] Smith 1928, pp. 98–9, 145.
[130] Smith 1928, p. 157. For F.W. Maitland cf. p. 296 above.
[131] Smith 1928, p. 320. Mr T.F.R.G. Braun kindly drew this to our attention.
[132] Quoted in Smith 1928, p. 218.

the authors of an important report on 'Oxford and Working Class Education'.[133] This led to the start of tutorial classes as a new department of extra-mural work and to the summer school for the W.E.A. which began at Balliol in 1907. For all this there was a price to pay. He had little time for literary works of scholarship. He published two lectures on Maitland, a set of Ford Lectures on *Church and State in the Middle Ages* and another on Stubbs's *Charters*, but judged by that unsatisfactory modern touchstone of 'publish or perish' this brilliant teacher might be thought to have failed. There was no respite when he became master of Balliol (1916–24) in the hard days of the First World War. Rather the reverse. He threw himself into the work of reconstruction at college and university which that cataclysm demanded. Smith was a personal friend of a Canadian, George Catlin (later Sir George Catlin), whom the Rhodes Trustees had made their agent after the death of Cecil Rhodes in 1902.[134] Mrs Smith described how she remembered one evening when she was allowed to be of the company in the study and 'five or six of our undergraduates sat spell-bound, closely together like sparrows on a bough, with eyes and beaks open . . . while the two talked "imperially" for nearly two hours. Visionaries they both were, but it is comforting to know that some at least of their wisdom materialized.'[135]

Rhodes himself, the fifth son of a vicar of Bishop's Stortford, had read the Pass School at Oriel before going out to South Africa to make a fortune which, when he died, was worth over £3,000,000. He had the vision of establishing a Trust which would bring to Oxford a steady flow of English-speaking young men (schoolboys originally, but later graduates) especially from the British colonies and the United States, but also from Germany, all of whom were to benefit from an Oxford education and become a ruling élite. They were to foster understanding between the three peoples and to make war impossible. The steady flow began in 1903 and by 1906 there were no less than 161 scholars in residence (71 from the British colonies, 79 from the United States and eleven from Germany).[136] The flow of Germans was twice stopped, but now once more there are German Rhodes Scholars at Oxford. Senator Fulbright and the former American Secretary of State, Dean Rusk, were Rhodes Scholars. So were Norman Manley, Dom Mintoff, and Bob Hawke, prime ministers respectively of Jamaica, Malta and Australia. Smith welcomed this development even if he complained of the testimonials of the first potential Rhodes Scholars. 'What are we to do? Every one of them is a cross between the Archangel Gabriel and C.B. Fry.'[137] For long Balliol easily received the largest number of first-choice applications.

Not many of them read Greats, however, no doubt because of a general lack of Greek. But although the highest point in the teaching of Greats at Balliol, with its centre in the analysis of argument and its most important component moral philosophy, lay in the 1860s,[138] a great flowering followed in the last decades of the nineteenth century and the beginning of the twentieth.

A notable representative of this generation was Ernest Barker. The son of a violin-playing miner from north-east Cheshire, he had been brought up in a cottage before going to Manchester Grammar School and winning a scholarship to Balliol.[139] Firsts in Mods,

[133] See Appendix IV in Smith 1928, pp. 317–18.

[134] We are grateful to Sir Edgar Williams for this reference.   [135] Smith 1928, pp. 189–90.

[136] We are indebted for these figures to the kindness of Sir Edgar Williams; cf. also Newbury 1982, chap. 4.

[137] Smith 1928, pp. 286–7.   [138] Schmidt 1982, p. 161.

[139] Catlin 1960, pp. 341–3; cf. Barker 1949, pp. 5–8. The college scholarship was worth £80 per annum; Manchester Grammar School granted a leaving scholarship of £45. This was not enough to live on and the deficit was made up by an interest-free loan from a local grocer (Barker 1949, pp. 67–8).

and Greats and the Craven Scholarship were followed by winning a prize fellowship at Merton. This was an important development, for fellowships which encouraged research were becoming more numerous and gave a man a chance to write before plunging off into the task of bread-winning. Barker used his years as prize fellow (1898–1905) to write an important book, *The Political Thought of Plato and Aristotle* (1906). This was to hold its place for over forty years and is still valuable. But he also kept up his teaching as lecturer for Wadham and St John's before becoming a full tutorial fellow of New College in 1913. His interests stretched out from classics to modern history, philosophy generally and political science. He lectured on all with distinction and became an outstanding tutor. As his book on *The Dominican Order and Convocation: The Growth of Representation in the Church during the 13th Century* (1913) and his *Social and Political Thought in Byzantium* (1961) showed, he was equally at home with the Middle Ages and with Greece and Rome. In 1920 he tried his hand at administration as principal of King's College, London, though he was probably happier as a teacher and returned to the life of lecturing when he was elected as the first professor of political science at Cambridge in 1928. It was typical of this large-hearted man that long after he had retired he answered a call to help the German universities get on their feet again, after the experience of Hitler, when he went out to take up in his seventies the post of professor of political science at the university of Cologne in 1947–8.[140]

When Rhodes had drawn up his project he had judged Oxford to be a centre of excellence in all departments 'except science'. What had happened to science at Oxford in the years after the construction of the University Museum, and why can one not name a great teacher of chemistry or physics at Oxford until the appointment of Harold Hartley as fellow of Balliol in 1901? The answer seems to lie in two bad appointments and to offer a demonstration that if electoral bodies make such mistakes there is no length to the harm that they can do.

R.B. Clifton, elected professor of experimental philosophy (that is, physics) in 1865, must have seemed a promising candidate.[141] He had been sixth Wrangler and a fellow of St John's College, Cambridge, before holding the chair of natural philosophy at Manchester (1860–5). He was to hold his chair at Oxford until he retired at the age of 79 in 1915. Lord Cherwell is reported to have said of him that he held up the development of physics at Oxford for fifty years. Nor did the electors to the Wayneflete chair of chemistry do any better in 1872 when they elected William Odling, a bright young man of 42 from London. He was to become notorious for his lack of interest in research.[142] He considered it beneath the dignity of a professor to appear in a laboratory. Odling did no research himself, nor did he encourage his students or colleagues to undertake any. The result was that the university chemistry department produced practically no published work for forty years.[143] In measured tones the authors of the report of the 1922 commission observed that 'There was a considerable period, during the most critical time in the history of modern science at Oxford, in which the Departments of Chemistry and Physics, the most fundamental of the new developments of the Museum, did not avail themselves of their opportunities for

---

[140] *Merton College Register, 1900–64*, p. 4.

[141] Foster 1888, p. 264. But see now the thorough analysis of the problem of Oxford science in this period in Howarth 1987.

[142] Foster 1888, p. 1036.

[143] Smith 1982, pp. 215–16. There were also more general factors at work: cf. Haig 1986 (the Warden of Merton kindly drew our attention to this important article).

vigorous progress, and this probably caused a serious delay in the growth of the Science school.'[144]

By an irony several of the colleges had erected their own small laboratories – Christ Church, Magdalen, Balliol (sharing with Trinity) – and they helped to sustain important research until around the turn of the century when a considerable revival in chemistry occurred. This was due chiefly to Vernon Harcourt at Christ Church and Harold Hartley at Balliol.[145] In the winter of 1899 Frederick Soddy, a Merton man who was to become Oxford's first Nobel prizewinner, was working in the Balliol–Trinity laboratory before going on to work with Rutherford at McGill.[146] In 1916 Balliol elected as a Brackenbury scholar Cyril Hinshelwood, another future Nobel prizewinner (jointly with Semenov), who became fellow of Balliol in 1920 and tutor at Trinity the year after that.[147] He was to become outstanding for his research on chemical kinetics, and as a tutor. Since he also mastered five European languages as well as Chinese, was to become president of the Classical Association and give an outstanding centenary essay on Dante's imagery, he also showed that professional skill in science at Oxford could go hand-in-hand with a polymathic versatility. His career links the age of William Perkin Junior[148] and the Balliol–Trinity, Christ Church and Magdalen laboratories with that of the Nuffield benefaction, since when Nuffield was persuaded to fund a chair in physical chemistry in 1937 it was Cyril Hinshelwood who became its first occupant. This time the electors got it right.

As many will think, the deepest of all the changes of late-Victorian days was the arrival of women, greeted with an ambivalent welcome. The foundation of Girton and Newnham at the turn of the 1860s and 1870s came mid-way between Tennyson's *The Princess* of 1847 and Gilbert and Sullivan's *Princess Ida* of 1884. It is hard to believe how great a step forward in women's education these foundations represented. Almost every century has produced its highly educated women, and Jane Austen had provided a case against almost all the generalisations on which the arguments to exclude women from enjoying a similar education to men were based; and the English colleges had been anticipated in America, as their founders well knew. Even so, Emily Davies of Girton and the group of enlightened men and women who summoned Miss Clough to found Newnham were heroic pioneers.[149] They owed much to J.S. Mill, who had nothing to do with Cambridge, and the Apostolic F.D. Maurice, who had much: but they owed more to a group of notable allies, led by Henry Sidgwick, one of the chief founders of Newnham – and most of all to themselves. Emily Davies gathered five students in Hitchin in 1869, which for some years was as near to Cambridge as she thought it safe to come; Miss Clough gathered five students in Regent Street in 1871 – and from this modest beginning two great colleges have grown. They were planted by members of the same circle of devoted supporters, but Emily Davies stuck to certain principles unacceptable to Sidgwick and his allies, so that they remained separate. Newnham passed after a short interval via Merton Hall (now part of St John's) to

---

[144] Smith 1982, p. 214.
[145] Smith 1982, p. 206.
[146] Smith 1982, p. 204. In a cellar on staircase XVI.
[147] H. Hartley in *DNB 1961–70*, pp. 516–19.
[148] William Perkin, Jr. assistant to Professor Dixon, professor of chemistry at Manchester, became in 1912 professor of chemistry at Oxford. His arrival and the construction of the Dyson Perrins Laboratory in 1916, thanks to the generosity of his patron, Dyson Perrins, had a most beneficial effect on his department.
[149] Bradbrook 1969, chaps. I, II; Hamilton 1936, esp. chaps. IV–IX; *VCH Cambs*, III, 490–5 (Jean Lindsay and Dorothy Brodie); Clough 1897; Sidgwick 1906, 1938.

200   *Cambridge, Newnham College, one of the group of original halls designed by Basil Champneys: Sidgwick Hall, completed in 1880, with the dining-hall of Clough to the left, 1888*

its present site, where Mrs Sidgwick was second principal and guiding genius from 1892 to 1910. The original buildings of Newnham followed quite a different pattern from men's colleges – a group of halls designed by Basil Champneys in the 'Dutch red-brick style' have an air considerably more domestic than the extensive new buildings of Alfred Waterhouse at Jesus and Pembroke and Caius so characteristic of Victorian endeavour in Cambridge.[150] Miss Davies was eventually prevailed on to allow her college to move to Girton, still at a much greater distance than Sidgwick and Miss Clough thought sensible. But Emily Davies had always wanted her girls to receive an education identical with men. So she and her helpers hired the leading college architect of the day, Alfred Waterhouse, and invited him to embark on a scheme in which the Tudor red brick of Jesus and Pembroke should predominate; and eventually her remorseless determination to build, kept alive by her

201–2

[150] Pevsner 1970, pp. 80–1, 90, 127, 190–2. For Waterhouse in Caius, see also Brooke 1985, pp. 215–17.

201 *Girton College, Cambridge, by Alfred Waterhouse: the entrance tower, completed in 1880*

202 *(opposite) Emily Davies Court, completed in 1873*

successors, led to the erection of a vast complex by a whole dynasty of Waterhouses.[151] For Cambridge, her buildings contained one major innovation, very recently anticipated at Keble. The rooms are linked by corridors, originally served by armies of maids, like a great Victorian country house – not by the staircases leading straight into the Cambridge weather of the traditional college. The corridors of Girton are the longest in Cambridge, and possibly in Christendom.

[151] Bradbrook 1969, esp. pp. 27–8, 59–64; Pevsner 1970, pp. 190–2.

312

203 *Waterhouse in Pembroke College, Cambridge: the Library, 1875 – with a corner of the chapel*

From early days Newnham and Girton were aided by many of the most enlightened of the men of Cambridge – Sidgwick, E.S. Roberts, John Peile, the master of Christ's (1887–1910), and many others; and they soon bred up their own distinguished academics. Stanley Spencer's portrait of Dame Mary Cartwright, one of the outstanding living Cambridge mathematicians, is a fitting monument to what the women's colleges have given both to the learning and the culture of Cambridge. Yet the university at large

314

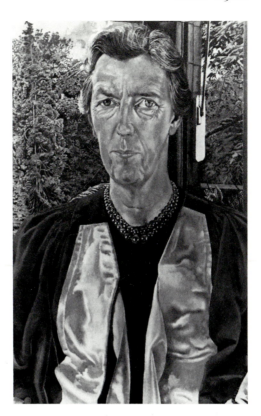

204 *Portrait of Dame Mary Cartwright, mistress of Girton, 1949–68, by Stanley Spencer*

was slow to welcome them. By the end of the Second World War they were still not members of the university. In 1921 the senate voted to keep them that way, and a foolish country clergyman cried out in his excitement, 'Now go and tell Girton and Newnham.'[152] The result was a riot in which a rabble of students severely damaged the Newnham gates – an event which caused a major reaction among the undergraduates, who whipped up a subscription to pay for their repair, and a minor reaction in the senate, which voted to allow women 'titular degrees'. Full admission came only in 1947–8 when the shame-faced men of the university did not dare even to raise a vote. But by then a new tide was flowing.

If Keble and Oxford anticipated the corridors of Girton, Cambridge had won the race for women's colleges, even if only by a few years. There had been hints in Oxford too that female influence in the university might grow. As in Cambridge, there was much debate on the abolition of celibacy; the tutors at Exeter College from 1858 might retain their tutorships on marriage, though not their fellowships. In 1869 New College altered its statutes to allow fellows who were also tutors to retain their fellowships on marriage;[153] and in 1872 Merton opened four of its fellowships to married dons, including Mandell Creighton, the future Dixie professor at Cambridge and Bishop of London; this brought to an end for Creighton and his fiancée a long and anxious courtship.[154] Many obstacles

---

[152] Howarth 1978, p. 42 – cf. *ibid.*, pp. 35–42.
[153] Engel 1983, p. 107 and n. 1.
[154] Creighton 1906, I, 80; Engel 1983, pp. 111–13.

205   *Oxford, Lady Margaret Hall, founded 1878: 'Talbot', by Reginald Blomfield, 1909–10; and to the right 'Toynbee', 1915*

remained, but these examples were catching. Already in 1866 a series of public lectures for women had been organised by Eleanor Smith, sister of the Savilian professor of geometry, although it had not been a great success.

A year later the Oxford Local Examinations were made available to schoolgirls and in 1871 Annie Rogers, daughter of Professor Thorold Rogers, gained marks which, had she been male, would have entitled her to an exhibition at Balliol or Worcester.[155] When the first halls of residence for women were opened at Hitchin in 1869 and in Cambridge in 1871, the argument for like foundations in Oxford grew warm. Characteristically it proved impossible to unite the would-be reformers. One group under the influence of high churchmen thought that a new hall should be governed according to church principles. Their leaders Edward and Lavinia Talbot were inspired by Pusey and the example of Keble

[155] Battiscombe 1978, p. 63.

316

College.[156] This was the Christ Church camp. Their rivals aimed at an undenominational foundation. They were inspired by Jowett and T.H. Green, and constituted the Balliol camp. Both groups proved successful. The former founded Lady Margaret Hall, named after the Lady Margaret Beaufort, in 1878, the latter Somerville, after Mary Somerville, the mathematician, a year later. Beyond these two residential halls an Association for the

---

[156] Battiscombe 1978, pp. 64–5.

Higher Education of Women was formed to make arrangements for the teaching of all women students in Oxford, whether at home or in lodgings or at L.M.H. or Somerville. Three more women's colleges were opened before the end of the century, St Hugh's,[157] St Hilda's and the Society of Home Students, the future St Anne's. St Hugh's is especially interesting since it pursued the aim of providing for poor students which Tractarians like

[157] Griffin 1986.

318

Charles Marriott had sought to foster. The attempt to bypass college fees and thus to lower costs had been made with the establishment of non-collegiate students in 1868 and the Society of Home Students. Keble College had tried to achieve the same end for men within a collegiate framework by giving its students 'the same educational advantages as members of other colleges' but together with 'economy and simplicity of living'. Much later, in 1928, Francis Chavasse, Bishop of Liverpool, once vicar of St Peter le Bailey and master of the theological college, Wycliffe Hall, followed this example in founding St Peter's Hall: he wished to found a place where university education at low cost should be combined – in his case – with evangelical churchmanship. He thus continued the evangelical tradition of the new foundation of Hertford. Now in 1886 the first principal of Lady Margaret Hall herself, when founding St Hugh's, observed that 'while there is a sufficient number of students willing to pay for the luxury of a room to themselves, and other things to correspond, there is a still larger, and we fear a growing number who find the charges of the present Halls at Oxford and Cambridge (even the most moderate) beyond their means. It may be added that many of the clergy especially are forced to send their daughters to "unsectarian" places of instruction because the Church has done so little for their needs.'[158]

All these colleges had to wait for their undergraduates to be admitted to degrees until 1920; not until 1960 were they made full colleges of the university. Their members have included the Nobel prizewinner Dorothy Hodgkin, and the outstanding pro-vice-chancellor and historian, Lucy Sutherland. In recent years the number of women at Oxford has greatly increased as a result of the decision of all the men's colleges to change their statutes and 'go mixed'. Three of the women's colleges have done the same. Though the total number of women in the university is now only a third of the whole student body, this proportion may thus be expected to rise steadily.

[158] Kemp 1986, pp. 15–16. We are grateful to Miss Kemp for this reference.

11 Epilogue: the mid twentieth century

> It seems that every show place gets every year more and more thronged, and it seems our destiny to turn into a show place. Learning will go elsewhere and we shall subside into cicerones. The typical Cambridge man will be the antiquarian personage who knows about the history of colleges, and is devoted to 'culture des ruines'.
>
> Henry Sidgwick, 1869, quoted in Sidgwick 1906; CC, p. 242

The refusal of the colleges after the agricultural depression effectively to finance the universities has led to a great divorce between the colleges and their parents. From the 1920s on, and far more since the Second World War, government finance and substantial investment from industry and elsewhere have created an immense machine of university departments and laboratories. It was mainly a large and immensely munificent gift from the Rockefeller Foundation which made possible the Cambridge University Library of 1934, when the ageing Sir Giles Gilbert Scott devised a monumental building which the benefactors asked him to crown with a tower.[1] But if its exterior is controversial, few who have grown up to serious study within its walls have doubted that it is one of the best libraries in the world to work in. After the Second World War university finance passed on to a higher plane altogether, and the state has become the greatest benefactor.

When the third royal commission sat in the early 1920s, its function was precisely to justify and quantify the first major injection of government financial support.[2] In a mood of considerable euphoria it prepared the way for growing government aid and the expanding work of the University Grants Committee, which had been founded in 1919. By 1927–8 the government grant amounted to 21 per cent of the total expenditure at Oxford. It had become obvious that the state alone could undertake the development of the scientific laboratories. The same was true for every British university.[3] By 1948–9 these grants covered more than half the total bill. Although Oxford and Cambridge were not singled out for major expansion in the 1960s, when new universities were founded and many of the old increased two- or three-fold, they had already grown substantially in student numbers and were to grow still further: from 5,023 at Oxford and 5,931 at Cambridge in 1938–9, to 8,800 and 9,150 in 1962–3, to 12,671 in Oxford and 12,342 at Cambridge in 1984–5.[4]

---

[1] See *Cambridge University Library 1400–1934* . . . (Cambridge, 1934); Pevsner 1970, p. 215. For what follows, Pevsner 1970, pp. 215–18.

[2] *Royal Commission 1922*; Roach 1959, pp. 290–3.   [3] *Whitaker's Almanack 1986*, p. 447.

[4] UGC, *Returns from Universities* . . . 1938–9, p. 7; *Committee on Higher Education* (Robbins Report), App. 2 (1963), p. 19; *VCH Oxon*, III, 35; *Oxford University Gazette* (supplement 1 to no. 4004, 3 October 1985, p. 75); *Cambridge University Reporter* 26 Sept. 1986, p. 2. These figures include both undergraduates and graduates.

208 *Oxford, Nuclear Physics Laboratory, c. 1960–70, by Philip Dowson of Arup Associates*

At Oxford, by 1984, grants covered just over half a total income of £80,000,000, and a substantial part of the rest came from students' fees, largely supplied by the state. Meanwhile there have been numerous large building projects, not only in the provision of modern laboratories. In Oxford the St Cross building of 1964 houses law and English and the Institute of Economics and Statistics. In Cambridge new buildings include the arts

209

209 *Oxford, St Cross Building,*
1961–4, by Sir Leslie Martin and
Colin St J. Wilson

complex first devised by Sir Hugh Casson and enlarged by many hands, including those of James Stirling, author of the most celebrated and the most controversial building in Cambridge of our day – to which pilgrims come from every architecture school in the world, and which the university seriously considered demolishing in the 1980s. It has many qualities and many problems, and has been saved for a great price. Almost all the colleges of both universities have extended their buildings in recent decades to ameliorate the need for accommodation. In recent years the number of undergraduates has been controlled and has expanded gradually. It is the graduates who have notably grown to reach a quarter of the total student body.

Jowett had observed that 'able men ought to go more often into a business career, the good they might do is simply endless'. Yet the emphasis of the Jowett ideal had been on public service and in his day more graduates entered upon commerce and the professions than industry. Oxford's great local industry, the manufacture of the motor-car, indeed has bred one great benefactor – Lord Nuffield. He became the greatest individual benefactor of the university and city of the present century. He began his benefactions to the university on quite a small scale in 1926. But ten years later he startled the university by offering to

322

210 *Cambridge, History
Faculty Building and Seeley
Library, 1964–8, by James
Stirling*

give a million and a quarter pounds for the Oxford medical school.[5] At the meeting of congregation at which this munificent gift was to be accepted in the presence of the chancellor, Lord Halifax, the donor rose to announce himself that he had increased the sum to £2,000,000 in order to make sure that it was enough. As a result five professorships and one readership in medical studies were founded; the chair in anaesthetics was particularly insisted on by the donor, and all the chairs played a major role in developing the clinical school after the Second World War.

[5] Cf. Andrews and Brunner 1955, pp. 288–9; Chester 1986, p. 66. The Nuffield Institute for Medical Research had been founded in 1935 (*Oxford University Calendar (1984–5)*, p. 137). Nuffield's intentions with regard to the Medical School were revealed at a private party given by Sir Farquhar Buzzard at All Souls on 20 July 1936 (A.M. Cooke, *Sir Farquhar Buzzard, Bt, KCVO* (1975), pp. 29–30).

211 *James Stirling in Oxford: the Florey Building of Queen's College, 1968–70*

212 *(opposite) Nuffield College, Oxford, 1949–60, by Harrison, Baines and Hubbard*

Individual existing colleges – St Peter's Hall, Worcester, Pembroke, Lady Margaret Hall, St Hilda's, St Hugh's, Somerville and Lincoln – all benefited from Nuffield's generosity. But in 1937 he began a process which was to lead to the foundation of the great new graduate college which bears his name. In July 1937 Lord Nuffield went to see the chancellor of the university and offered to pay for a college of engineering.[6] He said that he was ready to

[6] Andrews and Brunner 1955, pp. 288–9; Chester 1986, pp. 63–70.

spend £250,000 on a building which should be put up on a site which he had recently bought to the west of St Peter's Hall and at the same time 'to give beauty and dignity to the western approaches to the city'. He offered £750,000 for the college's endowment. In talks with the chancellor, the benefactor added the possibility of accountancy to that of engineering as a subject to which the new foundation should be directed. He wished to fill what he took to be a gap in Oxford's facilities as compared with those of Cambridge. However, the university had quite recently come to an agreement with Cambridge that each university should avoid unnecessary duplication. Moreover Oxford had also agreed that the major objectives of its future policy should include the development of social studies and the construction of a new physical chemistry laboratory. How could these different aims be reconciled? This was the task which faced the vice-chancellor, A.D. Lindsay, master of Balliol, and his highly efficient registrar, Sir Douglas Veale. They had in the same year been busy attending to an appeal for the extension of the Bodleian Library in order to benefit from a generous offer from the Rockefeller Foundation to do more than match any money which the appeal might raise; this resulted in the new Bodleian Library. Now they persuaded Lord Nuffield that the physical chemistry laboratory could be interpreted as filling a gap in the university's scientific facilities, while the college of engineering was to become a college 'to encourage research especially but not exclusively in the field of social studies, and especially by making easier cooperation of academic and non-academic persons'. The founder of Nuffield College thus drew attention to the needs of British industry which had not been much noticed since the days of Jowett.

Although since 1945 St Peter's Hall has become St Peter's College and St Edmund Hall has also become a full college (both have undergraduates and graduates), other new foundations have followed Nuffield in concentrating on the needs of graduates. In 1948 M. Antonin Besse of Aden gave £1,250,000 to found St Antony's College and another £250,000 to help seven existing colleges to extend their accommodation.[7] Under its first warden, Sir Bill Deakin, St Antony's specialised in the study of European history of the twentieth century and also began to turn its attention to areas of history previously overlooked, such as the Middle East and Latin America. The pattern of area studies has been followed for Africa at the Institute of Commonwealth Studies and Queen Elizabeth House and for Japan at the Nissan Institute, established by a benefaction from the Nissan Car Company.

In 1962 men and women graduates reading for advanced degrees were helped by the foundation of Linacre College.[8] Then to deal with the problem of senior members who had no university or college affiliation, two more colleges, Iffley and St Cross, were set up in 1965. They too were enabled to recruit graduate students. As a result of a substantial donation from the Wolfson Foundation, Iffley became Wolfson College and was thus able to erect an outstanding complex of modern buildings on a picturesque site beside the Cherwell. It includes a centre for socio-legal studies.[9] These benefactions were not limited to Wolfson. He also helped Pembroke and St Hilda's to add to their existing buildings. Oxford's two most recent colleges, Templeton and Green, are both for graduates. After the end of the Second World War a modest initiative was taken by the bursar of Brasenose towards setting up a Centre for Management Studies. The government had

[7] Footman 1986, p. 175.
[8] *Oxford University Calendar* (1984–5), p. 213.   [9] *Oxford University Calendar* (1984–5), pp. 307–8.

213 *Cambridge, New Hall, 1962–6, by Peter Chamberlin, Powell and Bon*

concentrated its attention in this field on the universities of London and Manchester, understandably enough. But a student of the Oxford centre decided to help to fill up this gap in Oxford's academic arrangements. Mr John Templeton is funding the transformation of the centre into a full-blown graduate college in management studies to be named after him.[10]

Of all the scientific discoveries to be made in Oxford's extensive range of scientific laboratories in the twentieth century there has been none more spectacular or haphazard in its initial stages than that part of the discovery of penicillin by Sir Howard Florey which was completed by his work with Sir Alexander Fleming and developed by Professor Abraham. The establishment of a clinical school and the building of a network of hospitals have made Oxford a centre of medical studies with a world-wide reputation. This was never more strikingly shown than when Dr and Mrs Cecil Green from Dallas, Texas, gave

[10] *Oxford University Calendar* (1984–5), p. 333.

214 The Founding of Wolfson College, Cambridge, *mural by Gordon Davies, 1980 (detail), a fantasy showing the symbols of academe in the foreground, and the building of Wolfson College: on the scaffolding are a group of fellows above, the architects below. Sir Isaac and Sir Leonard (Lord) Wolfson are on the left wing of the mural, not shown here. Behind is a pastiche of the Senate House, Caius, the Bridge of Sighs, Trinity, Pembroke and King's*

215 *Cambridge, Fitzwilliam College, 1961–7, by Sir Denys Lasdun, the hall*

£1,000,000 to a new college which was being designed to serve the interests of the growing number of medical teachers and students.[11] The Old Radcliffe Observatory forms the noble centrepiece of Green College, whose construction began in 1979.

In Oxford the colleges have never relaxed their grip on teaching appointments, and this saved the rift between the colleges and university from deepening. But in Cambridge, in contrast to Oxford, the revival and expansion of the university after the contraction and the pause inevitable in two world wars, led in the 1950s and 1960s to an even wider separation between the colleges and the university. There are no joint appointments. The majority of college teaching fellows also hold university appointments such as is the norm for college tutors in Oxford, who hold university lectureships; and all but a tiny handful of university professors and readers have fellowships – and there is an elaborate and bizarre

[11] Its first students were admitted in 1979 (*Oxford University Calendar* (1984–5), p. 193). The Observatory had been bought in 1930 by Lord Nuffield at a cost of £100,000 for the Radcliffe Infirmary (Andrews and Brunner 1955, p. 261).

330

216 *Cambridge, Churchill College, 1959–68, by Richard Sheppard*

machinery to ensure that professors from outside Cambridge are not left too long in the cold. But there were by the early 1950s a large and growing number of university teachers and other staff with no standing in any of the colleges, let alone fellowships, and whole departments with only a tiny proportion of college fellows. This separation, and other movements of the period, led to a series of creative measures. The division between university and college was the prime inspiration behind the formation of University College, which was planned to allow fellowships or membership at least to a large number of university officers without close ties to any other colleges; it was renamed Wolfson College after a major 214 benefaction from the Wolfson Foundation. The grave shortage of places for women and the extreme malaise about their opportunities in Cambridge led to the foundation of New Hall 213 in 1954. It was often observed that it was not only teaching staff but research students and other visitors from afar who were strangers to the colleges and their society. A prestigious committee under Lord Bridges recommended in 1962 many schemes for improvement, in

331

particular the formation of a graduate college. The same impulse led to the inspired idea of dividing Clare College into two. The other half of the amoeba, now called Clare Hall (to the eternal confusion of historians, since the college itself bore that name till quite recent times) is a new kind of collegiate society, untrammelled by the traditions and the taboos of the old, in which fellows and visitors and postgraduate students – and their families – can freely mingle. In 1964 Caius, St John's and Trinity – well aware that these problems could not be solved simply by expanding the existing colleges – joined to found another postgraduate society, Darwin College.[12] The system of student grants, of entry by U.C.C.A. and the immense increase in pressure for places at Cambridge – and the rising academic standards this inevitably brought forth in a world geared to fairness in such competition – made the old non-collegiate society, Fitzwilliam, formed in the nineteenth century to provide a cheaper home for poorer students, seem an anachronism. It has been converted into a full college of the traditional pattern; and beside it have been founded two more – Churchill in the 1950s as a memorial to Sir Winston, and Robinson in the 1970s named after the most recent, and one of the most princely of private benefactors, Sir David Robinson. Meanwhile several existing societies – St Edmund's House, Hughes Hall and Homerton – have received various degrees of recognition, and a group of women academics – originally formed of those who had no fellowships – came together to found the small society of Lucy Cavendish, which is specially designed to provide opportunities for mature women who had previously missed the chance for higher education.

At Oxford in 1962, as a result of the efforts of council's committee on the relationship between the university and the colleges, a sub-committee was set up to examine the problem that many of the university's academic staff were not fellows of colleges. One of the outcomes of its deliberations was the foundation of St Cross and Iffley (the future Wolfson). Meanwhile the commission of inquiry, known as the Franks Commission, since it sat under the chairmanship of Lord Franks, had begun in 1964 to seek to identify other necessary reforms throughout the structure of the university and to make recommendations for dealing with them. Among the results of the report which it made in 1966 was the establishment of a co-ordinating body known as the Conference of Colleges in order to improve the links between the colleges and the university. It also had a psychological and historical significance as an excruciating piece of self-examination.

A new wind has blown through the men's colleges of both universities in the 1970s and 1980s. As in the early nineteenth century, it has been rather the students than the dons who planned the next round of reform. In the 1960s student revolt led to a student presence on innumerable committees and even some college governing bodies; but the efforts to make Oxford and Cambridge mixed universities – not just male preserves with a few female strongholds within them – has had greater and more fundamental consequences. There have been many male dons who thought on principle that their societies should be mixed; there have been a number more who regarded it as a most undesirable revolution. But it seems likely that it was a pressure from the schools which was the chief solvent of change. More and more the state schools were mixed, and applicants looked for a mixed society in the universities as their natural milieu for study. Directors of studies and admission tutors discovered, or convinced themselves, that those colleges which were going mixed were proving more attractive to the abler students. It

[12] Young 1967. On Fitzwilliam Grave 1983, esp. chaps. VI, XIII.

217 *Cambridge, Robinson College, 1977–80, by Gillespie, Kidd and Coia*

took all the years between 1869 and 1948 to win legal equality of status in the university for women; but in the much shorter space of time between the mid 1960s and the present, Girton and all the men's colleges in Cambridge have become mixed; and in Oxford all but St Hilda's and Somerville.

In the 1960s the Robbins Committee made recommendations for the enhancement of the British universities which led to the rapid expansion of the modern universities and the foundation of new ones. But the enhancement that a Conservative government took in hand with considerable enthusiasm in the 1960s another has dismantled in the 1980s – and the effect that this will have on the future of Oxford and Cambridge and the relations of university and college is still to see. Meanwhile the constitutional structures of the 1920s – faculties and faculty boards and the General Board to direct their affairs – have survived

333

with little change; and the relations of the colleges and the university have only been significantly modified in the last sixty years as a consequence of financial pressures which put both under severe constraints – dictated by the government departments which finance both the university and most of the students.

Within this framework there have been academic changes in profusion: in the provision of new laboratories and libraries, of new departments and new areas of academic enterprise – an activity which has often strained the relations of universities and colleges to the utmost. Colleges may be slow to provide teaching in subjects which university opinion wishes to foster; and the university may be unable to meet the teaching demands of the colleges trying to respond to the demand of student applicants, whose admission they still control. Amid the galaxy of new disciplines the old faculties and schools and (in Cambridge) triposes in natural sciences have spread their wings and encompassed the earth and the stars; mechanical sciences or engineering have grown up and reared a family of fledgelings; social studies and social sciences have striven to find a place in the sun. Few of the new schools of the twentieth century have proved more successful than P.P.E. at Oxford – philosophy, politics and economics – a joint school from 1920 which rapidly came to vie with Classical Greats among the most prestigious of Oxbridge courses. But the conservatism of Cambridge kept social sciences at bay till the 1960s, and in Oxford archaeology is still not an undergraduate study.

Most Oxford and Cambridge students probably work a good deal harder than their predecessors fifty years ago. In this and other ways they follow the patterns and the fashions of the world. They still row on the river, fall out of punts, talk politics in the Union, debate the nature of the world in the Apostles, eat and drink and are merry and sad. But entry to Oxford and Cambridge has become very competitive, and its examinations even more so; and there is an anxiety, a universal rivalry, which in some measure is new. It can never be all-pervasive: as in the early nineteenth century an extraordinary concentration of young talent finds its own outlet. In the 1960s the students at Cambridge conformed to the pattern of the world and engaged in rebellion – not sufficiently to crack the structure of the university, but enough to bring a student presence to an infinite number of committees, and to create a new C.U.S.U. (Cambridge University Students' Union) to run the university. And now the world laughs with Cambridge, for an extraordinary concentration of the famous producers, actors, comedians and satirists (and at least one bishop) have been bred in the Footlights, especially between 1947 and 1963; they include Julian Slade, Jonathan Miller, David Frost, Eleanor Bron, John Cleese, Peter Cook – and Simon Phipps.[13] But for some Oxford had the last laugh by breeding Flanders and Swann.

In Cambridge the colleges and the university are as far apart as ever – much farther than in Oxford. The divorce has stimulated some of the creative measures of recent decades, and has stifled many more. A few years ago two Cambridge professors past the middle term of life fell to discussing the relation of colleges and university: 'A crazy system, and it doesn't work at all', said one; 'A crazy system, and it works miraculously', said the other. In another century or two, it may be, one will be seen to have adopted the stance of Sidgwick, the other of Whewell, in the endless debate on university reform; but if it can truly be said to work, it is indeed a miracle. Yet amid all the anxieties of the 1980s, it is heartening to recall

---

[13] Hewison 1983–4, esp. chaps. IV and V.

334

the resilience of the academic body in the past and the vigour with which the university and colleges responded to the challenges of the fifteenth century or the seventeenth. In the twentieth they cannot offer masses for the dead such as enabled them to make some recompense to their medieval benefactors. By contrast they can provide a comparable excellence of training to that which made Oxford attractive in, say, the thirteenth century. That the universities and colleges are going to have to work together today more closely than ever if they are to maintain the excellence of both is obvious.

Bibliographical References

OHS = Oxford Historical Society

Abbott, W.C. ed. 1937–47. *Writings and Speeches of Oliver Cromwell*, 4 vols., Cambridge, 1937–47

Addyman, P.V. and Biddle, M. 1965. 'Medieval Cambridge: recent finds and excavations', *Proceedings of the Cambridge Antiquarian Society*, LVIII (1965), 74–137

Allen, P. 1978. *The Cambridge Apostles: The Early Years*, Cambridge, 1978

Allen, P.S., and Garrod, H.W. eds. 1928. *Merton Muniments*, OHS, LXXXVI, 1928

Allen, W. 1969–70. *Translating for King James*, Nashville, 1969; London, 1970

Andrews, P.W.S., and Brunner, E. 1955. *The Life of Lord Nuffield*, Oxford, 1955

Annan, N. 1955. 'The intellectual aristocracy', in *Studies in Social History, A Tribute to G.M. Trevelyan*, ed. J.H. Plumb, London, 1955, pp. 241–87

Anstey, H. ed. 1898. *Epistolae Academicae*, 2 parts, OHS, XXXV–XXXVI, 1898

Arkell, W.J. 1947. *Oxford Stone*, London, 1947

Arnold, M. 1865. *Essays in Criticism*, 1865, cited from edn of London and New York, 1902

Aston, T.H. 1977. 'Oxford's medieval alumni', *Past and Present*, no. 74 (Feb. 1977), 3–40
    1984. 'The external administration and resources of Merton College to *circa* 1348', in Catto 1984, chap. 8, pp. 311–68

Aston, T.H., Duncan, G.D., and Evans, T.A.R. 1980. 'The medieval alumni of the university of Cambridge', *Past and Present*, no. 86 (Feb. 1980), 9–86

Attwater, D. 1979. *A Dictionary of Saints*, Harmondsworth, 1979

Aylmer, G.E. 1986. 'The economics and finances of the colleges and university, *c.* 1530–1640', in McConica 1986, chap. 8, pp. 521–58

Baker, J.N.L. 1971. *Jesus College, Oxford 1571–1971*, Oxford, 1971

Ball, W.W. Rouse, 1889. *A History of the Study of Mathematics at Cambridge*, Cambridge, 1889
    1918. *Cambridge Papers*, London, 1918

Barker, Sir E. 1949. *Father of the Man: Memories of Cheshire, Lancashire, and Oxford, 1874–1898*, London, 1949

Bartholomew, A.T. 1912. *Gunning's Last Years: Nine Letters from Miss Mary Beart to Professor Adam Sedgwick*, Cambridge, 1912

Barton, J. 1986. 'The faculty of law', in McConica 1986, chap. 4 (3), pp. 257–93

Bate, W.J. 1978. *Samuel Johnson*, London, 1978

Battiscombe, G. 1978. *Reluctant Pioneer: The Life of Elizabeth Wordsworth*, London, 1978

Bede, *Hist. Eccl.*: *Bede's Ecclesiastical History of the English People*, ed. B. Colgrave and R.A.B. Mynors, Oxford Medieval Texts, Oxford, 1969

Bede, C. 1853. *The Adventures of Mr Verdant Green*, n.p., 1853

Bennett, G.V. 1986a. 'Loyalist Oxford and the Revolution', in Sutherland and Mitchell 1986, chap. 1, pp. 9–29
    1986b. 'Against the tide: Oxford under William III', in Sutherland and Mitchell 1986, chap. 2, pp. 31–60
    1986c. 'The era of party zeal 1702–1714', in Sutherland and Mitchell 1986, chap. 3, pp. 61–97

1986d. 'University, society and church 1688–1714', in Sutherland and Mitchell 1986, chap. 12, pp. 359–400

Bentham, J. 1843. *The Works*, ed. J. Bowring, 11 vols., Edinburgh, 1843

Biddle, M., and Hill, D. 1971. 'Late Saxon planned towns', *Antiquaries Journal*, LI (1971), 70–85

Bill, E.G.W. 1973. *University Reform in Nineteenth-Century Oxford*, Oxford, 1973

Black, M.H. 1984. *Cambridge University Press, 1584–1984*, Cambridge, 1984

Blakiston, H.E.D. 1898. *Trinity College*, London, 1898

Boase, C.W. 1887. *Oxford* (Historic Towns), 2nd edn, London, 1887

  ed. 1894. *Registrum Collegii Exoniensis*, OHS, XXVII, 1894

Bourdillon, A.F.C. 1926. *The Order of Minoresses in England*, British Society of Franciscan Studies, XII, 1926

  1938. *A Survey of the Social Services in the Oxford District*, 2 vols., Oxford, 1938

Boyle, L.E. 1984. 'Canon law before 1380', in Catto 1984, chap. 14, pp. 531–64

Bradbrook, M.C. 1969. *'That Infidel Place': A Short History of Girton College 1869–1969*, London, 1969

Bradshaw, B., and Duffy, E. eds. *Humanism, Reform and the Reformation: The Career of Bishop John Fisher*, Cambridge, forthcoming

Brink, C.O. 1986. *English Classical Scholarship: Reflections on Bentley, Porson and Housman*, Cambridge, 1986

Brodrick, G.C. 1885. *Memorials of Merton College*, OHS, IV, 1885

Brooke, C.N.L. 1970. 'The missionary at home: the church in the towns 1000–1250', *Studies in Church History*, VI (ed. C.J. Cuming, 1970), 59–83

  1983. 'Homage to the Lady Margaret', *Cambridge Review*, CIV (1983), 14–17

  1985. *A History of Gonville and Caius College*, Woodbridge, 1985

  1985a. 'The churches of medieval Cambridge', in D. Beales and G. Best (eds.), *History, Society and the Churches: Essays in Honour of Owen Chadwick*, Cambridge, 1985, pp. 49–76

Brooke and Dumville 1986: C.N.L. Brooke, *The Church and the Welsh Border*, ed. D.N. Dumville and C.N.L. Brooke, Woodbridge, 1986

Brooke, C.N.L., and Keir, G. 1975. *London 800–1216: The Shaping of a City*, London, 1975

Buchan, John. 1898. *Brasenose College*, London, 1898

Buck, M. 1983. *Politics, Finance and the Church in the Reign of Edward II: Walter Stapeldon, Treasurer of England*, Cambridge, 1983

Burgon, J.W. 1891. *Lives of Twelve Good Men*, London, 1891

Burney, Frances. 1972–84. *The Journals and Letters*, ed. J. Twemlow *et al.*, 12 vols., Oxford, 1972–84

Burrows, M. ed. 1881. *The Register of the Visitors of the University of Oxford, from A.D. 1647 to A.D. 1658*, Camden Society, New Series, XXIX, 1881

Bury, J.P.T. 1952. *The College of Corpus Christi and of the Blessed Virgin Mary: A History from 1822–1952*, Cambridge, 1952

Busbridge, I. 1974. *Oxford Mathematics and Mathematicians*, Oxford, 1974

Bush, S., and Rasmussen, C.J. 1985. 'Emmanuel College Library first inventory', *Transactions of the Cambridge Bibliographical Society*, VIII, 5 (1985), 514–56

Bushell, W.D. 1948. *The Church of St Mary the Great*, Cambridge, 1948

Buxton, J., and Williams, P. eds. 1979. *New College, Oxford, 1379–1979*, Oxford, 1979

Caius, *Works: The Works of John Caius, M.D.*, ed. E.S. Roberts, Cambridge, 1912 (works separately paginated)

Cam, H.M. 1944. *Liberties and Communities in Medieval England*, Cambridge, 1944

Cambridge Plate (Fitzwilliam Museum catalogue by R.A. Crighton), Cambridge, 1975

Cambridge Portraits from Lely to Hockney (Fitzwilliam Museum catalogue), Cambridge, 1978

Campbell, J. 1975. 'Norwich', in Lobel and Johns 1975

  1979. 'The church in Anglo-Saxon towns', *Studies in Church History*, XVI (1979), ed. D. Baker, pp. 119–35

Carlyle, T., and Lomas, S.C. eds. 1904. *Letters and Speeches of Oliver Cromwell*, 3rd edn, 3 vols., London, 1904

Carpenter, E. 1936. *Thomas Sherlock, 1678–1761*, London, 1936

Carr, W. 1902. *University College*, London, 1902

Carter, H. 1975. *A History of the Oxford University Press*, 2 vols., Oxford, 1975

Catlin, G.E.G. 1960. 'Sir Ernest Barker', *Proceedings of the British Academy*, XLVI (1960), 341–3

Catto, J. 1984. *The History of the University of Oxford*, ed. T.H. Aston, I, *The Early Oxford Schools*, ed. J. Catto, Oxford, 1984

CC: *Cambridge Commemorated: An Anthology of University Life*, ed. L. and H. Fowler, Cambridge, 1984

Chadwick, O. 1984. 'Dr Samuel Johnson and the Dixie professorship of ecclesiastical history', *Journal of Ecclesiastical History*, XXXV (1984), 583–96

Chambers, R.W. 1948. *Thomas More*, London, 1948

Chester, N. 1986. *Economics, Politics and Social Studies in Oxford 1900–85*, Oxford, 1986

Chibnall, A.C. 1963. *Richard de Badew and the University of Cambridge, 1315–1340*, Cambridge, 1963

Clark, A. 1891. *See* Wood

Clark, J.W. 1900. *Old Friends at Cambridge and Elsewhere*, London, 1900

Clark, J.W., and Hughes, T. McK. 1890. *The Life and Letters of the Reverend Adam Sedgwick*, 2 vols., Cambridge, 1890

Clough, B.A. 1897. *A Memoir of Anne Jemima Clough*, London, 1897

Cobban, A.B. 1969. *The King's Hall within the University of Cambridge in the Later Middle Ages*, Cambridge, 1969

Cocke, T. 1984. *The Ingenious Mr Essex, Architect, 1722–1784* (catalogue of an exhibition at the Fitzwilliam Museum), Cambridge, 1984

Coleman, D.C. 1977. *Internal Trade in England, 1500–1700*, London, 1977

Collinson, P. 1967. *The Elizabethan Puritan Movement*, London, 1967

Colvin, C. 1985. 'A don's wife a century ago', *Oxoniensia*, L (1985), 267–78

Colvin, H.M. 1954. 'The architects of All Saints Church, Oxford', *Oxoniensia*, XIX (1954), 112–16
 1963–82. *The History of the King's Works*, 8 vols., London 1963–82
 1978. *A Biographical Dictionary of British Architects, 1600–1840*, London, 1978
 1981. *The Sheldonian Theatre and the Divinity School*, Oxford, 1981
 1983. *Unbuilt Oxford*, London, 1983
 1986. 'Architecture', in Sutherland and Mitchell 1986, chap. 30, pp. 831–56

Cooper, *Annals*: C.H. Cooper, *Annals of Cambridge*, 5 vols. (V, ed. J.W. Cooper), Cambridge, 1842–1908

Cornish, F.W. 1910. *The English Church in the Nineteenth Century*, 2 vols., London, 1910

Cragg, G.R. ed. 1968. *The Cambridge Platonists*, New York, 1968

Craster, E. 1981. *History of the Bodleian Library 1842–1945*, Oxford, 1981

Crawley, C. 1976. *Trinity Hall: The History of a Cambridge College, 1350–1975*, Cambridge, 1976

Creighton, L. 1906. *The Life and Letters of Mandell Creighton*, 2 vols., London, 1906

Cressy, D.A. 1970. 'The social composition of Caius College, Cambridge, 1580–1640', *Past and Present*, no. 47 (May 1970), 113–15
 1972. 'Education and literacy in London and East Anglia 1580–1700', University of Cambridge Ph.D. thesis, 1972

Cross, C. 1986. 'Oxford and the Tudor state from the accession of Henry VIII to the death of Mary', in McConica 1986, chap. 3, pp. 117–49

Cross, F.L., and Livingstone, E.A. eds. 1974. *The Oxford Dictionary of the Christian Church*, 2nd edn, London, 1974

Curtis, L.P. 1966. *Chichester Towers*, New Haven, 1966

Curtis, M.H. 1959. *Oxford and Cambridge in Transition 1558–1642*, Oxford, 1959
 1962. 'The alienated intellectuals of early Stuart England', *Past and Present*, no. 23 (November 1962), 25–43

Daniel, C.H., and Barker, R. 1900. *Worcester College*, London, 1900

Darby, H.C. ed. 1938. *The Cambridge Region*, Cambridge, 1938

    1974. *The Medieval Fenland*, 2nd edn, Cambridge, 1974

Davis, H.W.C. 1963. *A History of Balliol College*, 2nd edn, revised by R.H.C. Davis and R.W. Hunt, Oxford, 1963

Davis, R.H.C. 1946–7. 'The chronology of Perpendicular architecture in Oxford', *Oxoniensia*, XI and XII (1946–7), 75–89

    1973. 'The ford, the river and the city', *Oxoniensia*, XXXVIII (1973), 258–67

Dawson, J.E.A. 1984. 'The foundation of Christ Church, Oxford, and Trinity College, Cambridge, in 1546', *Bulletin of the Institute of Historical Research*, LVII (1984), 208–15

Dickins, B. 1972. 'The making of the Parker Library', *Transactions of the Cambridge Bibliographical Society*, VI, 1 (1972), 19–34

DNB: Dictionary of National Biography (reference by name); *DNB 1961–70*, ed. E.T. Williams and C.S. Nicholls, Oxford, 1981

Dobson, R.B. 1977. 'Urban decline in late medieval England', *Transactions of the Royal Historical Society*, 5th Series, XXVII (1977), 1–22

Documents 1852: Documents relating to the University and Colleges of Cambridge . . ., published by direction of the [University] Commissioners, 3 vols., London, 1852

Doolittle, I.G. 1986. 'College administration', in Sutherland and Mitchell 1986, chap. 9, pp. 227–68

Dowling, M. 1984. 'Anne Boleyn and reform', *Journal of Ecclesiastical History*, XXXV (1984), 30–46

    1986. *Humanism in the Age of Henry VIII*, Beckenham, 1986

Downes, K. 1979. *Hawksmoor*, London, 1979

    1982a. *The Architecture of Sir Christopher Wren*, London, 1982

    1982b. *Sir Christopher Wren, The Whitechapel Art Gallery*, London, 1982

DSB: Dictionary of Scientific Biography, ed. C.C. Gillespie, 16 vols., New York, 1970–80

Dunbabin, J. 1984. 'Careers and vocations', in Catto 1984, chap. 15, pp. 565–606

Dunbabin, J.P.D. 1986. 'College estates and wealth 1660–1815', in Sutherland and Mitchell 1986, chap. 10, pp. 269–307

Duncan, G.D. 1980. 'Heads of houses and religious change in Tudor Oxford', *Oxoniensia*, XLV (1980), 226–59

    1986. 'Public lectures and professorial chairs', in McConica 1986, chap. 4 (5), pp. 335–61

Elton, G.R. 1973. *Reform and Renewal: Thomas Cromwell and the Common Weal*, Cambridge, 1973

Emden, A.B. 1964. 'Northerners and southerners in the organisation of the university to 1509', in *Oxford Studies Presented to Daniel Callus*, OHS, New Series, XVI, 1964 for 1959–60, pp. 1–30

    1968. *An Oxford Hall in Medieval Times*, Oxford, 1968

Emden, *Cambridge*: Emden, A.B., *A Biographical Register of the University of Cambridge to 1500*, Cambridge, 1963

Emden, *Oxford*: Emden, A.B., *A Biographical Register of the University of Oxford to 1500*, 3 vols., Oxford, 1957–9

Emden, *Oxford, 1501–40*: Emden, A.B., *A Biographical Register of the University of Oxford, 1501–1540*, Oxford, 1974

Emmanuel Statutes: The Statutes of Sir Walter Mildmay Kt . . . authorised by him for the government of Emmanuel College founded by him, ed. F. Stubbings, Cambridge, 1983

Engel, A.J. 1983. *From Clergyman to Don; The Rise of the Academic Profession in Nineteenth-Century Oxford*, Oxford, 1983

Evelyn, John. 1955. *The Diary*, ed. J.S. de Beer, 6 vols., Oxford, 1955

Faber, G. 1957. *Jowett: A Portrait with Background*, London, 1957

Falkner, J.M. 1899. *A History of Oxfordshire*, London, 1899

Fasnacht, R. 1954. *A History of the City of Oxford*, Oxford, 1954

Feingold, M. 1984. *The Mathematician's Apprenticeship: Science, Universities and Society in England 1560–1640*, Cambridge, 1984

Ferguson, J.P. 1976. *An Eighteenth Century Heretic: Dr Samuel Clarke*, Kineton, 1976

Fletcher, J.M. ed. 1976. *Registrum annalium collegii Mertonensis 1567–1603*, OHS, New Series, XXIV, 1976

1977. 'Linacre's lands and lectureships', in Maddison, Pelling and Webster 1977, pp. 107–97

Fletcher, J.M., and Upton, C.A. 1983. 'Destruction, repair and removal: an Oxford college chapel during the Reformation', *Oxoniensia*, XLVIII (1983), 119–30

Footman, D. 1986. *Antonin Besse of Aden, The Founder of St Antony's College, Oxford*, Oxford, 1986

Foster, J. 1888. *Alumni Oxonienses, 1715–1886*, 4 vols., Oxford, 1888

Fowler, L. and H. See *CC*

Fowler, T. 1898. *Corpus Christi College* [Oxford], London, 1898

Fox, C. 1923. *The Archaeology of the Cambridge Region*, Cambridge, 1923, reissued with Appendix IV, 1948

Friedman, T. 1984. *James Gibbs*, New Haven and London, 1984

Fuller, T. 1840. *The History of the University of Cambridge* (1655), ed. M. Prickett and T. Wright, Cambridge, 1840

Garland, M.M. 1980. *Cambridge before Darwin: The Ideal of a Liberal Education, 1800–1860*, Cambridge, 1980

Garrod, H.W. 1931. *The Ancient Painted Glass in Merton College, Oxford*, London, 1931

1963. *The Study of Good Letters*, ed. J. Jones, Oxford, 1963

Gascoigne, J. 1983. 'Mathematics and meritocracy: the emergence of the Cambridge mathematical tripos', *Social Studies of Science*, XIV (1983), 547–84

Gaskell, P. 1980. *Trinity College Library: The First 150 Years*, Cambridge, 1980

Gaskell, P., and Robson, R. 1971. *The Library of Trinity College, Cambridge: A Short History*, Cambridge, 1971

Geison, G.L. 1978. *Michael Foster and the Cambridge School of Physiology*, Princeton, 1978

Gervers, M. 1972. 'Rotundae Anglicanae', in *Actes du XXIIe Congrès International d'Histoire de l'Art*, Budapest, 1969, publ. Budapest, 1972, pp. 359–76, and plates, pp. 109–14

Gibbon, E. *See* Murray 1896

Gibson, Strickland. ed. 1931. *Statuta Antiqua Universitatis Oxoniensis*, Oxford, 1931

Graham, M. 1972. *A Thousand Years of Folly Bridge*, Oxford, 1972

n.d. *On Foot in Oxford*, no. 4, *Folly Bridge and South Oxford*, Oxford, n.d.

Grave, W.W. 1983. *Fitzwilliam College Cambridge 1869–1969*, Cambridge, 1983

Gray, A. 1898. *The Priory of St Radegund, Cambridge*, Cambridge Antiquarian Society, Octavo Series XXXI, 1898

Gray, A., and Brittain, F. 1960. *A History of Jesus College, Cambridge*, London, 1960

Gray, J.M. 1932. *The School of Pythagoras*, Cambridge Antiquarian Society, 1932

Green, V.H.H. 1957. *Oxford Common Room: A Study of Lincoln College and Mark Pattison*, London, 1957

1964. *Religion at Oxford and Cambridge*, London, 1964

1979. *The Commonwealth of Lincoln College, 1427–1977*, Oxford, 1979

1986a. 'The university and social life', in Sutherland and Mitchell 1986, chap. 11, pp. 309–58

1986b. 'Religion in the colleges 1715–1800', in Sutherland and Mitchell 1986, chap. 14, pp. 425–67

1986c. 'Reformers and reform in the university', in Sutherland and Mitchell 1986, chap. 22, pp. 607–37

Greenslade, S.L. 1986. 'The faculty of theology', in McConica 1986, chap. 4 (4), pp. 295–334

Greenway, D.E. 1971. *John Le Neve, Fasti Ecclesiae Anglicanae 1066–1300*, II, *Monastic Cathedrals*, London, 1971

Griffin, P. ed. 1986. *St Hugh's: One Hundred Years of Women's Education in Oxford*, Oxford, 1986

Gunning, H. 1854. *Reminiscences of the University, Town, and County of Cambridge, from the Year 1780*, 2 vols., London and Cambridge, 1854

Hackett, M.B. 1970. *The Original Statutes of Cambridge University*, Cambridge, 1970

1984. 'The university as a corporate body', in Catto 1984, chap. 2, pp. 37–96

Haig, A.G.L. 1986. 'The church, the universities and learning in later Victorian England', *Historical Journal*, XXIX (1986), 187–201

Haigh, C. 1981. 'The continuity of Catholicism in the English Reformation', *Past and Present*, no. 93 (1981), pp. 37–69

Hall, C.P., and Ravensdale, J.R. 1976. *The West Fields of Cambridge*, Cambridge Antiquarian Records Society, III, 1976 for 1974–5

Hamilton, M.A. 1936. *Newnham: An Informal Biography*, London, 1936

Hamilton, S.G. 1903. *Hertford College*, London, 1903

Hammer, C.I., Jr. 1986. 'Oxford town and Oxford university', in McConica 1986, chap. 2, pp. 69–116

Hardy, Thomas. 1895. *Jude the Obscure*, London, 1895

Harris, B. 1979. *Chester*, London, 1979

Harrod, R.F. 1951. *The Life of John Maynard Keynes*, London, 1951

Harvey, J. 1943. 'The building works and architects of Cardinal Wolsey', *Journal of the British Archaeological Association*, 3rd Series, VIII (1943), 48–59

  1943–4. 'The building of Cardinal College, Oxford', *Oxoniensia*, VIII, IX (1943–4), 145–53

  1984. *English Mediaeval Architects: A Biographical Dictionary down to 1550*, 2nd edn, Gloucester, 1984

Haslam, J. 1982–3. 'The development and topography of Saxon Cambridge', *Proceedings of the Cambridge Antiquarian Society*, LXXII (1982–3), 13–29

Hassall, T.G. 1970. 'Excavations at Oxford 1969', *Oxoniensia*, XXXV (1970), 5–18

  1971. 'Excavations in Merton College, Oxford, 1970', *Oxoniensia*, XXXVI (1971), 34–48

  1973. 'Excavations at Oxford, 1972', *Oxoniensia*, XXXVIII (1973), 268–98

Hearne, T. 1885–1921. *Remarks and Collections of Thomas Hearne*, ed. C.E. Doble *et al.*, 11 vols., OHS, II, etc., 1885–1921

Henderson, B.W. 1899. *Merton College*, London, 1899

Hewison, R. 1983–4. *Footlights: A Hundred Years of Cambridge Comedy*, London, 1983, corr. repr. 1984

Heyworth, P. 1981. *The Oxford Guide to Oxford*, Oxford, 1981

Highfield, J.R.L. 1953. 'The promotion of William of Wickham to the See of Winchester', *Journal of Ecclesiastical History*, IV (1953), 37–54

  1963. 'An autograph manuscript commonplace book of Sir Henry Savile', *Bodleian Library Record*, VII (1963), 73–83

  ed. 1964. *The Early Rolls of Merton College, Oxford*, OHS, New Series XVIII, 1964 for 1963

  1984. 'The early colleges', in Catto 1984, chap. 6, pp. 225–63

Hill, C. 1956. *Economic Problems of the Church from Archbishop Whitgift to the Long Parliament*, Oxford, 1956

Hinnebusch, W.A. 1938. 'The pre-Reformation sites of the Oxford Blackfriars', *Oxoniensia*, III (1938), 57–82

  1951. *The Early English Friars Preachers*, Rome, 1951

Hodgkin, R.H. 1949. *Six Centuries of an Oxford College*, Oxford, 1949

Horn, J.M. 1969, 1971, 1974. John Le Neve, *Fasti Ecclesiae Anglicanae 1541–1857*, I–III, London, 1969, 1971, 1974

Howard, H.F. 1935. *An Account of the Finances of the College of St John the Evangelist in the University of Cambridge, 1511–1926*, Cambridge, 1935

Howarth, J. 1987. 'Science education in late-Victorian Oxford: a curious case of failure?', *English Historical Review*, CII (1987), 334–71

Howarth, T.E.B. 1978. *Cambridge between Two Wars*, London, 1978

Hoyle, D. 1986. 'A Commons investigation of Arminianism and Popery in Cambridge on the eve of the Civil War', *Historical Journal*, XXIX (1986), 419–25

Hunt, R.W., and Gibson, M. 1984. *The Schools and the Cloister, The Life and Writings of Alexander Nequam (1157–1217)*, Oxford, 1984

Hutton, W.H. 1898. *St John Baptist's College*, London, 1898

Ibish, J.S. 1985. 'Emmanuel College: the founding generation, with a biographical register of members of the college, 1584–1604', Harvard University Ph.D. thesis, 1985

Jackson, T.G. 1897. *The Church of St Mary the Virgin*, Oxford, 1897

Jacob, E.F. 1967. *Henry Chichele*, London, 1967

Jacob, M. 1976. *The Newtonians and the English Revolution, 1689–1720*, Hassocks, 1976

James, M.R. 1912. *A Descriptive Catalogue of the Manuscripts in the Library of Corpus Christi College, Cambridge*, 2 vols., Cambridge, 1912

Johnson, J., and Gibson, S. 1946. *Print and Privilege at Oxford to the Year 1700*, London, 1946

Jones, V.J. 1982. 'Sound religion and useful learning: the rise of Balliol under John Parsons and Richard Jenkyns, 1798–1854', in Prest 1982, chap. 5, pp. 89–123

Kearney, H. 1970. *Scholars and Gentlemen: Universities and Society in Pre-Industrial Britain, 1500–1700*, London, 1970

Keene, D. 1984. 'A new study of London before the Great Fire', *Urban History Yearbook*, 1984, pp. 11–21

　1985, *Survey of Medieval Winchester = Winchester Studies*, ed. M. Biddle, II, 2 parts, Oxford, 1985

Keene, D., and Harding, V. 1985. *A Survey of Documentary Sources for Property Holding in London before the Great Fire*, London Record Society, XXII, 1985

Kelly, H.A. 1976. *The Matrimonial Trials of Henry VIII*, Stanford, 1976

Kemble, J.M. ed. 1839–48. *Codex Diplomaticus Aevi Saxonici*, 6 vols., London, 1839–48

Kemp, B. 1986. 'The early history of St Hugh's College, Oxford', in Griffin 1986, pp. 15–47

Kersting, A.F., and Watkin, D. 1984. *Peterhouse 1284–1984; An Architectural Record*, Cambridge, 1984

Keynes, G. 1966. *The Life of William Harvey*, Oxford, 1966

Keynes, M.E. 1976. *A House by the River*, Cambridge, 1976

Knowles, (M.) D. 1948–59. *The Religious Orders in England*, 3 vols., Cambridge, 1948–59

　1963a. *The Historian and Character and Other Essays*, Cambridge, 1963

　1963b. *Great Historical Enterprises: Problems in Monastic History*, London, 1963

Knowles, (M.) D., and Hadcock, R.N. 1971. *Medieval Religious Houses, England and Wales*, 2nd edn, London, 1971

Knowles, (M.) D., Brooke, C.N.L., and London, V.C.M. eds. 1972. *The Heads of Religious Houses, England and Wales, 940–1216*, Cambridge, 1972

Lambrick, G. 1969. 'Some old roads of North Berkshire', *Oxoniensia*, XXXIV (1969), 78–93

Langford, P. 1986. 'Tories and Jacobites, 1714–1751', in Sutherland and Mitchell 1986, chap. 4, pp. 99–127

Lawrence, C.H. 1984. 'The university in state and church', in Catto 1984, chap. 3, pp. 97–150

Leader, D.R. 1981. 'The study of arts in Oxford and Cambridge at the end of the Middle Ages', University of Toronto Ph.D. thesis, 1981

　1988. *A History of the University of Cambridge*, I: *The University to 1546*, Cambridge, 1988

Legge, H.E. 1923. *The Divinity School, Oxford*, Oxford, 1923

Leland, J. 1745. *Cygnea Cantio*, ed. T. Hearne. London, 1745

Lewis, G. 1986. 'The faculty of medicine', in McConica 1986, chap. 4 (2), pp. 213–56

Lewis, J. 1855. *The Life of Dr John Fisher*, 2 vols., London, 1855

Liscombe, R.W. 1980. *William Wilkins 1788–1839*, Cambridge, 1980

Little, A.G. 1935. 'The friars v. the university of Cambridge', *English Historical Review*, L (1935), 686–96

　1943. *Franciscan Papers, Lists and Documents*, Manchester, 1943

Lloyd, A.H. 1934. *The Early History of Christ's College, Cambridge*, Cambridge, 1934

Loach, J. 1986. 'Reformation controversies', in McConica 1986, pp. 363–96

Lobel, M.D., and Johns, W.H. 1975. *The Atlas of Historic Towns*, ed. M.D. Lobel and W.H. Johns, II, London, 1975

Logan, F.D. 1977. 'The origins of the so-called regius professorships: an aspect of the Renaissance in Oxford and Cambridge', *Studies in Church History*, XIV (1977), 271–8

Loggan, D. 1675. *Oxonia Illustrata*, Oxford, [1675]
  1690, *Cantabrigia Illustrata*, Cambridge, [1690]
Lovatt, R. 1981. 'John Blacman: biographer of Henry VI', in R.H.C. Davis and J.M. Wallace-Hadrill (eds.), *The Writing of History in the Middle Ages: Essays Presented to Richard William Southern*, Oxford, 1981, pp. 415–44
  1983–4. 'The first century of the college library', *Peterhouse Record 1983–4*, pp. 60–73
Lucas, J.R. 1979. 'Wilberforce and Huxley: a legendary encounter', *Historical Journal*, XXII (1979), 315–30
Luckett, R. 1973. 'Church and college 1660–1745' in Rich 1973, pp. 110–37
McConica, J.K. 1965. *English Humanism and Reformation Politics under Henry VIII and Edward VI*, Oxford, 1965
  1975. 'Scholars and commoners in Renaissance Oxford', in Stone 1975, I, chap. 3, pp. 151–81
  1977. 'The social relations of Tudor Oxford', *Transactions of the Royal Historical Society*, 5th Series, XXVII (1977), 115–34
  1986. *The History of the University of Oxford*, ed. T.H. Aston, III, *The Collegiate University*, ed. J. McConica, Oxford, 1986
MacGregor, A.G. 1983. *Tradescant's Rarities. A Catalogue of the Early Collections in the Ashmolean Museum*, Oxford, 1983
McGregor, A.G., and Turner, A.J. 1986. 'The Ashmolean Museum', in Sutherland and Mitchell 1986, chap. 23, pp. 639–58
McLachlan, J.O. 1947–9. 'The origin and early development of the Cambridge historical tripos', *Cambridge Historical Journal*, IX (1947–9), 78–105
Macleane, D. 1900. *Pembroke College*, London, 1900
Macray, W.D. 1890. *Annals of the Bodleian Library*, Oxford, 1890
Madden, F., and Fieldhouse, D.K. eds. 1982. *Oxford and the Idea of Commonwealth: Essays Presented to Sir Edgar Williams*, London, 1982
Maddison, F., Pelling, M., and Webster, C. eds. 1977. *Essays on the Life and Work of Thomas Linacre c. 1460–1524*, Oxford, 1977
Magrath, J.R. 1921. *The Queen's College*, Oxford, 2 vols., Oxford, 1921
Maitland, F.W. 1898. *Township and Borough*, Cambridge, 1898
Mallet, C.E. 1924–7. *A History of the University of Oxford*, 3 vols., Oxford, 1924–7
Malmesbury, Earl of. 1844–5. *Diaries and Correspondence*, ed. the third Earl of Malmesbury, 2nd edn, 4 vols., London, 1844–5
Manuel, F.E. 1974. *The Religion of Isaac Newton*, Oxford, 1974
Massey, H., and Feather, N. 1976. 'Sir James Chadwick', in *Biographical Memoirs of Fellows of the Royal Society*, XXII (1976), 11–70
Matthews, A.G. 1948, *Walker Revised*, Oxford, 1948
Mayr-Harting, H. 1985. 'Functions of a twelfth-century shrine: the miracles of St Frideswide', in *Studies in Medieval History Presented to R.H.C. Davis*, ed. H. Mayr-Harting and R.I. Moore, London and Ronceverte, 1985, pp. 193–206
Merton College Register 1900–1964, Oxford, 1964
Miller, E. 1961. *Portrait of a College: A History of the College of St John the Evangelist*, Cambridge, Cambridge, 1961
Mitchell, L.G. 1986a. Introduction to Sutherland and Mitchell 1986, pp. 1–8
  1986b. 'Politics and revolution 1772–1800', in Sutherland and Mitchell 1986, chap. 6, pp. 163–90
Mitchell, W.T. ed. 1980a. *Epistolae Academicae 1508–1596*, OHS, New Series, XXVI, 1980
  1980b. *Registrum Cancellarii 1498–1506*, OHS, New Series, XXVII, 1980
Moberly, G.H. 1887. *Life of William of Wykeham*, Winchester and London, 1887
Monk, J.H. 1830. *The Life of Richard Bentley, D.D.*, London, 1830 (cited from one-vol. edn)
Moorman, J.R.H. 1952. *The Grey Friars in Cambridge 1225–1538*, Cambridge, 1952
Moorman, M. 1957. *William Wordsworth, A Biography*, I, Oxford, 1957

Morgan, V. 1975. 'Cambridge university and "the country" 1560–1640', in Stone 1975, I, 183–245

1984. 'Country, court and Cambridge university, 1558–1640: a study in the evolution of a political culture', University of East Anglia Ph.D. thesis, 1984

Morison, S.E. 1935. *The Founding of Harvard College*, Cambridge, Mass., 1935

Mullinger, J.B. 1873. *The University of Cambridge from the Earliest Times to the Royal Injunctions of 1535*, Cambridge, 1873

1884. *The University of Cambridge from the Royal Injunctions of 1535 to the Accession of Charles the First*, Cambridge, 1884

1911. *The University of Cambridge from the Election of Buckingham to the Chancellorship in 1626 to the Decline of the Platonist Movement*, Cambridge, 1911

Murphy, V. 1984. 'The debate over Henry VIII's first divorce: an analysis of the contemporary treatises', University of Cambridge Ph.D. thesis, 1984

Murray, J. ed. 1896. *The Autobiography of Edmund Gibbon*, London, 1896

Murray, J.A.H. ed. 1888–1928. *The Oxford English Dictionary* (formerly *New English Dictionary*), 13 vols., Oxford, 1888–1928

Neale, J.E. 1957. *Elizabeth I and her Parliaments 1584–1601*, London, 1957

Newbury, C. 1982. 'Cecil Rhodes and the South African connection: "a great imperial university?"', in Madden and Fieldhouse 1982, chap. 4, pp. 75–96

Newman, J. 1978. 'Oxford libraries before 1800', *Archaeological Journal*, cxxxv (1978), 248–57

1986. 'The physical setting: new building and adaptation', in McConica 1986, chap. 9, pp. 597–641

Newsome, D.H. 1984. 'Two Emmanuel historians', *Emmanuel College Magazine, Quatercentenary Issue*, 1984, pp. 104–14

Nutton, V. 1979. 'John Caius and the Linacre tradition', *Medical History*, xxiii (1979), 373–91

Oates, J.C.T. 1975. *The University Library, A Historical Sketch*, Cambridge, 1975

1986. *Cambridge University Library: A History from the Beginnings to the Copyright Act of Queen Anne*, Cambridge, 1986 (vol. ii by D. McKitterick, Cambridge, 1986)

Ogg, D. 1934. *England in the Reign of Charles II*, 2 vols., Oxford, 1934

1955. *England in the Reigns of James II and William III*, Oxford, 1955

Oman, C. 1972. 'Cambridge and Cornelimünster', *Aachener Kunstblätter*, Aachen, 1972, pp. 305–7

Page, R.I. 1981. 'The Parker Register and Matthew Parker's Anglo-Saxon manuscripts', *Transactions of the Cambridge Bibliographical Society*, viii, I (1981), 1–17

Pantin, W.A. 1964. 'The halls and schools of medieval Oxford: an attempt at reconstruction', in *Oxford Studies presented to Daniel Callus*, OHS, New Series, xvi, 1964 for 1959–60, pp. 31–100

1972. *Oxford Life in Oxford Archives*, Oxford, 1972

ed. 1985. *Canterbury College, Oxford*, iv, OHS, New Series, xxx, 1985

Panton, A. 1980. *Farewell St Ebbe's*, Oxford, 1980

Parker, M. 1853. *Correspondence of Matthew Parker*, ed. J. Bruce and T.T. Perowne, Parker Society, 1853

Parker, R. n.d. *A History of the University of Cambridge*, edn of London, n.d.

Partner, P. 1982. 'William of Wykeham and the historians', in *Winchester College: Sixth Centenary Essays*, ed. R. Custance, Oxford, 1982, pp. 1–36

Patrides, C.A. ed. 1969. *The Cambridge Platonists*, London, 1969

Pattison, M. 1875. *Isaac Casaubon*, Oxford, 1875

Pevsner, N. 1970. *The Buildings of England: Cambridgeshire*, 2nd edn, Harmondsworth, 1970

Philip, I.G. 1983. *The Bodleian Library in the Seventeenth and Eighteenth Centuries*, Oxford, 1983

1986. 'Libraries and the University Press', in Sutherland and Mitchell 1986, pp. 725–55

Pocock, J.G.A. 1950–2. 'Robert Brady, 1627–1700. A Cambridge historian of the Restoration', *Cambridge Historical Journal*, x (1950–2), 186–204

Porritt, E. 1909. *The Unreformed House of Commons*, 2 vols., Cambridge, 1909

Porter, H.C. 1958. *Reformation and Reaction in Tudor Cambridge*, Cambridge, 1958 (corr. reprint, Hamden, Connecticut, 1972, with new preface and bibliography)

Porter, S. 1984. 'The Oxford Fire of 1644', *Oxoniensia*, XLIX (1984), 289–300

Prest, J. ed. 1982. *Balliol Studies*, London, 1982

Preston, A.E. 1935. *The Church and Parish of St Nicholas, Abingdon*, OHS, XCIX, 1935

Prior, M. 1982. *Fisher Row*, Oxford, 1982

Quarrie, P. 1986. 'The Christ Church Collections Books', in Sutherland and Mitchell 1986, chap. 16, pp. 493–511

Rackham, H. ed. 1927. *Early Statutes of Christ's College, Cambridge*, Cambridge, 1927

Rannie, D.W. 1900. *Oriel College*, London, 1900

Rashdall, H. 1936. *The Universities of Europe in the Middle Ages*, ed. F.M. Powicke and A.B. Emden, 3 vols., Oxford, 1936

Raverat, G. 1952. *Period Piece: A Cambridge Childhood*, London, 1952

Rawle, T. 1985. *Cambridge Architecture*, London, 1985

RCHM Cambridge: Royal Commission on Historical Monuments for England, City of Cambridge, 2 parts, London, 1959

RCHM Oxford: Royal Commission on Historical Monuments for England, City of Oxford, London, 1939

Reynolds, J.S. 1975. *The Evangelicals at Oxford, 1735–1871*, Appleford, 1975

Rich, E.E. ed. 1973. *St Catharine's College, Cambridge, 1473–1973*, London, 1973

Roach, J.P.C. 1959. 'The university of Cambridge', in *VCH Cambs*, III (1959), 150–312

Robinson, J.M. 1979. *The Wyatts*, Oxford, 1979

Robson, R. 1967. 'Trinity College in the age of Peel', in *Ideas and Institutions of Victorian England, Essays in Honour of George Kitson Clark*, ed. R. Robson, London, 1967, pp. 312–35

Robson, R., and Cannon, W.F. 1964. 'William Whewell, F.R.S.', *Notes and Records of the Royal Society of London*, XIX (1964), 168–91

Roger of Wendover. 1886–9. *Flores Historiarum*, ed. H.G. Hewlett, 3 vols., Rolls Series, 1886–9

Rogers, J.E. Thorold. 1866–1902. *A History of Agriculture and Prices in England*, 7 vols., Oxford, 1866–1902

Roth, C. 1951. *The Jews of Medieval Oxford*, OHS, New Series, IX, 1951

   1966. 'Sir Thomas Bodley, Hebraist', *Bodleian Library Record*, VII (1966), 242–51

Roth, F. 1966. *The English Austin Friars 1249–1538*, New York, 1966

Rothblatt, S. 1981. *The Revolution of the Dons: Cambridge and Society in Victorian England*, 2nd edn, Cambridge, 1981

Rowse, A.L. 1950. *The England of Elizabeth*, London, 1950

Royal Commission 1852 (Cambridge): Report of Her Majesty's Commissioners appointed to inquire into the . . . University and Colleges of Cambridge, 1852

Royal Commission 1852 (Oxford): Report of Her Majesty's Commissioners appointed to inquire into the state, discipline, studies and revenues of the University and Colleges of Oxford, London, 1852

Royal Commission 1874: Report of the Commissioners appointed to inquire into the property and income of the Universities of Oxford and Cambridge, 3 vols., 1874

Royal Commission 1922: Royal Commission on Oxford and Cambridge Universities Report, 1922

Rubin, M. 1987. *Charity and Community in Medieval Cambridge*, Cambridge, 1987

Rupp, E.G. 1977. *Just Men: Historical Pieces*, London, 1977

   1981. 'A Cambridge centenary. The Selwyn Divinity School, 1879–1979', *Historical Journal*, XXIV, 2 (1981), 417–28

Russell, E. 1977. 'The influx of commoners into the university of Oxford before 1581: an optical illusion?', *English Historical Review*, XCII (1977), 721–45

   1985. 'Marian Oxford and the Counter-Reformation', in C.M. Barron and C. Harper-Bill (eds.), *The Church in Pre-Reformation Society: Essays in Honour of F.R.H. Du Boulay*, Woodbridge, 1985, pp. 212–27

Saint, A. 1970. 'Three Oxford architects', *Oxoniensia*, XXXV (1970), 53–102

Salter, H.E. ed. 1917. *Munimenta Civitatis Oxonie*, OHS, LXXI, 1920 for 1917

   1919. 'Geoffrey of Monmouth and Oxford', *English Historical Review*, XXXIV (1919), 382–5

   ed. 1920. *Surveys and Tokens*, OHS, LXXV, 1923 for 1920

   ed. 1923. *Registrum annalium collegii Mertonensis, 1483–1521*, OHS, LXXVI, 1923 ed. 1928. *Oxford Council Acts, 1583–1626*, OHS, LXXXVII, 1928

1936. *Medieval Oxford*, OHS, C, 1936

ed. 1960, 1969. *Survey of Oxford*, OHS, New Series, XIV, XX, 1960, 1969

Sandars, S. 1869. *Historical and Architectural Notes on Great St Mary's Church, Cambridge*, Cambridge Antiquarian Society, 1869

Scargill, I., and Crosby, A. 1982. *Oxford and its Countryside*, Oxford, 1982

Scarisbrick, J.J. 1968. *Henry VIII*, London, 1968

Schenk, W. 1950. *Reginald Pole Cardinal of England*, London, 1950

Schmidt, C. 1982. 'Classical studies at Balliol in the 1860s: the undergraduate essays of Gerard Manley Hopkins', in Prest 1982, pp. 159–84

Searle, W.G. 1867–71. *The History of the Queens' College of St Margaret and St Bernard in the University of Cambridge 1446–1662*, 2 vols., Cambridge Antiquarian Society, 1867–71

Shaw, J. Byam. 1976. *Drawings by Old Masters at Christ Church, Oxford*, 2 vols., Oxford, 1976

Sheehan, M.M. 1984. 'The religious orders 1220–1370', in Catto 1984, chap. 5, pp. 193–225

Sherwood, J., and Pevsner, N. 1974. *The Buildings of England: Oxfordshire*, Harmondsworth, 1974

Shuckburgh, E.S. 1904. *Emmanuel College*, London, 1904

Sidgwick, A. and E.M. 1906. *Henry Sidgwick, A Memoir*, London, 1906

Sidgwick, E. 1938. *Mrs Henry Sidgwick*, London, 1938

Simcock, A.V. 1984. *The Ashmolean Museum and Oxford Science, 1683–1983*, Oxford, 1984

ed. 1985. *Robert T. Gunther and the Old Ashmolean*, Oxford, 1985

Simon, J. 1963. 'The social origins of Cambridge students, 1603–1640', *Past and Present*, no. 26 (Nov. 1963), 58–67

Sinclair, H.M., and Robb-Smith, A.H.T. 1950. *A Short History of Anatomical Teaching in Oxford*, Oxford, 1950

Smith, Mrs A.L. 1928. *Arthur Lionel Smith, Master of Balliol, 1916–1924, A Biography and Some Reminiscences by his Wife*, London, 1928

Smith T. 1982. 'The Balliol-Trinity laboratories', in Prest 1982, pp. 185–224

Smyth, C. 1940. *Simeon and Church Order*, Cambridge, 1940

Southern, R.W. 1976. 'Master Vacarius and the beginning of an English academic tradition', in *Medieval Learning and Literature: Essays presented to R.W. Hunt*, ed. J.J.G. Alexander and M.T. Gibson, Oxford, 1976, pp. 257–86

1984. 'From schools to university', in Catto 1984, chap. 1, pp. 1–36

Stenton, F.M. 1936. 'St Frideswide and her times', *Oxoniensia*, I (1936), 103–12; repr. in *Preparatory to Anglo-Saxon England*, ed. D.M. Stenton, Oxford, 1970, pp. 224–33

1947. *Anglo-Saxon England*, 2nd edn, Oxford, 1947

Stephen, L. 1885. *Life of Henry Fawcett*, 2nd edn, London, 1885

Stephenson, C. 1933. *Borough and Town: A Study of Urban Origins in England*, Cambridge, Mass., 1933

Stevenson, W.H., and Salter, H.E. 1939. *The Early History of St John's College, Oxford*, OHS, New Series, I, 1939

Stokes, H.P. 1910. 'The old mills of Cambridge', *Cambridge Antiquarian Society Proceedings and Communications*, XIV (1910), 180–223

1924. *The Mediaeval Hostels of the University of Cambridge*, Cambridge Antiquarian Society, 1924

Stone, L. ed. 1975. *The University in Society: Oxford and Cambridge from the Fourteenth to the Early Nineteenth Century*, 2 vols., Princeton, 1975

Stride, W.K. 1900. *Exeter College*, London, 1900

Stroud, D. 1984. *Capability Brown*, edn of London, 1984

Strype, J. 1711. *The Life and Acts of Matthew Parker*, London, 1711

1812. *Memorials of Thomas Cranmer*, edn of Oxford, 1812, with corrections by Henry Ellis

Stubbings, F. 1983. *Forty-Nine Lives: An Anthology of Portraits of Emmanuel Men*, Cambridge, 1983

Sutcliffe, P. 1978. *The Oxford University Press, An Informal History*, Oxford, 1978

Sutherland, L.S., and Mitchell, L.G. eds. 1986. *The History of the University of Oxford*, ed. T.H. Aston, v, *The Eighteenth Century*, Oxford, 1986

Symonds, R. 1982. 'Oxford and India', in Madden and Fieldhouse 1982, pp. 49–72

    1986. *Oxford and Empire: The Last Lost Cause?*, London, 1986

Tanner, J.R. ed. 1917. *The Historical Register of the University of Cambridge*, Cambridge, 1917

Taylor, A.J. 1936. 'The royal visit to Oxford in 1632: a contemporary narrative', *Oxoniensia*, i (1936), 151–8

Taylor, C.C. 1973. *The Cambridgeshire Landscape*, London, 1973

Taylor, H.M. and J. 1965. *Anglo-Saxon Architecture*, i, ii, Cambridge, 1965 (and iii, 1978)

Thacker, F.S. 1909. *The Thames Highway*, 2 vols., London, 1909–14 (repr. Newton Abbot, 1968)

Thompson, A. Hamilton, 1935. 'William Bateman, Bishop of Norwich, 1344–1355', *Norfolk Archaeology*, xxv (1935), 102–37

Thompson, H.L. 1900. *Christ Church*, London, 1900

Thompson, P. 1971. *William Butterfield*, London, 1971

Thomson, D.F.S., and Porter, H.C. eds. 1963. *Erasmus and Cambridge*, Toronto, 1963

Town and Gown 1982: *Town and Gown: An Exhibition at the Bodleian Library*, Oxford, 1982

Toynbee, M., and Young, P. 1973. *Strangers in Oxford: A Sidelight on the First Civil War 1642–1646*, London and Chichester, 1973

Trevor-Roper, H.R. 1950. *Official Guide Book to Christ Church, Oxford*, Oxford, 1950

    1962. *Archbishop Laud*, 2nd edn, London, 1962

    1973. *Christ Church Oxford: The Portrait of a College*, Oxford, 1973

Turner, G. L'E. 1986. 'The physical sciences', in Sutherland and Mitchell 1986, pp. 659–81

Turner, R.S. 1975. 'University reforms and professional scholarship in Germany 1760–1806', in Stone 1975, ii, 495–531

Tuve, R. 1952. *A Reading of George Herbert*, London, 1952

Twigg, J.D. 1983. 'The university of Cambridge and the English Revolution, 1625–1688', University of Cambridge Ph.D. thesis, 1983

    1984. 'The limits of reform: some aspects of the debate on university education during the English Revolution', *History of Universities*, iv (1984), 99–114

    1987. *A History of Queens' College, Cambridge, 1448–1986*, Woodbridge, 1987

Underwood, M. 1979. 'Records of the foundress', *The Eagle* [St John's College magazine], Easter 1979, 8–23

    1982. 'The Lady Margaret and her Cambridge connection', *Sixteenth Century Journal*, xiii (1982), 67–82

    1983. 'Behind the early statutes', *The Eagle*, Easter 1983, 3–9

Varley, F.J. 1932. *The Siege of Oxford 1642–1644*, Oxford, 1932

VCH Cambs, iii: *The Victoria History of the Counties of England: A History of the County of Cambridge and the Isle of Ely*, iii, ed. J.P.C. Roach (*q.v.*), London, 1959. Some references also to ii, 1948

VCH Oxon, ii, iii: *The Victoria History of the Counties of England: A History of the County of Oxford*, ii, iii, ed. W. Page, H.E. Salter and M.D. Lobel, London, 1907, 1954

Venn: *Biographical History of Gonville and Caius College*, i–iii, ed. J. Venn, Cambridge, 1897–1901; iv, Part i, ed. E.S. Roberts, Part ii, *Chronicle of the College Estates*, ed. E.J. Gross, 1912; v–vii, ed. F.E.A. Trayes *et al.*, 1948–78

Venn, J. and S.C. 1887. *Admissions to Gonville and Caius College . . . March 1558/9 to June 1678/9*, London and Cambridge, 1887

Venn, J. 1901. *Caius College*, London, 1901

    1912. 'John Caius', repr. with corrections and additions, from Venn, iii, in Caius, *Works*, pp. 1–78

    1913. *Early Collegiate Life*, Cambridge, 1913

Venn, *Alumni: Alumni Cantabrigienses*, ed. J. and J.A. Venn, 2 parts (to 1751, 1752–1900), 4 and 6 vols., Cambridge, 1922–54

Walker, E.C. 1970. *William Dell: Master Puritan*, Cambridge, 1970

Walker, T.A. 1935. *Peterhouse*, edn of Cambridge, 1935

Ward, W.R. 1958. *Georgian Oxford: University Politics in the Eighteenth Century*, Oxford, 1958

Wayment, H.G. 1972. *The Windows of King's College Chapel, Cambridge*, Corpus Vitrearum Medii Aevi, London, 1972

Webster, C. 1986. 'The medical faculty and the physic garden', in Sutherland and Mitchell 1986, pp. 683–723

Wells, J. 1898. *Wadham College*, London, 1898

Westfall, R.S. 1980. *Never at Rest: A Biography of Isaac Newton*, Cambridge, 1980

Whitelock, D. ed. 1979. *English Historical Documents*, I, *c. 500–1042*, ed. D. Whitelock, 2nd edn, London, 1979

Wigglesworth, V.B. 1976. *Insects and the Life of Man*, London, 1976

Wigram, S.R. ed. 1895–6. *The Cartulary of the Monastery of St Frideswide at Oxford*, 2 vols., OHS, XXVIII, XXXI, 1895–6

Williams, P. 1986. 'Elizabethan Oxford: state, church and university', in McConica 1986, chap. 6, pp. 397–440

Willis, R., and Clark, J.W. 1886. *The Architectural History of the University of Cambridge and of the Colleges of Cambridge and Eton*, 4 vols., Cambridge, 1886

Wilson, H.A. 1899. *Magdalen College*, London, 1899

Winstanley, D.A. 1922. *The University of Cambridge in the Eighteenth Century*, Cambridge, 1922

 1935. *Unreformed Cambridge: A Study of Certain Aspects of the University in the Eighteenth Century*, Cambridge, 1935

 1940. *Early Victorian Cambridge*, Cambridge, 1940

 1947. *Later Victorian Cambridge*, Cambridge, 1947

Wood, A. 1813–20. *Athenae Oxonienses*, 3rd edn, ed. P. Bliss, 5 vols., London, 1813–20

 1891–1900. *The Life and Times of Anthony Wood, Antiquary, of Oxford, 1632–1695, described by Himself*, ed. A. Clark, 5 vols., OHS, XIX, XXI, XXVI, XXX, XL, 1891–1900

Woodforde, C. 1951. *The Stained Glass of New College, Oxford*, Oxford, 1951

Woodman, F. 1986. *The Architectural History of King's College Chapel*, London, 1986

Wordsworth, C. 1877. *Scholae Academicae*, Cambridge, 1877

Wormell, D. 1980. *Sir John Seeley and the Uses of History*, Cambridge, 1980

Wren, S. 1750. *Parentalia*, London, 1750

Young, F.G. 1967. *Darwin College 1963–66, and the University of Cambridge*, Cambridge, 1967

Index

Numbers in *italics* refer to plates and to references in captions to plates. Cambridge is sometimes abbreviated to C, Oxford to O. University institutions are indexed under Cambridge and Oxford; colleges and halls separately.